FAITH SEEKING UNDERSTANDING

FAITH SEEKING UNDERSTANDING

Essays Theological and Critical

by ROBERT E. CUSHMAN

DUKE UNIVERSITY PRESS

Durham, North Carolina 1981

BT
15
.C 87

Library of Congress Cataloging in Publication Data

Cushman, Robert Earl.
  Faith seeking understanding.

  Includes bibliographical references and index.
  1. Theology, Doctrinal—Collected works.
  2. Theology, Doctrinal—History—Collected works.
  3. Ecumenical movement—History—Collected works.
  I. Title.
  BT15.C87   230   80–69402
  ISBN 0–8223–0444–9

To
My Wife
Barbara Edgecomb Cushman
And to Our Children
Robert
Thomas
&
Beth

CONTENTS

THE ECUMENICAL MOVEMENT: WITNESS AND REFLECTIONS

PREFACE

These essays are, I suppose, a theological anthology—a selection mainly of published materials appearing in periodical form over many years. They are an overdue and only partial response to the longstanding request of students who have also honored me with engaged attention and engaging dialogue over the course of my years as teacher of philosophical and systematic theology. As I have selected, edited, revised, and added a few unpublished pieces, I have myself been struck by the measure to which the essays disclose a rather constant line of approach to presiding concerns of Christian theological reflection fermenting in our time. That line of approach is, partially sketched in bold strokes in the Introduction and, I believe, is variously illustrated in individual essays.

In other respects, the essays may be viewed as case studies of some problematics of modern theology, some in historical perspective. Functionally, they served as clearinghouses for treatment of stubborn issues recurrently confronted in teaching—primarily constructive theological reformulation, here, Christian doctrine. It is in the service of Christian doctrine, therefore, that I have included several essays of personal observation and reflection upon important phases of the ecumenical movement. The latter has not only contributed to the enrichment and vitality of 20th-century theology but has both uncovered and illuminated neglected areas and mooted issues that a responsible Protestant theology today can not ignore or presume to have settled.

As to the title of this volume, it seemed not inappropriate to use Anselm's *fides quaerens intellectum,* since it has been the dominant rationale of my work as theologian. Of its significance and claim to respect of all who seek Christian wisdom I have given some account in the Introduction and a further persuasive, I believe, in chapter 1.

As I relinquish these pages to the press, I wish especially to thank my colleagues Professor W. D. Davies for earlier and Professor D. Moody Smith for subsequent supportive initiatives eventuating, now, in this particular outcome. Their good will in the matter is worthy of at least this measure of fruition. To my long-time colleague and constant friend H. Shelton Smith, James B. Duke Professor Emeritus of American Religious Thought, and fellow ecumenist, I gratefully acknowledge unreserved encouragement to bring this book to completion and judicious assistance therein. This was crucial for one whose theological acumen had suffered the ravages of thirteen years of decanal preoccupation and the distraction of the late sixties. For cognate reasons I am grateful to Miss Harriet V. Leonard, always resourceful and supportive aid as reference librarian and bibliographical guide, for timely service of both late and earlier years.

It is perhaps fitting as it is also gratifying to have the Duke University Press, by action of the Editorial Board, accept this volume for publication with subsidy, and through the expert services of its Director Ashbel G. Brice and his staff. To Associate Director, Mr. Theodore A. Saros, I am indebted for particular counsel in preparation of manuscript. To the Duke University Research Council I express thanks both for good offices and for subsidy in support of publication.

ROBERT E. CUSHMAN

Duke University Divinity School
Ash Wednesday
February 28, 1979

INTRODUCTION

For myself, as one preoccupied with things theological over many years, it has always been, at one and the same time, both humbling and yet supportive to recall Aristotle's declared judgment that "although all other sciences are more necessary than Divinity, none is more excellent" (*Meta.*, 993a 10). On Aristotle's premises, this ranking of the sciences according to utility or excellence is understandable, since he did not expect much from God but enjoined contemplation of Him. However, I would side with the Psalmist that "the fear of the Lord is the beginning of wisdom." In this, furthermore, I suspect that I would have the support of another Athenian, Socrates, and his concurrence also in the surmise that wisdom, while surely elusive, is truly useful for humane life: that, both in the short and the long run, it is the difference between survival of humane life or the triumph of its opposite. I would likewise agree with Plato's *Republic* that for civilized and structured society humane life becomes problematic in the measure that it declines to consult beyond itself to avoid the nemesis of becoming its own norm of the Good. On this very point there is, I judge, near unanimity of Plato with the witness of the Old Testament prophets.

On such grounds as these, I find Divinity as necessary as it may, now and again, be excellent; and in the Western world—however we may define their relations—the age-old dialectic of church and state is, more than we realize, "the salt of the earth" for our corporate blessing in history.

Insofar as these things are worth pondering, the following essays may not be wholly unnecessary—whatever the measure of their excellence. There is, however, this proviso: it should be fully understood that they inquire after Christian wisdom. For, while they in no way mean to divorce Christian from philosophical wisdom, they do acknowledge—as my students will recognize—a radical difference and do rise to the Apostle Paul's challenge to the Corinthians respecting Jesus Christ "whom," he affirms, "God made our wisdom, our righteousness . . . and our redemption" (1 Cor. 2:30).

This witness of faith is an underlying *leitmotif* running through these essays, as it is also the prime grounding of the Christian wisdom they subscribe. It amounts to a first principle. Complementary to it is the insistence of St. Augustine on faith as the starting-point of Christian understanding: ". . . except ye believe ye shall in no wise understand."

In this, Augustine perpetuated the standpoint of the Greek and Latin Fathers—from Irenaeus and Tertullian onward—and mediated it to the Latin West to be encapsuled in St. Anselm's formulas: *Credo ut intelligam* or *fides quaerens intellectum*—faith seeking understanding. These things together, I am persuaded, are still the fundaments of any comprehension of the distinctive ground both of the way to and the substance of Christian wisdom. And this means that the primary *datum* of Christian wisdom is given, adventitious, in a particular history of which the New Testament is the decisive account.

Insofar, therefore, as these theological essays are also critical, their working principle falls back upon these premises, which I take to be rooted in biblical tradition and regnant in the Greek and Latin Fathers as well as in Latin Christianity through Anselm and on through the 12th century. Thereafter the story becomes mixed and, eventually, reversed in the High Middle Ages and the renaissance of Aristotelianism. Then, as Gerado Bruni has said: ". . . from the *fides quaerens intellectum* a transition is made to the *intellectus quaerens fidem*." Therewith, reason in search of faith led to the conception of a "twofold truth" of Divinity in which faith perfects reason. The breach of the Augustinian synthesis is accomplished.

In the 14th and 15th centuries the "two-fold truth" was to yield to the radical resurgence of faith under Scotist and Occamist influence. And faith, under the tutelage of Occamism, carried with it a virtual eclipse of the role of reason in Christian wisdom.

This was conjoined with, as it was also dependent upon, an awesome doctrine of God—the doctrine of absolute divine sovereignty. In provenance it was Augustinian, but, on grounds peculiar to itself, it incurred the extinction of any intelligible connections between nature and divine grace or between man and God. These were now at the absolute determination and, therefore, inscrutable will of omnipotent fiat. It was this philosophical background against which Reformation theology of the European continent was formulated and which it reflects. Consequently, as may be seen, it was formulated upon the urgently needed and near universally espoused premise of Luther's spiritual ordeal: salvation by grace *alone* through faith *alone*. Since, there is no way at all from man to God, Scripture *alone* shows an opened way from God to man. The *Deus absconditus* becomes, for Luther, *Deus revelatus*.

The undoubted positive truth of the Lutheran postulate—salvation by grace through faith—rests, to be sure, upon Luther's rediscovery of the Pauline gospel, but its republication was attended by a doctrine of God and a consequent doctrine of man, inherited, I believe, not from the New Testament but from the widely influential Occamistic philosophy. As alluded to already, the latter carried with it a breach of any intelligible relations—such as those between either the sovereign

Creator and the creation or between God and man—save those provided alone by God's immediate omnipotent will and act. Accordingly, the conception of the creation was rendered ambiguous, no longer conceived as in any sense God's established order of due process according to *inherent* secondary powers of nature or natures. Therefore, and moreover, the old distinction between "general" and "special Providence" tended to resolve into the latter only, lending to the creation the character of a perpetual miracle. From this derived an altered conception of man. Setting aside the Fall and total depravity, the official Reformed account of human being as such became largely told and, as it were, exhausted in such life-conferring relationship or salvation as, according to his eternal decrees, God conferred upon some and declined for others. With Calvin and his succession the story climaxed in "the eternal predestination of God," thereby depriving human nature of *inherent* dignity.

So the other side of the Occamistic coin—and almost certainly unintended by its progenitors—was the orphaning of man along with the dissolution of the *inherent structures* of the created order of due natural process, known as nature, *physis* or *Natura*. Meanwhile, man's orphaned status had, as time passed on into the 17th century, a quite unanticipated concomitant. In the consequent enforced isolation of the human being from his ground of Being, not a few thinkers of initiative discerned a silent invitation to explore, now eagerly, not alone a new-found *independence*—as a Galileo or a Francis Bacon—but also man's newly discovered and insistent *subjectivity*.

These became, together, the new and compelling incentives of the modern mind progressively visible in a far-ranging change in the cultural climate. The new incentives are presupposed in the rise of modern philosophy in its formative Cartesian posture—the *cogito ergo sum*—and moving onwards, either through Leibniz or Hume, to Kant's autonomous moral man, thence to Hegelian Idealism, or to Schleiermacher's philosophy of religion rooted in the original capacity of the human spirit "to give rise to the religious affections." Or onward through the positivistic altruism of Auguste Comte or the atheistic humanism of Feuerbach to Freud's probing of the superego, or Durkheim's referral and structuring of all meaning upon the communal self-consciousness.

Perhaps the scales were tipped in favor of pervasive subjectivity by the Reformation, but not by it alone; Occamism had a wider patronage. In its secular form, the tireless preoccupation of man with the universe of his own ego-self—having explored through the Enlightenment all the resources of "reason alone"—reemerged at the start of the 19th century in the vein of Romanticism. In the domain of religion, it took the form of what we usually speak of as "modern Protestant theology." And, at this point, Christian faith, in the New Testament sense, was successively translated into some species or other of the human self-consciousness. With Kant, it was the moral-consciousness, or the God-consciousness (Schleiermacher), the value-consciousness (Ritschl), the religious *a priori* (Troeltsch), religious experience (Wm. James), ultimate concern (Tillich), authentic self-understanding (Bultmann).

In each case, the presuppositions have been the same, the isolation of man as *de facto* starting point for theological understanding. In every case there is implicitly the same problem—the Cartesian problem. It is the question whether and how the human religious potential reaches as far as God, on the one hand, and, on the other, whether he is the same God whose thunders still sound from Sinai, whose Glory is radiated in the face of the Christ of the New Testament as the Word of God. How shall the two be brought together? In a word, that is the problem of modern Protestant theology.

Here it is out of place to explore these issues. It has been my purpose only to sketch in broad strokes the heritage of modern Protestant thought—a heritage with Occamistic rootage—left standing at its inception and, even now, largely unexamined. In the keeping of this theological tradition, the conception of Christian wisdom is altered as to its foundation. In it the order of faith and reason, or understanding, is reversed by Augustinian standards. With its distinctive rationale, method in theology is seen as *intellectus quaerens fidem*. For the Reformers, despite their Occamistic background, there was no question of the priority of faith to reason, no question, that is, of the divine initiative in the knowledge of faith. It was apperceived via the Word of God in Scripture and confirmed to faith by an inner witness of the Holy Spirit. The knowledge of faith was at the initiative of God's incalculable mercy self-manifest in Jesus Christ. Hence, in its way, Reforming Protestant theology subscribed to the priority of *fides quaerens intellectum* within certain limits. It was this Reformation standpoint that recaptured the attention of Karl Barth. In time, with recovery of the Reforming tradition, Barth also divined the pertinancy, not of Anselm's proof of God's existence, but of the correctness of Anselm's approach to the theological task in the *fides quaerens intellectum*, and Barth espoused the principle. He was attempting in his way to redirect Protestant theology once again along Augustinian-Anselmic lines. If he did not altogether succeed, it was, perhaps, because his stalwart efforts encountered obstacles of which he was not fully aware, namely, the largely unchallenged Occamistic presuppositions, standard equipment of the modern mind, and present, yet all but buried in his Reformed theological heritage. Above all, it may be that Barth, in dissociating his dogmatic task from all philosophy, was ill-prepared either to recognize the presence of a philosophy in the Reformed tradition he was restoring or to take note of it with tools appropriate to the task. However these things may be, Barth's vigorous attack upon Cartesianism in theology more nearly attended the symptoms than the endemic disease.

As, therefore, this author endeavors to read and unravel the thematic strands in the intellectual history of the West that go on entwining and silently unfold their influence upon the course of Reformed Protestant theology, the watchwords of the Reformation—*sola* gratia, *sola* fides, *sola* Scriptura—are valiant but, withal, deceptive. It is because, behind their bold program—including their enthronement of the Word of God—is a counterproductive philosophy of Reality, present but unacknowledged. It is a philosophy according to which there are no ways to comprehend significant relations between the Creator, his world, the creatures and man—save as by "special providences." In such a world, faith there may indeed be, but it can hardly advance to understanding. And, in such a world, the divorce of nature and grace persistently fosters the breaching of Christianity and culture and invites the progressive secularization of the work-a-day world. So, in spite of itself, this philosophy robs God of the glory. It does so in sundry tendencies recurrent in Protestant theology—from the 16th-century teaching on "imputed righteousness," to multiple instances in our time that refer to the Kingdom of God as beyond history. To do this, as has lately been widely urged, is to obstruct the proper fruitions in life of Christian wisdom.

This analysis, so far as it goes, has many implications, some of which are illustrated in the analysis and critique of the ensuing essays. If its main theses are sustained, it shows that one way of stating a pressing problem for future Protestant theology is: How might Protestantism recover a doctrine of Creation capable of affording a *rationale* for the Incarnation principle?

The following essays illustrate some aspects of this problem as it is represented in our theological heritage as Protestants. What is needed—and only just begun here—is the programmatic construction of an ontology on which to ground, as I see it, a restored Protestant doctrine of the Creation. Without this restoration, *fides quaerens intellectum*, as Christian wisdom, is well served as to its priorities but poorly served as to its consummation. To move toward this consummation is to emancipate ourselves from an exhausted tradition in theology that endlessly feeds on itself. How else, finally, shall we honor the Apostle's witness to Jesus Christ "whom God made our wisdom, our righteousness . . . and our redemption"?

HISTORICAL STUDIES

FAITH AND REASON IN THE THOUGHT OF ST. AUGUSTINE

I. THE PRIORITY OF FAITH

Christianity boldly asserted that the eternal Logos had been manifested in the personal history of Jesus called Christ. Once this claim began to receive wide acceptance, the older ways of philosophizing characteristic of the classical ages were shaken. On the one hand, Christians affirmed positively that God had drawn nigh, disclosing himself in history to those who believed. On the other hand, they held that, apart from reliance upon this divine disclosure, the efforts of scientific reason to apprehend God were pitifully inadequate and perverse.

From the beginning St. Paul had confronted the "wisdom of the world" with the "foolishness of the preaching." He did not scruple to declare openly the contradiction—asserting, nevertheless, that "the foolishness of God is wiser than men." It remained for Augustine to make clear exactly how this was so and why. He declared that "faith precedes reason" because *nisi credideritis, non intelligetis,* unless you believe, you will not understand.[1] He thus opposed Tertullian's view that faith recommends itself in proportion to its absurdity. The priority of *fides,* faith, he regarded as eminently reasonable. In showing how this was so, Augustine laid a new and definitive foundation for Christian philosophy.

For Augustine the Incarnation gave meaning to history, which it could not possess for those classical thinkers to whom history was, along with nature, the realm of the insubstantial and the changing. But the doctrine of the God-man signified henceforth that ultimate reality could be apprehended rightly only through a particular history in time, namely, Jesus Christ. Augustine perceived the offense of this view to the classical mind. Even the Platonists, whose point of view came nearest to that of Christianity in the opinion of Augustine, could make nothing of the Incarnation.[2] Augustine approved much of what was contained in their books; "But that the Word was made flesh and dwelt among us," he observed, "did I not read there."[3] Yet this which, together with the Cross of wood, was the rock of offense and the stone of stumbling to the philosophic mind, Augustine did not waver in regarding as the very core of Catholic Christianity.

Reprinted with permission of The Oxford University Press from an article in *A Companion to the Study of St. Augustine,* ed. Roy W. Battenhouse (New York: Oxford University Press, 1955).

It was because Augustine, with singular clarity of mind, located this cleft of conviction and disparity of standpoint between Christian and classical approaches to knowledge of reality that he was forced to make some settlement. What was a burning personal problem for Augustine was at the same time a prime intellectual problem of the Christian religion. The time was overdue, if Christianity was to be responsibly related to culture, for some elucidation from the Christian side of the antagonism between the standpoint of Christian faith on the one hand and autonomous reason on the other. Here was a contest whether faith or reason provided the most illuminating interpretation of the totality of human experience. The contest was the same between history and metaphysics, nature and grace, and the particular as opposed to the universal.

Augustine unflinchingly rejected any accommodation of the faith-standpoint to that of reason and culture. In his apologetic he undertook to exhibit the faith-factor in all knowledge. His apologetic also recommended the particular suitability of submission to Christ, the historical particular, as the indispensable corrective of a reason disabled by sinful pride. We are privileged to believe that the greatness of the Augustinian solution in no small part depends on the fact that it did not repudiate reason, philosophy, nature, or the universal while, nevertheless, it preserved to faith, history, grace, and the particular a certain primacy. Augustine's undeviating conviction was that *fides* is the gateway to understanding—the way to the Kingdom which none enters except as a little child. This, according to Augustine, is the Gospel wisdom, *sapientia,* which must replace the proud sufficiency of classical knowledge or *scientia.*[4] Faith is the lowly door by which the "heart," bowing to enter, is cleansed in order that at length the whole mind may apprehend the universal abiding Truth—may see God. The faithful shall at last see God by the instrument of reason; but reason cannot attain the vision of God uncorrected and unguided by faith. "For contemplation is the recompense of faith, for which recompense our hearts are purified by faith."[5]

This general point of view is not a pious opinion or an apology for Augustine's own tardy but eventual flight into Catholic Christianity. It is an expression in keeping with the principle most basic to his revolutionary conception of the knowledge process. The principle is the foundation stone of Augustinian theology. It is responsible for the first full-fledged Christian philosophy. Although it has periodically been influential, it has also frequently been lost to the sight of Christian philosophers; and, beginning with the ascendancy of Aristotelianism in the 13th century, was too largely obscured.

The principle may be stated simply. It is the doctrine of the primacy of the will in all knowledge. What is known cannot be divorced from what is loved. At the very minimum, all cognition is directly dependent on interest, and nothing is fully known to which the consent of the will has not been given. Yet there may be awareness of reality without completed cognition of that reality. The completion of cognition lies with affection. Thus full cognition is *re-cognition*. The possibility of so-called "objectivity" in knowledge is given in the fact that there may be *cognitio* without *agnitio*, acknowledgment. This is possible with respect to God. That is to say, God may be known while not being acknowledged. This is actually the center and depth of the plight of man. Therefore, the issue of man's destiny lies with the will. Faith is what moves the will, or, better, it is a certain movement of the will.

It is in this manner that faith serves reason. It does not supplant it. Harnack's opinion that "Augustine was never clear about the relation of faith and knowledge" and that "he handed over this problem to the future" [6] clearly indicates Harnack's failure to understand the essentials of the Augustinian epistemology. Augustine held that in knowledge the cognitive faculty *(ratio)* "takes in," according to its power, reality both eternal and temporal, but that being primarily passive or neutral it is directed to "recognize" what it *does* recognize in virtue of the will or dominant affection of the mind. Therefore, what is not effectually known is precisely what is not adequately loved. Man knows God not knowing that he knows God. The double knowledge, which is re-cognition or acknowledgment, is at the mercy of the will. In Augustine it is the will, hardly the reason, which is corrupt; and faith is the means of cleansing the will.

II. THE POWERS OF REASON

In accordance with his conviction that God is altogether good and the author only of good, Plato sought to formulate a rational theology, to moralize the inherited Greek religious world view. This involved the extrusion of the debased but more concrete mythological and historical elements in favor of the universal and rational.[7] Augustine clearly understood the preference of the philosophers for "natural theology" and their conviction of its superior truth-value to that of either "civil" or "mythological" theology.[8] He concurred with the estimate; but this only intensified his problem. He was obliged to relate the particular saving history in Jesus Christ to a manner of approaching God which, relying on mere reason, had eschewed all dependence on history.

Furthermore, while Augustine had no doubt that reason availed for apprehension of God's existence or that natural theology afforded knowledge, he was nevertheless convinced that, unguided by faith, it did equally afford mis-knowledge. He was not so much troubled that the ancient world doubted. It believed too much—a menagerie of error. Even the Platonists did not rise above polytheism to monolatry,[9] while so distinguished a philosopher as Porphyry toyed with theurgy and demonolatry,[10] and everywhere men looked to "curious and illicit arts" or to astrology rather than to the divine grace.[11] Perversely, men preferred the mediatorship of demons to that of Christ. Accordingly, Augustine declared in *The City of God* that he had not undertaken to refute "those who either deny that there is any divine power, or contend that it does not interfere with human affairs, but those who prefer their own god to our God." [12]

Withal, Augustine accepted with thanks what he regarded as the overwhelming weight of the Platonic theistic tradition founded upon reason. "It is evident," he said, "that none come nearer to us than the Platonists." [13] Their "gold and silver was dug out of the mines of God's providence which are everywhere scattered abroad." Such truth as the Platonists possess Christians ought to take away and "devote to their proper use in the preaching of the gospel." [14] Of the Platonists, Plato himself is to be preferred "to all the other philosophers of the gentiles," for he entertained "such an idea of God as to admit that in Him are to be found the cause of existence, the ultimate reason for the understanding, and the end in reference to which the whole life is to be regulated." [15] While admittedly this tripartite division of the conception of God does not expressly offer the doctrine of a trinity, yet Augustine allows that it does suggest the Christian Trinity. For Plato discerned "that God alone could be the author of nature, the bestower of intelligence, and the kindler of love by which life becomes good and blessed." [16] Augustine regarded this as defining essentially the several works of the Persons of the Trinity.

Augustine reads Plato as teaching that the "supreme God visits the mind of the wise with an intelligible and ineffable presence." [17] He agrees that the "higher light, by which the human mind is enlightened, is God"—God the Son.[18] This is Christ who already was in the world before He was sent.[19] The Platonists, says Augustine in *The Confessions,* teach that in the beginning was the Word and the Word was God, and that it is the Word which "lighteth every man coming into the world," by participation in which men are made wise.[20] Among the Platonists, therefore, reason approaches to the threshold of the Christian faith, yet does not enter in. It refuses to recognize "the grace of God in Jesus Christ our Lord, and that very incarnation of His." [21] It accepts the universal but not the universal in the particular—the discarnate not the Incarnate Word.

Notwithstanding, Augustine retains a high estimate of *ratio naturalis,* natural reason, for this reason is never fully "natural" or to be taken in isolation from the illuminating activity of God. Even reason wholly occupied with creatures and directed away from the Creator by the power of the will is yet empowered by divine illumination to apprehend the creatures which enthrall its interest. Reason in man is preeminently to be esteemed.[22] Reason is that in which our nature as man is fulfilled.[23] It is what constitutes man an image of God and thereby capable of being partaker of the divine nature.[24] By it God has left a witness to Himself among the Gentiles. For even in man's fallen condition, his reason is exalted by the divine *informing,* so that God is the light by which are known whatsoever things are known, temporal or eternal.[25] The Platonists are right: "the light of our understanding, by which all things are learned by us, they have affirmed to be that self-same God by whom all things were made."[26]

We may illustrate this general conception of knowledge by observing how Augustine employs it in the area of science, aesthetics, and moral values. As the sun is the condition of sensible intuition, so God, the inward "Illuminator," is the cause of "all the certainties of the sciences."[27] They presuppose the *informing* of our minds by the Truth apprehended *a priori.* The invariability of the propositions of the sciences cannot derive from the variability of sensuous experience. Mathematical propositions are valid because they are derived *a priori,* not *a posteriori.*[28] Man's memory contains "the reasons and innumerable laws of numbers and dimensions," none of which has been imprinted on the memory by any sense of the body.[29] Moreover, the foundational categories of all science, *esse, quid, quale* "we suck [*haurimus*] not in any images by our senses, but perceive them within by themselves." They were, says Augustine, "in my heart even before I learned them."[30] Inasmuch as the *forms* constitute things *what* they are, and yet are found only imperfectly in things, the Platonists are correct that their apprehension cannot be from experience.[31] It is because these *intelligibili* are "at hand to the glance of the mind" that science is possible:

It is part of the higher reason to judge of these corporeal things according to incorporeal and eternal reasons; which unless they were above the human mind, would certainly not be unchangeable; and, yet, unless something of our own were subjoined to them, we should not be able to employ them as our measure by which to judge corporeal things. But we judge of corporeal things from the rule of dimensions and figures, which the mind knows to remain unchangeably.[32]

Even physical knowledge, then, is available only by virtue of the omnipresence of the eternal Word. This is in a manner the prevenience of divine grace.[33] Yet there is a vast gulf between being enlightened by God and acknowledging the light by which we are enlightened. Both nature and the knowing mind are *informed* by God. Yet the knowledge of nature does not necessarily disclose but may in fact obscure God. It is true that St. Paul taught that the gentiles have a "natural" knowledge of God in holding "that what is known of God he manifested to them when His invisible things were seen by them, being understood by those things which have been made." [34] But Augustine does not interpret St. Paul as teaching that a knowledge of God may be had by a direct inspection of the outward world. Rather, he understands St. Paul to mean that reflection upon nature has theological value only for those "who compare that voice received from without by the senses, with Truth which is within." [35] Only because God, the eternal Word, is present within can His handiwork be discovered in nature without. The eye of the soul is blind which goes not within but dwells 'out of doors' while searching for God.[36]

As the divine visitation is the precondition of scientific knowledge, it is also the unchanging ground of all judgments of value. Aesthetic judgment upon corporeal beauty would be impossible "had there not existed in the mind itself a superior form of these things, without bulk, without noise of voice, without space and time." [37] In the aesthetic realm Augustine observed that he made judgments of worth in distinction from judgments of fact. He declared that some things *ought to be* irrespective of time or limiting conditions. He sought for a timeless principle as the sufficient ground for such value judgments. He could find no sufficient ground except the eternal and unchangeable truth and beauty which is above the mind and is God. Augustine therefore concluded that the mind necessarily has conversance with God.[38] With reference to moral worth, God likewise *informs* our minds with a rule of judgment which "rests firmly upon the utterly indestructible rules of its own right; and if it is covered as it were by cloudiness or corporeal images, yet it is not wrapt up and confounded in them." [39] This is a Word within us which does not depart from us when we are born.[40] By the discarnate Word we know what goodness or righteousness is; and, by means of it *a priori*, we love and approve a particular righteous man *a posteriori*.[41]

To summarize: God abides in the reason of man or in that more comprehensive vessel, his heart. God is, so to speak, used by many but known or recognized by none except those who go within to themselves. Except a man turn inward to God within, he will not discover the Author of the world by observing the things that are without.

He sees without "that they are, and within that they are good." [42]
Whether by *ratio* or by *fides*, it is the Son of God, either as the eternal
Word or as the Incarnate Word, who enlightens and gives understanding of the Father. The Word made flesh is the same eternal Word
that enlightens the reason of the gentiles and every man coming into
the world. He comes unto His own. He comes whither He already
was, but His own [the philosophers] receive Him not.

III. REASON IN NEED OF FAITH

Great, then, are the powers of the natural reason as illuminated by
the discarnate Son, the eternal Word of God. To be sure, since there
is a continuous divine illumination of the mind, the *ratio* is not in
Augustine's thought ever 'unaided' in its learning of God, as it can
be in the thought of Thomas Aquinas. But, now, given a reason divinely
sustained and empowered, what need is there of faith? Or, again, if
the Platonists acknowledge all that Augustine has attributed to them
concerning reason,[43] what need is there to force upon them what he
calls "the right rule of faith," namely, that 'we begin in faith, and
are made perfect in sight"? [44]

The answer is that in spite of all he has said to exalt the role of
reason, Augustine's pervasive insistence is that Jesus Christ, the eternal
Word *incognito*, disguised in the flesh, is the *principium* or the beginning point of knowledge.[45] Along with the Platonists, Augustine taught,
to be sure, a certain primacy of *ratio*. We comprehend something of
this primacy in Augustine's claim that the divine *informing* by the
eternal Word is the precondition of all *scientia*. But how shall we understand this insistence upon a deeper wisdom: that knowledge must necessarily begin with faith and its object—the historical and particular,
the Word made flesh?

Clearly, Augustine had not shown that the "natural" or "fallen" man
is entirely devoid of grace: though he has turned himself from the
light, the light still surrounds him.[46] Blindness is never complete while
a man has life.[47] Some residuum, some trace of awareness of God,
must remain in man though man recognize it not. This is essential
for the renewal of knowledge.[48] God cannot be recollected if absolutely
fogotten: "If I now find thee not in my memory, then am I unmindful
of thee; and how shall I find thee, if I do not remember thee?" [49]

In other words, the *imago Dei* may be obscured or defaced, but it
never ceases to be: the defacing "does not extend to taking away its
being an image." [50] Quite apart from the grace which is in Christ there
is a vestigial love of the Truth, for there is a *modicum lumen* not

altogether extinguished, and by it men have a desire after the Truth which is God.[51]

But reasons are to be found for Augustine's insistence against the rationalist that reason must begin with the Mediator and be "nourished by faith in the temporal history." [52] We are not glibly to suppose that this is required simply as an antidote to a lingering skepticism of Augustine's which must needs lean upon authority. It is true that, in the Scriptures and the Catholic faith, Augustine found a haven of calm after a stormy voyage in quest of certainty.[53] But the appeal to the primacy of faith is not to be identified simply and immediately with an appeal to authority. The fact is that the authoritativeness of both Church and Scripture wait upon the consent of a converted heart and will. The latter is faith and is the work of the Mediator.

If we are to understand Augustine's insistence upon the priority of faith, we must not assume that he was urging upon the pagan reason a sort of blind acquiescence to authority as the condition of understanding. Of course it is to be admitted that for Augustine, the churchman and apologist, the Scriptures offered infallible truth. He regarded Scripture as possessing "the highest, even the heavenly, pinnacle of authority." [54] And, in the debates with the Manicheans, Augustine was evidently driven by the logic of circumstances to espouse a view elicited by the exigencies of apologetic: "I should not believe the Gospel except as moved by the authority of the Catholic Church." [55] The battle of wits with heretics, if not with pagans, permitted no appeal against the misappropriation of Scripture except that lodged in the continuity of succession and the ubiquity of Catholic tradition.

It must, however, be affirmed that this utterance, which is solitary and conditioned by the immediate issues of the debate, cannot be regarded as exhibiting either the ground or the profound nature of *fides* in Augustine's thought. Augustine's own experience stood surely for the conviction that, although faith cannot do without authority, authority is impotent unless preceded by a redirection of the will through the operation of grace.

The function of authority is not primarily to provide an impregnable ground of certainty for the doubting intellect. Nor is it that of propounding a datum which, because *ex hypothesi* it is unamenable to comprehension, must therefore command uncomprehending acquiescence of the mind. It is not that I must believe because reason is inherently incompetent. It is rather that my reason is incompetent in virtue of the perversion of my will, so that I cannot understand until my pride and sinful will to independence are submissive to the Mediator—the eternal Word in the form of the Servant. The Word is, by historical circumstance, necessarily afforded me in a continuous tradition. This is the Church and the Scriptures in the keeping of the Church. The doctrine of the Church is what I believe. But I believe the Church because the grace of God in the Mediator has brought my will low even unto Christ's lowliness. Thus the Scriptures will not be authoritative to the uncleansed will.[56] Likewise, subjectively considered, the Church can be authority only to the heart that has become thankful rather than unthankful, that is, to the heart that has faith.[57]

No one knew better than Augustine, when not on polemical and apologetical business, that neither antiquity, nor continuity of apostolic succession, nor ubiquity [58] was of itself able to confirm the minds of men in the truth of Catholic Christianity. First of all men's minds had to be brought to self-knowledge and contrition. Thus, in his concluding word to Faustus, Augustine admonishes: "If you ask for demonstration, consider first *what you are*, how unfit for comprehending the nature of your own soul, not to speak of God." [59] The fact is that in the contest with heretics it became patent to Augustine—as it has become evident in history—that the appeal to either Scripture or Church as authority is convincing only to the warmed hearts of the faithful. As the perorations of Augustine's polemics against Donatist, Manichean, or Pelagian show, his final resort is a warning against perversity in the heart of the unbeliever and a call to repentance. Error, as well as truth, lodges with the state of the will. Augustine was resigned to the conviction that the mind is inclined toward the truth only by "the first elements of faith," which works *by love*—a love evoked only by Christ the Mediator.[60]

It comes to this, therefore: I do not believe *on authority*. Rather I have an authority in the Church because, through grace, my will has been made submissive to what the Church proffers. In addition (versus heretics) I cannot believe rightly apart from authority. This, then, is the dialectical truth about faith and authority. In the order of living experience, faith makes authority. In the order of historical actuality, the Church constitutes the persisting historical continuum mediating faith.

The indispensability of tradition was clear, moreover, to Augustine by virtue of his conception of the source of knowledge. Respecting this matter he declared that reason "must have its starting-point either in the bodily sense or in the intuitions of the mind." [61] Faith, however, has to do with the Incarnation, which is an event in time but in a time now vanished. As a past historical reality, it is, as Augustine designates it, a datum "adventitious" to the mind. That is, it does not qualify either as an object for the senses or for the "intuitions of the mind." In respect to the latter, the Incarnation is, therefore, not a universal truth accessible to rational reflection or deduction. In respect to sensi-

ble experience, nothing is clearer than that the temporal history of
the Mediator is forever withdrawn from possible present inspection.
Therefore the events done in time on our behalf *can only be transmitted to us* and offered as redemptive facts by church and Scripture
embodying a continuous historical tradition grounded in the testimony
of witnesses. Christianity is indefeasibly grounded in a "particular,"
not in a "universal." While, therefore, the grace which is in Christ is
operative so as to be independent of time, yet the specific saving character of grace can be apprehended only in association with the original
saving transaction in time. And this requires the maintenance of a
historical mediation in the midst of temporality.

The indispensability of authority, nevertheless, does not avail to clarify the deeper meaning of the primacy of faith in the epistemology
of Augustine. Faith must precede *ratio*, not because reason is intrinsi-
cally incompetent but because reason, in a man whose will has not
submitted to the grace of the Mediator, is an untrustworthy reason.

The primacy of faith in the process of knowledge rests on Augustine's
conviction that there is a dependency of reason and knowledge upon
the character of the will, whereas every actual will is corrupted. It is
an extension of the Socratic insight which Augustine clearly noted
and openly stated: that God can and will be known only by a purified
mind. Socrates

was unwilling that minds defiled by earthly desires should essay to raise themselves upward to divine things. For he saw that the causes of things were
sought for by them,—which causes he believed to be ultimately reducible to
nothing else than the will of the one true and supreme God,—*and on this
account they could only be comprehended by a purified mind;* and therefore
that all diligence ought to be given to the purification of the life by good
morals, in order that the mind, delivered from the depressing weight of lusts,
might raise itself upward by its native vigor to eternal things, and might,
with purified understanding, contemplate that nature which is incorporeal
and unchangeable light.[62]

With acuteness Augustine rightly construed the Socratic point of view
that right knowledge is dependent upon right love rather than right
love dependent upon right knowledge. Therefore faith, which was
first of all thankfulness, was the token of an unfeigning mind, a mind
shorn of *superbia*, pride.[63] This accorded with the word of Scripture,
urged constantly by Augustine: "Blessed are the pure in heart, for
they shall see God." [64]

Will you be able to lift up your heart unto God? Must it not first be healed,
in order that thou mayest see? Do you not show your pride, when you say,
First let me see, and then I will be healed? [65]

Inescapable it is, then, that "faith is in some way the starting point of knowledge."[66] The philosophic search even for God partakes of pride—a puffed-up and vain science.[67] Thus "if you believe not, you will not understand." Wherefore it behooves all men

to return and begin from faith in due order: perceiving at length how healthful a medicine has been provided for the faithful in the holy church, whereby a heedful piety, healing the feebleness of the mind, may render it able to perceive the unchangeable truth, and hinder it from falling headlong through disorderly rashness, into pestilent and false opinion.[68]

To be sure this is a generalization from Augustine's own experience, for he confesses "by believing might I have been cured, so that the eyesight of my soul being cleared, might some way or other have been directed toward thy truth . . . which could no ways be healed but by believing."[69] Therefore, everywhere Augustine's admonition is heard: we begin in faith and are made perfect in sight. Though, with Anselm of Canterbury, faith has acquired somewhat different denotations, the order is the same, *credo ut intelligam*, I believe in order to understand. It is, in Augustine's view, not that we begin with faith *and* go on to understanding. We begin in faith *in order* to go on to understanding. To obscure this distinction is to pass over the working principle of the Augustinian epistemology, for it is to ignore the determinative function of the will in knowledge. According to this conception, then, the Incarnate Christ, who moves the will, becomes the true first *principium* of knowledge, and the adequate starting point for the interpretation of the totality of human experience.[70]

IV. THE FUNCTION OF THE WILL IN KNOWLEDGE

The rational approach to God dispenses with the step of faith. Porphyry, that great light among the Platonists, scorns to accept "the flesh of the mediator." The Manicheans deride Christian credulity which begins with faith.[71] Augustine's reply to the detractors is that they wish to know God without acknowledging God, to have a God without trusting God. But there is no having or knowing God without having Him in the will. Men want God in the mind, not in the heart, for if God is held merely in the mind He is held tentatively, and the will is free to be its own master.

Augustine perceived in the merely rational approach to God an internal contradiction: it cannot reach God because it does not want to have God. It withholds commitment until it has sight, but it cannot achieve sight until it yields commitment. The rational approach to

God does not perceive that it founders upon the original sinfulness of the human heart. The Platonists do not perceive that man does not know God because he does not love God. These best of philosophers do not comprehend the plight of man.[72]

Augustine is not content with the easy diagnosis that a corruptible body "presseth down the soul" in the pursuit of divine knowledge.[73] It does so in virtue of a deeper disease, namely, that while God continually visits the mind of man with His light, men turn their backs to the light, preferring to pursue their own will among the creatures. We cannot justify this avoidance by holding that the mind is directed with greater ease toward things temporal. Augustine admits that we "handle things visible more easily . . . than things intelligible," and that this becomes habitual.[74] But the cause is found not in defective talent but in a certain ingratitude born of pride. Out of love of dominion, men employ the divine light for *scientia* or science whereby to exploit the creatures, rather than return thanks to the Light.[75]

Similarly it may be said of the philosophers that "knowing God, they glorified Him not as God; neither were thankful, but became vain in their imaginations. . . . Professing themselves wise, they became fools, and changed the glory of the incorruptible God into the likeness of corruptible men." [76] Even in the case of the Platonists Augustine believed this indictment was warranted, for they did not avoid idolatry but paid divine honors to many gods.[77] Nor was this idolatry attributable to anything else, in Augustine's opinion, than to awareness of God which failed to pass over into submission or commitment to God. The cause of this insubordination St. Paul had again rightly diagnosed: they "held down" or distorted the truth out of unrighteousness or perverted wills.[78] In place of submission to the inward Illuminator, the philosophers turn outward to the order of nature in an ostensible quest for God. It is a vain pursuit, and Augustine has a shrewd reply to the question why men go forth "and run to the heights of the heavens and the lowest parts of the earth, seeking Him who is within, if they wish to be with Him?" [79] The answer is widely explored in the *Confessions*. It is because we will, but do not fully will, to be with God. Our dominant preference is to be with ourselves.[80] Therefore we go abroad among the creatures to use them while pretending to seek God through them. In the case of God, as in the instance of all other cognition, full knowledge waits upon desire or love. It is appetition, love, or will that turns diffused awareness into true cognition. The crucial words of Augustine are these: "The bringing forth of the mind is preceded by some desire, by which through seeking and finding what we wish to know, the offspring, viz., knowledge, itself is born." [81]

In this manner Augustine founds a Christian theory of knowledge in opposition to Aristotelian intellectualism, in which Being has primacy over the Good and the "theoretical" has primacy over "the practical mind." [82] For while it is true, as Aristotle says, that appetite or desire (ὄρεξις) will be found in each of the parts of the Soul including the mind—in the reasoning faculty as purpose or wish—yet this desire is always there as a consequent and in no sense as either the effectual or even subsidiary determinant of knowledge.[83] For Aristotle this is as it ought to be; for the ideal of objectivity is served if all preferences regarding good or evil do not in the least direct but rather are derived from antecedent cognition of Being. Thus, all desire or appetition follows upon sensation, opinion, or thought.[84] Aristotle safeguards "pure truth" by rendering its acquisition independent of "practical considerations."

This is the ground of the subordination of the practical to the theoretical reason in Aristotle and generally in Western thought. It makes room for the idea of pure "objective" knowledge and the ideal of knowledge as pure contemplation of Being. For it is Aristotle's view that "the speculative mind thinks nothing practical [axiological] and does not comment on what is to be avoided or pursued." [85] It offers objectives to the practical mind (ὁ πρακτικὸς νοῦς) which, inspired by appetancy, calculates "with an end in view." [86]

The will is in all cases subservient to the intellect—the practical to the theoretical reason. Here is the triumph of the intellectual value— of the true over the good, of Being over value. In contrast, Augustine held that the noetic function of *nous* or reason is dependent for its direction and operation on the practical or valuative reason. The theoretical reason as well as the sensible nature has its predisposing affections.[87] Thus Augustine rendered explicit the integral association of the practical and theoretical functions that was implicit in Plato's *Symposium* and *Phaedrus*. The intellectualism of Aristotle, divorcing these two functions, destroyed therewith the Socratic-Platonic concept of *sophia*. This, Thomas Aquinas, laboring diligently, was unable to revive. Eventually, he himself contributed to the ascendency of science over wisdom in modern times.

With Aristotle belief (ὑπόληψις) involves an act of will or consent. It is not so with knowledge or even with opinion.[88] In knowledge, Being is apprehended (or not apprehended), and there is no place for preference or consent of the will. When there is knowledge or true opinion, it is because Being *prescribes itself* necessarily. On the contrary, Augustine regards knowledge as well as belief as involving a movement of the will or consent. Therefore, of the totality of divine and creaturely Being given for apprehension, what a man knows or acknowledges will depend on what portion of the continuum of Being a man most loves. With reference to God, as to anything else, this means that man's universal awareness of God cannot pass to knowledge without *appetitus* or desire or consent of the will.[89] Thus, the merely rational or contemplative approach to God is self-contradicted. It requires the consent of the will, but it is Augustine's immovable conviction that the will is perverse. Socrates and the Gospel are right, only the pure in heart shall see God; for "the more ardently we love God, the more certainly and the more calmly do we see Him."[90]

To man's awareness all reality is given, the temporal and the eternal. But in virture of his fallen condition man is turned from the Light to the creatures made luminous by the Light. The turned back is symbolic of the perverted love (Original Sin). Therefore the order of creatures becomes the dominant object of knowledge in virtue of the coercive inclination of man's will.[91] What else is love *(caritas)* except will, asks Augustine.[92] When this will is directed toward the creatures, the inclination toward God and, therefore, the awareness of God diminish. They decline in proportion to the liveliness of man's concupiscence toward the world of the senses. The immoderate love of the things of sense is derivative, however, and rests upon a foundational defection, namely, self-love or pride. It is through pride that man consents to the affections of the senses. "Pride is the beginning of all sin; and the beginning of man's sin is a falling away from God."[93] The first evil will, which preceded all man's evil acts, "was rather a kind of falling away from the work of God to its own work than any positive work. And therefore the acts resulting were evil, not having God, but the will itself for their end."[94] Thus man is the victim of an ambivalent will. His awareness of God and his *appetitus* toward God, with the attendant desire to be like God, are transformed into a desire to be independent of God.[95] Thus the philosophic quest for God may be only a pretense, a disguise by which the seeker hides, even from himself, his fleeing. Paradoxically, man would not flee from God if he were not secretly aware and did not secretly love God, but he fears to acknowledge or commit his will to God lest he lose his autonomy. He does not know that he who would save his life shall lose it. Thus, man is, in some way, touched by God even when turned away from him.[96]

v. THE MEDIATOR, THE WAY TO KNOWLEDGE

It is inevitable that even the Platonists should participate in the failure of the classical approach to God. The being of God is not altogether obscured from their vision, but the way to God—the way of the Mediator—they do not acknowledge.

You proclaim the Father and His Son, whom you call the Father's intellect or mind, and between these a third, by whom we suppose you mean the Holy Spirit, and in your own fashion you call these three Gods. In this, though your expressions are inaccurate, you do in some sort as through a veil, see what we should strive towards; but the Incarnation of the unchangeable Son of God, whereby we are saved, and are enabled to reach the things we believe, or in part understand, this is what you refuse to recognize. *You see in a fashion, although at a distance, the country in which we should abide; but the way to it you do not.*[97]

As Augustine will have it, men are born blind in Adam and need Christ to awaken them. But this is only a shorthand of his real meaning. Knowledge of God waits upon *re-cognition* of God. It is not that reason is impotent or that it is inherently corrupted, but that it is perverted by the will. To know, *cognoscere,* is to acknowledge, *agnoscere.* Thereby real cognition of God is at the same time the dissolution of the bondage of the will to self-love. The intellectualists among the philosophers failed to perceive that unless knowledge of the good involved acknowledgment, the consent of the will, right action would not necessarily follow upon right knowledge. Thus the contemplative conception of knowledge could no more solve the problem of ethics than it could the theological problem.

Out of soul travail and acute inward reflection, Augustine discovered in the will the key that at one time unlocked both the problem of theological knowledge and the problem of ethics. The same volition that turns awareness of God into recognition of God is the death of self-love that hitherto was the chain binding all benevolence tending beyond expediency. To the mind of Augustine, therefore, the conception of anaxiological or non-value-directed knowledge not only did not suffice to solve the problem of ethical motivation but was false of the cognitive process. It can explain neither ignorance nor knowledge. If Plato wrestled to account for the ignorance of the sophist and the materialist, neither was he altogether successful in explaining why any of the Cave dwellers emerged into the light. As Augustine conceived the matter, men are in the Cave and willingly committed to Cave-knowledge.

The will is the problem. The solution was the divine Visitant and the divine Emancipator. The Word made flesh, the Mediator, so moves the will that man is enabled to love the good of which he has been aware without acknowledgement, without *caritas.* As mover of the will, Christ becomes "the *Principium* by whose Incarnation we are purified." [98] Purified, that is, humbled, the will consents to the intimations of the Truth and the Good which had always been present to reason, and thus reason is made ready for eventual sight. This Christ is the wisdom of God. He is the "reason of wisdom" to which the

"reason of knowledge" must yield.[99] The latter, which clings tenaciously to the ideal of objective apprehension, usually contenting itself
with the investigation of nature, has been shown by Augustine to rest
upon a prior commitment of the will, namely, "the sensuous movement
of the soul." [100]

The products of this movement belong to *scientia* or science as distinguished from *sapientia* or wisdom, that is, to "the cognition of things
temporal and changeable." [101] They are, moreover, legitimate and necessary for the management of the affairs of this life.[102] But in so far
as the sensuous movement of the will becomes exclusive and directs
the reason away from the eternal and unchangeable objects of wisdom
or from the Word made flesh, it is the seduction of the serpent, who
is the satanic mediator of the Fall of man.[103]

Man is fallen, through pride, into an obsessive love and preoccupation
with the creatures, acquiring thereby the false opinion of their unconditional reality. It is *fides*, which alone apprehends the eternal within
the historical, that is the correction of man's perversity. Man can be
extricated from his unholy marriage to the creatures by God's appearance in the midst of the creatures. The sinner's submission to God
as God appears in the form of the Servant, which is *fides*, is the precise
antidote for the perverse love of the creatures. Only a new love can
expel the old perverse love and make way for the renewed understanding. Thus men are healed only "by means of the lowliness of the faith
of the history, which was transacted in time." [104] Nowhere is the principle more succinctly stated than in the following:

Then set I myself a means of gaining so much strength as should be sufficient
to enjoy thee; *but I could not find it, until I embraced that Mediator betwixt
God and man*, the man Jesus Christ; who is over all, God blessed for evermore,
then calling unto me and saying: I am the Way, the Truth, and the Life:
who mingled the food which I was unable to take [his own flesh] unto our
flesh. For the Word was made flesh, that by thy wisdom, by which thou creat-
edst all things, he might suckle our infancy.[105]

History becomes the medium of revelation and instrumental to the
fulfillment of knowledge. Time and change become, by the Incarnation,
the vehicle of the Eternal; whereas, in Platonism, the temporal tended
to bind *nous* in ignorance. Augustine has at length, through reflection
upon the Incarnation, succeeded in showing what Plato wrestled to
make plausible, namely, how, from the knowledge of the particulars,
the mind could mount up to the intuition of divine reality. It is because,
in a singular instance, the universal unfolds itself without deficiency
in the particular.

The Mediator comes to us in time, seeking us out where we are in bondage to things temporal from which "contraction of love" we must be cleansed.

But cleansed we could not be, so as to be tempered together with things eternal except it were through things temporal, wherewith we were already tempered together and held fast. . . . We then, now, put faith in things done in time on our account, and by that faith itself we are cleansed; in order that when we have come to sight as truth follows faith, so eternity may follow upon mortality.[106]

God was humbled in time, says Augustine. As such, He became the *principium* of knowledge, the wisdom of God.

It was therefore truly said that man is cleansed only by a *principium*, although the Platonists erred in speaking in the plural of *principles*. . . . The *principium* is neither the flesh nor the human soul in Christ, but the Word by which all things were made. The flesh, therefore, does not by its own virtue purify, but by virtue of the Word by which it was assumed when "the Word became flesh and dwelt among us." . . . The *principium*, therefore, having assumed a human soul and flesh, cleanses the soul and flesh of believers.[107]

But the work of the *principium* as the Mediator between man and God, who comes in "the form of the servant" and therefore veiled,[108] is not exhausted in exhibiting the condescension of God but in humbling man's pride in the condescension. Christ "by the drum of his cross hath opened the hearts of mortal men." [109] This is Christ the "troubler" who disquiets the ambivalent will of man until it turns in despair for healing.[110] As men had cast themselves down by pride, so there was no way to return but by humility: "Because pride has wounded us, humility maketh us whole. God came humbly that from such great wound of pride, He might heal men." [111] In this manner the Mediator converts the will in order that a man may know, remember, the God of whom he had always been aware. Such was the great astonishment of Augustine grounded in his own experience: "I fell off into those material things, and became bedarkened: but yet even thence, even thence, I came to love thee. I went astray and I remembered thee." [112]

Even of the *Confessions,* it is incautious and ill-considered to accentuate the "theo-centrism" of Augustine's form of piety. The Mediator is the indispensable instrument through whom confession is educed and without whom there could be none. Confession is by means of and through Jesus Christ our Lord "by whom Thou sought us, who sought not for Thee; yet didst Thous seek us, that we might seek Thee." [113]

What is *fides*? It is acknowledgment *(agnitio)* of the Word in the form of the Servant. Preeminently, it is love awakened by the lowly form of the historical. It is fundamentally "a motion of the heart." [114] It is the conversion of the will through the crumpling of pride. Whereas faith is elicited by an object in time "adventitious to the mind," its eventual object is the Son—not in the form of the Servant—but in the form of God.[115] As Augustine says: "Our milk is Christ in his humility; our meat, the self-same Christ equal with the Father." [116] For the present, this latter Christ, who shall be the object of sight and understanding in the world to come, is now an object of belief *(creditum)* rather than of faith. It is most important to note Augustine's distinction in this matter, best summarized in his own words: "For *fides* is not that which is believed *(creditur)*, but that by which it is believed; and the former is believed, the latter is seen." [117] It is the Servant seen who, abasing man's pride, evokes the *caritas* which, in its turn, requires belief that, in the flesh, the eternal Word is *incognito*. And by faith we shall at length arrive at sight of Him we have believed "whom, however, we shall never see unless now already we love." [118]

But, in the understanding of Augustine's thought, never should it be forgotten that no love could be evoked or faith implanted unless, in the servant, a man *re-cognize*, recall, remember the divine goodness from which, although always furtively aware, he has turned away to his own will. Nevertheless, not even the Word made flesh could induce faith and love to God had not the eternal Word already visited the reason of man. Of this visitation the heart retains vestiges. Were it not so, the eternal could not be discerned in the historical—wounding man's pride. Neither could the historical recall the heart to the eternal. Thus, of the mind, Augustine says ". . . unless the good remain in it from which it turns away, it cannot again turn itself back thither, if it should wish to amend." [119] Yet again: "And because our soul was troubled within us, we remembered thee." [120] The troubler, He who evokes crisis, is the Mediator. Confession is the will's consent to what was present to reason but was unacknowledged. Faith and reason are required one of the other. They are coimplicates; and it is error, in Augustine's view, to divorce them. Faith presupposes reason; reason urgently requires the correction of faith.

A final word about confession: it is the valid form of realized or completed knowledge of God. Confession, which is occasioned by the Mediator, signalizes the passage from God's being present to the mind to God's being penitently and therefore willingly entertained by the mind. The mind, that is, the willing-thinking-man, has become an eager host to God, whereas before he was inhospitable toward Him. It is confession, therefore, on the part of the converted mind, that betokens the dispersal of that sinful perversity of man in which he denies or distorts his knowledge of God's presence by turning from God in presumption.

The passage, therefore, from knowledge to acknowledgment, from philosophy to Christianity, is the transition, as Augustine so often declares, from "presumption" to "confession." But because of so great misunderstanding, it must be kept firmly in view that this is not a simple passage away from reason to credulity. It is a movement away from the standpoint of autonomous reason, as yet unhumbled by the Mediator, to a willing recognition of God in which reason is operative but at length, being cleansed, unambivalently and vigorously lays hold of God, not as an object but in eager and living conversation. This is, what Augustine's *Confessions* is—a penitent conversation with Him whom Augustine at length has come to know through acknowledgment. So does it become clear that sin is the cause and occasion of ignorance, and the ground of the aberrations of "natural" reason. Therefore, except a man have faith, he shall in no wise understand.

GREEK AND CHRISTIAN VIEWS OF TIME

It is commonly agreed that the Christian doctrine of the Word made flesh gives to history a significance it did not possess for classical Greek thought. Time ceases to be cyclical and acquires directionality. Directionality is constituted not only by *telos* but by *finis*. Time has beginning with creation, receives its *telos* through the Incarnation, and has its *finis* with the Last Judgment. Time, thus, acquires meaning as the interval of duration between creation and redemption. As such, it has an irreversible direction.

The purpose of this paper is a limited one. I propose to compare the Platonic-Aristotelian views of time with that of Augustine. Perhaps we shall be able to determine whether or not classical Greek thought attained to the concept of historical as distinct from physical time— if not, why not. We shall also be concerned to understand in what sense there are "kinds" of time, although time is essentially one thing, viz., duration. A certain directionality of time is a mode under which the Christian apprehends the power and purpose of God—the purpose of redemption. In such a perspective history becomes *Heilsgeschichte,* or saving history. But this perspective would be quite impossible for the Greek mind in so far as it did not attain to the conception of teleological or historical time. Actually, for the Greeks, humane existence as such is as assured of dissolution as of fulfilment.

I. PLATO CONCERNING TIME

Plato's treatment of time is meager and, apart from three pages of the *Timaeus* (36e–39e), entirely casual. In essentials, his position is twofold: (1) time is a concomitant of all change in the realm of Becoming; (2) time is a certain number or measure of all change, positional or organic. Both these views are expressly developed in the *Timaeus.* Elsewhere, Plato ordinarily conceives time as duration or interval.[1] Customarily, he conceives change always in conjunction with time lapse.[2]

Although Plato's explicit consideration of the nature of time is curiously fragmentary, the distinction between temporal and eternal is indispensable for his ontology and is continuously presupposed in the

A paper presented to the Duodecim Theological Society, New York, 1951, and published in *The Journal of Religion*, XXXIII, No. 4 (October 1953). Slight emendations have been made in this edition and a new section (IV) has been added by the author.

Dialogues. Time, *kronos*, is required to signalize the discontinuity between that "which is existent always and has no becoming" and that "which is always becoming and is never existent." [3] The "always becoming" is the realm of sensible and corporeal particulars. It is the sphere of generation where all things are subject to the endless process of coming to be and passing away. This is physical nature. When Plato declares that things of Becoming are "never existent," he does not signify that they have no being at all. He intends two things. First, that everything in the cosmos, perhaps the cosmos itself, is most radically in process, in process of coming-and-ceasing to be. Second, he means by "never existent" a condition contrary to that of eternal Being which everlastingly abides. He means, therefore, to specify a deficient degree of being in the "never existent." Accordingly, physical Becoming is "between" that kind of reality which "altogether is" and an abstract but real "material" substratum which, in Plato's defined sense, is not.[4]

We may say, then, that Plato's ontology requires that time shall be regarded as a condition inseverable from all that becomes. Time, whatever else it is, is the assurance that all Becoming shall be evanescent and finite. And, here, finitude involves *finis* of every particular, viz., its interval of existence is a curve limited in respect to duration. Accordingly, temporality is a mark of deficient being. The mark of complete Being is permanency; that of Becoming impermanency. As all particulars strive to actualize their Form and do so only deficiently, so all particulars strive after permanency, the Eternal; but their moment of partial attainment is succeeded by dissolution.[5] Limited duration or temporality is the ineluctable fate of all that becomes.

Plato's initial approach to time versus eternity was probably by way of reflection upon the nature of knowledge, *epistème*. Hitherto the word was highly ambiguous with no commonly acknowledged denotation. For Sophists, like Protagoras, knowledge was equated with sense perception. Aristotle's deductions are pretty reliable when he indicates that Plato abandoned the senses as avenues of knowledge because objects of sense are in continual flux and do not admit of stable apprehension. This is corroborated adequately in Plato's *Dialogues*.[6] Knowledge, therefore, must have to do with what "abides" and may be the object of common acknowledgment and communication. For this reason, Plato identified that which is "most intelligible" with that which "most truly is" (*Rep.*, 479a). Thus "essence" is taken to signify Being in the superlative degree. This sphere of reality is "divine, immortal, intellectual, uniform and ever unchanging." Reality, in the privileged sense, exists as an "eternal now." It is strictly timeless as well as spaceless.

In the *Timaeus* Plato first considers the nature of time systematically and in connection with cosmology. Of necessity the cosmos, which is always coming to be but never truly *is*, must be distinct from the eternal "Model" of which it is a likeness. This statement is followed by the famous assertion that the cosmos is an everlasting but moving image of eternity that moves according to number (*Tim.*, 37d). Now, it is the moving of the image according to number (κατ' ἀριθμὸν) which constitutes time. The *uranos*, heaven, is preeminently an image of eternity in the sense that its movement is all-embracing and majestic in order and measure. Hence, for certain purposes, time is said to come into existence along with the heaven; and, as the ideal "Model" of the cosmos exists through all eternity unchanging, the moving image exists through all time "continually having existed, existing, and being about to exist" (*Tim.*, 38c).

Time, then, comes into existence. It obtains wherever motion of bodies is measured according to some numerically determinate unit standard. Without orderly movement of the cosmos, there is no time. Because of time, as well as motion, the cosmos is an image of the eternal "Model." Time is the number or measure of motion. Generically considered, it does not matter what motion be designated, although the more uniform will be the more numerable. Strictly speaking, however, time is dependent upon any orderly motion whatever, whether the movement of the circle of "fixed stars" or the movement of any discrete body in space. In Plato's ontology, time is the indication that order and number have been superimposed upon the unordered and immoderate motions of the "material" substratum of Becoming.

If time is the measure of any motion whatever, it remains to inquire whether Plato envisions some universal standard of time. In ancient Greek religious tradition, *eniautos*, the year, signified the perennial round of the seasons. Time was popularly identified with the cyclical return of the seasons upon themselves.[7] Plato refers to this tradition in the *Cratylus* (410d). In the *Timaeus*, however, the influence of fifth-century astronomy becomes evident. Simultaneously with the "generation" of the heaven, days, months, and years come to be. The year, however, is not denoted by the return of the seasons but by the sun's completion of the ellipse of its own orbit. The year is the time required for the sun to leave and return to the degree longitude marked by the winter solstice. The month is time required for the moon to complete its phases. Hence, Plato speaks of sun, moon, and planets as "determining and preserving the numbers of time" (*Tim.*, 38c). Thus, the day, month, and year are convenient standard intervals by reference to which motions of all sublunary bodies are measurable in respect to duration. Length of time, then, is a coimplicate of the uniform movement of bodies through measured space, viz., degrees longitude. The standard interval of time is the correlate of distance covered by a specified body moving at uniform velocity. This is what we have come to call "clock time" or physical time. It is the amount of space traversed by a body in uniform motion. Directionality is here entirely accidental; the only requisite is uniform velocity in space.

There is, nevertheless, a manner in which time, for Plato, retains the cyclical character of *eniautos*, the revolving seasons. Also, in their common cyclical nature, both time and "generation" or Becoming are analagous to one another. In the *Phaedo* (72b) there is the striking statement that "generation" is "always curving back on itself." Plato's reasoning here is somewhat obscure, but other passages of the *Dialogues* make it clear that the inherent nature of *genesis* is elliptical, a continuous movement around two opposite or antithetical poles. It is axiomatic for Plato that "for everything that has come into being destruction is appointed." [8] Generation is an everlasting cycle, but everything "circles round according to number" (*Tim.*, 38a). Thus, the number or measure of generation is time, and time, accordingly, possesses the cyclical nature of generation. Whether, therefore, Plato makes time a correlate of uniform solar rotation or an analogue of the cycle of generation, the only direction of time is cyclical.

Before drawing a few implications of Plato's view, a word should be said about the "parts of time." Plato speaks of "past" and "future" as "generated forms" of time. Coming to be and passing away is the nature of all that becomes. Things are about to be or have been. Only in a very inaccurate sense may we speak of the "present," of the "is," of any particular (*Tim.*, 38b). No thing is what it is long enough to be called "this" but only "such-like." [9] Accordingly, the present-of-time is really specious. It is only respecting intelligible Being, which "abides ever the same," that we rightly use the present tense of the verb "to be." But that present, that "is," is an eternal now. The temporal does not admit of a "real" present. It is constituted of "will be," a fleeting indistinguishable present, and a "has been." The absence of a "real" present is, again, Plato's way of exhibiting the difference between Becoming and Being. Hence, in knowledge, as distinct from perception, the transition which the mind makes is from a specious to a real present—from time to eternity. Moreover, a specious present—a world to which the "real" present does not apply—is a world deficient in Being. If, however, the present-of-time were actual, there would cease to be difference between Becoming and Being, between time and eternity, between the *is* and the *ought*. There would be the end of process and becoming as was the case with Parmenides.

Finally, it should be observed that time and Becoming do not exist apart from the *contribution* of eternity and Being. Time does not exist apart from the existence of ordered as distinguished from unordered motion. There are both kinds in Plato's universe. It is number, the formal principle or *peras,* which, by ingression into the "material principle," imposes order upon "unorder" and accounts for the rhythmic processes of nature. The existence of time, then, is the indication that Becoming is a realm of deficient being between complete Being and its negation.

Time and Becoming are cyclical. Plato therefore leaves us the melancholy result that we can only have process, in contrast with Being, by having it in the form of everlasting recurrence. There is an important corollary. Plato does not look to any future "now," to any present in the future, for realization of the ideal Good. He does look for amendment of human existence in proportion as men acknowledge the sovereign authority of the divine measure, the Good. But he does not anticipate a perfected present in any future, some "far off divine event." For Plato a utopia in time is excluded.

If we complain that Plato has no place for salvation in history but only beyond history, we ought in justice to preface that observation with another. Plato did not attain to a conception of history at all; and one conspicuous reason is that he did not attain to the idea of historical time. Plato's time is either physical or organic; and, primarily, it is physical rather than organic. In so far as time was organic, Plato took his cue, not from growth-in-fulfilment, but from dissolution of every imperfect fulfilment. But, primarily, Plato's time was physical time or "clock time." This is the measurable movement of any body in uniform motion in space. It was only convenience which commended to him uniform solar rotation as standard. Strictly speaking, any measurable motion, viz., regular, would do. But it is wholly immaterial and accidental whether a physical magnitude moves in space in one direction or another. The fact that solar movements were elliptical accorded to time, therefore, the only direction it had, the cyclical. But cyclical motion is repetitious; and, hence, time, as its correlate, really has no direction at all. Thus, it is strange but true that Plato, the father of teleology, has no teleological time. And we cannot attain to history until time somehow acquires *telos.* But, first, time must be seen to be a continuum of duration not reducible to uniform physical motion in space. Aristotle was to make a step in this direction.

II. ARISTOTLE CONCERNING TIME

Although Aristotle asserted that no thinkers before him had illuminated the real nature of time, students of Plato and Aristotle are not surprised

to discover, on examination, that Aristotle's treatment of the time problem is dependent upon Plato's fragmentary but profound reflections.
Nevertheless, Aristotle is to be credited, not only with searching and
systematic elaboration of the thought of his great predecessor, but
also with a number of advances upon it.[10]

In the first place, Aristotle was aware that time was integral with
any treatment of physics in so far as physics was concerned, not merely
with physical magnitudes, but also with such magnitudes in process
of change. Changes might be any one of three varieties: local motion,
alteration, or growth (organic change).[11] Time is the measure of motion
in changing magnitudes. If, therefore, we are to render a rational account of bodies in motion, time is an indispensable correlate for expressing velocity. The physical context, then, for the most part, is the one
from which Aristotle approached the question of the nature of time.
This is most important, because, although Aristotle came near to attaining the concept of organic as distinct from physical time, he was finally
prevented because of the standpoint (physics) from which he approached the solution.

Aristotle shared Plato's two basic convictions regarding time: time
is a concomitant of all change and time is a certain numeration of
any change whatever. The latter thesis Aristotle articulated into the
dictum: time is the numerator or measure of motion.[12]

Although this formula is representative, it is not exhaustive of Aristotle's reflections on the nature of time. Plato's treatment of time in the
Timaeus left the impression that time had little or no existence apart
from orderly movement, preeminently, the orderly movement of the
outermost heaven. This numerable and numbered movement seemed
to constitute time itself.[13] Any other existence time might have was
certainly left undefined. In any case, Artistotle took Plato at his word
when the latter said time came into existence with the heaven. But
Aristotle's own reflections led him to oppose a simple reduction of
time to a measure of physical motion, even though the motions were
celestial and accounted divine. Time seemed to him somehow distinguishable from measured motion. He found himself obliged, it is true,
to concede that there is no time outside the outermost heaven.[14] Moreover, he was free to confess that, wherever motion was perceived,
time was perceived also; but he was persuaded that time could not
be identified with ordered physical motion without remainder.

In support of his persuasion of the partial independence of time,
Aristotle summoned three formal proofs, but behind the proofs stands
an intuition that time is a kind of continuum of duration, a sort of
omnipresent, all-embracing frame for mutable existence. Consequently, Aristotle argued, in the first place, that no heavenly revolution,
however orderly, could be arbitrarily selected as standard of time lapse.

He observed that a portion of the heavenly revolution is quite as much time as the whole of it.[15] Second, Aristotle argued that change is the changing of specified particulars in diverse phases of change, whereas "time is current everywhere alike and in relation to everything." [16] Finally, he pointed to the fact that velocity of change among bodies is faster or slower, but not so time; and, since the precise rapidity of change is calculated by reference to time, the latter must, consequently, be regarded as a constant.[17]

These observations lead to the following result: although time appears to us as "some kind of passing along and changing," it cannot forthwith be identified with the changes of any magnitudes however great or orderly. It is true that Aristotle, in the last resort, is obliged to follow Plato in deferring to a standard of time passage and to take as that *metron* the uniform rotation of the outermost sphere of the heaven.[18] But Aristotle is aware, as Plato was too, that any selection is an arbitrary, though inescapable, expedient. There must be, for pursuit of rational physics or cosmology, some universally applicable standard of time uniform enough to embrace all lesser times of change within its encompassing period. In due course, therefore, Aristotle was obliged to accredit Plato's view that time and the heaven have existence together; only Aristotle qualifies it: they have a correlative existence together.

Meanwhile, throughout Aristotle's analysis there is a pervasive indication that he conceives time as a quasi-independent continuum of duration, an even, regular flow of a "somewhat" that eludes comprehension because it can only be defined as a correlate of physical motion. Time is said to be identical everywhere.[19] Its "nows" are everywhere simultaneous. Like motion, it is a continual flux. Considered as a "scale," it possesses a dyadic character of more-or-less. As such, it is numerically calculable.[20] Moreover, things are said to be "embraced by time" after analogy with things embraced by place.[21] Altogether, Aristotle seems to be on the verge of according time independent existence—a kind of permanent possibility of change in changing things. However, this tendency to conceive time as a preexisting framework of mutability, is checked by Aristotle's agreement with Plato. Time is incomprehensible apart from its correlation with motion. Hence, Aristotle arrives at the somewhat equivocal solution that "time is neither identical with movement nor capable of being separated from it." [22]

The reasons for time's nonidentity with motion have been stated. The grounds of its inseparability Aristotle now undertakes to clarify. He observes that we are not conscious of time lapse unless we are simultaneously aware of change. The changes may be outward physical motions, or they may be successive moments of inward experience and reflection. Motion of thought, *dianoia,* or motion in the psyche, as well as motion of things, alerts us to time passage.[23] With this latter observation Aristotle was at the threshold of approaching a nonphysical and, possibly, teleological view of time; but he makes nothing of his observation concerning motion in the soul. He reverts to the exteriorized standpoint and proceeds to give a physical account of time.

In his analysis Aristotle holds that the primary denotation of "before and after" is the positional and spatial situation. There is, in point of fact, a sequential dependence of motion upon space or position and, in turn, of time upon motion. The "before and after" of time is, in rational physics, dependent upon the changed position of bodies in respect to space. Accordingly, Aristotle shortly concludes that physical displacement (motion) is the objective basis of "before-and-afterness" in time.[24] This is Aristotle's final word: the before-and-afterness of time is an "analogy" ($\alpha\nu\alpha\lambda o\gamma a i$) of the "behind-and-before" of spatial location.[25] Thus, as there is dependency of motion upon position (displacement), so, by the same token or "proportion," there is dependency of time upon motion. We determine a movement by defining its first and last limit; thereby we also recognize lapse of time. More exactly, awareness of time requires specification of two "nows" marking the start and the terminus of physical displacement.[26] It may be added, moreover, that the "now" of time, which is not a "part" of time itself, possesses "analogy" with the moving body in space, the atomic magnitude.[27]

From this analysis it appears at first sight that Aristotle has quite abandoned his intuition of time as continuum and has ended in reducing time to a function of motion, the sort of thing he had protested in Plato's treatment. Evidently this is not his intention, and he has protected himself by his concept of analogical relations among place, motion, and time. While there is "sequential dependency," the dependency is not direct and logical but analogical. This preserves the partial independence of time to motion as, on the same ground, independence from space is preserved to motion. Hence, Aristotle insists that the before-and-afterness of time is conceptually separable from motion, but in the actuality of physical change it is not so separable.

Following this analysis, Aristotle arrives at his definition of time as "measure" or "numeration of movement." We measure length of uniform movement by time and, conversely, length of time by uniform movement. The two mutually determine each other.[28] Time and motion, thus, are correlatives.

As a correlative of motion in space, the time Aristotle has defined is physical "clock time." It is apparent that Aristotle makes nothing of his observation that there is no consciousness of time where *nous* abides "in a single indivisible and undifferentiated state." [29] He does raise the question whether there would be time in the absence of consciousness or psyche. It was this question Augustine was to press. Aristotle's conclusion seems to have been that time, indeed, would not exist apart from some consciousness, because periods of motion would not be counted.[30] Here, he is on the verge of perceiving that the dependency of time is not upon physical motion primarily but upon the intelligent subject of experience for whom change is not merely outward but inward and, as Augustine was to show, in an irreversible direction. Aristotle might have discovered teleological and, therefore, historical time; but he failed to probe his own observations.

No more than Plato before him did Aristotle distinguish organic time from physical time. He did assert that time is the measure of any change whatever: local motion, alteration in quality and quantity, and growth. But he does not select organic development as a measure of time. It is not easily numerable, and it does not possess the uniformity of change that movements of sun or moon possess. Hence, like Plato, he resorts to the uniform rotation of the sun's orbit or to that of the outermost sphere because of the precise numerability of these revolutions—their greater rationality. So he remained imprisoned within the confines of physical and cyclical time, neither of which possesses direction or *telos*.

It is true that, like Plato, Aristotle considered the celestial cycles as analogous with the revolution of organic growth and decay. But, like Plato also, he fastened his eye upon the dissolving rather than augmenting pole of generation. It is the character of time to "crumble" all things. They grow old under the power of time. Time is still the great destroyer; for, says Aristotle, "we regard time in itself as destroying rather than producing." [31] In so far, therefore, as Aristotle considered organic time, it presented the somber spectacle of growth ending in decay. Whatever direction organic time might have apart from cyclical revolution—and that is no direction at all—it presented a movement toward death and dissolution. The aspiration of the temporal after the eternal, however strenuous was vain; and there was no conception of the eternal's taking upon itself the temporal. Time and eternity took their separate ways, and the fate of time was, as with Plato, forever to revolve upon itself. Aristotle made an important contribution, however. He indicated that time, as measure of change, is a continuum not identical to physical motion in space and, therefore, quite as capable of being the matrix of inward as of outward experience. This was a necessary intermediate step to the Augustinian view of historical time.

III. AUGUSTINE CONCERNING TIME

Augustine's reflections on time are distilled for us in Book XI of the *Confessions*.[32] Time is discussed within the larger framework of Augustine's treatment of creation. Creation is, of course, *ex nihilo;* therefore, we are prepared for the likelihood that time also will be considered an absolute creation of God. This Augustine expressly affirms in chapters 13 and 30.

The problem of time is ostensibly provoked by the irreverent question of the impious as to what God was doing in the time prior to creation and why, presumably, he had not made better use of time in delaying creation so long (XI. 10). Augustine states that he will not press the customary answer: that God was preparing hell for those bold enough to pry into mysteries too high for them. Instead, he will call attention to the fact that the creation of God is God's Word spoken in his Son from eternity (XI. 7 and 9). God neither speaks in time nor is He himself in time (XI. 6). If this were not so, and God partook of time and alteration, there would be no "true eternity" (XI. 7). Augustine is able to make the initial answer, then, that there was no time when God, as the inference was, had not made anything (XI. 14). God is the creator of all ages, of time itself (XI. 13). Augustine is now prepared to ask the prior and more fundamental question: *Quid est tempus?* "What is time?"

In the first place, Augustine takes note of the common notion of a threefold partition of time: past, present, and future (XI. 14 and 17). If nothing were passing away, there would be no past time. If nothing were coming to be, there would be no future time; and, if nothing were, there would be no present time (XI. 14). Now, Augustine takes explicit notice of something to which neither Plato nor Aristotle paid attention. *From the standpoint of immediate human experience, time always has direction.* Time passes from the future, through the present, into the past (XI. 21). The direction is one way and irreversible. This anthropological fact will have an effect upon the idea of cyclical process. It is imperative to note that Augustine seems to be following the line Aristotle opened but never developed when the latter observed that time is quite as much a correlate of psychical change as of physical change. Augustine's approach to the time problem is not from the outside primarily but from the inside, from the "psychological" standpoint. Augustine is going to ask: What is time *in human experience?* He observes that, in human experience, time flows out of the future, through the present, into the past.

Augustine now takes a closer look at the threefold partition of time.

With what right can we speak of future, present, and past time? If
we speak of a "long past" or a "long future," do we not speak nonsense?
(XI. 14). Time past is gone and is no more. Future time is not yet.
How, then, can we speak of length or shortness of past or future times?
Indeed, what existence can be accorded to times which are not, since
they are "not yet" or have passed away? [33] Augustine inspects the
present, but the present is passing away. In agreement with Plato,
Augustine remarks that, if the present did not pass but did abide, it
would not belong to time but to eternity. It would be an "eternal
now." Thus, also in agreement with Plato, in so far as the present is
passing away, it is not real but specious. The present is shown to be
a vanishing point: "If any instant of time be conceived, which cannot
be divided into none, or at least into the smallest particles of moments;
that is the only *it*, which may be called present; which little [it] yet
flies with such full speed from the future to the past, as that it is not
lengthened out with the very least stay." [34]

Augustine concludes that the present "takes not up any space." He
recognizes the predicament; if past and future times are not and the
present is a vanishing point, "where is the time which we may call
long?" Has time, then, any existence at all when it is analyzed as a
coimplicate of space? Under such treatment, does not the distinctive
reality of time dissolve into nonentity? Aristotle's analysis had all but
shown this; but his intuition of the reality of time would not permit
him to reduce time to displacement of bodies in space. Augustine is
about to honor the intuition by referring it to its ground in human
experience. Meanwhile, he remarks that it looks very much as though
time is illusory or else is not identifiable with future, present, and
past but is some sort of continuum in which events, prefigured in
the future, occur in the present, and are remembered in the past.
Time then will always require reference to the subject of experience.

Whenever Augustine probes his own consciousness, he is aware of
what he calls "intervals of time," *intervalla temporium* (XI. 16). These
intervalla are perceived as longer and shorter. The differences, however, are comparative. A longer interval is, comparatively speaking,
double or thrice as long as a shorter interval. But this in itself is paradoxical, because it is doubtful from previous analysis that past, present,
or future times have any existence. If they possess no existence, how
can they possess longer or shorter intervals? Time is always passing.
In its nature, it seems to be nothing but "flow" itself (XI. 16). If we
say it is measured *while passing*, we stumble again upon the fact that
no fragment of time, past, present, or future, exists in the sense of
interval of duration. Without interval of duration, how can we measure
time? Augustine wrestles with his problem. He reverts to it somewhat

later: "Does not my soul most truly confess to thee that I do measure times? Yea, I do indeed measure them, O my God, yet know not what I measure" (XI. 26). *Quid est tempus?* is still the unanswered question.

The problem is all the more acute for Augustine, because he refuses to employ the motion of some physical body in space as a standard interval of time. Here he departs from Plato and Aristotle. Referring explicitly to Plato, Augustine pronounces his disagreement with the "learned man" who declared that the motions of sun, moon, and stars are times themselves, *ipsa tempora* (XI. 23).

Augustine demands to know why the motions of these particular bodies should be taken as time or the measure of time. Why should not the motion of *any bodies*, even the potter's wheel, be taken as the measure of time? It seems to him that time is not constituted by the measured motion of any particular finite body (XI. 23). He concedes that the "lights of heaven" are *appointed* for "signs" of seasons, days, and years. Here, he may allude to God's appointment or merely to the arbitrary decision of men who select their motions as a measure of time. It is clear Augustine perceives the arbitrariness of the procedure. He perceives that, if time be measured by the motions of some finite bodies (creatures), there is no one of them which is preeminently the measure. Preeminence is a convenient but arbitrary human choice. Hence, there is, on this basis, no standard interval of time; but, as Aristotle had also declared, any interval is relative and comparative with all other intervals (e.g., the potter's wheel). Consequently, by the purely comparative method, we cannot determine the true certain measure of time (XI. 26).

From the deduction that no finite motion may be taken as the normative measure of time, as the certain interval of duration, Augustine proceeds to a second insistency. It is of crucial importance. He will not consent to the Platonic-Aristotelian equation: time is the measure of motion. He will not settle for the view that time is the numerically determinate distance traversed by a uniformly moving body from a known point. With great acuteness, Augustine discerned that this amounts to a translation of time into certain standard units of space, an effacement of its distinctive character. Augustine thought he perceived that there would still be time apart from the measured interval of any spatial motion (XI. 32). Time, he asserts, is not measured by movement of any finite bodies in space. He wants to know the force, *vis*, and nature of time "by which we measure the motions of bodies" (XI. 23). "I measure," says Augustine, "the motion of a body in time" (XI. 26). "That the motion of a body should *be* time, I never did hear" (XI. 24). "The motion of a body is one thing, and that by which we measure how long it is, is another thing," declared Augustine (XI.

24). Time is not the motion of a body. Rather, "I, by time, measure how long it may have moved" (XI. 24).

By careful inspection Augustine has hit upon the *sui generis* character of time as interval of duration in human experience. Time is not primarily displacement of a body uniformly moving through space. But what is time in itself, then? "Is my not knowing," Augustine asks, "only perchance a not hitting upon the way of expressing what I know?" (XI. 25). As if replying in the affirmative, Augustine shortly proceeds to suggest that time is nothing else but "a stretching out in length," a *distentione* (XI. 26). But the question returns, a stretching-out of *what?* Time is an interval, a continuum, in which bodies move according to number, no doubt, and in which events occur, but what is the nature of the continuum? Though the question persists, Augustine has made an advance over the "outlook" of Plato and Aristotle. By searching his own experience, he has discovered that time is, in experience, the consciousness of a certain duration, *distentione*, which is not exhaustively definable in nontemporal, viz., spatial terms. Otherwise stated, time is not the subject of an "analytical proposition" in which measured motion, as the predicate, exhausts the significant content of the subject.

We have now to find out, with Augustine, just what this interval, or distention, is. If it is an interval, it is an interval of *what?* The answer has already been alluded to and is gradually receiving focus in the course of the inquiry. In chapter 20 Augustine refers to the threefold division of time: future, present, and past. Events of past or future do not exist in the present, yet they endure somehow in time. In our soul, *in anima*, there is a present of the past, a present of present events, and a present of future events (XI. 20). Apart from this "present," viz., existence, there are no three times. The long past is retained in memory *(memoria)*. The present is entertained by beholding *(contuitus)*. The future event is present in expectation *(expectatio)* (XI. 20).

Is it, then, the mind which constitutes the interval of duration? Apparently, this is Augustine's conclusion. Time is the stretching-out of the mind itself (XI. 26). It is the mind that "I measure whenas I measure times," says Augustine (XI. 27).

The mind performs three acts *(acta)*. It expects, it marks attentively *(attendo)*, and it remembers. Therefore, there endures in the mind an expectation of things to come, a recollection of things past, and a beholding and attention to things present (XI. 28). The mind, thus, constitutes the direction of duration in which time is a movement from the future through the present into the past. Long future is an extended anticipation of future events. A long present is enduring attention in the present. A long past is a long memory of events passed away (XI. 28). Time, as the direction of duration, seems to be, then, the endurance and identity of the mind, and the mind's experience in three acts—memory, attention, and expectation.

In Augustine's view, time is basically continuum of duration. It is the duration of creaturely existence. Considered as a continuum, physical magnitudes endure and suffer change in time. But time has directionality only for mind. Time possesses direction only for creatures who possess *anima* or *nous* capable of three distinguishable acts: anticipation, attention, and memory. Teleological time, therefore, does not properly belong to the physical world of mechanical or organic change. From this it should be apparent why Augustine, but neither Plato nor Aristotle, attained to the notion of "history" as distinct from nature. Nature really possesses no history. Only *anima* is capable of history. It is because, for mind alone, events move or flow in an inalterable direction: out of the future, through the present, into the past. It is this which gives to human experience its *promise* to come, its realization, or nonrealization in the present, its happy, or it may be, its bitter memories of the past. Thus, by the inalterability of time flow in human experience, man's duration is susceptible of tragedy or fulfilment. This kind of duration is history or the raw material of historical existence.

For nature, on the other hand, duration either is not in one irreversible direction or else it is cyclical in movement. If cyclical, teleology is dissolved in everlasting recurrence. Or, if local motion be considered, it is all one whether a body accelerates uniformly through space in one direction or another. There are only the dimensions of space in which a physical magnitude moves. To such movement there does not properly belong the axiological dimension of historical, that is, teleological time.

That dimension properly obtains only where the continuum of duration—as for human experience—can "look before and after, and pine for what is not," or repent of the past and aspire to the not-yet. It is this axiological dimension of the human *anima* which Augustine intuits constitutes the possibility of history, as also the differentia of history as distinguished from nature, viz., of aspiration irrespective of what is so, of tragedy contrasted with instinctive fulfillment of function, of responsibility accepted or shunned. History seems to signify fateful alternatives together with what we call conscientious existence. Where this dimension of human existence is not attained or sustained, therewith, history relapses into nature and eternal recurrence.

IV. AUGUSTINE'S THEOLOGY OF HISTORY

Whether in fact Augustine elsewhere in his writings utilized his innova-
tive insights adumbrated in the *Confessions* may in some measure
be tested by consulting his historical reflections which comprise no
small part of his massive and profoundly influential work, *The City
of God.* This is the question whether we may discern traces therein
of history as axiologically determined or end-directed duration and
traces of an emerging distinction between nature and history. Something to be sure had happened to the concept of history between
Thucydides and late Hellenism. Among other things, Hellenism itself
had encouraged a transference of perspective from provincial to cos-
mopolitan, or world history, suited to the reach, first, of Alexander's
and, then, of the Roman empire. Augustine's *City of God* responded
to the momentous catastrophe of the sack of Rome by the Goths under
Alaric in 410 A.D. To the pagan mind it raised resurgent issues about
the role of the old gods in human destiny, and Augustine rose to the
defense of the Christian religion in answer to loud outcries of recrimina-
tion against the usurper Christ.

Turning then to the *City of God* in search of an altering concept
of history, we here and there catch sight in the text of a few matters
worthy of notice. First, the Latin word *historia* does make occasional
appearance and is classed among *studiae liberaliae*, liberal studies.[35]
Augustine refers to writers of history, *historici*,[36] and of what they
write and "commemorate" also as history, thus Sallust's account of
the decadence of Roman morals "can be read in his history," *in eius
historia legi potest.*[37] But, secondly, *historia* is also the thing itself,
that is, the "incidents" or "events" that the historian recounts.[38] If,
however, we look for the precise meaning of history, considered as
the object of observing and recounting, it is supplied by interesting
surrogates. Characteristically, they take the form of the substantive
re in the plural with a modifier in the genitive plural, thus: *principio
rerum gentium nationumque*, literally, "at the beginning of the affairs
of tribes and nations." Obviously established Latin idiom, it is nevertheless almost uniformly the case that when Augustine refers to the subject
matter of historical reflection and narration he uses some variant of
rerum humanarum, the things pertaining to men or human affairs.
Such things may be contrasted with *rerum divinarum* [39] or *rerum naturae*, things divine or the things or affairs of nature.[40] In the third place,
it must be noted that Augustine regularly speaks of "temporal duration," *temporibus diuturnibus*, of empires and of their history. Furthermore, almost uniformly he views this duration as divisible into eras.

The eras that lie behind, *alia retro tempora*, constitute the subject matter of historical memory—*tempora historiam memoriae*.[41] So Augustine introduces his account and defense of the city of God with the declaration of the onset, therewith, of the Christian era.[42] For him *Christianis temporibus* are the times of Christ, the Incarnation of the Word of God—times of the utmost moment for all humanity.

From this data certain observations offer themselves for consideration. Among them is the rather clear indication that the Latin word *historia*, which derives from the Greek ἰστορία, has suffered a significant alteration of meaning in late Hellenism, as with Augustine, when compared with its most characteristic usage in Greek philosophy well into the 4th century. There, its primary denotation was not inquiry or account of human affairs at all; rather it signified "the investigation of nature" in the pre-Socratic mode, and, as illustrated by Socrates' well-known usage and description in Plato's *Phaedo*.[43] It may be clear to some just how this metamorphosis is to be explained by way of the history of ideas; for us, only this much may be noted, namely, that with Augustine as perhaps with Cicero before him, the subject matter of "historical" inquiry is not nature, *rerum naturae*, but human affairs, *rerum humanarum*.

It is perhaps in the light of this finding that we may discern something cognate and something explanatory with reference to Augustine's conviction that historical time is inseparable from the mind of man—that is, its experience in three acts: memory, attention, and expectation—and that, therefore, only *anima* is capable of history. If this is so, then, to speak of history as object is to speak of human affairs. But to speak of human affairs is *eo ipso* to speak of duration as end-directed. Forthwith, what we speak of as history—the course of human events—takes on meaning specified by *telos*. The cyclical process of nature is transcended. Time becomes linear, moving, as Augustine says, out of the future into the present and on into the past. Therewith, also is provided the forward look, the expectancy and promise of the future, either by the provision of God, as in the biblical perspective, or by the provision of man as in secular humanisms. In any case, in Augustine, a philosophy of history is in formation which is predicated upon a solidifying distinction between nature and history.

But Augustine's formative philosophy of history is also a theology of history. Standing as he did, by faith, within the Christian era, his *City of God* is an account of human affairs over which divine purpose presides in a manner and measure hitherto unprecedented. In virtue of the Incarnation, it is a Lordship to be distinguished from God's sovereignty over nature, for although in this matter Augustine is not always consistent, it is a sovereignty not merely of power but of grace, redemptive in its purpose. Stated somewhat differently, God presides over and is determinative of human destiny, not just *secundum natu-ram*, according to nature, but in virtue of what faith acknowledges as the Word of God made flesh exceeding nature. In this word of grace is revealed a new status for humanity. It is a given relationship to sovereign Deity as sovereign grace but not so as to rescind judgment. This reinforces the long-standing issues of man before God, as in the Old Covenant, but now brings them to peak, that is, to a crisis of decision for all humanity.

The dominant theme of the *City of God* is therewith given. It is the issue that faces humanity with sharpened clarity, namely, whether human affairs are to be programmed by fallen man's "love of power" (autonomy) or whether they shall be made answerable to God's self-revelation in Christ who is God's manifest "power of love" (theonomy). The two alternatives are opposites. The latter is the mark and *telos* of the City of God, while the former, autonomy, is the dreadful fate of the city of earth and assurance of its negation. Its fate, unrelieved of its controlling dynamic—the love of power—is endless recurrence of the human struggle.

On such a premise, it seems to Augustine that the story of human history is recurring relapse into nature's cycle of generation and decay. The hope of a consummation of history derives to humanity by the advent of the "power of love," the redemptive Word made flesh. It is this Word of grace—wholly adventitious to the fallen human world—that alone supplies the alternative to the meaninglessness of eternal recurrence. So it is at once the word of salvation and the conferral of meaning upon man's history. Time, indeed, becomes end-directed and the concept of teleological time enters into the warp and woof of Western thought.

Withal, Augustine is more truly a systematizer of Christian under-standing in this matter than an innovator, since he too is dependent upon the biblical story of the history of salvation—now, however, fully extended to the Gentiles and universal in scope. Among New Testa-ment texts his thought reechoes the *Revelation* of St. John:

Behold I make all things new . . . and he said to me, "It is done! I am Alpha and Omega, the beginning and the end. To the thirsty I give water without price from the fountain of the water of life. He who conquers shall have this heritage, and I will be his God and he shall be my son." (Rev. 21:5–7.)

Here is the Christ-event that invades history for the amelioration of history, confers meaning, and constitutes an era of redemption as inter-val of duration between creation and the final Judgment—the latter as both *telos* and *finis.* The issue before humankind is the inescapable decision of every man to claim or reject the proffered heritage which is citizenship in the City of God.

If we ask Augustine whether or not history is finally meaningful for his theology of history, the answer he must give is that the creation, and with it human history, is possessed of such meaning as answers to God's sovereign purpose. That purpose is disclosed by the Word made flesh. By that advent a renovation of history is allowed,[44] but history itself is not a bearer of the consummation. The consummation of history is beyond history. "True justice," says Augustine, "exists only in that republic whose Founder and Ruler is Christ. . . ." [45] With Augustine, as with Socrates of the *Phaedo,* man's history is very much a vale of soul-making. If there is here an eschatology that is residually Platonic and, as some might claim, deficiently biblical, it remains only to answer that it is Augustine's.

HUMANISM SECULAR AND CHRISTIAN

I

For one address, it would perhaps suffice to attempt to unpack the meaning and import of Christian humanism, yet the assigned topic includes secular humanism as well. In my youth the issues, as between the two, were more openly in ferment and debate than they are today. Today, as yesterday, there are many who entertain doubts regarding "Christian humanism": some that it exists, some that it ought to exist, and some that it is either important or meaningful in the Christian tradition. On the other side, hardly any doubt that "secular humanism" exists in sundry expression, and the informed know that it has existed for a long time in bafflingly complex variety and that, like the Geresene Demoniac encountered by Jesus, its "name is legion" because it is many.

Humanism may be regarded as extant long before it acquired its name in and with the revival of learning in Italy beginning in the 14th century. The word "humanism," however, seems to be as old and no older than the Renaissance. In denotation it is not strictly a derivative either of Greek or of Latin. It is the Italian word *umanista* which found currency in the language of Francesco Petrarch (1304–74) and in that of his succession of the 15th century. It was sometime transliterated into the German word *humanismus* and, in our language, becomes "humanism." Among other things, *umanista* signified a lively renewal of interest in human culture as such and immense approbation for it—human culture, that is, represented either by classical antiquity or envisioned as the promise of a new unfolding future for humanity inherent in the intellectual powers of man. Humanism was optimistic about man and his potential in a way that contrasted with the retreating Middle Ages. It looked to a renaissance of arts and letters and went far to enstate the study of history as well as of philology—the latter conceived as an indispensable tool. Since it was still an offspring of the Christian tradition, the Renaissance view of history was not cyclical, as with the ancients, but linear in time. Therefore the future seemed loaded with something like illimitable promise, and humanism was, from its ripening in the 15th century, attended by somewhat utopian

An address to the Convocation of St. Olaf College, Northfield, Minnesota, October 30, 1978.

hopes for mankind. From the beginning humanism encouraged, in some respects, a secularization of human salvation; it tended to become this-worldly.

Although not regularly counted among humanists, the Elizabethan Francis Bacon may deserve a place among them. His affinity is suggested in his near ebullient confidence that, armed with his *Novum Organum* for "the investigation of nature," man's reach may extend, not to the Kingdom of God only, but to "the Kingdom of Man founded on the sciences." [1] Claimed Bacon: to understand "second causes" is to possess the means of interposing them upon nature.[2] Such knowledge is effectual power hitherto uncommanded. Commanded, it has for man unlimited promise for the management of his world, thus to advance, in Bacon's words, "the power and greatness of man." [3]

Umanista stands, then, not alone for the revival of classical learning and culture, the renewal of the arts, and creation of an historiography of human culture; it stands, as well, for the better instrumentation of human endeavor to human ends latent, but surely inherent, in the intellectual powers of man. If it is utopian in spirit, it is because it finds in human intellectual powers not only the promise of high culture but also, in some instances, the *sufficient reason* both of the end of man and of the attainment of that end. Insofar as the end of man is realized through his given intellectual potential, the desired outcome seems to lie more nearly in his own keeping. It is conditioned, no longer by an overruling divine sovereignty, but by a human initiative that fends for itself. So an expanding future opens with larger promise to men and nations. Such were the great expectations of the Renaissance. And, from them, men of the 18th-century Enlightenment nurtured a doctrine of illimitable human progress for which human felicity was the end, and the emancipation and proper tooling of human powers the means.

II

When we turn again to John A. Symonds's classical interpretation *The Revival of Learning*—published a hundred years ago as the second volume of his still notable work, *The Renaissance in Italy*—we may be struck by the evidence of linkage in the succession of humanisms right down to *Humanist Manifesto* II of 1973.[4] Symonds's exhibition of the linkage attends his discussion of Petrarch, whom he regards as "the inaugurator of the humanistic impulse of the fifteenth century." [5] Petrarch's originality, he says, was "eminently displayed in the revelation of humanism to the modern world." Symonds continues: "The essence of humanism consisted in a new and vital perception of the dignity of man as a rational being apart from theological determinations, and the further perception that classic literature alone displayed human nature in the plenitude of intellectual and moral freedom." [6]

Two points should not be missed. First, the revived and near exultant perception of "the dignity of man" as a rational being acquires renewed vitality because it is apprehended *apart* from received Church dogma such as that of the Fall and of original sin. Second, Symonds thinks that by contrast "classic literature" provided to Renaissance men an enhanced and unsullied view of human nature visible "in the plenitude of intellectual and moral freedom."

Knowing more, perhaps, than in the 14th century Petrarch knew of the witness of classic literature to the condition of humanity, we may today be surprised with this exorbitant estimate. Petrarch was not yet familiar with the Greek tragedians nor had he entered with Plato into the darkness of "the Cave" where men regularly confused the Truth for a lie—a lie that roots in the very soul and induces men to call evil good and the good evil.[7] Perhaps, then, it was the *discursive reason* of Cicero that Petrarch came first upon and also the Stoic consciousness of indefectible duty, defended with power by Gaius Cotta in Cicero's *De Natura Deorum.*[8] Through Cotta, Cicero had enforced an inalienable moral responsibility and freedom of man, as man. But it was also true that Augustine had, in refutation, rendered that freedom ambiguous in the fifth book of *The City of God* in the interest of an unambiguous divine sovereignty.[9] For a thousand years the reverberations echoed through the theology of the Middle Ages and, indeed, still echo. Perhaps it was the case, then, with Petrarch and his successors that to side with Gaius Cotta and Cicero in debate with St. Augustine over divine sovereignty and human responsibility also prompted renewed interest and respect for the *civitas terrana,* the city of earth, long sidetracked in favor of the City of God. This reversal of interest, attended by renewed loyalty to the city of earth, is a common tie among all humanisms from Petrarch's day until now.

Yet there are important differences between 15th-century Italian humanism and its many modern successors. From Cicero's *De Academica* as well as his other writings, Petrarch seems to have caught a glimpse—through the teacher of Cicero, Posidonius of Rhodes—of the morally enlightened intellect of Socrates of the *Phaedo* or of the *Republic* of Plato. In the measure this was so, Petrarch's humanism, like that of Pico della Mirandola a century later, retained for human intelligence a real if ineffable relationship to Plato's transcendent Divine Order of Being.[10] By way of this relation there inhered in the human spirit an ineffaceable higher responsibility. Man was indeed a "measure" because, as Socrates had taught all Hellenism, man is measured by an ultimate Good to which he is answerable. Without this inescapable accountability man does not acquire the dignity of *moral being*, the dignity of man *qua* man. This was the Socratic humanism.[11] Of these things Cicero in late antiquity was an eloquent expositor, and Petrarch surely did know his Cicero.

Therefore, the humanists of the early Italian Renaissance did not immediately sense in their nascent anthropocentrism a betrayal of their Christian inheritance. The reaffirmation of man remained still a reaffirmation under God. Revised, however, was their conception of the stature, role, and aptitude of man for the attainment of his cultural ends and of his moral vocation in the world. Down until the time of the French *encyclopedistes* and Condorcet, down to the 19th century, with its Auguste Comte, Karl Marx, or Emil Durkheim, humanism had retained, for the most part, as in Deism, this ineffaceable transcendental reference and affinity of the human spirit, which checked its secularizing momentum. Thereafter, this linkage, as with Condorcet or Comte, was lost in a return to the pristine humanism of Western thought—to the *metron anthropos* teaching of Protagoras of Abdera of the age of Pericles. It is met everywhere for refutation in the so-called "Socratic dialogues" of Plato. The Protagorean "humanism" is summed up in the report of Socrates regarding Protagoras in the *Theatetus:* "For he says somewhere that 'man is the measure of all things, of the existence of things that are, and the non-existence of the things that are not.' "[12]

This proposition becomes restrictive indeed when we add to it the attendant Protagorean dictum that the range of what men may know does not exceed what they can perceive with the senses. It is in great part this marriage of radical empiricism with anthropocentrism which in recent times went far to create the manifold species of naturalistic, sociological, political, so-called religious and,[13] in short, secular humanisms of our time. With Protagoras it took the form of theological agnosticism. Said he: "About the gods, I am not able to know whether they exist or not, nor what they are like in form; for the factors preventing knowledge are many: the obscurity of the subject, and the shortness of human life." [14] Among many implications of this view, if we may judge from the discussion between Protagoras and Socrates as provided by Plato, is this: In the absence of a higher responsibility of men to the gods, the moral vocation of men was defined by their obligation to the city-state. Accordingly, Protagoras conceded that his objective as a teacher of "civic science," *politikē technē,* is "undertaking to make men good citizens." [15]

III

It is fascinating how intellectual history keeps repeating itself. In the
latter half of the 18th century a similar rationale found expression
among a group of thinkers who, likewise, in varying measure, entertained a theological agnosticism and, like Protagoras, considered man
himself to be the *sufficient reason* of the end and also the means of
human endeavor. In that age, the prized objective was what J. B.
Bury has called "a condition of general happiness"—both individual
and communal.[16] And, in virtue of a new science of man, immense
confidence accrued in its attainment. Generalizing upon the emergent
and remarkable state of mind among some intellectuals of the later
18th century, Bury writes:

The idea of human progress is a theory which involves a synthesis of the
past and a prophecy of the future. It is based on an interpretation of history
which regards men as slowly advancing . . . in a definite and desirable direction, and infers that this progress will continue indefinitely. . . . *It must not
be at the mercy of an external will, otherwise there would be no guarantee
of its continuance . . . and the idea of progress would lapse into the idea of
Providence.*[17]

Somewhat more exactly, what is indicated here is that the "idea
of progress," which was to attain near-dogmatic status, is really premised upon a fixed preference for "general" over "special Providence"
among many thinkers of the late 18th century. It is this exclusion of
any divine intrusion into the human, as well as the natural order, which
decisively shapes the secularizing tendencies of the 18th-century Enlightenment. From Bacon onward, and whether with Descartes or
with Deistic thinkers of the 17th century, the primary presupposition
of the latent but formulating "idea of progress" was the assured uniformity of nature. This secured the retirement of "special providences"
by way of the dictum of Francis Bacon that "God worketh nothing
in nature save by second causes." [18] These, taken to be invariable by
Bacon, were identified with the "laws of nature." They were ascertainable by the inductive method of the *Novum Organon*.[19]

With the flowering of the full-orbed idea of progress in the late
18th century only an additional step was needed. Bacon's hypothetical
uniformity of nature was assumed applicable and was applied to the
study of man. Therewith, a science of human nature supplemented
the science of physical nature, posing as no less a "science." Moreover,
as Bacon had extolled experimental knowledge as the self-evident
power to control nature for human ends, so a fledgling science of man
now aspired to a comparable control of human nature, purposing to

alter it for the better. The end was taken as manifest, namely, the greatest happiness of the greatest number. Thus the new "science" of man implemented, as it also rationalized, the idea of inevitable progress.

The bearing and verity of Bury's study of the "idea of progress" may be case-tested by reference to certain English writers of the second half of the 18th century together with the Physiocrats and, particularly, among French Philosophes associated with the Revolution and with democratic political theory. Thus, for example, was the English physician and philosopher, David Hartley, powerfully influential upon contemporaries—Joseph Priestly, Jeremy Bentham, and Thomas Paine. Directly, and through Priestly and Bentham, Hartley was influential upon the political thought of Condorcet and, probably, Diderot. It was Hartley who had at mid-century laid a new basis for the science of man in his massive two volume work, *Observations on Man,* 1749.[20]

Hartley's meticulous study is reflected in Joseph Priestly's *Essay on the First Principles of Government.* It is clear Priestly had made his choice. He had cast his lot with the greater efficacy of human betterment and social progress through the application of Hartley's "association psychology" rather than by way of "special providences," whether in the form of the Sacraments or Reformation justification by faith. This commitment was at the root of the Unitarianism that he brought to America. He looked to the state, not to the Church, for initiative in advancing the program of human moralization. Where there is a science of man there is knowledge. With knowledge, there is power to socialize humanity. It was suitable that the state exercise it as an instrument of social control for re-education of instinctual human affections. Priestly looked for utopia. He did not doubt that "our progress towards perfection must be continually accelerated, and that nothing but a future . . . is requisite to advance a mere man above everything we can conceive of excellence and perfection." [21]

Such sentiments and aspirations disclose a species of humanism fermenting in the Age of Reason. As has been said of the age ". . . man was its goal and starting point, humanity its sole standard of worth." [22] So Alexander Pope sounded the *desideratum* of the age: "The proper study of mankind is man." Sylvia Benians is near correct: "One of the main impulses in the aesthetic Renaissance of Italy had been the conviction that human life as lived on this earth is beautiful and good in and for itself. It was from this point of view that Bacon looked on knowledge. Knowledge is not needed to prepare men for a future life but to help them in this world." [23] Yet, in the matter of the future life, always for the record, Bacon deferred to the "Word of God" seeking, as he claimed, only "the advancement of learning" of God's work, that is nature, better to advance "the Kingdom of man founded on the sciences." [24]

Thus, in the course of the Age of Reason, the subordination of divine Providence to the uniform laws of nature, the erosion of received doctrines of original sin and salvation by grace, opened the way for a more relevant way of salvation. The *novum organum* in this enlightened age would be a new science of man. It was this which came to early bud in Hartley's psycho-physical explorations of the dynamics of the human person. It was a frail harbinger of things to come, but in many minds it emboldened expectations of human transformation and unlimited perfectability. So, M. Condorcet could declare with revolutionary import:

No bounds have been fixed to the improvement of the human faculties; the perfectability of man is absolutely indefinite; the progress of that perfectability is henceforth above the control of every power that would impede it and has no other limit than the duration of the globe upon which nature has placed us. The course of this may doubtless be more or less rapid, but it can never be retrograde.[25]

Here the idea of progress becomes dogma that requires proper implementation by government adequate to the new vision. With Condorcet and Diderot this was revolutionary democracy as the way of social salvation. Baroness Stael de Holstein stated in a word the rationale of her fellow travelers: "In the study of government, we must propose happiness as the end, and liberty as the means." [26] As the sciences of society advanced in the 19th century at the hands of such as Comte, Marx, and Sumner, the ultimate end in view was hardly altered and, certainly, not the presuppositions on which a science of man had been founded. What was changed was the means for application of the scientific truth about man. With Marx and Engels the truth was enforced by the dictatorship of those who had mastered the science of society. With scientific truth in hand, difference of opinion became intolerable!

IV

There are, then, profound divisions between Renaissance humanism and its successors of the 18th and 19th centuries, and there is much more to say of these differences. Is there, then, any single standpoint they yet share in common? Perhaps it comes to this: together they highly esteem human culture as primary *desideratum* and, in contrast with certain emphases of historic Christian teaching, view mankind

as endowed with sufficient intellectual powers for its proper advancement. Gone is a fall of man by which he is disqualified for self-fulfill-
ment. Humanism becomes expressly secular when it is assumed, with
Protagoras, that culture is all the world man has and that, with him
alone, rests the outsome of this world. Then, man is not only the "measure" but also the sole arbiter of his destiny. His calling is, as in the
daring language of Francis Bacon, "to become a god to man." In his
way, a quite different way, Thomas Hobbes in the mid-17th century
was to show how this might be accomplished respecting the political
organization of mankind. By the last quarter of the 18th century a
science of society, mated with democratic political theory, emerged
as alternative to the monarchial absolutism of Hobbes, while, in the
19th century, Karl Marx was to formulate a fateful and competitive
science of society premised upon an economic determinism of history.
With Marx, however, humanism becomes unambiguously secular, i.e.,
programmatically atheistic. With him the latent utopianism of all humanism becomes explicit in the peculiar form of the "dictatorship of
the proletariat."

With such an outcome as this we confront, not paradox, but hard
contradiction in the history of post-Renaissance humanism. What began
with the Italian humanists as a program for the liberation of the human
spirit and the emancipation of the inherent powers of the intellect
is, in Marxist "humanism," and by way of the *Communist Manifesto,*
transposed into "scientific" reasons for the enslavement of men *in
their own best interest.* The state, it turns out, must become a god to
man to establish the kingdom of man founded, now, on the social
sciences! Moreover, it turns out that it is only the state or the élite,
and not men as such, who may be trusted! Is it so, then, that Thomas
Hobbes was right in the mid-17th century: "Where there is no Absolute
in heaven there must needs be one upon earth"? [27]

V

We come now as we must, and belatedly, to what some venture to
call "Christian humanism." Is there such? If so, what is its rationale
and its legitimacy? To begin, there is undoubtedly a long-standing
rift, even clash, between the Renaissance and the Reformation roots
of modern Western culture. Now and again, at conspicuous turning
points and with conspicuous persons, a "Christian humanism" of a
kind seems to have found influential representation—as in the case
of the Oxford Reformers: [28] John Colet, Erasmus, and Sir Thomas More
or, perhaps, in The Mayflower Compact of 1620. Some think it was

rebuffed and, others, reaffirmed by Roger Williams at Providence in the 1630s. Some find it surfacing in the antislavery movement in Britain under Wilberforce, issuing in part, out of the 18th-century revival of the Wesleys. Still others find evidence of Christian humanism in the whole Arminian tradition and find a distinctive articulation in the late 19th-century Ritschlian theology, which helped spawn the so-called "social gospel" and its successors—the "renewal" theologies of our time of which Dietrich Bonhoeffer was a moving spirit.

Insofar as Renaissance humanism rejoiced in the inherent intellectual powers of man or found in this endowment and its employment a sufficient index to the true end of man, it was expressly rebutted by *The Westminster Shorter Catechism:* "The end of man is to glorify God and enjoy him forever." [29] Insofar as Renaissance humanism rejoiced in man's moral vocation and the sufficiency of man for its fulfillment, Luther would be—as indicated in his debate with Erasmus— in vehement dissent. Luther might share with Petrarch the judgment that the conscience of man does indeed alert him to his calling under God. But the conscience was always, for Luther, a guilty one, notifying men not of the sufficiency but of the bondage of their wills when devoid of justifying Grace. Moreover, justification by faith was not entire liberation. Men remained at once justified, and yet sinners. Utopianism, therefore, was completely alien to Luther's viewpoint, and on at least two grounds: first, the condition of man in present bondage to Satan, and, second, the *end* of man as, not the kingdom of man founded either upon the arts or the sciences, but the Kingdon of God founded by faith alone in Jesus Christ. This kingdom men enter, not at their own initiative, but wholly by the over-ruling grace of God. These two grounds, with their corollaries, remove Luther, as also Calvin, from the province of even the moderate humanism of Petrarch or Mirandola and make them irreconcilable adversaries of modern secular humanisms of whatever species.

VI

Is there, then, any legitimacy in a Christian humanism? I will not argue with Luther or Calvin over either the sinful condition of mankind or the pivotal question of divine sovereignty which Luther thrashed out with Erasmus in 1525 respecting the freedom or bondage of the human will. I will note that Erasmus has long been viewed as, in some sense, a Christian humanist by the standards of his age. [30]

Instead, I shall resort in good Lutheran fashion to Scripture—to Genesis 1:26: "Then, God said, 'Let us make man in our image, after our likeness; and let them have dominion over the fish of the sea, and over the birds of the air, and over the cattle, and over all the earth.' . . . So God created man in his own image . . . and blessed them. . . ."

There are several things to notice about this passage, but, in unpacking these briefly, we should remember that we are searching for answer to the question, What does it mean to be human beings? What is man? It was answer to this question that Petrarch, and his succession, rejoiced to find in the classic literature which "alone displayed human nature in the plenitude of intellectual and moral freedom." This we saw was the judgment of J. A. Symonds, and he added of "the plenitude of human nature" that it was found by Petrarch "within the mind restored to the consciousness of its own sovereign faculty." [31]

Perhaps this is so, but the account of man in Genesis 1:26 f. varies somewhat from this perspective. We do not quite start from a "sovereign faculty" possessed by men. Second, along with other creatures, man too is a creature of God. Third, his creaturehood has no standing in itself but, like that of the other creatures, is wholly conferred by sovereign power. Yet it is sovereign power *entirely referable to sovereign grace.* Fourth, the sovereign grace of God is in the case of man distinctively signalized: man is made "in the image of God." This means that man, like the creatures, is not only endowed with a special nature and, by nature, with a distinctive vocation but also that this particular nature and calling defines both man's dignity and also his end. Man's dignity is partly symbolized by his *delegated* dominion over the creatures of sea, air, land, and all the earth. But, in the final analysis, man's dignity is ultimately given in and with his end or his destiny. And his end or destiny is inherent in his *endowment.* This is, again, the "image of God" in which he is made. He is made for responsible companionship with his maker.

The rest of the Old and New Testament is preoccupied with man's failure, or unequal success, in discharging the given role and vocation inherent in the *imago Dei.* It is climaxed by the perfect fulfillment of that vocation in and by Jesus called Christ. In Christ the lost or vagrant image is restored and so actualized in the kind of response to the grace of the Creator that all the time had been the given mandate laid upon man, and, incident to his being made in "the image of God." This is why St. Paul looked upon our Lord as the "New Adam" and those justified by faith as, after the analogy, a "new creation."

We may ask then, what would a Christian humanism look like? It would not view human culture, however splendid, as the end of man. It surely would not understand the vocation of man simply as the Baconian sovereignty over, or exploitation of, the creatures. It would indeed extol man's fulfillment of his endowment or given potential,

but it would understand that endowment as suitable response to the
sovereignty of grace. This the Apostle Paul otherwise described as
"the obedience of faith" (Rom. 1:5). Christian humanism, then would
take the form of faithful discharge of all that is entailed in this divine
endowment—that of the image of God. More exactly, proper response
would take the form of divine-human community specified by the
first together with the second great commandment. In the language
of Jesus, and especially of the Sermon on the Mount, the end of man
would take the form of the Kingdom of God (Matt. 6:33). In a word,
in contrast with secular humanism, Christian humanism holds that
man is not man who spurns his birthright, or, that man is self-deprived
of both his dignity and his divine destiny who pockets his patrimony,
like the Prodigal, and departs to a far country to capitalize on his
inheritance quite to his own ends.

There is much more to say, but this much, I think, we may gather
from Genesis 1:26 f. Christian humanism is responsible existence under
God dedicated to seeking *first* "the Kingdom of God and his righteousness." And, to the contrast of this vocation with that of secular humanism, the words of Robert Browning in his assessment of Andrea del
Sarto, the "faultless painter" of the Italian Renaissance come to mind.
With all his unerring skill, his survey of accomplishments—his or Raphael's—Andrea del Sarto voices Browning's own critique of Renaissance
humanism: "Ah, but a man's reach must exceed his grasp or what's
a Heaven for!" [32] Such in Browning's view is the *ennui*, the finitude,
which overtakes the ultimate products of human genius, even the finest
exempla of the human potential. To reach this point with Browning
is to be open to the Kingdom of God and, by God's grace, a restored
humanity.

THEOLOGICAL LANDMARKS OF THE WESLEYAN REVIVAL

I. DOCTRINE COMES TO LIFE

Thomas Coke and Henry Moore, in the introduction to their *Life of the Rev. John Wesley,* directed this sober and challenging word "to the preachers of the Gospel, late in connection with John Wesley":

The God of this world has hitherto triumphed over every revival of the true religion. Yet the gates of hell have never wholly prevailed. The Lord has raised up another holy temple out of the scattered living stones of the once beautiful building. And this he will do again, if those who now serve him 'leave their first love.' " [1]

Then speaking directly to the successors of Wesley in the gospel, Coke and Moore continue: "On you it chiefly rests, whether the present revival shall continue, and keep its rank in that universal spread of righteousness, which we expect from the sure word of prophecy, when the earth shall be full of the knowledge of the Lord." [2]

Whether Coke and Moore's words, following hard upon the death of Wesley in 1791, already disclose misgivings about the future of the revival is a fair question, which, however, cannot detain us here. Also I leave aside the question whether, in Methodism of mid-20th-century America, "the God of this world" has contrived to bank the fires of that living faith which gave earlier Methodists their identity and reason for being. I leave that aside too for a prior question, one that has often been asked and just as often deserves a fresh answer, namely, What was it that lighted the fire of the revival under the Wesleys and kept it burning for at least a century? What was it in the thought and experience of the early Methodists that made them channels of a new and living movement within Christianity? Or, better, what was it that they recovered out of historic Christian tradition which made them fit instruments of the grace of God?

These are suitable questions, for it is a solid lesson of church history that every *bona fide* revival within historic Christianity has been, in good part, a recapturing of authentic elements of Christian faith—those which in the course of time have fallen out of focus, lapsed, or

A paper before *The Wesley Society*, Minneapolis, April 1956. First published in *District Evangelism*, Board of Evangelism, The Methodist Church, Nashville, Tenn., 1956. Republished in *Religion in Life*, XXVII, No. 1 (Winter 1957–58). Here slightly abridged.

been obstructed. Coke and Moore seem to allude to this fact in referring to the scattered but "still living stones" of the once coherent structure that, lying scattered, may need again and again to be reassembled into the balanced edifice of reformed Christian faith and life. In their eyes the then recent revival under Wesley was no exception to our generalization. It was a gathering up, setting in place, of stones which the builders of Restoration Anglicanism had rejected. These stones were fundamental ingredients of Christian faith and experience. Wesley himself always protested they were firmly fixed in the *Articles of Religion* and the *Homilies* of the Church of England.[3] Nevertheless, they were consistently ignored, and he had to cut them again out of that common quarry of all revitalized Christianity, the Bible.

Wesley indeed called himself *homo unius libri*, a man of one book.[4] How little he is to be taken literally and how vast was his literary range, both his *Journal* and his massive editing labors show. Nevertheless, he was *homo unius libri* in this respect that, after 1730, by his own account, the Bible was for him the standard of Christian doctrine and life. The adoption of this standpoint by John and Charles Wesley may deserve to be considered the first positive step in the direction of the revival that was to come. For it is true to say that the revival, which had its decisive beginning some years later in 1738, consisted, at the core, in a living experiential recovery of biblical faith. Thus, in his *Short History of Methodism* (1764), and referring to the early Oxford Methodists, Wesley declares:

They were all zealous members of the Church of England; not only tenacious of all her doctrines, so far as they knew them, but of all her discipline, to the minutest circumstance. . . . But they observed neither these nor anything else any farther than they conceived it was bound upon them by their one book, the Bible; it being their one desire and design to be downright Bible Christians; taking the Bible, as interpreted by the Primitive Church and our own, for their whole and sole rule.[5]

When, therefore, we look for the genesis of the revival and for foundational and moving causes, we should take careful notice of the vigorous return to the biblical standard of faith and practice by the Oxford Methodists. Anyone acquainted in whatever degree with the controversial literature of English theology between the Restoration and 1738, when the revival got under way, will know that Deistic rationalism, natural religion, and philosophical ethics had well-nigh usurped the place of the Bible and historic Protestant doctrine within the precincts of the Church. There is, moreover, little doubt that the 18th-century revival, both in England and America, was a powerful answer—probably the really effective one—to the rationalistic emaciation of Christian faith and life that had weakened religion for half a century.

In probing for the roots of the revival, then, it is reckless disregard of the evidence to treat slightingly the fact that Oxford Methodism and the recovery of the Word of God in Holy Scripture went hand in hand. Scriptural Christianity was, in this period, not only under attack from without, it had been for some years on the wane within the Anglican establishment. This obvious point, together with the reversal of the tendency by the Methodists, is too little attended to by the historians of that "surprizing work of grace" in the 18th century. Implied in it was a most emphatic protest, from within the Church, against the substitution of philosophy and ethics for the faith and doctrine of the Bible.

However, the return of the Oxford Methodists to the Bible was not a return to dead literalism and the worship of the text. It is undoubtedly true that Wesley accepted something like plenary inspiration of the Scriptures.[6] His work was done before the task of critical Bible study was fairly begun. Nevertheless, Wesley was far from making Christian faith consist in believing all that is written in Old or New Testament. "This the devils believe," he said, "and yet still for all this faith, they are but devils; they remain still in their damnable estate, lacking the true Christian faith." [7] What, then, is the true faith according to Wesley? His answer is plain:

The true Christian faith is not only to believe the Holy Scriptures and the articles of our faith; but also to have "a sure trust and confidence to be saved from everlasting damnation by Christ" whereof doth follow a loving heart, to obey his commandments. And this faith neither any devil hath, nor any wicked man.[8]

What this means for Wesley is that the Bible doctrine of salvation through Christ is known to be true when, and only when, it is experienced as true. Wesley was a man of one book because he found, and innumerable others under his preaching found, that the redemption of man, his justification by and reconciliation to God through Christ, as witnessed to in Holy Scripture, could and did have abundant representation in the present experience of men. The Bible promises verified themselves by coming to life in the recurring response of men and women touched by the power of the Word.

The Word was life. It came to life under the power of the Holy Spirit. Doctrines of the New Testament—justification, new birth, sanctification—took on flesh and blood in the lives of individuals. Here are visible and ample experiential proof of the truth of Scripture. And it was in this context that Wesley was able to distinguish between mere assent to the truth of Holy Scripture, which the "devils" might have, and living faith which a man possessed who knew and had "assurance" of new life. It is also in this manner that we are to understand Wesley's oft-mentioned dismissal of *opinion* and *orthodoxy* in religion.[9] Even true opinions are empty if their substance is not appropriated in life. For Wesley, true Christian faith is *doctrine* come to life in the soul of man.

A great deal of misleading talk has centered upon Wesley's opening remarks in *The Character of a Methodist:* "The distinguishing marks of a Methodist," he said, "are not his opinions of any sort. His assenting to this or that scheme of religion, his embracing any particular set of notions, his espousing the judgment of one man or another, are all quite wide of the point." [10] In recent times these words have been commandeered by some of Wesley's nominal successors to depreciate and dismiss any precise doctrinal standards within the church or to condone a latitudinarianism that opens the doors to all good causes. This, however, is a deceptive and even silly reading of Wesley's meaning.

Wesley was, to be sure, a foe of *orthodoxy*, that is, making relgion consist in right opinions. In his sermon "On the Trinity" his reasons are clear: "Whatsoever the generality of people think, it is certain that opinion is not religion: no, not right opinion; assent to one, or to ten thousand truths. . . . Persons may be quite right in their opinion; and yet have no religion at all; and on the other hand, persons may be truly religious, who hold many wrong opinions." [11] The question is, then, what is religion? And the answer is undoubted: It is *faith*, justifying and sanctifying faith, which works by love. It is, as Wesley declares, "the faith which enables every true Christian believer to testify with St. Paul, 'The life which I now live, I live by faith in the Son of God, who loved me, and gave himself for me.' " [12]

There is a mine of theology embedded in that witness, and we must shortly ferret it out; but for the moment there is this remaining word. While Wesley is a foe of right opinion as a substitute for living faith, he nevertheless believes that Christian faith implies doctrine, the doctrine of the Bible come to life. But he is equally sure that until doctrine has come to life in appropriating faith, it is empty and profitless to entertain opinions and dispute about them. Opinions do not save, only grace does, through faith. For Wesley, Christian truth is what in some circles today is called existential truth, and until it is appropriated, until it becomes true for me, it is dead orthodoxy. And dead orthodoxy was, indeed, one deadly disease of established religion for which the revival sought to be a cure.

II. FOUR DOCTRINAL PILLARS OF THE REVIVAL

On the occasion of Wesley's first visit to the North and to Epworth, and under the *Journal* dateline, "Wednesday June 9, 1742," the following incident is recorded:

> I rode over to a neighbouring town to wait upon a Justice of Peace, a man of candour and understanding; before whom (I was informed) their angry neighbours had carried a whole wagon-load of these new heretics. But when he asked what they had done there was a deep silence; for that was a point their conductors had forgot. At length one said, 'Why, they pretended to be better than other people; and, besides, they prayed from morning to night.' Mr. S[tovin] asked, 'But have they done nothing besides?' 'Yes, sir,' said an old man: 'an't please your worship, they have *converted* my wife. Till she went among them, she had such a tongue! And now she is as quiet as a lamb.' 'Carry them back, carry them back,' replied the Justice, 'and let them convert all the scolds in the town.' [13]

Wesley was single of eye and purpose, absolutely given to the Lord's business, without patience for levity—but not without whimsical sense for the ludicrous. Yet the truth about the revival was that men and women were changed, even gossips and scolds. This was often the unintended witness of its enemies, such as the perplexed husband who deduced his wife had been "converted" because her vinegar and irrepressible tongue had lapsed.

To read Wesley's *Journal* is to have sight of a thousand and one such transformations, and many of them far more spectacular. No one has yet mined for the study of conversion the vast riches of Wesley's *Journal*. I mention conversion here, because no man in the history of Christianity was witness to and a more thorough observer of so much empirical evidence of the power of the Christian proclamation upon human lives. For Wesley, it was the work of God of which he, his brother Charles, and his itinerant preachers were but instruments. Again and again, in the biography of Wesley by Coke and Moore, John Wesley is spoken of only as "the chief and most honored *instrument*" of the great revival of religion.

This gives us our cue: the revival was understood by the revivalists and their earlier successors as a "work of God," an action of the divine grace, and in no sense a contrivance of men save in so far as men became answerable and pliant to the divine working. In this respect the revival was in fact a reassertion of the Reformation watchword, *sola gratia*, by grace alone. Indeed, it was Wesley's recovery of this pillar of Pauline Christianity which precipitated the revival in 1739. But in order to see how this is true, we must consider certain basic motifs in the experience and thought of the Wesleys.

While every exact count will be arbitrary, I find four great moments in John Wesley's pilgrimage of faith. Corresponding to them are four phrases embodying four pivotal doctrines. These are: Christian perfection, justification by faith, radical sinfulness, and faith working by love. By no means do these four phrases represent Wesley's compendium of Christian theology, but they do represent the full cycle of his thought respecting the *nature,* the *obstacle,* and the *way* of salvation.

(1) First, then, let us consider Christian perfection or holiness. In his *Plain Account of Christian Perfection* (1777), Wesley reviews the history of his thought upon the subject. He tells us that from the reading of Jeremy Taylor's *Holy Living and Dying* in the year 1725, he formed an instant resolve: "I resolved to dedicate all my life to God, all my thoughts, and words and actions; being thoroughly convinced, there was no medium, but that every part of my life must either be a sacrifice to God, or myself, that is, in effect to the devil." [14] Further, from a reading of Thomas à Kempis a year later he was impelled to believe that he must yield not only his whole life and action but his whole heart. From the reading of William Law's *Christian Perfection,* Wesley was convinced of "the absolute impossibility of being half a Christian"— a rare and bitter insight indeed! Then, in 1729, Wesley reports that he began "not only to read but to study the Bible," that it became for him "the only standard of truth, and the only model of pure religion."

Then it was that he acquired the conviction never thereafter to be lost that "the indispensable necessity of having 'the mind which was in Christ,' and of 'walking as Christ also walked.' " [15] This conviction, as he himself observes, he enforced in his earliest published sermon preached at St. Mary's Oxford, 1733, under the title "The Circumcision of the Heart." Therein Wesley declared the nature of Christian perfection in terms which ever after were only to be reiterated. He held that "the distinguishing mark" of a true follower of Christ is "a mind and spirit renewed after the image of him that created it." [16] A spirit so renewed is one that loves the Lord its God with all the heart, soul, mind and strength, and the neighbor, as a natural consequence.[17] Here we have Wesley's conception of holiness or of Christian perfection, for these are not distinct.

Accordingly, we have the impulse of the Oxford Holy Club, the preaching to prisoners and ministration to the poor and needy, and his mission to Savannah and the Indians. For, as Wesley explains much later in 1777, "this was the light, wherein at this time I generally considered religion as a uniform following of Christ, an entire inward and outward conformity to our Master. Nor was I afraid of anything more, than of allowing myself in any the least disconformity to our grand Exemplar." [18]

Although these words regarding conformity of the whole life to Christ as "our grand Exemplar" could have been and, indeed, were used by the moralistic rationalizers of Christianity in the Age of Reason, they possessed for Wesley a rich doctrinal content, not intended by the rationalists. The conformity of the whole life to Christ meant for Wesley "a renewal of the heart in the whole image of God." [19] Christian life, therefore, was for Wesley the restoration of the image of God in man. It was a new and different order of existence, so that it seemed to him in later years that those who attacked Christian perfection were fighting, as he said, "against the image of God" and so depriving the Christian of his birthright.[20]

Surely anyone having so exalted a view of the Christian life would seem to have good claim of being a Christian. But the story of John and Charles Wesley from the year 1729 to 1738 is the story of disciplined and strenuous effort to attain the goal, yet dogged by an increasingly painful disenchantment respecting human power to achieve it and a progressive consciousness of self-depreciation and impotency. This, indeed, comes to expression in Wesley's bitter confession homeward bound from America, January 24, 1738, on shipboard: "I went to America, to convert the Indians; but oh, who shall convert me? Who, what is he that will deliver me from this evil heart of unbelief? I have a fair summer religion. I can talk well; nay, and believe myself, while no danger is near. But let death look me in the face, and my spirit is troubled. Nor can I say, 'To die is gain.' " [21]

It is true that Wesley's insights were high and his self-exactions severe and unrelenting, but we should not dismiss his real dilemma. For years he had affirmed that the *whole* life "must be a sacrifice to God, or to myself, that is, in effect, to the devil." And it had become terrifyingly clear that his commitment was really withheld and his life was not entire sacrifice. He could not meet the test: "To die is gain." He was still pledged to himself, in effect, to the devil. He lived in the stark and bitter realization of his impotency. The nature of the Christian life he understood; the way to it he had not found. This was his condition on returning to England in 1738.

(2) Wesley was now ripe for the second and decisive moment in his pilgrimage of faith. Under his *Journal* dateline, "February 7, 1738," is the opening parenthetical phrase that may have been a later insertion—"A day much to be remembered." On that day Wesley met Peter Böhler, the German Moravian. A month later on March 5, finding Böhler in Oxford with his brother Charles, he records these words:

"I found my brother at Oxford recovering from his pleurisy; and with him Peter Böhler, by whom (in the hand of the Great God) I was, on Sunday the 5th, clearly convinced of unbelief, of the want of that faith whereby alone we are saved." [22]

From a reading of the *Journal* for the spring of 1738 there is no doubt that Wesley had made and appropriated to himself a formative discovery. The nature and source of faith was the heart of his new insight. As to its nature, Wesley says under dateline April 22, 1738, "I met with Peter Böhler once more. I had now no objection to what he said of the nature of faith; namely, that it is (to use the words of our Church) 'a sure trust and confidence which a man hath in God, that through the merits of Christ his sins are forgiven and he reconciled to the favour of God.' " [23]

This conception of faith, with variations and enlargements, runs through Wesley's every treatment of the subject thereafter. But the full significance of this view of faith rests upon understanding its source and ground; and here we may best rely upon the great manifesto sermon of the revival entitled "Salvation by Faith," which Wesley preached at St. Mary's Oxford, before the University, June 18, 1738. Therein he affirmed that faith is not belief or assent, or "a train of ideas in the head," but "a disposition of the heart." Moreover this disposition presupposes what Christ has done for us, that he was delivered up for our sons, and rose again for our justification. Faith is trusting the work of Christ; first, that our sins are forgiven and, second, that we are reconciled to God's favor. Faith is "recumbancy" upon Christ. It is no trust in ourselves or in our works, but in Christ's working. Christ is the objective ground and cause of faith.

But there is a subjective ground, and here we come closer to faith's basis. "Of yourselves," declares Wesley to the unversity congregation, "cometh neither your faith nor your salvation: It is a gift of God; the free undeserved gift. . . . That ye believe, is one instance of his grace; that believing ye are saved, another. . . . For all our works, all our righteousness, which were before our believing, merited nothing of God but condemnation." [24] Here is the doctrine of justification by grace alone through faith. It not only dismayed Wesley's university hearers; it was at first received with offence by Charles Wesley and with his severe protest.[25]

That Wesley had really recovered the Reformation standpoint and put his semi-Pelagian religion behind him is clear enough from the evidence that, in January of that year, he still regarded the Lutheran theology as erroneous in magnifying "faith to such an amazing size that it quite hid all the other commandments." [26] Even at that date Wesley was so far from understanding justification by faith that he

still regarded faith as among the "commandments." Five months later
his view is fully altered: faith is "a gift of God" and the real and only
true beginning of the Christian life. Wesley had now arrived at the
doctrinal center at which he was always thereafter to remain. It was
a position, as he was prepared to admit, coming within a "hair's breadth
of Calvinism." This proximity to Calvinism is defined in the *Conference
Minutes* of 1744 in three points. Obviously, the prime one is grace as
the sole ground of faith. But the second is crucial, and with it Wesley
puts behind him forever all his earlier religion of self-help. He does
so in "denying all natural free-will, and all power antecedent to
grace." [27]

Wesley had found the weak link in the armor of his strenuous and
pelagian Christianity and, with the discovery, he found the cure. It
was a personal discovery and appropriation. In faith, as the gift of
grace, he had found not only release from the burden and "guilt" of
sin but also, as he asserts, from the "power" of sin.[28] Faith, which he
had formerly taken for a "commandment," he now received as a gift;
and, in forgiveness of sin, he found release from its "dominion." Sin
still remains, but it no longer reigns.[29] Thus Wesley found in his own
experience, what he was subsequently to see illustrated in the lives
of countless others, that the Christian life—life in the image of God—
is begun through a work of God in justification—a work he could not
refer to man but, by experience, exclusively to the grace of the Holy
Spirit. To the "religious man" it was affrontery, for it had left him
nothing wherewith to boast.[30]

(3) It must have seemed almost childish to Wesley as, in retrospect,
he looked back, from the vantage-point of 1739 and the succeeding
years, upon his earlier hectic striving to conform his life inwardly and
outwardly to "the grand Exemplar" when all the time, there had been
no provision in his previous version of Christianity for the forgiveness
of sins. In those days he had only fastened his eyes upon the goal,
girt his loins, multiplied his duties, and cherished self-discipline. Returning to England in January 1738, depressed in spirit, he hitched
his belt a little tigher and renewed his former resolutions.[31] It had
not yet occurred to him that sin might be a "power," a barrier to
Christian perfection, that would require voiding before the goal could
be won. By personal realization he had to learn, what later he was
impelled to state, that no fitness for grace is required, but one thing
only, a sense "of our utter sinfulness and helplessness; everyone who
knows he is fit for hell being just fit to come to Christ." [32]

Accordingly, and in order to explain what happened before and
after Aldersgate, Wesley wrote in his *Journal:* "All the time I was in
Savannah I was thus beating the air. Being ignorant of the righteousness

of Christ. . . . I sought to establish my own righteousness, and so labored in the fire all my days." Then, referring to the warfare in the members, Wesley continues: "In this vile, abject state of bondage to sin, I was indeed fighting continually, but not conquering. Before, I had willingly served sin: now it was unwillingly; but still I served it." [33] In retrospect, Wesley now saw the meaning of the radical sinfulness of man apart from justifying grace. He identified it by its disabling power. Later in his great sermon on "The Spirit of Bondage and Adoption," he graphically described the bondage of sin, its dominion over the life in which grace through faith has not yet wrought its emancipating work.

It was undoubtedly this faith which Wesley found through the instrumentality of Peter Böhler. First he was convicted of the sin of unbelief, viz., unfaith in the working of God. And, secondly, and probably at Aldersgate, Wesley became subject of the grace which works a change in the heart by faith. Speaking of the whole transaction he reflected: "I was quite amazed, and looked upon it as a new gospel." [34] But finally, if justifying faith entails pardon, then, plainly, the new gospel of justification has sin for its presupposition. On this point Wesley is quite emphatic; for it is "sin alone which admits of being forgiven." [35]

(4) The fourth towering moment in Wesley's pilgrimage is represented in the phrase, "faith working by love." In the *Conference Minutes* of 1746 it is declared: "In asserting salvation by faith, we mean this: (1) That pardon (salvation begun) is received by faith, producing works. (2) That holiness (salvation continued) is faith working by love. (3) That heaven (salvation finished) is the reward of this faith." It is an axiom with Wesley that faith brings forth good works. It is also an axiom that "all truly good works *follow after justification*." [36] The original Methodists, Wesley declared in 1779, set out with the "grand principle" that "there is no power in man, till it is given from above, to do one good work, to speak one good word, or to form one good desire." [37] After 1738 it was plain to Wesley that the "heart is necessarily, essentially evil, till the love of God is shed abroad therein. And while the tree is corrupt, so are its fruits." [38] This was Wesley's seasoned explanation of the barrenness of his earlier version of Christianity.

Wesley's later Christianity rests upon justification, which is not only forgiveness of sin but a new centering of the whole life in God. He once called it "therapy of the soul." It is the change which the Spirit of God works in the soul "when it raises it from the death of sin to the life of righteousness." It is the renewal of the "image of God in righteousness and true holiness." [39] Says Wesley, "Gospel holiness is no less than the image of God stamped upon the heart; it is no other than the whole mind which was in Christ." [40]

But, in so describing the work of salvation begun and continued, Wesley is actually describing Christian perfection. His conception of its nature has not changed with the passing years, *but his understanding of its basis has completely altered.* Christian perfection is still inward and outward holiness; it is still love of God and love of neighbor, but it is now dependent upon a change wrought in the heart by faith. The change may not be total. The "corruption of nature" still remains, but it no longer has dominion. And now, the righteousness of faith working by love, that is, love of God, completely replaces the righteousness of works. And it is this righteousness of faith of which Wesley, in 1746, expressly declares he knew nothing in his Oxford days.[41] Now at last the yoke is easy and the burden light. Now the good tree brings forth good fruits, for faith works by love. Faith is no more among the "commandments" but is the spring and motive of their fulfillment.

III. OBSERVATIONS IN RETROSPECT

The four living stones, foundational for the structure of early Methodism, have been scanned. They are: Christian perfection as the goal of human life, justification by faith as the way to it, radical sinfulness as the barrier to be overcome, and faith that works by love as the normal fruit of the renovated life. What we have seen is that, always clear as he was about the nature of the Christian life, Wesley, until 1738, did not understand the way of attainment. In 1733 he was requiring "circumcision of the heart" and unqualified love to God and man. But he did not yet acknowledge these as the fruits of faith, that faith itself is a gift of grace, and that the gifting carries with it a renewal of the image of God in man, that is, in St. Paul's language, a "new creation."

Wesley had come to maturity not untouched by the prevailing ambiguities of post-Restoration Anglicanism for which the earlier Anglican Reformer's stress upon "justification by grace through faith" had become obscured if not eclipsed. Moreover, prior to 1738, I find Wesley's practice of the Christian religion, however relentless, to have shared— if it was not tempered by—the unselfconscious pelagian tendencies of Richard Allestree's widely read *The Whole Duty of Man*.[42] Along with that popular and comprehensive *scalae disciplinae* of Christian life and devotion, John Wesley was about equally innocent of inhering human inability to conform to the rule of Christian practice he so rigorously imposed upon himself. In the winter and spring of 1738, he came, cumulatively, to perceive that his program of Christian perfection evidently presupposed something in addition to disciplined human resources, even of baptized Christians at prayers. Surely, these things must be viewed as the background of his dawning impression of Peter Böhler's teaching as, truly, a "new gospel."

John Wesley, the ardent Christian practitioner, came reluctantly to acknowledge that there is a bondage of the will, as Luther had testified, until it is transcended, and that, although a man may "strive with all his might, he cannot conquer: sin is mightier than he." [43] Those who think that Wesley overdoes the case will have the right to dissent in the measure, that, having defined the standard of Christian life as rigorously as he, they have also striven and with comparable exertion to attain it. Wesley at first underestimated the task by overestimating dedicated human powers. When bondage to sin became an acknowledged reality, he was evidently ripe for Pauline salvation by faith through God's restorative grace.

Evidence is not wanting for the judgment that the 18th-century revival was, on a vast scale, a recapitulation in human experience of salvation by faith which Wesley himself had come personally to know—in his own view, belatedly. Primarily, perhaps mainly, it is this existential realization, conceptualized in doctrine, that related the Wesleys most directly to the Lutheran 16th-century Reformation. As the revivalists held a mirror up to man's plight and offered to all God's pardoning grace, grace was amazingly appropriated in renewal of life. The presupposition was as simple as it was potent: God's forgiveness was at hand but for the taking. Through the grace of forgiveness in Christ, God became, for Wesley, the God of the living, not of the dead. God acted, and men received a jolt; but it was a jolt out of the old ways into the way of God's righteousness—not man's, that is, but the new creation. It was frequently not gradual, but sudden. This at first startled both Wesleys, and John records his disbelief.[44] There were reasons: hitherto, his Christian life had been something he had been at pains to contrive, and his progress had been both laborious and disheartening. But now the result was taken out of man's hands, and Wesley was obliged to acknowledge that what he had supposed could only be diligently achieved was, in fact, in its inception, a gift to be received. Henceforth, faith became for John, as for Charles Wesley, no longer reserved acceptance of God's acceptance in and through the merits of Jesus Christ. We might say that John Wesley recovered a vital Christology as well as what he took to be "the gospel way of salvation."

SALVATION FOR ALL—JOHN WESLEY
AND CALVINISM

I. WESLEY AND CALVINISM

Wesley's *Journal,* for the first year of the revival, has the following entry under April 26, 1739:

> While I was preaching at Newgate on these words, "He that believeth hath everlasting life," I was sensibly led, without any previous design, to declare strongly and explicitly that God willeth "all men to be" thus "saved"; and to pray that, "if this were not the truth of God, he would not suffer the blind (i.e. Wesley) to go out of the way; but if it were, He would bear witness to His word." Immediately one, and another, and another sunk to earth; they dropped on every side as thunderstruck. . . . In the evening I was again pressed in spirit to declare that "Christ gave himself a ransom for all." [1]

The manner of this statement indicates Wesley's awareness of an awakening criticism toward his teaching on grace. Apart from the manifesto sermon "On Free Grace," preached at Bristol, April 29, 1739, in which M. Piette says Wesley declared war on the doctrine of eternal decrees,[2] a reading of the *Journal* from as early a date as May 7, 1738, will indicate that Wesley was preaching "grace for all" as well as salvation by faith. Faith is a gift, but a gift impartially extended to all, and Wesley presumes to offer it.

At Newgate, September 17, 1738, seven months prior to the April visit, Wesley offered the prisoners "free salvation." [3] A characteristic report of this period is: "I offered to about a thousand souls the free grace of God." [4] Time and again his sermon text is: "Ho! everyone that thirsteth, come ye to the waters." [5] Under the date line of May 20, 1739, Wesley declares, God is "not willing that any should perish, but that *all* should come to repentance." On that occasion "a strong assertor of the contrary doctrine" who stood by was among those who "dropped down." [6] Whether this gave Wesley cause for amusement, he studiously omits to say.

Very shortly both John and Charles were astonished and perplexed at the opposition which even "familiar friends" expressed toward their teaching on grace.[7] At Bradford, as early as October 9, 1739, where

Reprinted here, by permission, from *Methodism,* ed. W. K. Anderson (New York: The Methodist Publishing House, 1947). Dedicated, with happiest recollections of thirty years' colleagueship, to Ray C. Petry, Professor Emeritus of Church History, Duke Divinity School, eminent medievalist, prompter of this study.

Charles sought to correct the impression that a previous sermon had asserted reprobation by declaring "in plain and strong words, that God willeth all men to be saved," John reports that some others "were equally offended at this." [8]

By 1744 Wesley was answering charges of persons from the Calvinist wing of the English clergy on the indictment of "popery." For this criticism he could educe but two explanations: either "to excite hatred" of the Methodists or because the Wesleys, rejecting predestination, held a "doctrine of universal redemption." [9]

But the cry of "popery" had already been sounded within the society itself at Kingswood in the spring of 1741. Here the issue came to an open dispute between the Wesleys and certain predestinarians led by John Cennick, a lay leader employed by Wesley to superintend certain interests of the local society. Cennick sought to involve George Whitefield in the dispute and gain his support against the Wesleys, probably a questionable procedure in view of his responsibility to Wesley.[10] The Kingswood crisis was only an outbreak of fires which had been smoldering during the year since Wesley's Bristol sermon "On Free Grace." Whitefield had roundly attacked Wesley for this utterance in a private letter. The letter, secured by some Calvinist Methodist, was published for the promotion of their cause against Wesley, and circulated without consent of either Whitefield or Wesley.[11] Interpreting Whitefield's sentiments (rightly or wrongly) and expressing his own, Wesley had publicly destroyed the printed document at a London meeting of the society.[12]

The expulsion of Cennick and his fellows from the Kingswood society, February 28, 1741, was followed by an open break between Whitefield and Wesley a month later. Whitefield voiced his resolution to preach publicly against Charles and John.[13]

While Wesley insisted that the expulsion of the Cennick group was not on the ground of doctrinal opinion, but upon that of insubordinate and slanderous behavior toward ministers, it is pretty clear that fundamental considerations touching the heart of the revival were at stake.[14] Cennick asserted that the Wesleys were many times heard to preach "popery." His words were : (1) the Wesleys preached against predestination, as any atheist; (2) they "please the world" with a promise of "universal redemption"; (3) the Wesleys teach that men have "nothing whereon to rest but their own faithfulness." [15]

The last point was to awaken Wesley to the realization that however close his preaching to the Reformation, his doctrine of salvation by faith not works still did not permit him to go all the way with Calvin. Cennick was keen enough to perceive that, in Wesley's assertion that faith is altogether the gracious gift of God,[16] yet in denying the doctrine of "eternal decrees" and holding universal justifying grace, Wesley was really rejecting the Calvinist exclusiveness of the divine causality in salvation.

However much Wesley protested that all is of grace, if he denied predestination, he must necessarily, it would seem, allow man some causality in his redemption, thereby robbing God of the glory. In Cennick's mind Wesley was really attributing to man some potency to goodness, in spite of Wesley's denial, and thus, as Cennick claimed, resting man's salvation upon his "own faithfulness." This was impeccable Calvinist logic. Cennick saw vividly the connection between *sola fide* and election joined by the middle term "grace."

If salvation is by faith, and faith is altogether God's gift (grace); then clearly if a man is saved, it is because he was chosen, i.e., God willed to give him the gift. If a man is not saved (justified), it is because he was not given the gift of grace unto faith; therefore he was not chosen. Thus, if salvation is not by works, it must be by decrees. If it is not by decrees, then it must be by works.

Eventually Wesley came to understand this logic.[17] His Calvinist opponents never formulated this dilemma explicitly, so far as I know, but it was implicit from the beginning in Cennick's opposition to Wesley. As the case stands, it justified Hervey's charge that Wesley was "halting between Protestantism and Popery." [18] The argument itself may be regarded as the classic predestinarian demonstration. For fifty years Wesley wrestled to show that the argument did not touch him. That it actually did not is his momentous and little understood contribution to the progress of Christian thought. We shall see that the decisive difference between Wesley and the Calvinists is that he viewed the process of faith from an empirical vantage point as well as from a speculative one; they from a predominantly scholastic and rationalistic perspective.

II. WESLEY AND PREDESTINATION

In order to get the flavor of Wesley's onslaught against the doctrine of eternal decrees, one should read his sermon "On Free Grace, or Predestination Calmly Considered" (!). His reasoning against this blasphemy" is impressive. It is blasphemy because it makes God more malicious than the devil, and contradicts the tenor of the entire New Testament teaching on the gracious love of God.[19] If the Calvinists argue from the divine sovereignty, Wesley replies that God is not exalted but dishonored in despising the works at his own hands.[20] If his opponents take refuge in the inscrutable counsels of God, Wesley stands upon the *declared* Word in the New Testament. All this is interesting, but it does not bring us to the irreducible issue which divides Wesley from his opponents. They declare that if salvation is by grace and not by any work of man, as Wesley admits, then Wesley ought to go along with them in holding double predestination. If all causality in salvation is of God, what other ground can there be for the operation of that causality than the divine determination to operate or not to operate? But Wesley holds back. Somehow experience defies logic, formidable as it is.

What then is the inconsequence in Wesley's teaching and preaching in the opinion of his opponents? This: that Wesley not only preached salvation by faith but that in doing so he emphatically affirmed man's "utter inability to think one good thought, or to form one good desire; and much more to speak one word aright, or to perform one good action, but through his free [!], almighty grace." [21] They heard Wesley declare: "Neither is salvation of the works we do when we believe: for *it is then God that worketh in us:* and, therefore, that he giveth us a reward for what he himself worketh, only commendeth the riches of his mercy, but leaveth us nothing whereof to glory." [22]

This they heard continually, and Wesley reasserted it until his dying day, but his opponents also heard Wesley call sinners to repentance urging them to work out their own salvation with fear and trembling, as though they could of themselves initiate the process of salvation with works meet for repentance.[23] They heard his appeal to the wills of his listeners: "What is your choice? Let there be no delay: now take one or the other! I take heaven and earth to record this day, that I set before you life and death, blessing and cursing. Oh choose life! the life of peace and love now; the life of glory forever!" [24] His opponents did not hear him add, for they were angry by this time: *"By the grace of God,* now choose that better part, which shall never be taken from you." [25] If they had heard, they would have regarded it as self-contradictory; for except the grace of God be possessed, how can a man choose *by it?* If it is possessed, he will *necessarily* choose as it empowers and directs.

To the Calvinists this then is the inconsequence in Wesley's thought: on the one hand he makes everything dependent on the divine grace, while on the other he speaks as if there were some efficacious causality in man instrumental to his own salvation. In the opinion of the Calvinists, the sure indication of this was Wesley's assertion that grace is resistable.[26] Is Wesley really in self-contradiction? Is he holding at one time that salvation is attributable altogether to the divine causality, and that it is attributable to the cooperating causality of man? It would seem that he is, and some of the latest and best treatments of Wesley seem willing to accept the contradiction by attributing to Wesley the conception of an inherent freedom to good, "a genuine cooperation of man with God," to be sure, in the context of a prevenient grace.[27]

But let us be candid. If salvation is of grace, even prevenient, it is of God, not of man. In the light of all the evidence I cannot find that Wesley ever receded from the position that the slightest stirring of man toward faith is other than through the inner working of the divine causality. And, just as firmly I believe he is not in the contradiction ascribed to him by the Calvinists. Our problem is one of saving Wesley from the too soft treatment of his admirers as well as from the allegedly annihilating logic of his foes.

It is desirable here to suggest briefly an hypothesis for the solution of our problem before undertaking to evaluate it. Part of the confusion has been the Calvinist assumption that liberty meant for Wesley liberty to righteousness apart from grace—a Pelagianism or semi-Pelagianism.[28] This was Cennick's assumption. The fact is, Wesley repeatedly asserts that he means only a liberty to "disbelieve" and rebel against God. The will of man, once parallel to God's, now is directly contrary to it, and "leads from God." [29] This liberty is wholly negative, as Dr. Cannon is clearly aware.[30] Nevertheless it requires to be reckoned with in the process of redemption. As a brute given, it confronts the grace of God and may finally resist that grace.

How shall it be extirpated? It cannot be extirpated by God independently of man. It cannot be extirpated by man himself, for the will cannot extirpate itself. But Wesley can say that when it is vanquished, the immanent operation of grace attending, it is through a climactic realization of the self-destructive and self-stultifying consequences of self-affirmation or pride. The man has "come to himself" through despair. Sometimes this may be elicited through *representation* in the preached word; sometimes natural freedom to self-love must ripen its fruit of misery before the omnipresent grace of God can have its perfect work. Despair is the neutralization of man's perverse volition wherewith human causality ceases to resist so that divine causality effectually can begin to operate.

This construction enables one to account for Wesley's admission, derived from experience, that "most believers do, at some other times, find God irresistibly acting upon their souls." [31] Is it not precisely at those times when the will to perversity is reduced to zero? If this is Wesley's understanding of the matter, it derived from observation of his own conversion experience and that of innumerable others. It comes to this: positively, man's will, turned from God, cannot come to God but only to itself and to the "creatures." That will must be rooted out through a certain despair or self-disgust. Any faith or love of God which eventuates is thenceforth attributable altogether to the efficacious operation of grace. Salvation is then altogether of God, yet Wesley is not in contradiction in holding man's will to be a condition, a not-to-be-neglected factor.

III. WESLEY AND GRACE

A presupposition entertained by Wesley's Calvinist critics is that the natural man is totally corrupt and effectually devoid of grace. Cennick and Whitefield must then necessarily conclude that, if human causality has any part as a condition in salvation, then Wesley eventually must be driven to confess that men "have nothing whereon to rest but their own faithfulness." [32] This was "Popery" it seemed.

As has been pointed out, Wesley rejects the presupposition. Dr. Lee has correctly shown that man without grace, the "natural man," is for Wesley a fictional abstraction.[33] Unlike Calvin, one must always remember that Wesley retains, in spite of the "fall," what we may designate as a continuity between God and man, *from God's side*. To be sure, Wesley stands by the total and inbred corruption of man's nature whereby he is "very far gone from original righteousness." The doctrine of "the entire depravation of the whole human nature" Wesley declared to be the distinguishing difference "between heathenism and Christianity." [34] If this overdoes the point, at least it settles the issue. Elsewhere he declares: "Without the spirit of God, we can do nothing but add sin to sin; that it is he alone who worketh in us by his almighty power, either to will or to do that which is good." [35] Such is the natural man, conceived independently of grace of whatever kind. But does any man, devoid of grace, actually exist *as God made him?*

Let us look more closely into man's condition for an answer. Man's original righteousness, in his pristine condition, consisted in a three-fold endowment: understanding, will or "various affections," and "liberty or a power of directing his own affections." [36] He possessed a power to sin *(posse péccare)* and a power not to sin *(posse non peccare)*.[37] With the actualization of the will to unbelief, born of pride, he lost *posse non pecarre*, retaining only *posse peccare*. Thus, in his natural condition, man has no freedom to good, but only to evil.

Wesley knows what he is about, then, when in the *Minutes* of 1745 he affirms that he comes to the "very edge of Calvinism: (1) In ascribing all good to the free grace of God. (2) In denying all natural free-will, and all power antecedent to grace." [38] This position seems not to have been abandoned concerning man's bondage, for in 1772 Wesley writes: "But indeed, both Mr. Fletcher and Mr. Wesley absolutely deny natural free will. We both steadily assert that the will of man is by nature free only to evil. Yet we both believe that every man has a measure of free will restored to him by grace." [39]

So does Wesley make void the power of man *qua* man to work, of his own causality, salvation. But no man is merely natural. The definitive statement here, as well as the most important single utterance Wesley made upon the process of salvation, is found in his sermon "Working Out Our Own Salvation." Here he declares:

It is God only that must quicken us; for we cannot quicken our own souls. For allowing that all the souls of men are dead by nature, this excuses none, seeing there is no man that is in a state of mere nature; there is no man, unless he has quenched the spirit, that is wholly void of the grace of God. No man living is entirely destitute of what is vulgarly called *natural* conscience. But this is not natural: it is more properly termed preventing grace.[40]

We hit here upon what Wesley indifferently terms assisting or preventing grace.[41] This is a knowledge of God independent of the Mediator and antecedent to justification. It is of grace not of nature; for all is of grace, and nothing is really nature *in actualis*, that is, nothing except the man who has quenched the spirit, if such there be. This knowledge man may willfully obscure by neglect through self-love. This grace is universal and universally operative. It is the presupposition for the very beginning of the life of the spirit: "Salvation begins with what is usually termed preventing grace; including the first transient conviction of having sinned against him." [42]

Preventing grace, moreover, must be presupposed as prerequisite to the possibility of sin (resistance of grace) and the consciousness of it. Thus "no man sins because he has not grace, but because he does not use the grace which he hath." [43] Or "it is his Spirit who giveth thee an inward check, who causeth thee to feel uneasy." [44] Sin is "grieving the Holy Spirit," presupposing the universal immanence of grace.

The ubiquity of grace is a conception carried over by Wesley from his "pre-conversion" period to remain forever integral to his thought; hence his word to Chicali, the Georgian Indian: "I told him, if red men will learn the good book, they may know as much as white men. But neither we nor you can understand that book, unless we are taught of him that is above; *and he will not teach, unless you avoid what you already know is not good.*" [45]

From all of this it is apparent Wesley makes no sharp divorcement between nature and grace, in the sense that man's whole existence is enveloped by the wooing activity of God, who "enlighteneth every man coming into the world" with some knowledge of himself—a knowledge that allures and disquiets.[46] Temples of the Holy Spirit we are.[47]

But we are at liberty to grieve the Spirit, yet not without disquiet, and the disquietude and compunction is our hope of eventual redemption. Salvation is the resolution of the tension between "the drawings of the father" (prevenient grace) and man's rebellious introversion. For Wesley justifying grace is prevenient grace becoming triumphant; but it is God working, not man.

We see then that Wesley's conception of man, whereby he is continually confronted by grace and against which he rebels, does not diminish man's corruption of will but rather exhibits it in its depravity. It is not that man has not grace and, therefore, is corrupt (Calvinism). It is that *despite grace*, he continues to rebel. Also we see, contrary to the supposition of Cennick and others, it is not true to hold of Wesley that, if salvation has some other condition than the grace of God, men are thereby reduced to resting upon "their own faithfulness." If men are saved, it is by the grace of God alone, nothing else. But the effectual operation of grace is contingent, *not* upon man's co-operative assistance, but upon his nonresistance. Nothing is clearer in Wesley than that man cannot of himself will God. Let that be settled.

How then can a man be saved if he cannot will not to resist? Man is at liberty to resist grace but he is unfree, of his own volition, to concur with or confirm the prevenient grace of God. We are here at the very nadir of the problem of freedom and salvation for the whole of Christian thought. With Wesley as guide we have tracked it to its center. But observe, prevenient grace does not solve the problem. Granted even that the Calvinist disjunction between Nature and Grace is an untenable artificiality, Wesley's provision for prevenient grace only pushes the problem a step back.

If grace can be resisted, how is resitance removable? The Calvinists cut the Gordian knot with a *deus ex machina*, the overwhelming and exclusive divine causality. Who has not been made uneasy by the profound contradiction ensuing in the Christian conception of God? But let us not boast; there is here a severe problem for any who take a serious view of sin. How is salvation possible if man's will is bound? Wesley affirms that it can *only* resist.

IV. SALVATION BY GRACE

It has been suggested by some that Wesley at length withdrew from his position of salvation by grace alone. They refer us to a short essay "Thoughts on Salvation by Faith" (1779).[48] Here Wesley recounts how, at length perceiving that there is no "medium between salvation by

works and salvation by absolute decrees," he adopted salvation by
works "in a scriptural sense." This is supposed to signalize Wesley's
retreat. But it actually does not when we observe what Wesley means
by "works in the scriptural sense." He tells us. It means the holiness
characteristic of a Christian but *consequential to faith*, the faith "which
worketh by love." [49] Even if Wesley intended this as a way out it fails,
for it does not even touch the prior question how faith, which is unto
holiness, is possible in the first place. Wesley was only saying what
he always had said that the evidence of justification is its fruit in
sanctification.[50] In support of Wesley's retraction, Dr. Lee refers to
the *Long Minutes* of 1770.[51] Here, it seems, unblushing emphasis is
put upon man's faithfulness. On the authority of Christ's word, it is
declared that salvation is "not by the merit of works, but by works
as a condition. . . . Whoever desires to find favour with God. . . .
Whoever repents, should do works meet for repentance." [52]

If this means, as Dr. Lee supposes, that Wesley is here falling back
upon human causality in salvation, then we must be content with a
final unresolved contradiction in Wesley's thought. Wesley has rendered man powerless and, in spite of that, requires him to respond
freely to grace. Wesley is not only in contradiction, he does not truly
possess an understanding of how salvation is possible.

Are the *Long Minutes* and the *Thoughts on Salvation* to be regarded
as definitive and countermanding the whole body of Wesley's utterance? I think not. The former in particular indicates a growing exasper-
ation with predestinarianism as a "pitfall to the revival" and a "device
of satan" to unsettle believers. The passages do indicate a conviction
that faith is hollow if "unholy tempers" exhibit themselves in bitterness
of spirit among orthodox contenders for opinions.[53] But in any case
the *Minutes* do not cut the issue; for, granted that there should be
both works appropriate to repentance and to faith, no comment is
made nor any explanation given for either faith or repentance.
*Moreover it is distinctly not said that works are antecedent conditions
of grace unto faith.*

The case for retraction falls to the ground and is, I think, buried
by the words of Wesley in his sermon on the death of Whitefield,
preached at Greenwich on December 23, following the August Conference of 1770.[54] Therein, reiterating "the grand principle" of the Whitefield and Oxford Methodists, Wesley summarized:

There is no power, by nature, and *no merit*, in man. They insisted, all power
to think, speak, or act aright, is in and from the spirit of Christ; and all merit
is . . . in the blood of Christ. . . . There is no power in man, till it is given

him from above, to do one good work, to speak one good word, or to form one good desire. . . . For "who can bring a clean thing out of an unclean?" None, less than the Almighty. . . . These are the fundamental doctrines. . . . These let us insist upon with all boldness.[55]

Having answered the retractionists, we are forced back to the issue. Again, how is salvation possible if man cannot do it and God does not override man's resistance? Dr. Cannon [56] relies here upon a vague word of Wesley's, the only one of its kind I know: "By some awful providence, or by his word applied with the demonstration of his Spirit, God touches the heart of him that lay asleep." [57] But if this is the answer, then Dr. Cannon, contrary to his intent, forces Wesley into Calvinism at the crucial point.

The solution, not merely of Wesley's problem but perhaps of the problem of freedom and grace itself, turns upon an alternative. If Wesley holds that man by inheritance is such a being as the "natural man," described in Sermon IX, utterly ignorant and asleep to God, then if that man ever awakes, it can only be through some chance or the overpowering causality and decree of God. If, however, no man is so, since enlightenment by grace is an inalienable endowment of his nature, then salvation is possible without irresistible divine causality.

Now what Wesley taught was that no man is by endowment utterly asleep to God. The "natural man" is not the native man but the man who, by resisting the light that he has, succeeds in virtually quenching the Spirit. This is not the native state but an acquired state.[58] The "natural man" is not the first man; the first man is "the man under the law." This man, by the light that enlightens him, recognizes the contradiction between his will and a good of which he is aware but cannot willingly affirm. He is the man who is in degree disquieted by his sin but cannot conquer it.[59] But the tension is itself the ground of hope, for it unsettles man in his self-reliance and may at length reduce him to despair, that zero-point of the will whence comes the imperceptible transition from man's futile working to God's working. Man cannot be reconciled to God in his own working because his very struggle is an effort to assimilate himself to God independent of God—a contradiction.

The necessity of *inactivation* of the will through despair appears in Wesley's writing from 1736 to 1790. Wherever it appears it presupposes man under law, that is, attended by grace and in some measure *wittingly* attended. Examples of this phenomenon appears many times in the *Journal:* "It pleased God to give us in that hour two living examples . . . of man's inability either to remove the power, or to atone for the guilt, of sin (called by the world despair); *in which prop-*

erly consist that poverty of spirit, and mourning which are the gate of Christian blessedness."[60]

The "travail of the whole creation" is that productive misery which culminates in the emergence of man from bondage into the glorious liberty of the children of God.[61] Wesley observed the frustrated futility and contradiction in the frontal attack of the will upon righteousness:

> But though he strive with all his might, he cannot conquer: sin is mightier than he. . . . He resolves against sin, yet sins on: he sees the snare, and abhors it; and runs into it. . . . And the more he frets against it, the more it prevails; he may bite but he cannot break the chain. Thus he toils without end, repenting and sinning . . . till at length the poor, sinful, helpless wretch, is even at his wits end.[62]

How like this is to Wesley's depiction of his own early condition: "In this vile, abject state of bondage of sin, I was indeed fighting continually, but not conquering. Before, I had willingly served sin: now it was unwillingly [!?]; but still I served it."[63]

Here is the state of disquiet and despair in which a man is not far from the Kingdom of God. No fitness in man is required but a sense "of our utter sinfulness and helplessness; every one who knows he is fit for hell being just fit to come to Christ."[64] So he declares: "We must be cut off from dependence upon ourselves, before we can truly depend upon Christ. . . . First, we receive the sentence of death in ourselves; then we trust in Him that lived and died for us."[65] Thus our despair is our healing; for it is then that we "go out of ourselves, in order to be swallowed up in him; when we sink into nothing, that he may be all in all."[66]

From limitless observation Wesley learned the secret of Paul's word about "dying with Christ," and saw, recapitulated in his own experience and in that of others, the truth that Paul discerned: *that freedom from the will to evil can never be effected by the operation of that will.* A will bent upon self-assertion, attempting to affirm God, only affirms itself. Every effort to goodness stumbles upon self-contradiction. The will must die subsiding in the despair of exhaustion. Then the grace, the presence of which inaugurated the struggle, completes in the chastened and humbled spirit the work which long since it had begun. Strangely a man *does* believe!

Somehow Wesley was not able to translate this observation of experience into the language of abstract thought, coming thus to terms with predestinarian logic. He could only assert that salvation is by grace and yet that something else was a condition. That condition was the inactivation of the will through despair.[67] This is not the work of man but the death of man's working. In the last resort Wesley is not a predestinarian because he rejects the practically absolute disjunction between Nature and Grace—that philosophical and theological ineptitude of the Reformation.

Wesley called men to repent and to receive God's free grace; but his appeal was successful insofar as, with the Socratic art of midwifery, he was able to elicit in his listeners abdication of self through despair.

A STUDY OF FREEDOM AND GRACE IN RESPONSE TO RECENT INTERPRETATION OF THE GOSPEL ETHIC

I. AN ALLEGED ANTINOMY IN CHRISTIAN ETHICS

For more than a decade Reinhold Niebuhr has strongly contested an "implicit assumption" of liberal Christianity, viz., "that human nature has the resources to fulfill what the gospel demands." [1] Apparently, Niebuhr's denial rests, in part, upon the premise that when human "life is seen in its total dimension, the sense of God and the sense of sin are involved in the same act of self-consciousness. . . ." [2] Consequently, according to Niebuhr, when "this religious feeling is translated into ethical terms it becomes the tension between the principle of love and the impulse of egoism, between the obligation to affirm the ultimate unity of life and the urge to establish the ego against all competing forms of life." [3] So difficult is a resolution of this antimony that Niebuhr's realism in ethics inclines him to the view that the "love perfectionism" of Jesus' ethical demands "are incapable of fulfillment in the present existence of man." [4] Yet he acknowledges that they remain "the mythical expression of the impossible-possibility under which all human life stands." [5]

In Niebuhr's trenchant assessment of the human situation one discerns a heavy dependency both upon Luther's somber estimate of human bondage to sin and upon Luther's view of the justified sinner—repeatedly underscored in the reformer's *Commentary on Galatians*—"God reigns but sin remains." It is so with Niebuhr: if justification is sure warrant of forgiveness of sins, much less is it empowerment for "newness of life" as in the language of St. Paul. If indeed salvation is by God's grace through faith, it often appears that neither the Reformers nor their successors are disposed to look for the "new creation" of whom the Apostle long since had spoken (2 Cor. 5:16–17; Rom 6:4).

This, indeed, Niebuhr both concedes and explains in his more recent Gifford Lectures. Contrasting Reformation with pre-Reformation Christianity for which latter "grace had healed the hurt of sin," Niebuhr observes:

First published in *The Journal of Religion*, XXV, No. 3 (July 1945), 197–212. To this article an introduction is added which was omitted in the original publication. In addition to emendation of the text, revision includes new material, hopefully, to the end of greater clarity and exhibition of issues in somewhat wider context. Republished with permission of the Editor.

The Reformation took the fact of sin as a perennial category of historic existence more seriously and maintained that there is no point in history where history is fulfilled and where man's self-contradiction is ended. It therefore defined divine "grace" not so much as a divine power in man which completes his incompletion but a divine mercy which brings his uneasy conscience to rest despite the continued self-contradiction of human effort upon every level of achievement.[6]

It is one thing to challenge the assumption of liberalism that human nature *as such* possesses the resources to fulfill gospel demands, but it seems quite another to foreclose upon such fulfillment as more than human power may enable. Is the grace that justifies of no greater efficacy than Niebuhr's neo-Reformation thought allows? Is it not, rather, human nature, in its *essence,* that proves to be intransigent to the operations of divine grace and so justifies Niebuhr's "pessimism"? Of man he teaches as follows:

The Christian estimate of human evil is so serious precisely because it places evil at the very center of human personality: the will of man. Man is a sinner. His sin is defined as rebellion against God. . . . Man contradicts himself within the terms of his true essence. *His essence is free self-determination.*[7]

If man is essentially "free self-determination"—no other and no more—we have indeed, problems in assimilating to it a New Testament understanding of the work of divine grace in human redemption. Such, however, seems to be incompatible with the paradox of Nature-and-Grace immemorially lodged in St. Paul's admonition: "Work out your own salvation with fear and trembling; for it is God who worketh in you both to will and to work, for his good pleasure" (Phil. 2:12–13). Nor is this wholly unrelated to Jesus' observation to Peter about things not possible with men but possible for God (Mark 10:27). If, as is commonplace in the New Testament, God is truly at work for human redemption, it may be, as John Wesley once persuasively urged, that the repentant and justified sinner is precisely such a one as "can work," that is, is *empowered* so to do.[8]

In any event these considerations that stand close to the mainstream of Christian thought on the relation of Nature to Grace, alert us to questions about the verity of a neo-Reformed view of man as sinner insofar as this view leaves the issue of "works fit for repentance" entirely to a human being unrelieved of his "essence" as "free self-determination." Such a voluntarism has, to be sure, recognizable antecedents, including, in some measure, Kant. It is also surprisingly Pelagian in its implications. Yet, even for Kant the exercise of volition was always subject primarily to dictates of the "moral consciousness" as qualifying, and inseparable from, essential human nature. Freedom in the dominant tradition of Western thought—whether Greek or Christian—is regularly qualified and never the essence of humanity as such. In a great part of that tradition, man's real freedom is not freedom *from*, or self-affirmation, but freedom *for*, or affirmation of and consent to Being.

If, now, we add to Niebuhr's identification of man's essence with "free self-determination" his further description of the human condition as "the tension between the principle of love and the impulse of egoism . . .," i.e., "the urge to establish the ego against all competing forms of life," we have a conception of the plight of man strongly reminiscent of that entertained by Benedict Spinoza. But, for Spinoza the remedy was precisely not further exercise of self-determination but *acceptance of an appropriate ultimate dependency* as the way of salvation, which earned for Spinoza the title of "God-intoxicated philosopher." So we propose now to look at Niebuhr's doctrine of man together with the alleged "perfectionism" of Jesus' ethic against a relevant background of the history of ideas, and so to assess it more largely in that perspective.

II. KANT'S CONCEPT OF FREEDOM AND THE CHRISTIAN ETHIC

Scarcely is anything more familiar to students of moral theory than that Immanuel Kant considered freedom of the will to be the indispensable presupposition of morality. In this respect he stood firmly in the succession of Aristotle. It is less familiar that Benedict Spinoza abandoned the dependency of morality upon an autonomous will, although he did not dissociate his own distinctive conception of freedom from virtue.

So far as I am aware, it appears all but unnoticed that Jesus of the Gospels, in his teaching on the role of faith as indispensable empowerment for the life of God's Kingdom, is quite opposed to Kant and nearly at one with Spinoza regarding the springs of so-called ethical action. This raises the question whether Spinoza's major philosophical writing, the *Ethics*, in fact is "ethics" as Kant understands morality and whether, by the same standard, Jesus' "ethic of the Kingdom" at all qualifies as "morals" in the understanding of Kant. A failure to have faced this question squarely may account for much confusion in post-Kantian liberal theology of the recent past. It may enlighten the long-standing issue attending the Ritschlian liberal tradition in theology, namely, whether the latter is not misleading in its recurring tendency to reduce Christianity to an ethic that is, in fact, foreign to the New Testament understanding of the life of faith. Whatever else that life is, it is surely not grounded upon the inscrutable autonomy of Kant's free will.

In plain language our question is this: is the life of the Kingdom a *morality* in the sense in which Kant defines the concept? It is to be acknowledged that Kant's masterful delineation of the dutiful life is unsurpassed in the history of Western thought. In some respects it is the culmination of one of the two mainstreams of the *philosophia perennis*, in ethics, mainly, the Aristotelian. These facts do not, however, necessarily qualify Kantian ethics as biblical. Nor should the Kantian ethic provide the Procrustean bed to which "the ethic of the Kingdom," so-called, may uncritically be conformed. Our suspicion is that whenever the term "perfectionism" is used with reference to the life suited to the Kingdom its very use suggests an undue deferral to the Kantian conception of morality.

It is hoped that by bringing the above issues into clear relief, by illustration from the thought of Spinoza and Kant, some illumination also may be accorded the old antithesis in Christian ethics between Nature and Grace. The same was formulated in paradoxical synthesis by Paul in the famous Phillipians passage already cited. It may well be that the rigoristic interpretation of Jesus' ethic,[9] historically, is, in a measure, due to Paul's inability to let go one horn of his dilemma— the horn of freedom integral to a good deal of late Jewish thought and the teaching of the Rabbis.[10] In this, Paul may have failed to accept the full implications of his experience of the "mind of Christ" [11] in the believer as the only sufficient ground for the possibility of an *apapē* which "seeketh not its own."

Be these things as they may, viewed through the teaching of Kant, the ethic of love becomes an appeal to the will belonging to man as "the character of his species." [12] So construed, the maxims contained in the Sermon on the Mount are, as Kant well understood, "impossible possibilities" only. And in his contention that the form of morality must be duty, he necessarily declared that action springing even "from love to men and from sympathetic good will" is not of "moral worth." [13] In this, Kant places himself in opposition to both Jesus and Spinoza, for whom goodness is possible because it emanates, not from freedom of an autonomous will, but from *beatitude* conceived as consciousness of a peculiar relation to the ultimate ground of Being and accompanied by love of that ground.[14]

My thesis is that, for both Spinoza and Jesus, the modes of conduct "prescribed" in the Sermon on the Mount are not only, as Kant saw, statistical impossibilities when conceived as appeals to the natural will;

they are even absurdities apart from a revolution in the life-focus of personality. Jesus understood it this way; and no student of the New Testament, as I am aware, has grasped the matter more clearly than T. W. Manson, who says: *"What Jesus offers in his ethical teaching is not a set of rules of conduct, but a number of illustrations of the way in which a transformed character will express itself in conduct."* [15] If we accept for the moment Kant's understanding of the preconditions of the possibility of an ethic, the Christian ethic is not an "ethic" at all. It is simply the statement of the necessary consequence, on the horizontal dimension of human existence, of a prior relationship of man to God in the vertical dimension. Jesus defines that relationship by the word *faith*. As we shall see, since Kant completely eliminated the possibility of the vertical relationship by his negative epistemological conclusions regarding God in the *Critique of Pure Reason*, he was obliged to generate ethics from man in isolation from God, that is, from the autonomy of an absolute individual.

The Kantian Ethic

Freedom, in the form of a will whose action—to use Kant's words— is "subjectively contingent," [16] is not held by Spinoza to be the condition of morality. In contrast, morality is unthinkable for Kant apart from an absolutely contingent will that may accede, on grounds inscrutable to reason, either to the law of duty or to the inclinations of sensibility. [17] *Freedom must be actual because obligation is the only possible form of ethics.* Obligation is the only possible form of ethics because the proper end of the will can never be what *is* desired but only what *ought* to be desired. [18] Again, what *ought* to be desired can alone be the proper principle of volition because only so can there be a universally valid object for the wills of all rational beings in place of a relativity of human preferences. [19]

Since God was unknowable, there remained but two grounds to furnish the possible norms of conduct: the objects of sensibility and a universally legislating "practical reason" in man. To provide a universally valid morality, Kant chose the latter. Just as he had made synthetic judgments *a priori*, that is, science, possible by making the manifold of experience conform to the cognitive modes of the knowing subject, so, in the sphere of ethics, Kant abandoned empiricism and effected a "Copernican revolution" in the notion of the derivation of the principles of conduct. They are given by the *pure practical reason* quite as the forms of sensibility and the categories are the contribution of the subject of experience in the first *Critique*. Kant believed that principles of conduct could not be derived from experience.[20] In such a case, morality would be wanting in universality and necessity.[21] Relativity would prevail:

The ends which a rational being proposes to himself at pleasure as effects of his actions (material ends) are all only relative, for it is only their relation to the particular desires of the subject that gives them their worth, which therefore cannot furnish principles universal and necessary for all rational beings and for every volition, that is to say, practical laws.[22]

Subjectivistic, then, is Kant's conception of value, which may be defined as "any object of any interest." No value, therefore, could provide a universal and necessarily valid end of conduct. Pure reason, universal in all men, must give it.

The consequence must be that Kant radically divorces Nature from Morality, or inclination and happiness from duty. Happiness is simply the idea of all inclinations (valuations) combined in a total.[23] The very conception of morality decrees that happiness must "for the most part be postponed." [24] Happiness is the consequence of morality when felicity, commensurate with worth, shall, through the agency of God, be accorded to the man of good will—when God at length shall have joined together what Kant had put asunder.

And now the necessity of freedom in such a scheme of things is manifest. Morality consists in respect for the law while involving "an inevitable constraint put upon all inclinations or a painful resistance to the motives of sensibility." [25] This divorce of happiness and duty (which really is the ground for the requirement of the "categorical" as distinguished from the "hypothetical" imperative) [26] urges the need of an irrational, viz., absolutely free will. Kant argues that the will, in giving itself the law, is not "lawless" but is "objectively determined" by the law.[27] Nevertheless, the will cannot be "necessarily in unison with the law," for, then, it would be *holy* and determined to goodness.[28] The will, therefore, must adopt the law on grounds, subjectively considered, altogether contingent and, hence, irrational. By divorcing moral worth from holiness—conceived as a character or disposition—*Kant made the willing of maxims conformable to the law quite as inexplicable as the adoption of maxims contrary to the law. The action of the will has no ground other than itself; and morality comes to be the absolutely free or unintelligible affirmation of the law in opposition to the inclinations of sensibility.* Thus Kant declares: "When we say then, Man is by nature good, or, Man is by nature evil, this means only that there is in him an ultimate ground (inscrutable to us) of the adoption of good maxims or of evil maxims." [29] Such is morality—

"simply respect for the Law, is the spring which gives actions moral worth." [30]

We need not quarrel with Kant concerning his definition of moral worth, but if morality requires freedom, we may, nonetheless, recall that Kant's primary evidence for freedom is its necessity for morality. The real question, therefore, is why should we have morality (worth) when goodness can be achieved without it? If we find "morality" unnecessary, we may therewith find absolute freedom gratuitous.

The New Testament teaching on the God-man relationship does not allow an isolation of man from God or of God from man, presupposed by Kantian Deism. On the contrary, in Jesus' utterance, the *agapē* of God is the antecedent environment and precondition of creation and of human existence as such. As humanity exists in the mindfulness of God (Ps. 8:4), so human response in faith is acknowledgment of God's mindfulness. In faith, the believer is already possessed of his worth. As one reads the Sermon on The Mount, moreover, it appears to be God's gracious predisposition, which, when acknowledged by faith, liberates and, so, constitutes a good will in the believer.

With Kant all this is reversed. In the ascending logic of his "moral argument" for the existence of God, it is man's autonomous moral achievement—for which immortality is postulated—which also justifies God's final vindication, namely, the reunification of happiness (nature) with duty (obligation) or morality.[31] Only in eternity is there to be the re-integration of *duty* (the Ought) with *holiness* or, as we may say of nature with grace. Salvation is a human achievement—contingent upon an autonomous will—the hard-won price of a *true* morality. Holiness is reserved for eternity—perhaps in good Lutheran fashion! Thus, for the decisive difference between Kant and the thought of Spinoza and Jesus, we shall not look to the fact that Kant makes much of freedom, as the condition of morality, while the latter make little of it. Rather, we shall find the difference in this: that, whereas for Kant, actions are morally worthless if they derive from *holiness*, for Spinoza and Jesus no nonegotistical actions are possible save as deriving from a kind of holiness (a certain relation to God), and the matter of worth is irrelevant because it is conferred with creation.

The Ethics of Spinoza

Of the title of Spinoza's principal philosophical work, *Ethica ordine geometrico demonstrata* (1677), more attention has been given the qualifying phrase, "demonstrated according to geometrical method," than to his exceptional choice of "ethics" to encompass an entire philosophy of Reality. However oblique the reference, it is fairly clear that this exceptional title points backward in time to what W. L. Davidson rightly called "the Stoic creed." [32] Not only does Spinoza adopt the Stoic ontology that equates God and Nature *(Deus sive Natura)*, but he shared with the Stoics a profound soteriological concern and, with them, finds in *ethikē* the way of human salvation. In this fundamental respect he is a fountainhead of the thought of G. E. Lessing and, therewith, of the German Enlightenment.

While vice, as well as virtue, was considered by Kant the consequence of absolute freedom, Spinoza conceived vice and social evils to be consequents of wrongly directed love, namely, determination by the "passions." Passions are "affects" of the body of which man himself is not the "adequate cause." [33] Subject to passions, man suffers rather than acts, viz., is conscious of joy, sorrow, or desire accompanied by the idea of an external cause perceived through *imaginatio* or sensible cognition.[34] Human bondage consists in this: that man conceives the objects of sensibility to be the factors upon which his *conatus* [35] or effort to persevere in being is dependent—all the time ignorant that his salvation is conditioned upon a knowledge of the true object of his *conatus* or essence (namely, God) who is knowable through *ratio* as opposed to *imaginatio* and in the knowledge of whom man becomes active and ceases to suffer. That is, he becomes the adequate cause of his affects.

It is familiar enough that Spinoza denies any "absolute faculty of willing or not willing." [36] Men are deceived in thinking themselves free, and "the sole reason for thinking so is that they are conscious of their actions, and ignorant of the causes by which those actions are determined." [37] It hardly needs mention that Spinoza's determinism derives from his metaphysical monism and his espousal of "immanent" as opposed to "transitive" causality. Respecting man, the heart of the matter is this: that his essence is given in his *conatus* or effort to persevere in being; and, with that *conatus*, is also given the ends of his striving.[38] The *conatus* defines the good for man.[39] But man is deceived about the true end of his being and is bound, therefore, to the pursuit of material values moved by his "passions."

Man is a focus-point reflecting reality. He is determined as mind and body in the nexus of immanent universal causality. But man reflects the universe according to two principal modes corresponding to two cognitive functions. According to the *imaginatio,* he reflects the world of discrete objects transitively causal, while, according to *ratio,* discreteness resolves into unity and transitive into immanent causality. Corresponding to these cognitive modes are given the possibility of two modes of human determination: either (1) to be determined by

material objects accompanied by *passio* or suffering or (2) to be determined by God. But the latter determination is not passive, as is the
former. It is active, for man *participates* joyously from both love and
fulfillment in God's determination of his being. This is so because a
man cannot but perceive with joy the unity of his "superior part"
(ratio) with God or the whole of Nature.[40] *The love of God is man's
true happiness or beatitude, which is, at the same time, the source of
his freedom from bondage to the passions.* The love of God is an "affect"
of which a man is himself the adequate cause as reintegrated into
Being. As an "affect," it is able to overcome the opposing affects of
the body (passions) of which man is not the adequate cause. Passions
arise in men whose awareness is confined to space-time existence and
who, therefore, are obsessed with the impossible task of persevering
in being as mere centers of physical energy but whose power is "infi-
nitely surpassed by the power of external causes." [41] Only the love
of God can overcome the anxiety of self-defensiveness wherein are
rooted, at the same time, the antisocial passions.

The *intellectual love of God* constitutes blessedness and is at once
freedom itself and the possibility of freedom *for* goodness. It is freedom
itself, in Spinoza's peculiar sense, because, in the knowledge and love
of God man has realized his true essence. He is almost wholly active
in the actualization of his being which *is* his perfection. Beatitude is
freedom *for* goodness because it is "quietness of mind" permitting a
diminishing dependency upon material values, which, in turn, affords
an amelioration of the struggle for existence by effecting a surcease
of anxiety. Beatitude is freedom for "morality" precisely because being
is no longer, as it is with *imaginatio,* confined within the limits of
space-time existence.

Spinoza observed two possible strategies for the achievement of human well-being: (1) a frontal attack to secure material goods and socially
accepted values or (2) a reorientation of personality by a shift in the
value focus. He favors the second. Only the knowledge and love of
God could dispel the obsessive self-concern of the isolated individual
and, thereby, achieve a reduction of social tensions attendant upon
the exclusive pursuit of mundane goods.[42]

Man's reliance upon *imaginatio* (the sensible self-consciousness) accounts for man's ignorance of "general providence." [43] The same ignorance deludes man in the supposition that his perseverance in being
depends alone upon the provision of goods or the avoidance of evils
known to him through the sensible self-consciousness. General providence, the conception of all things as produced and sustained by Nature, *Natura naturans,* is specifically contrasted with "special providence" as "the striving of each thing separately to preserve its

existence, . . . considered not as a part of Nature, but as a whole (by itself)." [44] Paradoxically, this quest for autonomy is man's bondage. Thus, for Spinoza, salvation depends upon knowledge of God accompanied by a love of Him that reveals a universal order sustaining the individual and freeing him from the agony of seeming autonomy with its inevitable counterpart of defensiveness. In a state of defensiveness freedom *for* goodness is unthinkable. Therefore, Spinoza declared in the closing passage of the *Ethics:*

> Blessedness consists in love towards God. . . . Again, the more the mind delights in this divine love or blessedness, . . . the greater is the power it has over the affects, and the less it suffers from affects which are evil. Therefore, it is because the mind delights in this divine love or blessedness that it possesses power of restraining the lusts; . . . no one, therefore, delights in blessedness because he has restrained his affects, but on the contrary, the power of restraining his lusts springs from blessedness itself.[45]

Whereas Kant taught that moral worth was the precondition of happiness and, freedom, the presupposition of the possibility of moral worth, Spinoza's God or Nature has already accorded man whatever "worth" he needs in constituting him a being whose true end (given in his essence) is the knowledge and love of God.[46] Morality is not, with Spinoza, the precondition of happiness; rather, happiness is the precondition of morality or goodness. Moral action is not the achievement of an imperfect and contingent will but the ripe fruit of "peace of soul." Freedom, therefore, as absolute contingency of will, is gratuitous because social goodness is possible without it. Moral worth was the lever with which Kant pried God into existence as the guarantor of felicity commensurate with man's goodness. Spinoza required no such lever because God was as accessible as Nature itself.

The Life of the Kingdom

Jesus is at one with Spinoza that goodness is not the product of a radically contingent will conforming to a law, even a divine imperative, but the action of a self, functioning in social situations, as liberated from the bondage of obsessive self-consciousness, a liberation accomplished by a *faithful* relation to ultimate Reality. While Spinoza and Jesus understood the nature of this Reality in ways diametrically opposed—only witness Spinoza's complete rejection of teleology—and, while, for Spinoza the cognitive pathway to Reality was a purely rational intuition of the involvement of finitude *(natura naturata)* in the One, they are yet agreed that the possibility of social goodness derives from an apprehension of the dependence of all creaturehood upon God together with the *dependability* of God. Man's good becomes contingent upon the eager and, therefore, voluntary, acceptance of God's determination, viz., man's given role, through the constraint of love.

Apparently, the "ethic" of Jesus falls within this context, and one will look vainly, I believe, in the Gospels for anything resembling the Kantian absolutely contingent will. Rather does the pattern, with respect to Kingdom membership, seem to be: "With men it is impossible, but not with God: for all things are possible with God." [47] Yet the common manner of reading the Sermon on the Mount is to suppose that the apparent injunctions constitute options for unmotivated freedom and, therefore, considering their source, are unconditional obligations upon everyone. The clear indication of their extreme rigor, on such a supposition, is exhibited in numerous attempts of late to make them palatable by explanation in terms of Jesus' eschatological worldview. Thus we have variations on Schweitzer's "interim ethic" or Reinhold Niebuhr's "impossible possibility" of the ethic of love—impossible because the "ethical demands" of Jesus presuppose, contrary to fact, "a transcendent and divine unity of essential reality." [48] What is this but a tacit adoption of Kant's separation of Nature and Morality, duty and happiness, goodness and holiness, and an understanding of Jesus' ethic by way of the presuppositions of Kant, for whom the "right," not the "good," must always proceed from an *irrational freedom* rather than from blessedness deriving from knowledge and love of God?

All this might be necessary if God were unknowable to Jesus as he was to Kant, but Jesus assumed the opposite and knew nothing of the absolute individual. For Jesus there is no unconditional ought confronting a free will. Ethics is not a discipline of the will but is rather doing what God is doing out of a confident heart. The so-called "ethical" demands of Jesus are, rather, descriptions of conduct characterizing those who are within the Kingdom in contrast to those who are without—those who have faith in contrast to those who have it not.[49] The "demands" of Jesus describe the pertinent tasks of the Kingdom and depend upon a prior status—the status of present community with God defined by the word "faith." The ethical demands of Jesus are not conditions but consequents of participation in the Kingdom. They are the good treasure which the man of faith produces out of his heart.[50] Faith is acceptance of the *agapē* of God toward all creatures, with joy or love, as Spinoza would say, accompanied by the idea of the object. Joined with this, and in proportion to it, is the present possibility of love of neighbor. Professor Manson says it well: "In the light of God's love to himself a man sees other men, as it were, through God's eyes: and to see them in this way is to love them." [51]

The man of faith is one in whose life disabling anxiety for self has given way to the certainty of God. In accepted community with God, man's isolation is dissolved, and his autonomy—seen now to be sterile and fruitless—is cast aside, while, in its place, comes an *eager* acceptance of divine determination *as* the constraint of a thankful heart. Faith is a quietness of mind, banishing defensiveness, that makes goodness possible. The source of Jesus' own ease in goodness derives from the certainty, inaugurating his career, "Thou art my Son." [52]

The life of Jesus, as Manson declares, issues out of a single fact, namely, "The Father was the supreme reality of His own life." It is the vertical reference of life-in-faith which empowers the horizontal by making freedom from self-concern unnecessary and, thereby, making freedom for goodness possible. Such it seems was the view of Spinoza and Jesus. Indeed, Spinoza himself, straining perhaps a little at the point, observed the affinity. "Being led by the Spirit of Christ," is, he affirmed, to be led "by the idea of God, which alone can make a man free, and cause him to desire for other men the good he desires for himself." [53] Somewhere herein is contained the secret of the possibility of the Golden Rule, and no one perhaps has stated the matter more clearly than Spinoza. Both Jesus and Spinoza agree that man can have either of two masters: either he may be determined by God through love of him or he may, confronted by the not-self, be determined by self-love. The self's affirmation of itself is bondage, while the self's affirmation of God, through love, is freedom.

III. THE ISSUE OF NATURE AND GRACE

There is truth in Santayana's remark upon Kant: "In the categorical imperative we see something native and inward to the private soul, in some of its moods, quietly claiming to rule the invisible world, to set God on his throne and open eternity to the human spirit." [54] Magnificent indeed is man's role in Kantianism—giving the law of duty to himself *a priori* out of the rich resources of his "pure practical reason" and by the exercise of a wholly autonomous will assenting or dissenting to the mandates of his own moral consciousness. These mandates register themselves not as "hypothetical," that is, as conditional, but as "categorical imperatives" of the same practical reason. Nor is this majesty, as Santayana notes, limited to man's self-legislation. The full range of its authorization becomes visible in Kant's famous "moral argument" for the existence of God.[55] There, this majesterial moral consciousness is found by Kant to have as its logically warranted coimplicates, not merely human freedom, but in succession: immortality, felicity (the mating of duty and happiness), and God himself as the guarantor of it all. Thus, Kant is so far a man of his age and so far under the leading of Descartes that there remains no way from God to man but only a way from man to God. But, departing from Descartes, it is no longer the way of the "theoretical" but of the "practical reason," that is, the *moral consciousness*.

It is of the first importance that Kant recovered from Greek thought the distinction between the "theoretical" and "practical" functions of reason, presupposed by Plato and declared by Aristotle.[56] That Kant held in "theology" that we do and must begin from the "practical reason" undoubtedly created an epoch in Protestant theology. Moreover, the same insistence that, in theology, we move toward God from the positive *datum* of the "moral consciousness" is of greater interest than is customarily allowed, since it was from the witness of the moral consciousness that the Platonic Socrates started *philosophia* upon its long course in the twilight of the Periclean Age.[57] With Socrates the witness of conscience was the "sign" of an unbroken continuity between the human spirit and divine Being. With Kant the continuity is broken, and his Cartesianism becomes evident in his acquiescence to the primary and undoubted self-certainty of the human consciousness, its privacy, and its querulous isolation from its ground of Being.

Somehow, somewhere in the intervening intellectual history of the West, the ties between God and man had been cut, and Kant did not so much create a hiatus as articulate one he had inherited. It was this received apperception of man, wholly on his own, which sponsored and then enforced, for a nest of reasons, Kant's version of human freedom as the absolutely contingent liberty of indifference conjoined with a pure practical reason—integral in its own right—that legislates the "categorial imperative of duty" out of its somehow abundant resources. In this schema, Grace no longer *converts* nature as with Augustine, nor does it *perfect* nature as with Thomas Aquinas.

In Kant's now fully articulated world of the autonomous man—that of the "transcendental self," presided over by "the moral law within"— all that was received of the Christian tradition respecting divine grace in creation and preservation has vanished. On strictly positive grounds—that is, in consulting the full range of human experience *as given*—Kant can testify only to two prime data, viz., "the order of the starry heavens above and the moral law within." In nature, determinism prevails according to the uniform laws of the Copernican and Newtonian universe. In the other, the human world, the determinate order of external nature is excluded because the "transcendental subject" of experience is *never* an "object" external to the knower. So far forth, the subject is free. He, moreover, testifies to his freedom in his acknowledgment of *obligation* to the moral law within as unconditionally binding. If he *must*, he *can*—was self-evident to Kant! Thus, the human subject is free in legislating the law of duty to itself and in electing to consent or not to consent to the law. Taken together, this is the meaning of man's "autonomy." Its radical character lies in the utter contingency of the will itself. Its act is without a sufficient reason other than itself on pain of negating its entire freedom. Explanation of its exercise can be given neither by reference to the "empirical" self, that is, to sensuous "inclination" or "nature," nor to society, nor to God. To attempt this is to invite *heteronomy* or extrinsic determination of the will.

In this picture, Reality has fallen asunder. There is the objective and determinate order of the phenomenal world and the inner world of the moral consciousness with absolute freedom. Each implies the other. But the sundering does not end with bifurcation but with trifurcation, for nature and man are not alone divorced the one from the other, but God from both. God, the ground of Being in the *philosophia perennis* remains, perhaps *Noumenon*, but for Kant, his status attains no more than that of hypothetical reference-point of the moral consciousness. We may perhaps put it this way, God has no *community-in-being* either with nature or with man. Of his relation to nature, "knowledge" has been so defined by Kant in the first *Critique*, as that we have no theoretical knowledge of God. Of God's relation to man *qua* man, we are somewhat better off in this: that we have the moral certitude that, without God, "the 'moral law within' " and the moral task without do not make sense.

In Kant's conception of Reality, not unlike Aristotle's, God *does* nothing.[58] But he does remain a "necessary coimplicate" of the *datum* of the moral consciousness—a reasonable hypothesis, we may say, required to explain man's existence as a moral being over against nature, and as Albrecht Ritschl once said, claiming the right to transcend nature.[59] In such a world-view as this, the biblical understanding of the gracious action of God in creation, preservation, and redemption has all but vanished. Moreover, in contrast with the Platonic tradition in Western thought, man—Kant's transcendental moral subject— stands in splendid isolation, apart both from nature and from God. It was out of this perspective that philosophy, theology, and ethics was destined to work in the succeeding 19th and 20th centuries.

Yet Kant is not the creator but the masterly articulator of a line of philosophical development which antedates the Reformation and the Renaissance. He must be credited, moreover, in no small part with salvaging the moral dignity of man in face of the ascendant and near regnant mechanistic naturalism of his time.[60] Yet he so decisively

shaped the intellectual framework in which discussion of human freedom and dignity proceeded that the freedom at issue has been styled
far more a freedom *from* all heteronomy than a freedom *for* goodness.

From the Christian standpoint, as also from the Platonic, freedom
is measured, not by a "liberty of indifference" as with Aristotle and
Kant, but by a liberty for fulfillment of being in accordance with the
ultimate and antecedent structure of Being. Thus, in the Christian
view, the freedom proposed by Kant is a preposterous freedom of
absolute autonomy, i.e., man's entire determination of his destiny.
Given his premises, with immense cogency Kant secures man's autonomy and, therewith, his dignity and worth over nature, but at the
heavy cost not only of cleaving Reality into *phenomena* and *noumena*
but, among *noumena,* banishing divine sovereignty from the known
world and leaving moral man quite to his own resources.

A Christian position would regard moral goodness, not as the product
of a Herculean will, but of human nature—and party to its own reclama-
tion—brought to moral integrity by a divine Grace that has not been
excluded, *ex hypothesi,* either from the process of Creation or from
its normal workings in the unfolding permutations of the human spirit
created in the image of God. Hence, it is the bearing of this study
that Grace may not be divorced from Nature, and that the thought
of Spinoza, in this matter, as well as that of Jesus of the Gospels, give
us a lead. Both assume the freedom of man, not in the sense of autonomy, but in the mode suited to a quite different context. It is freedom
in the form of confident action issuing from *beatitude* or conformation
of life to antecedent Reality. Therewith, the divine Grace is becoming
effectual in, through, and together with human nature. In this view,
freedom is liberation of human powers for good that also presupposes
and entails man's recovery of and reassimilation to the divine center
of Being.

In an idiom somewhat closer to the New Testament, man's self-in-
curred alienation from God, his flight from God, may be conceived as
his *initial* freedom. It is the freedom to resist his Maker. But, in the
words of Jesus of the Gospels, and not alone of the Sermon on the
Mount, the call to faith is invitation to an alteration of existence in
which the prevailing resistence to the divine leading is being resolved
in and with the onset of faith. So faith is also enablement of the love
of neighbor as faith itself is both acknowledgment and acceptance of
the antecedent and ceaseless grace of God. Thus, in the New Testament, faith emancipates the will for goodness. This emancipative
process is man's new freedom. It is the freedom suited to the abiding
context of divine Grace. It is authentic freedom. In the declaration
of Mark 1:14, Jesus' call to repentance suited to faith, signifies a transi-

tion in process. It is a switch of loyalty—from self-affirmation, or indifference to God, to God-affirmation. With faith, grace converts nature.
Likewise, in the sermon, the faith that is wanting in the men of "little
faith" is the *sine qua non* for seeking first God's "kingdom and his
righteousness" (Matt. 6:33). Hence, while faith entails insight with a
reversal of loyalties, it seems to be at the same time, transformation
of life. And, rather plainly, the new freedom for righteousness, attending the transformation, is a constitutive part of it. We do not see here
the absolute contingency of an unmotivated will, as with Kant. Rather,
we discern a revolution of commitment and, with it, freedom *for* all
that the Kingdom may imply for the sundry occasions and demands
of life itself in aspiring fidelity to the Kingdom.

If, then, we may speak of faith in the way described by Jesus of
the Gospels, namely, as transformation of existence in the context of
a converting divine Grace, may we not also invoke, without strain,
the idea of "holiness" as *beatitude* and as a renovation of human nature
where faith is regnant and from whence, in the subjects of faith, new
motivation emanates voluntarily? Such, it appears, is indeed the indication of the language of the *Beatitudes*. Jesus' familiar words are:
"Blessed are the pure in heart" with the consequent, "for they shall
see God" (Matt. 5:8). The antecendent clause may be simply converted,
thus: "The pure in heart *are* blessed," that is, they attain a certain
condition of life. The consequent vision of God, the *renewed* vision,
is an outcome of the cleansed heart. Vision depends upon newness
of life and attends what Jesus calls faith, and this is a revolution of
loyalties.

With Immanuel Kant, however, no renewed insight is possible, since
there is no such reach of the "understanding," limited as it is in the
first *Critique* to only an "empirical employment." As for the "moral
consciousness," its reach does not carry beyond the human self-consciousness enlightened by "the moral law within." Under the condition
of such isolation, the discharge of *indubitable obligation* must necessarily be resigned to the initiative and free will of the human moral
subject. Moreover, since morality—namely, all that elevates man above
nature—is dependent upon the exercise of human initiative, man, for
his vindication, must both legislate the law of duty to himself and
must fulfill it by reference to no standard other than the law itself.
Therefore, also, man's voluntary action can be referred to nothing
but the free will that is contingent upon nothing at all but itself.

For our purposes, it is essential to perceive that the high price of
this remarkable human autonomy is, precisely, the abandonment of
beatitude as the gifting grace of antecedent Being and as the final
motivation of human behavior. Autonomy excludes beatitude, and the

autonomous man has no alternative but to earn his salvation. Not even Pelagius had so completely divorced nature from Grace. Yet with the Lutheran dictum, *simul iustus et peccator,* and as a part of his Protestant inheritance, Kant had some justification for the rigor of his ethic. But his understanding of beatitude was wholly governed by the structure of his system. Accordingly, his final rejection is as follows: *"Now the perfect accordance of the will with the moral law is holiness, a perfection of which no rational being of the sensible world is capable at any moment of his existing."* [61] Here also there is an echo of Luther's exegesis of Romans VII, but the main point is that "holiness" has been redefined to accord with the morality, alone, of the "pure practical reason" isolated, as Kant had made it, from the ground of Being. It is against this background that we may now turn to Reinhold Niebuhr's interesting word about the "impossible-possibility" of Jesus' ethic.

The Alleged Perfectionism of the Gospel Ethic

Earlier we took note that Reinhold Niebuhr challenges and denies the assumption of much "liberal" theology that human nature is in fact possessed of resources sufficient to fulfill the Gospel demands when the measure of man's sinfulness is faced in the light of the realistic Reformation understanding of the disqualifying power of sin. With this judgment we take no issue. The issue emerges as Niebuhr proceeds with his own interpretation of the "ethic" of Jesus of the Gospels as, for example, when he speaks of the Gospel "demands," of the "love perfectionism" of Jesus ethic, of the "impossible-possibility" of such an ethic "in the present existence of man," and of the reason supplied, that fulfillment of this ethic presupposes "a transcendent and divine unity of essential reality." [62] The issue invoked by this phraseology with its attendant concepts is whether Niebuhr has quite freed himself from the same post-Kantianism on which, in great part, the "liberalism" he strongly opposes was in fact nurtured.

For reasons already offered it is doubtful that an "ethic" of Jesus, in Kant's terms, exists in the New Testament or that it can be referred to at all in the form of "mandate" or "demand." Niebuhr's alleged "love perfectionism" of the Gospels would more surely be derived from the long prevailing post-Ritschlian reading of them and, hence, better attributed to that liberal interpretation itself. The epithet, "perfectionism," has warrant only in relation to a conception of morality such as Kant's where, indeed, *obligation*—as the express form of the ethical as such—presupposes necessarily, a commensurate ability to fulfill the obligation in the context of unconditional freedom. But if Jesus, in any connection, presupposed such freedom, surely it was not

with him a presupposition of human nature *as such*. We have suggested
that Jesus "ethic" is not that of obligation but of transformation and
enablement. It is more like salvation by Grace through faith. It is dubious, then, whether "perfectionism" is apropos the so-called "Gospel
ethic" at all. Perfectionism, like "moralism," is more nearly Kant's
morality gone compulsive or the "categorical imperative of duty" become an obsession. It may have an analogue in Pharisaism, but it does
not ring true for Jesus. Every perfectionism is usually keyed to a pru-
dence motif that looks for reward of which the perfection is the condition. But this, surely, was not the message of the Gospel.

The issue invoked by Niebuhr's critique of the "Gospel ethic" is
whether it reveals an undue dependency upon the Kantian inheritance.
Does this question, then, also emerge in connection with Niebuhr's
expressed view that, in the end, the ethic of love is impossible because
it presupposes "a transcendent and divine unity of essential reality"?
In his discussion of the ethic of Jesus he rejects Schweitzer's "interim
ethic" as unconvincing. Yet he allows an "eschatological element" to
be operative in the ethic of Jesus. He conveys his meaning as follows:
"The ethical demands made by Jesus are incapable of fulfillment in
the present existence of man. They proceed from a transcendent and
divine unity of essential reality, and their final fulfillment is possible
only when God transmutes the present chaos of this world into its
final unity." [63]

For Kant, of course, this transmutation is referred not to history at
all but to a beyond history where the *summum bonum*, the concurrence
of duty fulfilled (the Ought) and happiness (the Is), is brought about
by God in a blessed immortality. Here, the cleavage between *nature*
(including history) and *fulfilled obligation* coalesce, and the claim of
man as a moral subject over against mere nature has its transcendental
vindication. This too, as the substance of Kant's "moral argument,"
became for Ritschl the heart and core of religious interest as such.[64]
Now it is just exactly the absence of this coalescence between the *Is*
and the *Ought*, or the "transcendent and divine unity of essential
reality," as in Niebuhr's phraseology, which presently obtains in the
human historical world. It is this intransigent obstacle to "the ethical
demands of Jesus" that renders them "incapable of fulfillment in the
present existence of man." It renders the ethical demands impossible,
and yet, somehow, too, impossible-possibilities by which paradox Niebuhr alludes to the divine and eternal mandate "under which all human
life stands." [65]

The issue before us is not whether an eternal mandate is the ultimate
sign under which all human life stands. That is the testimony alike
of the prophetic consciousness, as Niebuhr declares, and of the moral

consciousness of Socrates. Here is a unanimity in the "springs" of Western thought. It is here affirmed, not contested. But suppose that the
eternal mandate does not find man, as with Kant, simply in the form
of absolute *obligation* calling for fulfillment by an equally absolute
human free will in a context that *prescribes* the isolation of man! Suppose, not the cleavage of nature and Grace but Grace either perfecting
or converting nature, then, for the mandate and its fulfillment, enablement commensurate with the mandate might be acknowledged and
something like St. Paul's paradox heeded: "Work out your own salvation
with fear and trembling, for God is at work in you, both to will and
to work" (Phil. 2:12). In such a case, the impossible-possibility shifts
from man as "nature" to a grounding in more-than-nature, and the
ethic of absolute obligation and autonomy is therewith transcended.

Niebuhr's version, however, of the "impossible-possibility"—carrying, as it does, the solemn judgment that "the ethical demands of
Jesus are incapable of fulfillment in the present existence of man"—
clearly presupposes the trifurcated world-view in the context of which
Kant was required to understand morality—the ethic of categorical
obligation—as the product of the pure practical reason *alone* together
with human autonomy in complete isolation. Accordingly, Niebuhr's
ethical thought also presupposes the Kantian divorce of the Ought
and the Is, the cleavage that is, at least partially, represented in man
by the antagonism of impulse and reason. Therefore, morality must
take, as with Kant, the form of obligation, while goodness must be
the achievement of volition conceived as absolutely free.

Three consequences of the view, in the present connection, need
to be remarked: (1) the perfection of an absolutely contingent will is
an absurdity because perfection is contradictory to the will's freedom,
as Kant saw; (2) the ground of obligation must always be a law with
which one's will is not necessarily in conformity; if it were not so,
one's will would be holy and I should *not* be *obliged;* (3) goodness in
man cannot be conceived as emanating from nature because *nature
in man* presupposes the cleavage between the Ought and the Is (the
good and the desired); to assume otherwise would be to suppose mistak-
enly that Niebuhr's "transcendent unity of essence and existence" holds
of the historical world.

The charge of "perfectionism" is based, therefore, upon the implicit
assumption of the validity of the Kantain separation of nature and
morality or the Is and the Ought. Accepting this cleavage as ineradica-
bly in man's being, an "ethic of love" is not only impossible; it is, as
Kant held, no "ethic" at all. Presuming the cleavage, morality presupposes the necessary disjunction between duty and inclination. It is
very beautiful, said Kant, to seek men's good from love of them, "but

this is not the true moral maxim of our conduct which is suitable to our position amongst rational beings as men, when we pretend with fanciful pride to set ourselves above the thought of duty, like volunteers, and, as if we were independent of the command." [66] Moreover, says Kant, love to men is possible, no doubt, "but cannot be commanded." [67] And Niebuhr concurs: "To command love is a paradox, love cannot be commanded or demanded." [68] The tacit assumption is the same as Kant's. The love ethic of Jesus is taken to be *commandment* and, as such, can only be conceived as possible when "God transmutes the present chaos of the world into it final unity." [69] In the meantime, the true form of ethics is a free will conforming to the law in opposition to nature—*precisely not* emanating from inclination or love which *is* nature. The ethic of love, therefore, is "perfectionistic" because it assumes what is not so, namely, the coalescence of the Ought and the Is. For the same reason it is impossible, because it assumes that what I desire to do and what I ought to do are the same. Kant has forbidden such an assumption.

Regarded from Kant's standpoint, the charge of perfectionism stings (1) because of the absurdity of a perfect will, which, by definition, being free, must be imperfect, i.e, not necessarily in accord with the law, and (2) because of the moral worthlessness of action deriving from love or inclination. Abandon the presuppositions of Kant and the sting is drawn; but Niebuhr actually makes them the basis of his ethical criticism. Assuming that autonomy must be the ground of ethics, he supposes in Kantian fashion that love of God is "uncoerced giving of the self." [70] The truth seems to be that love is always coerced as the necessary commitment of the self to the esteemed object. It is will which follows love, not love which is constrained by will. True it is that love cannot be coerced. It does not have to be. It is impelled out of its own eagerness. But, for Kant, God could not be known. How then could he be loved? [71]

The heart of the matter is this: for Kant, as for Niebuhr, the *natural man,* alienated from God both in knowledge and in will, is the only man possible. It must remain so until God effects a union of the real and the ideal. Directly consequential to the dualism of the Is and the Ought is Niebuhr's view of grace as merely "justifying," as "pardon rather than power." [72] Grace may not be regarded as conferring "an actual power of righteousness." [73] Goodness would then derive from nature in some sense, and Kant does not allow it. Yet there are numerous glimpses of an opposing truth in Niebuhr, as when it is said: "What men are able to will depends not upon the strength of their willing, but upon the strength which enters their will and over which their will has little control." [74] It is just possible that a Christian doctrine of grace should mean that, of the man of faith, what Niebuhr holds ought to be true is becoming true, namely, that "in perfect love all law is transcended and what is and what ought to be are one." [75] The thesis of this essay is that Jesus supposed it to be so—that, in this sense, all things, even goodness, are possible to faith.

With Kant this eventuality is excluded because of his separation of the Is and the Ought, whereby, duty fulfilled must always derive from imperfection and freedom but never from nature. In Kant's thinking, *moral man* bridges the gap between *phenomena* and *Noumenon*—nature and God. There is no way from man to God by way of theoretical knowledge. The *causa noumenon* is not open to any intuition since intuition has but one form—the sensible.[76] However, happiness (the second factor of the *summum bonum*), which by nature all men seek, cannot forever be postponed in man's performance of his duty; therefore, a sufficient reason adequate to effect the conjunction of morality and nature (i.e., happiness) must be postulated "as the necessary condition of the possibility of the *summum bonum.*" That condition is the existence of God.[77] Man's moral achievement, therefore, implicated necessarily the postulate of God's existence. There is, then, a way from man to God through man's morality.

Reality and Perfection

The coalescence of the Is and the Ought is what Spinoza does assume, not in all men, but in him who attains to *amor intellectualis Dei.* For such, there is a comprehension of "the union existing between the mind and total Nature." [78] To view things *sub specie aeternitatis* is a purely rational function in man, but one in which—active rather than passive—he fulfills his true essence or *conatus.* The true end of man's *conatus,* that is, of his effort to persevere in being, is knowledge conjoined with the love of God. Here man's existence will have become identical with his essence. Such is Spinoza's demythologized version of the first commandment.

Central to Spinoza's thought, of course, is the postulate: *perfection* and *reality* are one and the same.[79] With this definition he hopes to eliminate the conceptions of final cause and teleology from the world, for all created being derives from God with the necessity of a mathematical deduction.[80] Everything is deduced according to the necessity of God's nature, from which nature God himself cannot vary.[81] Therefore, what is, is as it ought to be, for it is as it must be. There is no appeal beyond *what is* to a hypothetical Ought. The world is rational. Imperfection is absent from it; how, then, is ethics a serious problem?

Whether Spinoza admitted it or not, there was a little item of irrationality and nonbeing left in his world. Man suffered under the conditions of existence and was in bondage to the passions. By Spinoza's admission, all this *ought not to be*. There is, plainly, a difference between life according to *imaginatio* (sensibility), in which man is in bondage to the "affects," and life according to *ratio*, in which man is "active" and in which his blessedness consists. The latter condition ought to obtain rather than the former. *At one point in reality, then, Spinoza runs upon the nonidentity of realitas and perfectio, namely, in man.* Here he finds an incongruence between the Is and the Ought, between existence and essence, indeed a contradiction. And, precisely, in this disjunction is the plight and misery of man. But in it also is indicated both the possibility and the necessity of the "ethics," which Spinoza understands as the way of salvation.

Spinoza recognized his problem. To those who might ask "why has God not created all men in such a manner that they might be controlled by the dictates of reason alone?" Spinoza replies, because in God "material was not wanting for the creation of everything, from the highest down to the very lowest grade of perfection." [82] In this reply to the question about evil in the order of Being, Spinoza resorts to the Plotinian or Neoplatonic *principle of plenitude* but now employed by Spinoza in a pantheistic framework that equates God and Nature, Essence and Existence. In such a context the appeal to the principle of plenitude is illicit, since for Plotinus, the author, all derivation is imperfection. The doubt is not that there is a hierarchy of beings and perfections but why there should be an existent being at all in whom his existence is not identical with his essence, or, how any reality can be imperfect, viz., nonidentical with its essence in a world in which reality and perfection are one and the same. Spinoza's theoretical denial of this item of nonbeing in man was countered by his practical admission of it which actually eventuated in making ethics the main end of his philosophizing. [83]

The pertinency for the present essay is this: goodness is derived from a renewed nature. It derives from blessedness in which man is released from bondage to the "affects which are evil." [84] "The more the mind delights in the divine love or blessedness . . . the greater is the power it has over the affects." [85] Goodness derives, therefore, from Being. Not from man's original being, as alienated from God by ignorance of him, but from man's acquired being. Moreover, goodness emanates from a kind of holiness. It is not holiness defined as the necessary conformity of a will to the law. Rather, it is love which is directed to God and which is the token of being or community shared with Him. It is a metaphysical, not, as Kant made it, a moral

category. By making possible a transition in man's nature from existence to essence, Spinoza made room both for an ethic not based upon
autonomy and for goodness instead of "morality."

The Way of the Kingdom

It is very much the same in the view of Jesus. Holiness or purity of
heart has its primary and secondary, or consequential, aspect. Primarily, it signifies a relationship of the human subject with God, initiated by God and confirmed, on man's side, in all that Jesus signifies
by the word *faith*. As confirming that relationship, faith is not simply
cognitive; it is a mode of experience being realized as an altered-way-
of-being-together-with-God, viz., one of community *(koinonia)* with
the Father. So the name *Abba*, in Jesus' usage, stands for communion-
being-realized. Secondarily, the consequential aspect of *beatitude* is
the resultant, the life both transformed and in process of transfigura-
tion. This transformation manifests itself in ways illustrated by Jesus'
Beatitudes (Matt. 5:3–11). What is primary is beatitude itself—the transformation in process. What *we* customarily call goodness issues out
of life-in-faith.

At least once Jesus refers to the good man, saying: "The good man
out of the treasure of his heart bringeth forth that which is good.
. . ." [86] T. W. Manson's claim seems to be vindicated in that faith signifies a "transformation of character" with a commensurate overflow.
In the Sermon of Matthew, Jesus says: "By their fruits ye shall know
them" (Matt. 7:16). But, apart from a few references, Jesus does not
mention nor accent the "good man," and never the "moral" man in
Kant's sense, nor "virtue" either, in the tradition of the Greeks. In
the interchange with a certain ruler who addressed him as "good
teacher," in the Lukan account, the response of Jesus is usually regarded as troublesome: "Why callest thou me good? none is good,
save one, even God." [87] Yet this is wholly consistent with the twofold
point we have been making: (1) What Jesus signalizes is *life-in-faith*,
that is, a relationship to God the Father *confirmed*—not initiated—in
and with the appropriate response of a Son of the Kingdom. In its
primary denotation and essential meaning, then, the *beatitude* of the
Gospels is not a moral quality of the man himself but a relationship—
that of faith—by which he is constituted a member of the community
of faith. (2) In its secondary sense, *beatitude* is the source of which
the "fruits" are the ripe outgrowth. How, then, can the so-called "love-
ethic" of Jesus be viewed as "perfectionism" when it falls wholly outside
a "morality" from which the very word is inseparable? What Jesus
calls for is faith *as* transformation of human existence, acceptance of

Sonship to the Father and a love of the neighbor commensurate therewith, but also empowered thereby.

Accordingly, even the secondary aspect is not holiness in the moral sense that Kant gave to it—"perfect accordance of the will with the moral law." In the New Testament salvation is by faith, not by works of the Law. Kant had no other way to God than through the astounding miracle of man's morality. With Jesus, beatitude even in its derivative aspect, impelled as it is by faith or *answering* love to God the Father, is not conformation to the Divine-will-over-against that of an autonomous subject. Rather, it is eager participation in the manifest redemptive activity of God out of thanksgiving and nerved by love. The transformation by life-in-faith has, as its other side, emancipation from an obsessive self-concern. The man of faith, in Jesus' view, is freed for "fruits worthy of repentance" as faith replaces anxiety.[88]

Through this faith the Kantian cleavage between nature and Grace, between the Is and the Ought, is surmounted by restoration of community with God. Man is no longer alienated from God; accordingly, St. Paul spoke of reconciliation. If there is a Christian "ethic," it is the way of reconciliation by which the hiatus between the Is and the Ought, or nature and Grace is being overcome—not at the solitary initiative of man, as with Kant, or even as with Socrates—but at the initiative of the God and Father of Jesus of the Gospels. Moreover, this transcendence of the hiatus is virtually identical with the establishment of the Kingdom *as present.* It is the Kingdom which Jesus says is "received" ($\delta\epsilon\xi\eta\tau\alpha\iota$) [89] on the condition of faith analogous to that of the little child.[90] This constitutes God's present, not just future, transmutation of essence into existence, the ideal into the actual. This is, we propose, the actualization in time and persons (as existence-points) of the "transcendent and divine unity of essential reality" of which Niebuhr speaks. Henceforth, goodness proceeds from "nature," as against Kant, although it is not human nature as alienated from God but as reconciled. Thus, for Jesus, there is open to man through community with God a renovated nature. It overcomes or is overcoming self-defensiveness or, as Spinoza described it, the anxiety to persevere in being.

iv. CONCLUDING OBSERVATIONS

In this study I have had no quarrel with a major premise of Reinhold Niebuhr: that, for humanity as we find it, and, on the witness of the prophetic tradition, "the sense of God and the sense of sin are involved in the same act of consciousness." On the contrary, I regard this judgment as a starting-point of Christian theology. My discontent arises with Niebuhr's succeeding "translation" of this proposition into, as he says, "ethical terms." In translation, he finds that the premise "becomes the tension between the principle of love and the impulse of egoism. . . ." This, while an oversimplification, is not without truth, but its usefulness for the interpretation of Jesus' so-called ethic is entirely dependent upon what tradition of ethical thought is employed to unpack the meaning of either the love-principle or the "impulse of egoism."

Niebuhr has employed Kantain "morality," conjoined with "autonomy," to probe the meaning of the love-principle in the Gospels. The result is a misreading of the Gospels. The "impulse of egoism" is understood, wittingly or unwittingly, more nearly in Spinoza's terms. These two systems of ethics are incompatible. The largely unnoticed inconsequence to which Niebuhr brings us is the total incapacity of the Kantian ethic to illuminate the so-called gospel "ethic." Yet, in this, Niebuhr adopts a course of which the predominant line of post-Kantian "liberal" Christian ethics is precursor.

What is needed, I judge, has as yet no precedent. It is, namely, to recognize that the 'moral consciousness," as conceived by Kant, and as received by him from the *philosophia perennis,* has yet to be assessed precisely from the standpoint of the prophetic consciousness of either Testament. When examined, the two will be found to be complementary but, quite certainly, not identical. It is the error of Protestant "liberal theology" to assume a simple identity, and this, I think, Niebuhr has perpetuated. It is, moreover, this unexamined assumption of near identity, together with the long privileged position of the Kantian ethic, in liberal Protestantism, which fosters a recurrent phenomenon in Protestant thought. It is the recurring tendency—fully visible in all species of Ritschlian theology and its offspring—toward a reduction of Christianity to ethics. How can it be otherwise, when, under the aegis of Kantianism, morality is at the initiative of man's autonomy and the precondition of his *beatitude?* This nonbiblical viewpoint was the price of Kant's acceptance of a long-standing cleavage in Western thought between Nature and Grace.

CONTEMPORARY THEOLOGY
IN REVIEW

BARTH'S ATTACK UPON CARTESIANISM AND THE FUTURE IN THEOLOGY

I. THE ISSUE IN THEOLOGY TODAY

Whither are we going in theology today? That is the question. In order, at the beginning, to put the import of this discussion in focus, I immediately hazard the judgment that a central issue in contemporary theology centers on the question whether or not the radically theocentric or, perhaps, Christocentric theology of Barth will prove able to withstand an already perceptible drift back in the direction of the anthropocentric standpoint of Schleiermacher. With reference to the drift, no one should read carelessly Paul Tillich's remark in the masterly Introduction to his *Systematic Theology:* "No present-day theology should avoid a discussion of Schleiermacher's experiential method." And he continues: "One of the causes for the disquieting effect of neo-orthodox theology was that it detached itself completely from Schleiermacher's method, consequently denying the theological developments of the last two hundred years." It is wholly intentional when Tillich adds: "The crucial question of theology today is whether or not, or to what degree, this denial is justified." [1]

As long ago as 1932 Barth was fully aware this was the issue. He took the stand that the denial was not only justified but imperative, and he has only elaborated his reasons in the interim. Some years later, in his *Die protestantische Theologie im 19. Jahrhundert* (1947), Barth paid tribute to the great master in asserting that "at the summit of the history of theology of recent times there belongs and will for all time belong the name of Schleiermacher, and with none beside him" (p. 379). Barth observes that Schleiermacher, like Frederick the Great, "did not found a school but an age." So great was his influence that the field of theology in the 19th century may be described as a medley of greater or smaller curves which always at length sweep back again to Schleiermacher as their origin. This situation prevailed, Barth affirms, until the year 1924. At this point he singles out the work of Emil Brunner (probably *Der Mittler*) as the first real attack upon Schleiermacher's standpoint which is truly taken outside the circle of Schleiermacher's influence. Obviously, Barth means to specify in

A paper presented to *Concilium*, theological group of the doctoral Program in Religion of the Graduate School of Arts and Sciences, Duke University, March 1956. Published in *The Journal of Religion*, XXXVI, No. 4 (October 1956). Republished with permission of the Editor.

Brunner's work a pole antithetical to Schleiermacher with which he associates himself.

In this essay Barth makes it clear that Schleiermacher's "anthropocentric theology" is exhibited, among other things, in the fact that "a mode of human apprehension comes to be equivalent to the outpouring of the Holy Spirit and, at the same time, of the pious self-consciousness as such" (p. 414). In Barth's view, man, that is, the human self-consciousness in its determination as the pious self-consciousness, has undoubtedly become for Schleiermacher the object of theological reflection (p. 410). For him piety or religious experience takes the place which, in Reformation thought, was occupied by the Word of God. Knowledge is understood as *Erlebnis* of men rather than as God's self-revelation through the objective Word made flesh and appropriated in faith through the work of the Holy Spirit (p. 414). To sum it up: "The Word in its self-identity over against faith is [in Schleiermacher] not really secure, as, necessarily it must be if this theology of 'faith' were a true theology of the Holy Spirit" (p. 422). A real difference between Christ and the Christian cannot be made out, thinks Barth. We are reduced to man's universal capacity for pious experience. This is the reduction of theology to anthropology. Barth is opposed.

Adverting once more to Tillich, there can scarcely be much doubt that Tillich's theology is, as Barth long ago recognized,[2] rather forthrightly directed to showing to what degree the denial of Schleiermacher's method in theology is *not* justified; and there is no doubt whose side Tillich takes in the recently prevailing contest between Schleiermacher and so-called neo-orthodoxy. Like many another religious thinker who has been strongly influenced by existentialism in both its theological and philosophical expressions, Tillich's sympathies lie with Schleiermacher. The reason is clear: 20th-century existentialism roots in an anthropology and is, like Schleiermacher, commonly monistic in ontology. Taking its start from man's self-consciousness, together with the problem of man under "the conditions of existence," whatever it may say in ontology will issue from man's understanding of his existence. Ontology will be the illuminating interpretation of the import of that understanding. It is hard to escape the impression that Tillich's "theology of correlation (which is itself reminiscent of Schleiermacher's method) is premised upon other than the proper human self-understanding. It is therefore, and furthermore, not surprising that Tillich looks for religious knowledge or "revelation" as reason in man becomes "transparent" to its "depth" or "ground." Revelation ensues as reason, under the conditions of existence, is transformed through "ecstasy" and "sign-event" into essential reason. This reason "must be understood as reason in ecstasy or fulfilling reason."[3]

In order to make good this program, it is necessary, among other things, for Tillich to begin by establishing the diffference between "technical," or "controlling reason," and ontological reason. This analysis Tillich has executed more cogently, I believe, than perhaps any contemporary thinker, although he is dependent upon such predecessors as Dilthey, Rickert, and Buber, not to mention Plato. Technical reason is concerned with and competent for knowledge and management of the world which lies to hand—the "I-It" world of Martin Buber and Karl Heim. Much like Kant's theoretical understanding, technical reason has phenomenal employment only. Ontological reason, on the other hand, is the structure of mind (or *logos*) by which human reason is primordially conformed to the structure of Being (or *Logos*), and it is the transparency of this reason to its "depth" to the "abyss" of Being, which is revelation of Being.

Apparently, it is Tillich's intention to assert that transparency of reason to the ground of Being is an actual event in time and under the conditions of existence in Jesus as the Christ. However, as Brunner charged against Schleiermacher with good effect, it remains at least highly ambiguous in what sense Jesus as the Christ is to be considered more than the "subject of religion" or the subject of redemption.[4] If Jesus Christ is no more than this, and I do not confidently assert it in the absence of the second volume of the *Systematic,* we have again something reminiscent of Schleiermacher, namely, Christ as the realization of the capacity of "the higher self-consciousness" to disclose its divine ground.

Such motifs as have been sketched in the thought of Tillich serve at least two purposes which can be mentioned here. One is to demythologize, by means of rational anthropology, the Christian *Weltanschauung* along with its kerygma and eschatology. The other is avoidance of head-on clash with a scientific world-view for which revelation, in Barth's sense, offends as a scandalous intrusion of divine causality—a scandal which Schleiermacher sought to obviate more than a century ago.[5]

The program of Tillich comes to something like this: Just as 19th-century theology—following Kant and Schleiermacher—differentiated the theoretical from the practical reason, with Kant, or the "sensible" from the "higher self-consciousness," with Schleiermacher, so Tillich differentiates technical from ontological reason. Then, as the 19th century found surety of religious knowledge either in the "practical reason" or in the distinctive religious consciousness, so Tillich finds the assurance of religious knowledge in ontological reason's recovery of its "depth." And, just as either the Kantian bifurcation of experience and that of Schleiermacher made provision for scientific knowledge without jeopardizing distinctive religious truth, so Tillich secures an independent domain for revelation through probing the resources of ontological reason. To this, the findings of science are hardly relevant and certainly never a threat.[6] At this point the similarity with Kant ceases, but the connection with Schleiermacher remains; for as, with Schleiermacher, there is an immediate and direct ontal import of "pious feeling" so, with Tillich, ontological reason in man is continuous with its "ground," and, where it attains transparency, revelation is assured in ontal and epistemic union. This is ontologism, but of an alarmingly monistic provenance.

II. THE ANTHROPOLOGICAL STANDPOINT REVERSED

I have a clear recollection of the appearance of Wilhelm Pauck's *Karl Barth, Prophet of a New Christianity?* upon my father's desk in the year 1931. Shortly thereafter the storm of neo-orthodoxy—already over a decade advanced in Europe—broke upon the American theological scene. By 1938 it was sweeping all before it. By that time, when indeed I was studying theology with D. C. Macintosh at Yale, the empirical theology he had influentially represented was already heavily on the defensive and, almost month by month, was increasingly in disrepute among theological students of my generation. Hitherto bright lights in American theology—represented in the names of Mathews, Wieman, Macintosh, and Lyman—dimmed and then disappeared to be replaced by various spokesmen of the new persuasion. The vanguard was led by that admirable whirlwind of theological virtuosity, Reinhold Niebuhr, and by Emil Brunner, whose voice now sounded for a time out of the environs of Princeton and decisively influenced, I believe, the form in which, in America, neo-orthodoxy was appropriated.

It is fair to say, I think, that Barth has been known in America rather more through the writings of those who shared the temper and tendency of his thought than through his own more formidable and exacting theological productions. The result is that there has been a good deal more discussion of Barthianism than of Barth and a good deal more conversancy with refractions of his thought than with his closely knit language itself.

From the standpoint of Barth's detractors this circumstance is, no doubt, a matter of relief, yet one would be blind to the complexion of contemporary theology if he did not at least acknowledge two things: first, that Barth avowedly set himself "against the stream" of more than a century of modern Protestant theology with unsurpassed resourcefulness, and, accordingly, in the second place, that he has been exceptionally responsible for having raised the significant questions around which serious theological discussion has flooded for a generation. Whatever be the estimate which history at length sets upon the worth of Barth's system, it will most probably sustain the judgment that Protestant theology in the 20th century was decisively shifted in its course by Barth's work. I surmise, moreover, that the immediate future of theology will turn upon the manner in which it finds its way and takes its course between two poles represented, the one, by Schleiermacher, the other, by Barth. For, in an unusually precise respect, either of these two thinkers is the antithesis of the other. This antithesis is perhaps crucial, because the polarity here represented is a permanent possibility inherent in the structure of the Christian world-view. The one takes man as starting point and finds God a co-implicate of the properly interpreted human self-consciousness. The other unyieldingly makes the "sovereign freedom of God" the alpha and omega and consents to understand man only so far as he is the *object* of gracious divine activity in creation and redemption.[7]

We can go further, perhaps, and say that the antithesis is, in fact, and fundamentally, a permanent possibility inherent in the polarity structure of all experience, that is, the subject-object polarity. the polarity not only entails the question of primacy or priority of object to subject or vice versa; it also, by its very nature, engenders the problem and need of a "reconciliation," the one to the other. Methods of reconciliation in the history of human thought have tended alternately to subordinate the subject to the object (in realism) or, conversely, the object to the subject (in idealism). Christian theology has in fact participated in this oscillation of preference. Tendency to give priority to the subject certainly preponderates in post-Schleiermacherian theology. On the other hand, a tendency to give priority to the object becomes fully recognizable in nominalism and every theology which depreciates *theologia naturalis* and general revelation or accentuates grace over nature.

In terms of this polarity situation, Barth's choice is clear and unyielding. The determining focus is God in his sovereign freedom. As for man, theology cannot rightly speak of him considered in himself over against God (*Doct.*, p. 197) or "in abstraction" from the relation in which he stands to God and God to him (II. 1. 167; III. 2. 174). Everywhere it is characteristic of Barth, after about 1930, to assert, especially against existentialism, that theology cannot rest upon an "autonomous human self-understanding" independent of the Word of God (III. 2. 148). He declares, "We know nothing of our created state, from our created state, but only through the Word of God" (*Doct.*, p. 148). This position is normative and is amply reiterated in subsequent sections of the *Dogmatik*, where, for example, it is affirmed: "Man will be an object of the theological knowledge in so far as, through the Word of God, his relation to God is made manifest" (III. 2. 20). It is made manifest exclusively in the "humanity" of Jesus Christ, the revealed Word (III. 2. 47, 50, 413). Understandings of man—philosophical, historical, or psychological—can well be outside the standpoint of faith. In principle they are permissible and even called for, although they treat only the phenomenal man (III. 2. 286). Hence they do not unfold the "truth of the human being" whose nature is knowable only as it is apprehended in the relation with which God stands to it (III. 2. 21). Man is defined, not especially by the relation in which he stands to God, but by the relation in which God wills to stand in Jesus Christ with respect to him (III. 2. 49). In this connection it is worthy of utmost emphasis to add that we quite misunderstand Barth if, supposing him to be the theologian of "transcendence," we fail to recognize that, for him, God is fundamentally *Being-in-relation*, first, with himself in his own *Lebensform* and then with man (III. 2. 391).

With Barth, however, there is always the ontological priority of God. We may say—and with this we come to the epistemological theme we are to pursue—that Barth has so vivid a sense of antecedent reality in the order of being that, in the order of knowing, he must regard the object as determining the subject. Thus Barth was saying in 1932 that, while we cannot speak of man in himself over against God, nevertheless, in theology, "we must speak of God in Himself in His isolation over against man" (*Doct.*, p. 197). Extreme as this statement may appear, it is calculated to countermand "Cartesianism" in theology which, according to Barth, characteristically derives the knowledge of God from a prior and self-confirming knowledge of man.[8] Nevertheless, in subsequent writings it is everywhere manifest that God is not understood by Barth to be a "solitary one" (III. 2. 260). It is of the nature of God, not only in his inner being to be "existence with one another" (II. 2. 261), but, in virtue of his grace, to be in relation with the creature and, in the humanity of Jesus Christ, to set forth the reality of his being for man (III. 2. 260). When, therefore, Barth spoke of God in his isolation over against man, he meant to affirm, as the context shows, that any "correlation" between God and man or the world is entirely dependent upon the prior gracious initiative of the Creator and that, consequently, the knowledge of God is extractable not from man as such but from the action in which God wills to make himself known (II. 1. 68).

In all this we properly observe a bold stress upon what, in epistemological language, is called "antecedent reality." Barth knows precisely what he is about. Already in the Prolegomena to the *Dogmatik* we find him repudiating even Gogarten's "anthropological programme," namely, no understanding of man without understanding of God and no understanding of God without *prior* understanding of man. With this Barth puts behind him all that remains of Schleiermacher's antropological method in theology (*Doct.*, p. 145). He even corrects the questionable impression fostered by Calvin, who, in the first sentences of his *Institutes*, left it doubtful as to which of the two—knowledge of God or of ourselves—precedes and gives rise to the other.[9] Barth has no doubt, for he holds that "to understand God, starting from man, is either impossible in itself, or such a view as can only be described in the form of Christology" (*Doct.*, p. 148). By this he means to assert—as he was to make fully explicit later—that the only true understanding of man, the only true anthropology, is Christology.[10] Indeed, it is only in the man Jesus Christ, the revealed Word, that both the *status corruptionis* and the *status integritatis* are disclosed.[11]

The following words in the Prolegomena are about as suitable to convey Barth's point as any. Speaking of *analogia entis*, he asserts: "This direct discernment of the original connection between God and man, discernment of the creation of man which as such is also the revelation of God, is, according to Reformed principles as to the seriousness of sin, taken from us by the Fall and only restored in the Gospel, in *revelatia specialis*" (*Doct.*, p. 147). It is upon this ground, of course, that Barth is obliged to replace *analogia entis* with *analogia fidei.* This signifies the conformation of the whole man to the Word of God, through the Holy Spirit's working, in such fashion that a man acknowledges the truth in faith.[12]

Everywhere, plainly, it is Barth's earnest intention to safeguard the sovereign freedom, the absolute priority, of God. To this end, and as an integral part of his program, Barth shows a distinctive emphasis in epistemology which has received less comment than it deserves. Corresponding to the ontological priority of God is an insistence upon the entire priority of the divine causality in the knowledge of faith and, one may add, in man's knowledge of himself. This position, having been fully attained by Barth before the year 1932, makes it entirely clear why Barth, by that time, felt obliged to cut all ties with the existentialist standpoint. Kierkegaard must go along with Heidegger (*Doct.*, p. 21). Therewith, Barth rejected root and branch all dependency upon the human self-consciousness as revelation or ground of revelation. The radical character of this negation was calculated to enforce, with a stringency Kierkegaard's existentialism could not attain, the dictum: "By God alone can God be known" (II. 1. 86). And not only so, in particular it enforces, in Barth's explicit intention, a radical and entire dependence upon the *dynamis* of the Holy Spirit for the event of faith (*Doct.*, pp. 207–8). So palpable is this consequence that to Barth is almost certainly to be attributed the first really influential resuscitation of pneumatology in modern theology since the Enlightenment.

III. BARTH'S REALISM IN EPISTEMOLOGY

Attending once more to the priority of Being and to the correlative concept of antecedent reality, we are in a position, now, to look more closely at the structure of knowledge which Barth formulates apropos thereto. He has committed himself irrevocably to the view that the order of knowing is determined absolutely by the order of Being. How, then, is this expressed in theory of knowledge? The difficulty of answering this question inheres in the fact that, as theologian, Barth acknowledges no responsibility for supplying a general theory of knowledge. He will not, as is well known, specify any particular faculty—intellect, will, affections, or conscience—as point of meeting for the divine-human encounter (*Doct.*, pp. 230–31). He is neither favorable nor indisposed in a special way toward any of these faculties. He is neither antirationalistic nor voluntaristic; but, if there were any preference, he would commend the entire rational human nature, the whole self-determining man, as the subject of the divine determination, and says so (*Doct.*, p. 233). In his later writing it is indeed the "entirety" and true integrity of human nature in Christ which is a concomitant of his status as Revealer (III. 2. 394–95). But location and designation of "anthropological centers" as points of divine-human connection are foregone by Barth precisely with the dismissal of the anthropological method itself.[13] Since causality in theological knowledge lies with the *object* rather than the *subject*, it is fruitless as it is also grievously mistaken—a mark of disbelief—to take man, the subject, more seriously than God the sovereign agent.[14]

The one passage of which I have knowledge where Barth supplies a generalization to enbrace this conception of divine causality in cognition is to be found in the first half-volume of the *Dogmatik* dealing with the "knowability of the Word of God" and the nature of "experience of the Word of God" (*Doct.*, pp. 213–37). Even here the formulation is very guarded. We shall, Barth warns, have to frame the concept of knowledge "so generally with such philosophical and epistemological indefiniteness that the possibility is kept open of any revision, restriction, or reversal that might befall from the side of the object of knowledge" (*Doct.*, p. 216). Behind this caution, of course, stands Barth's avowal of the sovereign freedom of God. The divine causality cannot be allowed to suffer even so restricted a limitation as is implied in a normative *description* of its operation if that description were to be entertained in such a way as would counterdetermine divine causality to a particular form or mode. This would be the epistemological way of laying violent hands upon God, of conditioning from the side of the creature the gracious freedom of the Creator. However, with this admonitory self-restriction, Barth does allow himself a definition of the nature of knowledge—presumably knowledge of the Word of God as well as of knowledge in general. He also permits himself a characterization of its dynamics.

Let us, in the first place, consider its *nature*. The following is a crucial definition: "By the knowledge of an object by men we understand the proof of their acquaintance with its reality in respect of its being there (or its existence) and in respect of its being thus and so (or its nature)." Barth continues: "But 'proof of their acquaintance' implies that the reality of the object in question, its existence and its nature, now becomes, while true in itself, somehow and with some degree of clarity and definition also true for them" (*Doct.*, p. 214). Each of these sentences carries a particular stress. In the first we are once more alerted to the fundamental realism of Barth's outlook. The whatness is given in and with the thatness of the object. In the second statement it is clear that in veridical cognition the "trueness" of the thing, which we may perhaps call, albeit awkwardly, its whatness-in-its-thatness, becomes entertained as a datum of consciousness.

If these deductions are valid, three comments seem warranted. (1) Knowledge, as Barth understands it, obtains when, as distinguished from ontic, there is nonetheless noetic identity or conformity between the known and the knower. (2) Knowledge involves something we may perhaps describe as the *recapitulation* of the antecedent in the consequent, that is, of the potency of the known in the knower. This is confirmed by the insistence in the same context that, in acquaintance which is knowledge, the relation between the object and the subject is transformed. From being only "accidental," it becomes "necessary" or integral; and, from being merely external, the relation becomes an "inward determination" of the subject's own existence by the object (*Doct.*, p. 214). Thus Barth asserts a few pages farther on: "We defined knowledge as that confirmation of human acquaintance with an object whereby its trueness becomes a determining factor in the existence of the man who knows" (*Doct.*, p. 226). (3) This comment is derivative of the preceding two. We do discern in this conception of knowledge—and contrary to the estimate of D. C. Macintosh [15]—a marked departure from Kantian phenomenalism, and this on two grounds: first, knowledge here is in no sense constitutive but derivative of reality, and second, an *epistemic* difference between the object and the subject, as confirmed in immediate acquaintance, is not asserted, although an ontic difference remains. This provides the basis for Barth's characteristic insistence that, in "the event of divine encroachment" (II. 1. 86), God is known truly, or he is truly self-revealed in his *act* of revelation.[16] God is truly known in so far as he wills and acts so as to be known. In both respects, then, we see a withdrawal from Kantian critical agnosticism and, in its place, a sort of critical realism in epistemology. But it is *critical* realism because God remains veiled in his revealedness (*Doct.*, pp. 191–92).

Now, concerning the dynamics of knowledge, a few words are in order. For Barth, knowledge is "event." Perhaps more exactly, it is an eventuation. In part, it is what eventuates in the subject on the condition solely of the causality of the object. In knowledge there is a necessary and inward determination of the subject's existence by the object.[17] Barth's way of putting the matter is as noteworthy as it is casual. Speaking of knowing subject, he says: "As knowers they are got at by the known object" (*Doct.*, p. 214). Or, again, he puts it thus: "Man exists not abstractly but concretely, i.e., in experiences, in determinations of his existence by objects, by something external distinct from himself" (*Doct.*, p. 226).

IV. ANTI-CARTESIANISM DEFINED

In this last statement we can once more perceive the powerfully realistic outlook of Barth in ontology and epistemology. When he declares that man exists "not abstractly but concretely," he means to *deny* something and also to *affirm* something. What he means to deny is all "Cartesianism" in philosophy and theology (*Doct.*, p. 223). For Barth, "Cartesianism" means the way of thought which draws the knowledge of the world and of God out of the alleged prior knowledge of the self [18] or that places "self-certainty," not merely before "God-certainty," but before certainty of all else whatever (*Doct.*, p. 223).

Barth shares with William Temple a lively conviction that the whole day Descartes spent "shut up alone in a stove" was a disastrous moment in the history of Europe.[19] His long excursus on Descartes in the third volume of the *Dogmatik* (III. 1. 401–15) is in many respects directed to ends similar to those of Temple in the latter's now famous chapter, "The Cartesian Faux-Pas." He comes close to agreement with Temple's summary judgment that the Cartesian *faux pas* consists in "the inherent error of its initial assumption that in knowledge the mind begins with itself and proceeds to the apprehension of the external world by way of construction and inference." [20] In like manner, Barth accuses

Descartes—and this is fairly standard criticism—of deriving the existence of God from the prior certainty of self-existence. But what is derived from the *cogito* is only the *Gottesidee*, only an idea still quite within "the circle of necessary thought" (III. 1. 411). Descartes is "hopelessly inside the world," and God is hopelessly inside the circle of Descartes's reflection and dependent upon an act of the creature's thought (III. 1. 412). God is alleged to be a necessary inference from either the "sufficiency" or the "deficiency" of the human spirit (III. 1. 410). Honor is due Descartes in so far as he intended, albeit he failed, to ground the certainty both of self-consciousness and of world-consciousness upon the existence of God. But, having started with self-consciousness and finding God its logical but merely ideal co-implicate, Descartes was never able to establish the priority, the real antecedence, of God's being (III. 1. 410).

This is to pick up the stick at the wrong end. There is no way from man to God but only from God to man—a way he himself provides, which is altogether suitable to his sovereign lordship and ontological priority. Descartes aspires to demonstrate God rather than, like Anselm, to "acknowledge" and submit to God's demonstration of himself (III. 1. 412). Already by 1932 Barth was vigorously declaiming against such a view as holds that the "I-experience is for men the foundation of the surest certainty of reality that is thinkable, that is possible for him at all. [Or] is the presupposition . . of all validation of reality connected with the external world." [21] In his opposition to this standpoint, Barth is setting his face, as the context makes clear, against a Cartesianism that derives man's "proof of God from man's certainty of himself" (*Doct.*, p. 222). And now, later, Barth asks how the real presence of God can become evident "as long as the highest force of proof consists only in logical necessity under the pressure of which a man can scribble no more than the object of his own concepts of present reality out of himself . . . ?" (III. 1. 412).

In consistency with his realistic position, Barth urges that Descartes's *Gottesidee* does not reach beyond the circle of subjectivity to the "other side," to reality over against. In order for the "other side," the reality of God, to be known, God's causality must move toward and "reach man" (III. 1. 412). In this Barth not only opposes Descartes and every form of idealism but, in addition, he sets himself against the "Copernican revolution" of Kant, wherein attainment of knowledge is partially the work of the subject who knows.[22] Barth's denial here is characteristically a denial of Pelagianism, that is, of Pelagianism in theory of knowledge. Indeed, so resolutely does Barth assert the antecedence of the divine causality—the object's determination of the subject—that he rejects as semi-Pelagian any doctrine of concurrence or "synthesis" in causality between the two (*Doct.*, p. 228). In all this we have an indication of what Barth means to deny in the proposition that man exists "not abstractly but concretely." *Against Cartesianism in all its forms he denies that man can be considered abstractly, that is, in independence of determination from without, whether by mundane or divine realities.* As for divine causality, in particular, it evidently seemed clear to Barth that the only assurance we have that we are not imprisoned within our own experience—and thus that Feuerbach was right—is that God breaks into our experience from without.[23] Only the breakthrough of divine causality can preserve us from anthropological solipsism in theology. With this insight established, Schleiermacher's doctrine of immanent causality becomes finally and definitively unacceptable.

The divine intrusion or breakthrough finds clear representation in Barth's unusual conception of experience *(Erfahrung)*, as set forth in the first half-volume of the *Dogmatik*, and this leads to an examination of what Barth means to *affirm* in his statement that man exists "not abstractly but concretely." The context, it will be recalled, is a general epistemological discussion of "the concept of experience" and one of the few statements of a merely philosophic nature which Barth indulges himself. He declares that man exists not abstractly but concretely, and this is to say he exists in *Erfahrungen,* in experiences. But, in turn, this means that man exists "in determinations of his existence by objects, by something or other external to himself" (*Doct.*, p. 226). Judging by the language of this passage, the point to get is that, in describing the dynamics of the knowing relationship, Barth explicitly reverses both the Cartesian and the Kantian positions. Previously we saw that he described the knowledge situation as an "inward determination by the object of the subject's existence" (*Doct.*, p. 214). "As knowers," he says, "they are got at by the known objects" (*Doct.*, p. 214). Reality "comes home to men" so that they no longer exist without it but only with it (*Doct.*, p. 215). Now, in a subsequent passage, this general view is reaffirmed with clearer definition. The man experiencing becomes the *object* of the causality of realities external to him. This causality constitutes man, alike in his being and in his knowing. Now, says Barth, "it is precisely this factor determining the existence of the man who knows that we call *Erfahrung,* experience" (*Doct.*, p. 226).

The "Copernican revolution" of Kant is here violently reversed. In no degree whatever will Barth accede to a view of the subject's causality in knowing which would make the human cognitive act constitutive of the result.[24] Knowledge is something that happens to him in the determination of his existence. In this way, Barth continues to enforce the view that man cannot be known or know himself out of relation with the determinative environment considered either as subpersonal or personal, mundane or divine.

It should be plain, once analyzed, that this general epistemological standpoint reverses the field of post-Cartesian epistemology and reverts to something like the realism of the Greeks and of Aristotle. Barth is aware of this shift, for he expressly observes that we must beware of opposing to Cartesianism "another philosophy somewhat better in accord with the instinct of theology, or, weary of Descartes, of throwing ourselves into the arms of Aristotle, which means Thomas. At this stage, having our suspicions of the other side, too, we merely make the point that in theology at least thought cannot proceed along Cartesian lines" (*Doct.*, p. 223).

But alliance with Aristotle is not really possible, in any case, simply by the reassertion of the causality of antecedent reality in knowledge. It would be indispensable to resurrect the "substantial Form" as the mediating link between subject and object; and neither here nor elsewhere does Barth show any inclination to go behind the nominalism of Luther or Ockham. As a result, there is really no historical antecedent for the sort of epistemological theory which he has adumbrated unless we are to find a counterpart in Francis Bacon's direct physical realism and pervasive insistence upon the humble submission of the mind to the impressions of nature as the condition of knowledge.

But, however eccentric to previous epistemological theory, we should not miss the point that, as a general conception, this theory serves Barth's purpose in theology quite well. The question which provoked his modest excursion into general epistemology was the question of the "knowability of the Word of God." Barth had rejected all basis in human nature for this possibility. If God is to be known only through God, then the "event" of knowledge must rest solely with the divine determination, and the event of knowledge will be the eventuation of the divine activity, thus entirely the work of grace (*Doct.*, p. 183). Accordingly, we can see the relevance of the general statement that knowledge is the determination by the object of the existence of the subject who knows. But now it is to be noted that the object is really the energizing divine Subject, and the human subject is really the energized object (*Doct.*, pp. 280–81). Thus, in the "event" of revelation, we deal with the divine subject,[25] with God the addresser and man the addressee (*Doct.*, p. 218).

We are now fully prepared to understand Barth's pervasive view that, in the knowledge of faith, our "self-determination" suffers the determination of God (*Doct.*, pp. 227–28). This must be the case if "experience" is defined as "the factor determining the existence of the man who knows." His examination of Cartesianism early convinced Barth that, for knowledge of the Word of God beyond and above man's own word, "our very self-determination needs this determination by God in order to be experience of His Word" (*Doct.*, p. 228).

Barth is emphatic that this divine determination does not entail the evacuation or extinction of man's "self-determination" in the actual event of revelation.[26] However, the paradox of the determination of man's self-determination is apparently soluble at last for Barth only by appeal to the "miracle" of God's working through the Holy Spirit (*Doct.*, p. 208). This, however, is only to say that the real ground for man's "openness" to the Word of God cannot in any way be exhibited from man's side. "The fact that we know God is his work not ours," says Barth (II. 1. 43). No account of the fact, therefore, can be rendered from the side of man. Here reference must be exclusively to the Holy Spirit (*Doct.*, p. 208). Accordingly, Barth declares: "By the outpouring of the Holy Spirit it becomes possible in the freedom of man for God's relevation to befall him" (I. 2. 269). Thus, against Schleiermacher, who identified the outpouring of the Holy Spirit with the potentiality of the human self-consciousness to give rise to "pious affections," Barth has reaffirmed the scandal of the divine intrusion.

V. THE STATUS OF MAN IN CHRIST

Clearly, such a theory of knowledge contributes solidly to Barth's program of giving glory to God. For over thirty years Barth has been striking blows against the Schleiermacherian program in theology, which understands revelation as "the realization of a religious potentiality in man" (*Doct.*, p. 219). For Barth this is the decisive and sinful folly of taking man more seriously than God's grace, "self-certainty" more seriously than "God-certainty" (*Doct.*, p. 225). It presupposes an "openness of man for God" which, though widely affirmed, is not the less an illusion.[27] It is an illusion in which Roman Catholic theology also participates in giving place to "natural knowledge" of God as complementary to that in Christ, while, in point of fact, such knowledge can only be considered a "foreign body" in Christian teaching.[28]

But, returning to our theme, can we say that in his sweeping rejection of Cartesianism in theology—whether Augustinian, Schleiermacherian, or Kierkegaardian[29]—Barth has entirely repudiated the anthropological approach? Is it true that, as Schleiermacher certainly obscured and denatured the divine causality by regarding human spirituality as its secret equivalent, Barth, conversely, has denatured man in his jealousy for God's initiative in creation and redemption? Did Schleiermacher render God ambiguous, while, in reaction, Barth has rendered man ambiguous? To what extent are these apparent eventuations real consequences of their basic antithetical standpoints? I will not here pretend to face the question about Schleiermacher but only that about Barth. He has one thing in his favor. In theology God *is* a sort of first, an ordinarily acknowledged *prius.* I suppose every Christian, and possibly every Christian theologian, is prepared to affirm with Barth that man is nothing without God. Now the question is whether, in the decisive determination of man by God's causality, both in being and in the knowledge of faith, there is any remainder left to man as his own to which some dignity may be attached or even identified; or has the sovereignty of God so overshadowed man as to annihilate him?

If we attend to Barth's later writing, the answer is, plainly, that man has both existence and dignity, and that on two grounds: (1) on the one hand, man is a being who, in his "closedness to God," not only *serves* notice of his "existence," he effectually demonstrates it in his power of resistance to grace; (2) on the other hand, man *receives* notice of his essential and real being in faith. In faith he possesses his true being and destiny in hope, viz., in Jesus Christ.[30] On the one hand, man possesses the dignity of being a sinner. On the other, in faith he has his existence *in* the "real man," that is, Jesus Christ (III. 2. 410). Let us look more closely at both sides.

It must be recognized in the first place that Barth does not reject but permits phenomenological knowledge of man and considers the range of this knowledge in a lengthy section of Volume III of the *Dogmatik* (III. 2. 82–157). But his contention is that the "exact sciences" of man do not get to the true but only to the phenomenal man (III. 2. 29–28). In Volume III, 1 he had already stated that "the knowledge of creaturely existence rests entirely and exclusively upon God's self-disclosure and revelation. It is entirely and exclusively an echo and an answer of the creature to what his Creator has said to him."[31] And it is the error of Cartesianism generally that it proceeds not from God's own self-witness but from the testimony of man's own intellect (III. 1. 414). Much earlier Barth had stated his essential program in this domain. In the first half-volume of the *Dogmatik* he said: "There is a way from Christology to anthropology. There is no way from anthropology to Christology."[32]

What, then, is the truth about man in the light of Jesus Christ? Barth's answer is clear: "The revelation of God shows us in the first place not man in the uprightness of his being as created by God; it reveals man in his perversity and corruption" (III. 2. 29). It displays man not merely as an opponent of God; but, *as a creature* and in rebellion, it shows man to be actually a traitor to himself, in contrariety to his own created nature—one who in his strife against God is rendering himself "impossible" (III. 2. 29, 34, 162). This is revolt against our onto-logical status as creatures of the Creator, and, as such, it no doubt incurs the peril of our lapsing into "not-being"; for the positive meaning of man's *Dasein* (real existence), the purpose of his creation, is to be in community with God in the likeness of Jesus Christ (III. 1. 430). Despite his self-antagonism and perversity, however, man retains his "proper creaturely nature." We are "nevertheless" God's creatures (III. 2. 34).

But now it is important to understand that between the knowledge of our sin and the knowledge of our creaturely nature there is a "neces-sary connection" (III. 2. 34). We *know* we are sinners because we are under the judgment of God's Word in Christ, because in Christ we discern our real nature by which our actual nature is measured (III. 2. 269). Man becomes known to himself at last, and this reflected self-knowledge portends that man is "the counter-part of God's grace" (III. 2. 35), made according to God's image and for community with him (III. 2. 385). This change of perspective, supplied through Christ, is no doubt precisely what Barth calls for: "a transformation of autono-mous into theonomous self-understanding" (III. 2. 148). It comes to this then: "What the human creaturely nature is we have to learn by way of a look to the revealed grace of God and, concretely by way of a look to the man Jesus through whom we have sight of an unaltered and unchangeable nature that is ours despite the fact of sin" (III. 2. 50).

Our first authentic knowledge of ourselves, then, the true theono-mous knowledge of man as it is afforded in Christ, is that of man created *for* community with God, and so called and elected, but pres-ently in revolt. It is in the resistance of man to grace, his power of being contrary, his power of willing his own nothingness, that we have the token of his independence—an independence, however, which has inherent dignity only because of the creating and redeeming grace which "nevertheless" constitutes man and his *telos.* In Barth's view the "closedness" of man to God, his unreadiness for God, is his own. His readiness for God, his openness for grace—even his consciousness of "need for Grace"—is of God (II. 1. 143). "There can be no readiness for God without God's grace" (II. 1. 150). For Barth declares again and again: "We are ready for God in Jesus Christ through the Holy Ghost" (II. 1. 176).

Our sin is our own; our salvation is God's working. But there is an obverse side of our sin in which inheres our dignity. We *can* be sinners just because, as creatures of God and with our creation, we are called to existence with him in Jesus Christ. *This is the ontological truth about man.* The ontological truth of man, which becomes manifest to faith in Jesus Christ, is, despite man's God-antagonism, the very presupposition of his being a sinner. Sin presupposes grace, but sin is self-existence in hostility to grace. In this outcome there is nothing especially bizarre or without antecedence in the thought of Augustine, Fénelon, and Wesley.

This brings us to a consideration of the second proposition above: man *receives* notice of his essential and real being *(wirklicke Sein)* in faith, viz., through Jesus Christ. *It is now time to state forcibly that Barth does not, in point of fact, abandon root and branch the anthropological approach in theology. What he does is baptize it in Christ.* In retrospect one can see that this was always his intention in his assertion that "there is a way from Christology to anthropology" and that this entails a "new understanding of man" based on God's Word *(Doct.,* p. 148). And now much later in 1948 Barth is explicit: "The nature of man, in our unnature, is not hidden in the person of the man Jesus but is revealed; because we can once again know, in the human nature of Jesus, the nature [*Natur*] of each man" (III. 2. 50). A "theological anthropology" is possible "in so far as it stands in the light of the Word of God" (III. 2. 21); and man "will be an object of theological knowledge in so far as, through the Word of God, his relation to God is made manifest," in the man Jesus (III. 2. 20). "This man is man, primarily and properly and he alone, so that we are assured of God's relation to sinful man first properly and quite alone through God's conduct toward Him and, through Him, of God's conduct toward us" (III. 2. 49). This leads to the basic proposition of Barth's theological anthropology; *"The choice of this starting-point means not more and not less than the grounding of anthropology upon Christology."* [33]

It is in Christ that we are given knowledge of the "real man" (III. 2. 51). But, when one finds the real man in Christ, what does he find? He finds in the man Jesus the man *for* God, "co-existent" with God and *with* his fellow man.[34] In Christ humanity means "fundamentally and indissolubly being together with God" (III. 2. 161). Here also man is *imago Dei,* in Christ.[35] In him, man is not only by nature *Bundesgenosse,* covenant-ally with the fellow man, but by grace he becomes *Gottes Bundesgenosse,* God's covenant ally (III. 2. 385). We are not "by nature" God's "covenant-partners." We are not created *as* such but *for* such partnership (III. 2. 386). And, in faith in Christ, we possess it but, as yet, only in hope (III. 2. 391). But elsewhere Barth speaks somewhat more positively: "Faith is fundamentally more than any attendant change in man: it is, as the work of the Holy Ghost, a new birth of man from God, upon the basis of which a man ought already here and now to live from it, that is, he ought to live what there in Jesus Christ, and consequently in truth, he is. Faith is the temporal form of his eternal being in Jesus Christ" (II. 1, 177). In faith we may say that we grasp the "ontological," therefore the "true definition" of our nature (III. 2, 158). In faith there is attainment, however imperfectly, of true manhood as existence together with God. "Menschsein heisst: mit Gott zusammen sein" (III. 2. 167).

Cartesianism had affirmed in its way, the *immediate* way, that man is a being together with God. Barth has altered the statement: man is the being together with God in the *mediate* way, viz., in Jesus Christ (III. 2. 161). Even as sinner, man is not shorn of his reality and independence. On the contrary, his very resistance to grace notifies him that he both is and is not his own. He is God's creature in his resistance (II. 1, 158). However, he receives his true status and dignity in his openness for grace, but that is only by faith in the man Jesus. In the man Jesus the resistance of man to God proved not to be irresistible (II. 1. 159); and through him, in the power of the Holy Spirit, the resistance of other men is replaced by readiness for God.

VI. THE ALTERNATIVES BEFORE US

Investigation of Barth's developed thought indicates, I think, that he cannot fairly be charged with swallowing up man in the sovereignty of God. In principle, Barth believes he has banished this possibility in holding firmly to the thesis that the sovereignty of God is revealed in Christ exclusively as the sovereignty of grace (II. 2. 115). This contention deserves to be honored with deliberate consideration. If sustained, the key to Barth's thought turns out to be not bare sovereignty but sovereignty as disclosed in the Redeemer. This is, indeed, Barth's crucial revision of Calvinism; but, at the same time, it provides him with the antidote to Cartesianism, its anthropological method and, as he believes, its epistemological subjectivism.

With his emphatic Christocentricism, Christology becomes the reliable way to a valid anthropology. In the man Jesus Christ there is a way from man to God because the man Jesus, through God's determination or deed, is God's man. Here the for-ness of God for man is reciprocated in the man for God. This man, who is the truth of man (II. 1. 177), the ontological as distinct from the actual man, and in history but not of history, this man is the point of decisive divine breakthrough into the circle of mere human self-understanding. It is the man Jesus who really specifies the place where the divine determination "befalls" man's self-determination finally and definitively. There is the miracle of the Incarnation, and, specifically corresponding to it and correlative with it, and through the Holy Spirit, there too is the miracle of faith (*Doct.*, p. 282). But, once again, the miracle lies in this—that, if God is God, if he is absolutely antecedent being, then the conditioning determination of the antecedent cannot be derivable from the consequent. The conditions cannot be extracted from the creature as such or identified by attention to grounds within the human subject of faith (*Doct.*, p. 257). If God is God, then the grounds of being and knowing alike must be referred to the Antecedent, not to the consequent, to the Creator, not to the creature.

Obviously, according to such a view as this, neither the world nor man can be self-explanatory or self-contained. Such a view as this is the ultimate theological challenge to naturalism as well as to its theological next of kin, viz., the doctrine of exclusively immanent divine causality, favored by Schleiermacher. Thus, Barth's doctrine of causality *ab extra* stands as the most formidable opponent to all demythologizing existentialism which proposes to eliminate or "relocate" the *scandalon* of the Christian world view by translating a decisive divine intrusion into a metaphysical truth according to which ontological reason in man becomes transparent to its ground or, according to which, the great decision is fundamentally man's rather than God's as man somehow realizes his inherent possibility of transition from "existence" to "essence." Let us be candid; here is the issue of theology today. Here and about we discern the real dividing of the way between a Barth and a Tillich. With Barth God is to be taken more seriously than man. Tillich's "ultimate concern," on the other hand, almost surely is not God but "to be or not to be," [36] and, in this dire extremity, God makes all the difference to man! Barth, however, cannot take man seriously except as man is alerted to both God's judgment and mercy by confrontation from without the circle of his own subjectivity.

It is, however, not possible to accept Barth's unduly narrow restriction of divine causality in knowledge to faith in the Mediator through the effectual power of the Holy Spirit. On this important matter it is possible to say only that classical theology has never sanctioned the view that the Holy Spirit proceeds alone from the Son or is inaugurated in his working by the advent of the Redeemer. The "filioque *clause*" is, no doubt, not retroactive; yet God spoke to the fathers aforetime in divers portions and manners albeit he has spoken unto us in his Son. Doubtless we can say that the decisive working of the Spirit presupposes the manifest work of the Son.

In terms of the foregoing study, it now remains for the Christian theologian to decide really only one thing; namely, in what form he will entertain the divine causality. This is actually what is involved in Tillich's invitation to reconsider Schleiermacher's experiential method and anthropological standpoint. Shall the theologian, with Schleiermacher, settle for a theory of immanent causality? If so, is he ready, with Schleiermacher, to identify creation with preservation and revelation with the dominance of the "higher self-consciousness" or, again, as the resumption of reason's continuity with its depth through *ecstasis?* Or will the theologian of the future take God more seriously than either the world or the human self-understanding and regard the divine causality, not as immanent exclusively, but as reserved and adventitious? Here, I think, is the central issue and the choice before us.

Barth has made his choice. His candor and resoluteness on this point constitute his distinctive stature in 20th-century theology. Nevertheless, Barth is justly aware that, in decision respecting these alternatives the choice will rest upon an ultimate preference (*Doct.*, pp. 224–25). It is not merely a preference as between an incompletely manageable world intellectually and an intellectually manageable one. It is that. But more exactly it is an alternative that will be decided on the basis of the lust for autonomy or the lure of theonomy. It is, perhaps, represented in the preference for the "actual" as opposed to the "real man" in Jesus Christ. And here, for Barth and exasperating as it may be, the decision is really taken out of the theologian's hands, and the last and effectual word is spoken of the Holy Spirit. For Barth, error would be assured if, in point of fact, the last word were uttered by man, even the theologian!

CHRISTOLOGY OR ECCLESIOLOGY? A CRITICAL EXAMINATION OF THE CHRISTOLOGY OF JOHN KNOX

I. THE STANDPOINT

In a series of small but impressive and influential books published over the years since 1941, Professor John Knox has doubtless made, among American theologians, the most sustained and boldy creative contribution to contemporary Christological thought outside the European scene.[1] He regularly approaches the Christological question from the side of New Testament studies which are, indeed, the field of his professional labors. As an exegete he is uniformly insightful and profound. But, while he works as a historical scholar, his program and the import of his work are unquestionably theological or doctrinal. There is even some indication, as, for example, his insistence "that biblical historical criticism not only has no stranglehold on Christian faith, but does not have it in its power to destroy one jot or one tittle of the gospel," that Dr. Knox is paradoxically eager to emancipate faith and doctrine from history.[2] In consequence, it would seem, he casts some considerable doubt upon the usefulness of his own peculiar task as historian.

The "doctrine" just referred to is, however, in fact indistinguishable in Knox's view from the faith and faith-engendering experience of the Christian Church—whether the early Church or its *bona fide* succession—and it is not really so much the case that Knox has abdicated the historical task as that he has consistently contended for the reidentification or relocation of its proper subject matter.

Quite abruptly, therefore, it may be stated that the proper subject matter of Christian historical understanding is an "event," an "eschatological" one, which includes within itself Jesus as remembered as well as the believing community. The subject matter is, therefore, not the person of Jesus,[3] and not especially "the historical life of Jesus." It is not Jesus' consciousness regarding his own significance, nor his *ipsissima verba*.[4] It is rather the faith-interpreted experience of the early Christian community *within* which "the miracle of the resurrection" occurred as constitutive of the church itself. That "miracle" is

Published in *Religion and Life*, XXVII, No. 4 (Autumn 1958). Reprinted here with permission of the Editor.

recurrently defined as "the coming of the Spirit," [5] or as the "inexplicable fact" of the "realized identity" of Jesus as he was remembered with the Lord, living and presently known.[6] Further, what is available to historical investigation, according to Knox, is a Christ-event culminating in the coming of the Spirit together with the identification, in the community's experience of the living Christ, both with Jesus as remembered and with the Spirit. Or, defined still more closely, the subject matter is the church as "the new order of the Spirit." [7]

Dr. Knox uniformly stresses the reality of "a new kind of life" which entered the world with the community.[8] This is, manifestly, subject matter available to historical inquiry, and is, at the same time, appropriable in the recurring experience of faith. This datum, Knox evidently believes, is the business of historical understanding faithfully to delineate, and its honest exposition will be, in point of fact, one important condition of recurring participation as, also, its explication will supply the content of Christian doctrine. Herein is perhaps one reason for the way in which Knox regularly seems to pass from history to dogmatic. For dogmatic is the faithful account of the faith of the Christian church; it is, I think, *kirchliche dogmatik*. In all this, revelation is kept explicitly historical by identifying it with an "event" which includes within itself the distinctively new life of the community. Indeed, it is declared that revelation took place in an "event," not a person,[9] and is located within the experience of the Church.[10]

From this, and for Christology, certain important consequences are, it would seem, involved. We are recurrently reminded that in Christology we have not to do with the person of Christ, a messianic consciousness of Jesus, an incarnation of the Word in him,[11] or with the resurrection considered as an objective event. Even of the Cross, Knox says, "Faith had a part in creating it." [12] Such questions about Jesus as "Who is he?" or "Whose Son is he?" are discouraged and, according to Knox, should be replaced by such questions about the community as "What is the *reality* in which these persons who knew Jesus and now remember him participate, and which constitutes the essential principle of the community's existence?" [13]

In the light of these suggestions, one is prompted to ask in all candor whether we do not have here a daring alteration of the Christological standpoint. When the Church has discussed Christology, it has usually supposed it was referring to the dignity of Jesus Christ's person, not to itself. Such was the concern classically represented by Chalcedon, but Knox warns against Hellenism, metaphysics, and Chalcedon in a way certainly reminiscent of Herrmann and Harnack. He proffers as the "reality" for Christological reflection "the eschatological event," [14] namely, the new life in the Spirit, realization of the resurrection,[15] or "the experience of the divine life in the community." [16]

Dr. Knox's thought on these lines comes, I think, to conspicuous ripeness in his volume, *The Early Church*. There he seems to me to complete his effort to relocate the miracle of Christian origins. It is notable in his contention that the early Christians did not believe "that the event and the community were divine because they also believed that Jesus was divine; but rather he was seen to be divine because of the way in which he was related to an event and a community whose divine significance was a matter of intimate and indubitable conviction." [17] Plainly, Knox is reversing the order of dependency and is deriving the dignity of Christ from the community of faith, though not fully intending it so.

It is a fact quite unmistakable that in the whole range of Knox's writings there is a pervasive effort to shift the locus of the Incarnation from Jesus as the Christ and to relocate it in a more comprehensive total event which Knox understands to embrace the historical career of Jesus, the coming of the Spirit, and the new life of the Church. Long before Lund, Knox was affirming the inseparable unity of Christ and his Church; but, in this conjugation, it is clear that Knox continually leans toward a higher ecclesiology than Christology, or perhaps we might say that ecclesiology has come to embrace Christology.

This seems to me to be openly spelled out in Knox's latest writings. Raising the question whether Christology refers to person, event, or community, and having declared earlier that the term "Christ" in the New Testament encompasses, in its amplitude, event and community as well as person,[18] Knox declares: "It follows from this that the Christological question does not need to be construed as a question about the person; it can be just as appropriately be thought of as a question about the event or the community." [19] Plainly, for Knox, it involves all three, but one does not escape the strong impression that Knox's real stress falls upon the last two. They are accorded a causal antecedence which Knox does not fully intend but which follows ineluctably from his theory of the knowledge of history as "event" in which the subject is constitutive of the event and possesses a necessary antecedence *in ordine cognoscendi* to the object of knowledge. In addition, the stress falls upon the event and the community because these, happily, are positively identifiable by historical scholarship and are also appropriable in living faith. Of the Incarnation, therefore, all that Knox can confidently affirm is "the eschatological event," embracing Jesus as perceived by the community and constituting thereby the event.

Here, I believe, is a new form of historical and Christological positivism: when the Jesus of history became too elusive for historical science to recover—a fact early acknowledged by Knox [20]—a historical substitute seemed indispensable, namely, the kerygmatic and Spirit-filled community. So with profundity and daring, Knox set about clarifying a basic issue of contemporary theology. Confronted with a choice between Christology, in the traditional sense, and ecclesiology, Knox proposes to incorporate Christology within ecclesiology—Christ within the Church.

II. THE ISSUE

It is well nigh indubitable that Knox relinquishes very nearly all responsibility for a doctrine of the person of Jesus Christ. It is now our business to inquire of Knox's writings the grounds of this stringency.

Although there are evidences of a surviving realism in historical knowledge in *The Man Christ Jesus*—a realism Knox clings to tenaciously, if ambiguously, throughout his writings—already in this early book the basic critical problem of Knox's work stands disclosed. Although the historicity of Jesus may not be seriously questioned, Knox concedes that "the amount of knowledge of Jesus that we may properly claim has been materially reduced." [21] The memory of Jesus in the Church preserves continuity with his historical existence, but already Knox is prepared to refer the messiahship of Jesus to the "creativity" of the community—an estimate of the latter in which he is always conspicuously generous.

The messianic self-consciousness of Jesus is, for Knox, psychologically incredible,[22] but he acknowledges that Jesus "did regard himself as sustaining a relation of peculiar intimacy and responsibility to the kingdom of God." [23] There was a "mystery about his consciousness of himself," and "the Christian church had its origin in a mystery, if not in a miracle. . . ." [24] And this "mystery," which is the objective *prius* of the Church's memory is, apparently, about all that can be asserted with confidence about the person of Jesus by way of historical reconstruction. The reason is that "the historical student tracing backward the history of the Church can proceed facilely enough until he reaches the vigorous, joyous faith of the primitive Christian community." [25] But when he attempts to get behind the faith of the early Church "he immediately runs into insuperable difficulties." [26] For the historian "cannot lay his finger on a cause even approximately adequate to the effect." [27] If the cause was the personality of Jesus, then we must face the fact that "Jesus' personality cannot be fully recovered and no historical reconstruction of it on the basis of the Gospels quite accounts for the effects. . . ." [28]

Reflection indicates then that the "effect," but not the "cause adequate to the effect," is the surviving assured content of positive historical knowledge. Perhaps, then, it will be necessary in some measure to derive the cause from the effect conceived as entailed *in* the effect. Hereafter Knox's program will be the twofold effort, on the one hand to avoid historical skepticism by finding the career of Jesus implied in the effect,[29] and, on the other hand, to reconceive the Christ-event as possessed of sufficient capaciousness to include Jesus, the coming of the Spirit, and the community of new life in an inseverable unity—the true Christological datum.

III. THE METHOD

It is now our task to indicate the various lines of approach by which Professor Knox has methodically advanced the program just mentioned. In *The Man Christ Jesus*, Knox adopted a principle thereafter to be retained, a principle held in common with form criticism, that "we cannot know the historical Jesus—Jesus 'simply as he was'—until we have some realization of what he meant to those who stood nearest to him." [30] Consequently, it is denied that we can "really separate between the Jesus of history and the Jesus of early Christian faith." [31] This is the first step; and the second is to make a virtue of necessity, that is, to endeavor to find in the only surviving historical datum, the Jesus of faith, adequate grounds for assurance of its authenticity. In the last analysis, the appeal must always be to the Church, to the community of Christian apperception. Whether he was then fully aware of it or not, in his book *The Man Christ Jesus* I find evidence that Knox was already on the way to abandoning "objective" history for the theological circle.

What was begun in the first book was advanced with greater sureness of touch in its sequel, *Christ the Lord*. There Knox began, as he has continued, to speak of the "career of Jesus" as the "center" of a complex of events which, collectively, we know in the New Testament as Jesus Christ. Herewith the revelation occurence is beginning to be depersonalized and more inclusive. "Fact" and "interpretation" of fact are said to be inseparable—softening thereby the loss of the "bare fact" by accenting the receiving subject which apprehends it. The meaning attaching to the "occurrence," as entertained by responsive subjects, becomes contributory to, even constitutive of, the occurrence itself.

Warning is issued by Knox, as with Bultmann's *Jesus*, against a historiography of "false objectivity." Imaginative participation is seen to be essential for true historical understanding.[32] If the public career of Jesus "may be stated in a few ingredient essentials," the meaning of it can be ascertained only by attention to its realized significance in the life of the early community.

Gradually we see "fact" being replaced by something called "the event." This is comprised of Jesus as remembered, as interpreted, and as known still.[33] Jesus, as "known still," is the resurrection, that is, the realization of "the present and living Lord." This in turn is shortly identified with the coming of the Holy Spirit.[34] And Knox asserts that it "was in the experience of that spiritual reality that the faith of the resurrection really consisted." [35] In all this, I think we discern a shift of focus from the so-called "fact" to the interior life of the community, thus to provide a new location for both the historical and the Christological datum. The way out of skepticism, attending the older quest for the historical Jesus, is by way of redefinition of the *datum* so as to embrace object and subject in it as one reality. But this must in the nature of things, I think, give a certain primacy to the subject (i.e., the community of faith), because it alone is really accessible to knowledge.

So we are prepared for the flowering of Knox's theory of the historical *and* revelatory event as set forth in two succeeding works, *On the Meaning of Christ* and *Criticism and Faith*. It was already apparent in *The Man Christ Jesus* that "event" had come to embrace "a new kind of life" which had found expression in the church.[36] In *Christ the Lord*, the event was Jesus, remembered, interpreted, and known still. Now, in these later works, the event is declared to encompass: (1) a series of events through which God made himself known, (2) a person who was the center of that complex of events, and (3) the community which both came into existence with the event and provided the locus of it.[37]

Knox has now defined the more capacious Christological datum toward which he had been working. A "true Christology," he asserts, is concerned with this threefold complex considered as a unitary reality, but he also urges that the category of "event" (1) has a certain primacy over both person (2) and community (3). It is more appropriate and adequate.[38] His reason is, I think, that the complex of events which conveyed "the revelation of God in Christ" embraces and unites what had been sundered by historical skepticism, namely, the one remembered and the community that remembers. The "total event," therefore, Knox asserts, is the "reality" with which we are concerned. In it the "fact" is given *in and with* the faithful response of the community.[39] Thus the event becomes the Christ-event, and it is summarily defined "as that historical occurrence or cluster of occurrences which culminated in the coming of the Spirit and the creation of the Church." [40] As the "fact" has become wholly implicated with the "response," so the Jesus of history has become forever transformed into the Christ-faith-event.

This outcome was implemented by Knox's developing conception of the social nature of any and every historical event.[41] It always has two sides: "the external occasion and the human response, the thing 'out there' and the way in which this objective element is received and appropriated." [42] The response is said to be "a constitutent and creative element in the event itself, *and the event had not fully happened* [speaking of Christ] until this response of faith had been fully made." [43] On this view, Knox's earlier contention of the inseparability of the Jesus of history and the Christ of faith is not only substantiated but demonstrated. The former, *ex hypothesi*, cannot be known to exist in independence. Therefore, a form of epistemological idealism becomes explicit in Knox's assertion that a historical event "Is not something hypothetical and unrecoverable which lies before or back of the experience of the persons to whom it occurred." [44] Thus, of an historical event, including the Jesus of history, it surely follows that the knower becomes causally determinative of the event, so much so, indeed, as at least to suggest Berkeley's *esse est percipi.*

IV. THE RESULTS

In barest outline Professor Knox's solution to the problem of historical skepticism, which has consistently engaged his scholarly concern, has been sketched, it is hoped with fidelity to his own exposition. The solution, especially as it relates to the social nature of "event," is not unlike C. H. Dodd's, although more explicit.[45] By means of it a number of vexing problems are partly resolved.

In the first place, it suggests that the quest of the historical Jesus, apart from the response of faith to him, is either, in principle, misconceived if not impossible, or else can disclose nothing but the most superficial "accidents" as opposed to the substance of his career. Second, Knox's theory requires a redefinition of the true historical Jesus as the Christ of the early Church's faith, so that the early contention of Knox that we cannot "really separate" the two is vindicated. Third, the problem of historical skepticism, entailed in the "objective" quest, and as a consequence of it, is overcome or transcended. For now it will be recognized that the only historical Christ-event of which we can intelligibly speak is also indubitably the empirical emergent life of the community of the Spirit. In a quite recent statement Knox reminds us that, while we may uncritically believe that we have contact with the event other than through the community, "is it not obvious, when one reflects on it," he asks, "that the sole residuum of the event was the Church?" [46] Fourth, therefore, since "the event and the community are indissolubly involved with each other," [47] we have assurance, not alone of the ready accessibility of the event, we may also avoid all the inadequacies of "historicism." For, with Herrmann and Bultmann, Knox has all along been aware of the impossibility of grounding faith upon the shifting and merely probable findings of historical research in the unrevised objective sense. Existential participation, that is faith, is possible if it is participation in the life of the community.

In the fifth place, and here we come to the heart of the Christological question, the Christ-event is so enlarged in compass that it is understood to include, not alone the career of Jesus, but the coming of the Spirit or the realization of the resurrection in the life of the community. We have here an empirical reality not only positively identifiable and appropriable, but, in addition, we are no longer obliged to restrict the Christological question to the person of Jesus Christ. In principle, to speak of Jesus Christ is to involve ourselves, as believers, as well. Now we can include in Christology what is "latent or implicit in that empirical fact," including the new life in the Church, and we can avoid, furthermore, historically divisive and insoluble disputes as when Christology wrongly ranges beyond "the empirical meaning of the fact" to formulate speculative metaphysical answers about the divinity of Jesus Christ or the divine dignity of his person.[48]

And finally, in the sixth place, it is possible to see that Knox is now equipped to relocate the miracle of Christian origins and to avoid the scandal of particularity.[49] It is not to be located in the career or self-consciousness of Jesus, not in *his* incarnation, nor *his* sacrificial death, nor *his* resurrection considered as *objects* of faith. It is around such questions that the profitless strife between fundamentalism and modernism has centered.[50] Rather, the miracle is what God did through Christ to effect "the eschatological event," the empirically determinable new order of life in the Christian community.[51] The divinity of the remembered Jesus "rested on the experience of the divine in the life of the community," says Knox.[52] And doubtless this is true in the order of knowing; but is it true according to the order of being? Jesus Christ is known in his benefits, but does this warrant us in locating the miracle there and making the object depend upon the subject— the divinity of Jesus a reflection of the new divine life in the community? Evidently, the christological event has received literally a polar shift and relocation. It now centers in the Church rather than in Jesus Christ, since *Jesus* Christ cannot be located except in the Church. The medium of this polar transference has been the social theory of historical event.

V. THE OUTCOME

In evaluating the Christological developments in Knox's thought, one should recognize the problems which he has truly faced with both candor and profound concern. These problems, latent in late 19th-century biblical criticism, were fully recognized only in the recent past. With Knox there is the open recognition that historical study of the New Testament sources cannot supply a cause in Jesus adequate to the emergence of a new community of the Spirit, the Church. Very early in this century W. Herrmann had recognized that the certainties of faith could never be made to rest upon the mere probabilities of history. And the bearing of form criticism has been that the only Jesus we can know is Jesus as Christ and Lord of the community of faith. Professor Knox therefore has conceived the task as that of indicating *how* the Jesus of history, the originative "center" of the event, could be reunited with the Christ of the Church's faith.

Now there are always two basic ways to solve the problem of correlating subject and object in experience, namely, to start from one side or the other. Knox has chosen to solve the problem from the side of the subject of experience. What Knox has actually done is to effect a "Copernican revolution" after the manner of Kant in the sphere of Christological knowledge. A problem quite analogous to that which confronted Kant in the matter of knowledge of the world confronts Knox in the problem of the knowledge of Jesus Christ: he can find no ground of adequation between the objective "cause," Jesus in his history, and the content (effect) of the subject's, that is, the church's, experience. The cause he complains is not adequate to the effect because the cause has dwindled to less and less under the acids of New Testament criticism.

In this extremity there is for Knox but one solution, namely, to affirm as Kant affirmed in his "transcendental analytic" that the "matter" or raw material of knowledge is apprehensible only as structured and formed by the subject of cognition. This, I believe, is plainly what is involved in Knox's theory of the social nature of the "event." The "event" entails reference to an antecedent given, but the given is known only as it is received and constituted in its specific form by the participating response of the subject of experience, in this instance, the community of faith.[53]

In short, very much in the manner of Kant's critical idealism, the community of apperception, the Church, is constitutive of the event; the subject determines the object, not in its being, but in its being what it is known as. What the given, the "matter," is in itself—that is, the career and person of Jesus, the *ding-an-sich*—must necessarily remain unknowable. Thus, recurrently, Knox refers to Jesus in his history as the "something that happened" because he concedes that what it is in itself is mostly inaccessible to critical historical knowledge.[54] It *is* only as it is known *as*. So Knox redefines the Christological datum, the event, as he must on this view, to include within itself both the objective and subjective factors in one moment of experience of the Spirit. The event is, therefore, "primary," as Knox claims, in the sense that it is inclusive of both subject and object.

Since, then, the response of faith is constitutive of the event, there is no legitimate appeal beyond the community of apperception. The criterion of truth, also Kantian, is not adequation but a certain universality. In this instance, it is the *consensus fidelum* within the community of faith. Thus we emerge in this theory of Christological knowledge with an undoubted phenomenalism. We have Christ Jesus *as he is received* (i.e., the eschatological event) in the church. This is the datum of Christology. Thus the so-called historical Jesus is dissolved in the amalgam of critical epistemological idealism.

As I understand it, this means that Christology now unquestionably includes ecclesiology or, rather, ecclesiology includes Christology and that, indeed, without the church, Christology is impossible. This latter point would be an innocuous truism if it did not entail some thought-provoking consequences. The first is that we must now, I think, inescapably accord to the church a certain "divinity" we have been unable to ascribe to Jesus. This indeed is necessarily implicated in the theory that the Church is constitutive of the event and also that there is no appeal beyond this community of apperception regarding the truth of Jesus Christ. Since, furthermore, Knox insists that the event only fully occurred in the Church,[55] the identifiable locus of the Incarnation must be there. In this cumulative outcome, I do not see that the end of the most radical Protestant scholarship in New Testament studies is many steps away from Rome.

Another outcome seems to be this: if we can no longer talk of the event of Jesus Christ out of relation with the apperceiving community, we seem to be finally bereaved of the "humanity" of Jesus Christ as well as of his word in all ages *against* the Church. Clearly the humanity of Jesus has some relation of dependence upon the historicity. But, in all strictness, Knox cannot on his ground argue for the availability of the humanity except as it is allegedly implicit in the remembering community, which, however, knows only the Lord the Spirit. Intended or not, this is methodological docetism. It has, I think, no way out except to view the Church as the sole residuum of Christ's humanity, as quite literally the body of Christ.[56] Christ and his church have drawn so close together as to become well nigh indistinguishable.

Professor Knox has conceded to holding a "high" doctrine of the church.[57] This is an understatement. But he has himself warned against docetism [58] and any tendency "to absorb the event completely within the life of the Church." [59] This, however, is exactly the tendency of his own thought. I would have to say that, on the basis of his phenomenalistic epistemology, he cannot despite his protests, any more than Kant, affirm anything with certainty about the antecedent reality of the "object," Jesus Christ. He can only affirm the availability of the *phenomenon*, that is, "the new order of the Spirit"—the Church.[60] It is an axiom with Knox that to "objectify" the event Jesus Christ is to destroy it; thus the resurrection occurred *"within* the experience of the first disciples." [61] This surely is to "objectify" the event in the church; and there, it seems, the event of Christ occurred.

Ecclesiology has, I think, embraced if not replaced Christology. The program is complete: "historical criticism . . . does not have it in its power to destroy one jot or one tittle of the gospel." No, nor is there any assured standard by which the historical Church may be brought before the judgment of Christ, for Christ is at one with his Church. Which Church?

THE INCARNATION—A SYMBOL OF WHAT? AN INQUIRY INTO THE CHRISTOLOGY OF RUDOLF BULTMANN

I. THE ISSUES

Rudolf Bultmann has declared with emphasis that "the incarnation is an eschatological event and not a datable event of the past." He has added that "it is an event which is continually being re-enacted in the event of the proclamation" of the of the Word of God.[1] It is his view that the Incarnation is not an identifiable event of objective history *(Historie)* but, instead, an "historic event" *(Geschichte)*. A *geschichtlich* event is an "eschatological" one or, as he prefers to understand that word, an existential "moment" of encounter, crisis, and decision. The latter is an event in which I myself am involved in such a way that the "moment" is experienced as a passage from anxiety to faith, from self-defensiveness to surrender, from saving the life to losing it, in short, from inauthentic to authentic existence.

Thus, as Bultmann recurrently insists, we cannot talk about an "act of God" as something objective to us, open to the observation of just anyone who happens along. For he declares "to speak of an act of God means to speak at the same time of my existence."[2] The subject is involved; perspective is involved; faith is involved. And for this reason we cannot speak of the Incarnation as a datable or specifiable "world event." The Incarnation takes place within a kind of inner history, eschatological history, history which is disclosed only to the eyes of faith. And this kind of faith "is not a knowledge possessed once and for all, not a *Weltanschauung.*"[3] To give this event a cosmic setting, even a setting commensurate with a modern scientific cosmology, such as that of William Temple or Karl Heim, would be to support with scientific and theoretical buttressing that which had its origin in a totally different context. Faith has its own *sui generis* foundation, and so radical is Bultmann's insistence upon *sola fide* that he regards himself, following Herrmann, as standing in the true Reformation tradition.[4] Like many another neo-Protestant, Bultmann looks upon himself as the true interpreter of Luther, although the justification, in the sphere of Christology, admits of doubt.

First published in *Theology Today*, XV, 2 (July 1958). In the present rendering, this study has been altered by some revision and additions. Republished with the permission of the Editor.

II. HISTORICAL SKEPTICISM AND METHODOLOGY

As I read Bultmann, two bases of his aversion to an objective view of the Incarnation plainly suggest themselves: the one is methodological and critical, the other theological and philosophical.

It is worthy of notice that Bultmann's methodology in New Testament study presupposes certain formative antecedents. The first important influence is W. Wrede's view set forth in *The Messianic Secret in the Gospels* (1901), establishing the threefold thesis that: (1) Mark, the oldest Gospel, cannot be accepted as an exact narrative of the history of Jesus; (2) Mark is "really dominated by the theology of the Church and by a dogmatic conception of Christ"; (3) one cannot make out from Mark either the fact or the development of a messianic consciousness of Jesus.[5]

Secondly, Bultmann accepted as demonstrated the contention of the history-of-religions school, especially as represented in the work of W. Bousset, that Palestinian-Jewish Christianity is distinct from that of Hellenistic-Gentile Christianity in a decisive way. The former asserted that Jesus was the Messiah "whose return as Son of Man was ardently expected," while Hellenistic Christianity viewed Jesus primarily as Lord who was worshipped in the common cult and whose presence was *now* experienced in the activities of the Spirit.[6] Bousset thus showed the way to demythologize Palestinian New Testament eschatology; and Bultmann was to find that John's Gospel had already accomplished the task by the opening decade of the 2nd century.

A third factor seems to be a powerful reaction on the part of Bultmann to the "wholly futuristic eschatology" of Schweitzer's historical interpretation of the mind of Jesus. As I examine Bultmann, the impression deepens that Schweitzer's reconstruction of Christian origins was a rock of offense.[7] It not only refuted Wrede but it made the figure of Christian devotion not merely unknown but inherently unknowable and incredibly fantastic to the modern mind. This provoked the basic apologetic program of Bultmann, which has ever been that of locating the *skandalon* of the Gospel where, rather than repelling the modern mind by its bizarre irrelevancy, it would instead challenge that mind on its own ground. This program called not alone for demythologizing, which is already underway in Bultmann's *Jesus* (1926), but also for a distinctive and challenging reconception of the *eschaton*. The clue to Bultmann's revision of the concept of the *eschaton* is foreshadowed in his observation that the whole idea of God is endangered "if God is not thought of as the power which determines man in his present existence." [8]

In the fourth place, it is entirely clear that Bultmann received and absorbed the influence of W. Herrmann at the point of the latter's relinquishing any effort to rest the decisions of faith upon the relativities of historical criticism of the New Testament.[9] He also gave close attention to Herrmann's reminder that the decision which the Christian reaches in faith is not derived from an objectively determinable body of historical evidence but "proceeds from our own independent activity." [10] And, while Bultmann doubtless rejects the possibility of entering with Herrmann, in faith, into "the inner life of Jesus," he would affirm that the Christ-event, as Herrmann suggests, "speaks to us from the New Testament, as the disciples' testimony to their faith, but which, when we perceive it, always comes home to us as a miraculous revelation." [11]

In short, there is in Bultmann the same tendency as in Herrmann to constitute the "act of God" in revelation as a "moment" of experience which authenticates itself. Bultmann would prefer a "moment" of *existence* rather than of "experience." Be that as it may, it is clear that he shares with Herrmann the view that the genuine "miracle" is an inner, if existential one, since, as he says, "we cannot speak of an act of God without speaking simultaneously of our own existence." [12] If we regard miracles as ascertainable processes in nature or history, we ignore the "hidden character of God's activity" and surrender "the acts of God to objective observation." [13]

To summarize: it was Wrede who taught Bultmann to take with utter seriousness the formative influence of the community mind in shaping the Gospel record. It was Bousset who isolated the two mainstreams of theological tradition within the apostolic age, each giving its distinctive shape to the *historisch datum* behind the tradition. It was "wholly futuristic eschatology" that reduced the quest of the historical Jesus to absurdity. And it was Herrmann who taught Bultmann the folly of "historicism" and provided him with the suggestion as to how faith in Christ could persist without explicit dependency upon the historical Jesus. Whereas Herrmann was mainly content to have recourse to the moral consciousness as the clue to history, Bultmann was to find his alternative in the existentialist moment of transition from inauthentic existence to authentic being. This would be the way to understand the Word of God in the *kerygma*. In the face of historical relativities, the philosophy of existence would come to the rescue of faith!

These, then, are some important antecedents of the methodological grounds for Bultmann's aversion to an "objective" view of the Incarnation. But brief reference must be made to this methodological standpoint itself. It is of course tied up with Bultmann's conclusions resulting from his vigorous employment of the form-critical method. This method postulates a freely circulating oral tradition "behind" the earliest written sources. It understands that this tradition tended to crystallize in the shape of stylized structures or forms characteristic of all folk-tradition. Further, it holds that the surviving forms, whether narratives, apothegms, miracle stories, or proverbial sayings, were selected and propagated by the community, not out of historical or repertorial concern, but on two grounds: the developing Christology of the Church and the exigencies in the midst of which the Church found itself as an embattled missionary and cultic community.

The outcome of all this for the knowledge of Christian origins is soon told. It presses with greatest seriousness the question whether there is any possibility at all of tearing away the veil of the Church's faith in Jesus as Messiah, or Jesus as Lord, and so peering through to the *originative* event, something we may call Jesus-as-he-was. Bultmann's answer seems to be all but negative. In the book, *Jesus,* he was prepared to preserve for us an expurgated version of the "message of Jesus," but he warned that we "can now know almost nothing concerning the life and personality of Jesus." [14] Of the factuality of the Cross we can have high confidence. It is "no mere mythical event, but a permanent historical fact originating in the past historical event which is the crucifixion of Jesus." [15] Yet the interest of Bultmann seems invariably to fall not upon the past event but upon its universal significance as "the eschatological event in and beyond time, for as far as its meaning—that is, its meaning for faith—is concerned, it is an ever-present reality." [16] Interpreted, this seems to mean that the Cross is *eschaton* in the sense that it represents the prototypal situation—challenge to radical obedience through decision—as "a necessity constituting the essential part of his [man's] human nature" as such.[17] When Julius Schniewind shrewdly observes that "everything Bultmann says about the Cross is located not at Calvary but in our human experience" and that the *eschaton* thus tends to be made timeless, Bultmann regards it as a sufficient reply to reaffirm that the *existential moment* is mine precisely in the midst of the concrete encounters of my present existence.[18]

What then does this come to? Quite simply it comes to the methodological denial that we can know with any confidence the person, the mind, or the intention of Jesus. We are left with what we can reconstruct (always strictly problematical) of the *message* of Jesus and what this indicates concerning his life purpose: "It is precisely this complex of ideas in the oldest layer of synoptic tradition which is the object of our consideration." [19] I think it is worthy of the clearest recognition that, with this stated conclusion of historical research, the long-extended quest of the historical Jesus comes to its end and with an open confession of failure. The resulting conclusion is obvious and is stated recurrently by Bultmann—as previously, if prematurely, by Herrmann—that faith "cannot be dependent upon a historian's labor." [20] This view, which was fully anticipated by Kant, has been verified by the most strenuous efforts of more than a hundred years of scholarship to gainsay it.

Now then what to do? Before giving Bultmann's answer let us make one further observation. It should be obvious that if, on the grounds of scientific historical knowledge—taken by Bultmann to be the accredited way of "historical" knowing—we cannot identify the subject of the Church's messianic claim, we can scarcely accept that claim as true. Or, again, if we cannot locate the "historical" subject of the Incarnation claim, we can hardly put much stock in a past event reputed to have possessed such dignity. In short, we can hardly be asked to put our faith in an "objective" event of past time alleged to have absolute divine significance if we cannot even identify the event. Jesus, where art thou? And the answer is: gone beyond recall—*so far as the most refined use of our adopted scientific method can say.* This then seems to be the *methodological* basis for Bultmann's aversion to the Incarnation considered as an "objective" event in *Historie.*

III. THE PHILOSOPHICAL SUPPOSITIONS

What then of the theological and philosophical basis for the aversion to the Incarnation as "objective" event? If *Historie* has failed us, perhaps *Geschichte* may serve us better. Indeed it is, according to Bultmann, neither in *Historie* nor in *Weltanschauung* that faith, the Christian faith, has its ground, but in *Geschichte.* This word is really "loaded" in Bultmann's usage and he himself, I think, needs a systematic interpreter to make his whole meaning coherent, indeed, intelligible.

It is at those places where the historian turns philosopher, and regularly without notice, that interpretation becomes most difficult and uncertain. In perhaps the primary sense, the distinction between *Historie* and *Geschichte*—as we shall see later—rests upon a theory of the knowledge of history, the latter, i.e., "history," contrasted with the world of external relations. But every epistemology has a corresponding reality appropriate to its mode of cognition. It is understandable, therefore, that *Geschichte* may come to stand for a mode or dimension of Being. With Bultmann, such appears to be the case, namely, a mode of Being borrowed—it seems without explicit acknowledgment—from an "ontology of Being" unfolded by existentialist philosophies in the 1920s and 30s. It is an "ontology," so-called, deriving from multiple but rather cognate sources, among them the maturing work of Bultmann's colleague at Marburg, Martin Hiedegger, the writings of Martin Buber, and Karl Heim of Tübingen.

The influence of Heidegger may easily be exaggerated. It is fairly clear, however, that in Heidegger's *Sein und Zeit* Bultmann found a significant advance over Wilhelm Dilthey's earlier quest for the distinctive character of history and a greater understanding of historical knowledge as distinguished from nature and the knowledge of nature. This is indicated by Bultmann's passing statement regarding the problem of "historical understanding"—namely, that it "has been brought into decisive clarity by Heidegger's demonstration of understanding as something existential, . . . but above all by his analysis of the problem of history and his interpretation of the historical nature of existence." [21] It is the phrase *the historical nature of existence* that commands Bultmann's interest. It does so because the "existence" referred to in Heidegger's nomenclature is *Dasein*, that is Human Being as such. It is this to which John Macquarrie calls our attention in referring to Heidegger's "ontological analysis of Being" as analysis of "the being which shows itself in *Dasein's* own understanding of itself." [22]

The consequence is three-fold: (1) historical understanding and, therefore, hermeneutics, is fundamentally self-understanding; (2) what we speak of as history *(Geschichte)* and what we denote by "Human Being" are coordinates; (3) the realm or subject-matter of historical understanding is, as it were, possessed of an ontological status not to be confused with nor to be reduced to nature. It is *Geschichte* in Bultmann's usage, if not in his precise acknowledgment.

By the time of Bultmann's publication of the book *Jesus* (1926), *Geschichte* is silently acquiring the status of a "dimension" of existence, that is, of human existence. It may be described, moreover, as existence in encounter.[23] It is not the "I-It" dimension but belongs to the "I-Thou" dimension of Being as described either in Martin Buber's phenomenological analysis of human experience or in Karl Heim's analytic of the human consciousness.[24] In the book *Jesus* this dimension includes a range of human experience capacious enough to embrace an I-Thou encounter between man and God, or man before God.[25] In this encounter is given an option of destiny: either of man's decision for God in entire obedience of life and acceptance of God's future in the *present,* or the contrary; either forgiveness of sins and reconciliation or self-exclusion and condemnation.[26]

Geschichte then denotes the specifically "historic" as distinct from natural process or merely objective "historical" world events. In making this distinction Bultmann is also dependent at once on Kant, Ritschl, and Herrmann. But he goes well beyond these, not only sharply distinguishing between nature and history, but between history considered in the I-it dimension and history in the I-Thou dimension. It is in the latter sphere alone (i.e., *Geschichte*) that we can speak either of revelation or of the "Christ-event."

Now, as I understand it, this conception of things requires that the knowledge of which faith consists shall involve not only the *activity* of the object but the "agitated," "concerned," and "decisive" involvement of the subject. Or, stated more exactly, in this dimension of existence knowledge expressly presupposes the existential engagement of the subject. This is why Bultmann is always saying in a variety of ways and has been saying since 1926 that "we cannot speak of an act of God without speaking simultaneously of our own existence," or that "when the believer speaks of an act of God he is *ipso facto* speaking of himself as well." [27] Quite plainly revelation is understood to occur in personal, even individual, encounter with the divine Thou.[28]

It is a defect, and very misleading, that rarely is this general view directly addressed in Bultmann's writing. Indeed, so wanting is express declaration on this point that not a few responsible critics suspect that Bultmann is not only radically anthropocentric but, even more, that he is replacing theology with existentialist anthropology of the Heideggerian sort. But Bultmann protests that from the fact that, in speaking of an act of God, man is *"ipso facto* speaking of himself as well, it by no means follows that God has no real existence apart from the believer or the act of believing." [29] It is in the I-Thou dimension of existence, involving personal encounter either between man and man or between man and God, that we may speak of "revelation," or "act of God," or "eschatological event." And this is precisely the sphere of *Geschichte*.

We have then the basis for Bultmann's longstanding rejection of both mythology and *Weltanschauung*. Any effort to conceive the deed of God, the Christ-event, or the ground of faith in the context of the subject-object antithesis, external objective relations, or in terms of the time-eternity duality, or simply in terms of any cosmology at all ignores and *faith*lessly seeks to transcend the *dimension* of Reality in which alone revelation is given and faith is entertained. One can say of Bultmann, on the one hand, that he takes his place in the line of antimetaphysical post-Kantians, that he is a foe of "natural theology" in the preexistentialist sense, and that faith neither requires nor should be allowed to rely upon the exercise of Kant's "theoretical reason." Or, one can say that he is the unyielding foe of all substantialistic metaphysics either of the Platonic or Aristotelian variety, that he approves the nominalism of Luther, and that, therefore, any effort to establish the Incarnation by an employment of *substance metaphysics* draws upon a standpoint which would seek to objectify within a cosmic frame a testimony to Jesus as Christ that comes from a wholly different quarter.[30]

It is in this context that we are to understand Bultmann's denial of any but the most ambiguous revelation of God in "nature" or in "history," [31] and it is against this background that Bultmann brands as both sinful and illusory all talk of God's transcendence outside the standpoint of God's *act* in personal encounter. "It is wishful thinking," he says, "to imagine the things of this world as a screen on which we can view the transcendent, and to hear in this world—in nature and history—the rushing current of the divine lifestream." [32] Likewise man "cannot ascribe to himself as a man a relationship to the eternal, nor press on into the realm of the eternal with himself as starting-point." Quite to the contrary, "man can speak of the transcendent as a positive reality if the transcendent makes a gift of itself to him." [33] In this manner and to this extent, Bultmann joins Barth in subscribing to the dictum: "By God alone may God be known."

IV. HISTORICITY REDEFINED

In this context Bultmann finds himself in position to redefine the "eschatological event." This he had always felt incumbent upon the Christian apologist after Schweitzer had rendered the *eschaton* a gratuitous offense and absurdity to the modern mind. The program was fully outlined in Bultmann's early work, *Jesus*. There he ventured to understand Jesus' message of the Kingdom as implying the call to absolute obedience, confronting man with an absolute "either-or" and demanding decision.[34] The "Kingdom of God is a power which, although it is entirely future, wholly determines the present." [35] But Bultmann shortly makes it clear that what Jesus' message proclaims as beginning, as if in time, is in fact the perennial or universal requirement of decision. "The coming of the Kingdom of God is therefore not really an event in the course of time, which is due to occur sometime and toward which man can either take a definite attitude or hold himself neutral. Before he takes any attitude, he is already constrained to make his choice, and therefore *he must understand that just this necessity of decision constitutes the essential part of his human nature.*" [36]

With this last statement in italics the eschatological event is plainly withdrawn from the outer world of nature and history and is given a universal and permanent abiding place in a quite different dimension of existence, the eschatological dimension of "encounter," or of *Geschichte*, that history where God can and does meet man, first in "crisis" and then in "forgiveness." It is forgiveness that not only frees man from the past, his past, with its "care," "anxiety," and "dread," but opens to him the "future" which now at last can determine the present.[37] It is this openness for the future that marks the transition from bondage under existence to "new life," "new being," "life in the Spirit." [38] Through crisis and decision man becomes "what he is meant to be." He has "freedom to obey." Thus man is released not only from the guilt but from the power of sin.[39] And this critical transition depicts the crucifixion which is not alone that of Jesus but every man's as the way of salvation. Thus "the cross is not just an event of the past," rather, "it is an ever-present reality." [40] The Cross is, it appears, the cruciform nature of human existence itself. It is, we might say, the universal vocation of man inasmuch as it is "the essential part of his human nature." Bultmann asks, can we "read off" this significance from the cross of Jesus? His answer: "For us the cross cannot disclose its own meaning: it is an event of the past. We can never recover it as an event in our own lives." [41] What then? The answer seems to be that the Cross is the eschatological event, the Christ-event, *as we realize in experience the cruciform nature of human existence as illuminated by the existential analysis of essential human nature.* The cross of Jesus is prototypal of the way to essential being if, indeed, there was, as is probable, a Cross of Jesus. The Cross of Jesus is universalized.

What then is the *eschaton?* Bultmann calls it the "Christ-event" or the eschatological event. But it is clear that this event is not an event in past time, not the cross of Jesus, because scientific history does not verify this event so that we can "read off" the significance of it. The point seems to be that the *eschaton* is not recognizable as an event in *Historie* at all. Thus, as late as 1952, Bultmann declared: "Christ is everything that is asserted of him insofar as he is the Eschatological Event. But he is not this in such a way that it would be expressible in terms of a world event." [42] This kind of assurance is ambiguous. Admittedly the whole issue we are airing is of greatest subtlety, but plainly this means either of two things: either we cannot predicate *Christ* of Jesus because we cannot identify Jesus for lack of knowledge, or else, despite our disclaimer of knowledge of Jesus, we refer our faith to him as "Eschatological Event" when our actual referent is the resurrection faith of the earliest community in which we participate by hearing of the Word preached. In either case we are deprived of Jesus, and the "eschatological event" turns out to be only an event in *Geschichte,* that is, in the "moment." The latter is the timeless option—open to those who heed—of encountering God's judgment and his mercy in forgiveness.[43] Salvation, then, is indeed by faith! The *eschaton* is the "moment" of faith, the faith, first of the primitive community, and thereafter, successively, the faith of those to whom it is given to hear and heed the Word of God continually "re-presented" in the proclamation of the Church.[44] In this we may see the indication that ecclesiology is replacing Christology.

The *eschaton* is causally inseparable from the faith of the believer and the community. This surely is what it comes to. But not only so, the *eschaton* is Christ, i.e., the "Christ-event," the *geschichtlich* event. It is the event that happens in my concrete "here and now" and is "realized invariably and solely" just in that concrete "here and now." [45] And this, moreover, is the true and proper meaning of the *ephapax!* On the strength of all this Bultmann exclaims: "It seems high time that Christology was emancipated from its subordination to an ontology of objective thought and re-stated in a new ontological terminology." [46] Bultmann has tried valiantly to lay the groundwork: it is the new ontology of *Geschichte*..

It seems all but impossible to avoid the consequence that, for Bultmann, the Incarnation is indistinguishable from the eschatological moment of faith which the Church experiences and proclaims and which, also, the individual believer may experience and proclaim. Indeed, this is evidently what portends in Bultmann's explicit assertion that "the incarnation is continually being re-enacted in the event of the proclamation." [47] The Incarnation takes place where the Word of God wins its own acceptance by faith. On these premises it is rather evident that the only permissible locale of or for the Incarnation is the sphere of *Geschichte*, that is, in Bultmann's understanding, the moment of faith *coram Deo*. It is this and only this, it seems, which Bultmann allows us to signify when the Church speaks, as it has long spoken, of the Incarnation of the Word of God. On these premises, however, we are prevented from speaking of the Word incarnate in Jesus Christ. The later invokes erroneously an ontology of external relations.

v. THE LOCUS OF THE ACT OF GOD IN CHRIST

But, now, Bultmann faces a problem of some gravity. We might put it this way: either Bultmann must find a way of deriving the Word of God from the historical event Jesus-Christ, as its originative *prius*, or he is, in all candor, bound to admit that the Christian faith has all the marks of being a cruciform interpretation of essential human existence now definitively illuminated by existentialist ontological analysis. More simply stated, Bultmann will have to decide whether Christianity is based upon a unique revelation or is simply the most soteriologically effective philosophy of salvation. It is simply not true that the "eschatological moment," the moment of faith, the "Christ-event" that Bultmann favors, is unique, although it does have a singular life-history in the history of the Church. When, nevertheless, he protests its uniqueness, it is so only according to his own refined and special meaning. The *eschaton* is unique as the *geschichtlich* personal realization of "forgiveness" and "new life," mine or yours, for which John Doe's can be no substitute.

But the hard point is that the Christ-event is not, according to Bultmann, *historisch* unique but *geschichtlich* unique—dubious though it is that any event that is not historical can be unique. Accordingly, so far as our strictly "scientific" historical knowledge takes us, its origin is the existential or eschatological moment which informed the faith of the primitive community and constituted the *kerygma*. But, since Bultmann's historico-methodological skepticism does not permit of finding any reliable connection between the historical figure of Jesus of the past and the historically identifiable mind of the Church, it becomes apparent that the mind of the Church became, once upon a time, the *locus* of the "act of God." From that moment of faith, the Word of God in the *kerygma* goes forth to be both "re-presented" and "re-enacted" among successive hearers of the Word.

If this is an accurate representation of the case, then several things are quite plain in consequence. The first is that Christianity turns out to be a cruciform interpretation of essential human existence existentially appropriated, and the "Christ-event" is identical with this interpretation *as appropriated* by Peter or Paul, Luther or Bultmann. Second, the "act of God" becomes an internal transaction between God and the believer—in some unspecifiable way related to the message and death of Jesus of Nazareth. The cruciform interpretation and *realization* of essential human existence is apparently a given and ubiquitous possibility inherent in the *geschichtlich* form of human existence.

Third, this same *realization*, moreover, stands for the substance and locus of revelation. It is itself the revised meaning of "historicity" and, therefore, of historical revelation. Hence, in the fourth place, Bultmann is really to be understood as supplying us, in Schleiermacher's train, with a distinctive and, withal, an exciting philosophy of religion. But, so far as I can see, this is a substitute for classical Christian faith with its affirmation of the Incarnation of the Word in the *person* of Jesus-Christ as the absolute, if paradoxical, *prius* to the churchly *kerygma*. With Bultmann, the name Jesus-Christ is not hyphenated and cannot be because, while he can invariably tell us much about Christ, he can say little about Jesus. The hyphenated name stands in the tradition for the "hypostatic union," but, with Bultmann's Christology we are seemingly, despite his later protests, deprived of the humanity *in ordine cognoscendi.*

None of these consequences, I think, has Bultmann quite openly admitted. This is often the dilemma of the Christian apologist: he does not wish to give offense to good people while he woos the "unbelievers." Heresy was ever so incurred! *Bultmann's excruciating dilemma is really this: how can he so universalize the eschaton as to make it relevant to the modern mind while at the same time he transmits to that mind the challenge and key to salvation resident, as he believes, in the Christian kerygma?* He can do so only by removing the *skandalon* of an objective "act of God" in outward nature and history. He chooses an old technique with different apparatus—the old technique of Schleiermacher. *It is that of relocating the "miracle."* The miracle is the "eschatological moment," the crisis, the moment of decision, in which God meets man in judgment and in mercy and opens to him a new freedom to love and service. This is surely a miracle, the miracle of redemption; but is it the miracle of the Redeemer?

VI. RE-ASSESSMENT OF THE BULTMANNIAN CHRISTOLOGY

In the unfolding thought of Bultmann, it seems two things primarily combine to effect what may be called a new definition of *historicity,* or, of an ontology of history. They are the "historical skepticism" regarding the Jesus of history inherent in the form-critical method as applied to the New Testament witness; and, secondly, a program of universalization of the *eschaton,* or the act of God in Christ, so conceived as to minimize offense to the scientific awareness of modern man. In tandem the two conspire to postulate a philosophy of religion of which the *rationale* is to relocate, as we have noted, the miracle. It seems no longer an "outward" event of history in the positive sense. It is withdrawn, in fact, from the sphere of operation of Kant's "theoretical reason" as all post-Kantian Protestant theology had consented to do. In view of this withdrawal, the problem that Bultmann will now face, as his predecessors before him in German theology, is whether, on these premises, he can still affirm the "finality" of the *kerygma* or the uniqueness of the Christian religion. Are the steps he has taken such as to render the Christian claim to God's decisive self-revelation in Christ simply *illustrative* and so subordinate to a universal access of man to God as delineated by a "proper" philosophy of religion? This was the old pitfall of "liberalism" from which the dialectical theologians, in concert, reacted in the earlier period.

Toward an Epistemology of History

Let us look more closely into Bultmann's apparent relocation of the miracle—its identification of the Incarnation with the "Christ-event" rather than with the Redeemer. By the Christ-event, we understand Bultmann, in much of his writing, to mean a cruciform interpretation of human experience existentially *(existentiell)* appropriated by faith. Faith is preeminently decision. It is a passage from "inauthentic" to "authentic self-understanding" by openness and commitment to God's future *for me* (Luther's *pro nobis*). Thus, it is the *eschaton* realized in human existence—whether of the individual or of the community of faith, and its *depositum* is the *kerygma*. We might say that my faith is the evangelical moment recapitulated and that *this* is the primary denotation of the Christ-event—the Redeemer becomes the redeemed, the community of the faithful. Finally, it appears that this passage from a closed existence to open existence toward God is, at least, the destiny of man and, perhaps, a possibility inherent in human nature as such—much as Schleiermacher regarded the "God-consciousness" to be implied in "the original perfection of the creation." [48] All of this comes to the first and fundamental function of demythologization pervasive of Bultmann's program and firmly established long before the appearance of his new hermeneutic in the essays, *New Testament and Mythology*.[49]

Our procedure so far has sought mainly to clarify Christological issues from the vantage point of Bultmann's treatment of the question of the knowledge of history wherein he functions primarily, but not exclusively, as accomplished historian and historiographer. In this phase and function, there comes to be established and illustrated his most important distinction between *Historie* and *Geschichte*, which had antecedents in the work of W. Dilthey and powerful suggestions from the teaching of Martin Kähler, as well the Ritschlians. But, as historiographer, Bultmann always functioned at the same time as a philosopher of history, not in the grand manner of Hegel, but specifically, as student of the *epistemology of history*. This function and its early results are fully apparent as the very substance of the preface to Bultmann's *Jesus*, first published in 1926, where the foundations are already laid for what we may properly call an "existentialist" philosophy of the knowledge of history.

There, in express dependence upon Kierkegaard, Bultmann adopts the view that a proper "subjectivity" alone can assure access to history as distinct from nature.[50] The "subjectivity" is not clearly defined, but, as illustrated, it is the problematic of human existence as such. It is the given and inherent urgency of human beings to pass from "fallenness" to what came to be denominated as authentic existence in the language of the current "existentialism" and which was to become regular usage in that of Bultmann. In the *Preface* it is declared that we are deprived of the "objective element" in history as distinct from nature unless we approach history profoundly concerned—concerned for our own transition to authentic self-understanding and, thus, open to decision by way of "a highly personal encounter with history"—in the present instance, with Jesus of the New Testament.

Not to understand this first principle of Bultmann's epistemology of history is to be deprived both of the ground-work of his entire historiography (his methodology of historical inquiry) and, at the same time, of its outworkings both in his theology as "kerygmatic" and in his resultant Christology.

From this epistemological first principle of historical knowledge a corollary derives. In simplest terms it is that we do not and cannot apperceive the historical Jesus apart from ourselves, that is, apart from the existential *problematic* we carry with us as human beings. From this, moreover, it follows that we do not cognize and, therefore, speak of the historical Jesus from a neutral zone.[51] We do not speak of him apart, as we may, say, from the momentous response of the decision he invokes—either the decision of the early Church or of ourselves. This I judge is what we may term the Lutheran postulate in Bultmann's thought, for it identifies the momentous response silently with justification by faith, and faith alone.

But, as always, epistemological first principles, from Plato onwards, have their ontological coordinates. Accordingly, Bultmann—and without explicit acknowledgment—proceeds on the postulate that we do not and cannot have "the object" of Christian affirmation apart from the faithful *subject* who affirms the *object* by faith.[52] Therefore, we do not "have" (i.e., cognize) the Redeemer apart from the redeemed, or Jesus *as* the Christ apart from the "Christ-event," which *is* the moment of faith. On these premises then we may discern that it is not alone Bultmann's chosen method of historiographical inquiry (form-criticism) as applied to the New Testament which places the *kerygma*, so to speak, as a screen between the historian and the Jesus of history, it is finally an epistemology of history that has its sources both in Kant and in Kierkegaard.

Whatever its cogencies for historiography—and it has many—Bultmann, on this understanding, has adopted and employed for historical cognition a version of the "Copernican revolution" of Kant's "critical idealism" as in his *Critique of Pure Reason*. This "critical idealism" means that, in knowledge of external relations *(phenomena)* the subject governs every apperception of the object. So in the "knowledge" of history, for Bultmann, the object is not given without the coordinates supplied by the subject. It follows that Bultmann may not speak of Christ save qualifiedly as the Christ-event and, correspondingly, he cannot speak of the Redeemer in abstraction from the redeemed. This, of course prescribes that the primary *datum* of Christian theology is not Jesus Christ but the *kerygma*. But, eventually, it became clear that this too required critical understanding—a hermeneutic of demythologization to which we briefly turn.

Demythologization and Christology

The first phase of Bultmann's theological endeavor was as historian and historiographer. When we come to the promulgation of his demythologizing program, it is desirable to see that the Christological problem and task, while it presupposes his developed epistemology of history, is approached from a correspondingly different standpoint and problematic. Simply stated, it is the task of differentiating between the historic *(Geschichtlich)* affirmation of the New Testament *kerygma* in its essentials and the "mythological" eschatology and language in which it is couched. Having in the first period vindicated the *kerygma* as the prime *datum* of Christian life and thought, it was, at length, necessary to distinguish truth from error within the primary *datum* itself. Liberal criticism had been doing this for years with the New Testament documents. Now, it had to be done with the *kerygma*, that is, the existentially apperceived *depositum* of faith.

The program is inaugurated, perhaps, decisively in two essays: "New Testament and Mythology" and "Demythologizing in Outline" which first appeared in English translation in Volume I of Hans W. Bartsch's *Kerygma and Myth*.[53] The word "decisively" is used because, from the start, Bultmann's historical criticism was not discontinuous with the demythologizing endeavors of his predecessors of the 19th-century "liberal" period, although, as with others of the time, it was given vigorous impetus, for Bultmann, by the impact of Schweitzer's theory of "wholly futuristic eschatology" coming at the turn of the century.

In the essays on the New Testament and mythology, Bultmann takes the position that, in contrast with the "older liberals" who used criticism to "eliminate" mythology altogether from the New Testament, "our task today," he proposes, "is to use criticism to interpret it."[54] The motive for doing so is the incompatibility of the preaching of the New Testament with the kind of preaching (*kerygma*) acceptable to modern man who has long since abandoned "the mythical view of the world as true."[55]

The mythical view of the world in which the Gospel message is set carries at least two offenses. The "event of redemption" is set in a cosmological framework of apocalyptic expectancy which has had no fulfillment in history and which is conceptually obsolete for the scientific world-view. Secondly, the New Testament *kerygma* conceives man as subject to the direct intrusion of supernatural powers, whereas modern man conceives himself as "essentially a unity" capable both of "self-mastery" and "mastery over nature." [56] It is on these premises that Bultmann propounds the question: ". . . does the New Testament embody a truth which is quite independent of its mythical setting?" If such is the case, then the program is given: "Theology must undertake the task of stripping the *kerygma* from its mythical framework, of 'demythologizing' it." [57] The method is not to "strip" so as to "eliminate," but, as already noted, to strip by way of interpretation. The ambiguity here is relieved in Bultmann's *Shaffer Lectures,* 1951, where it is declared of the new program: "Its aim is not to eliminate the mythological statements but to interpret them. It is a method of hermeneutics." [58]

In the *Shaffer Lectures* it becomes evident that as mythology "expresses a certain understanding of human existence," [59] so the new hermeneutic in prospect will be concerned to provide an alternative. It will prove to be the updated understanding of human existence, in the main, afforded by Bultmann's version of existentialist philosophy, and "screened" from the writers of that school. In this manner—still resting on the foundations of his earlier epistemology of history—we move to the phase of his philosophy of religion proper. Here the enterprise takes on, quite evidently, a methodology fully established in multiple expression by 19th-century liberal theologies, either of the Schleiermacherian or Ritschlian lines. The difference will be this: the vehicle of reinterpretation of the *kerygma* will be the self-understanding of human existence as illuminated by the recent ontology of human Being. It is with this instrument that we may hope to provide the needed hermeneutic for the preaching of the Gospel today! There is no way to understand what Bultmann is doing in the doctrine of the person of Jesus Christ save in the context of the methodologies that serve to meet, for him, the problematics of theology as it faces its task in the modern world, that is, if it is to be, as Schleiermacher prescribed, "scientific dogmatics."

Results for the Role of the Redeemer

Turning now from methodology, let us look more closely, once again, into the "miracle" of the Redeemer and his role in redemption in the later context of the new hermeneutic and as this is set out in

Bultmann's *Shaffer Lectures* already referred to. Their merit for us is both the clarity and candor with which they state the rationale of his demythologizing program.

We are told, in the first place, that "the whole conception of the world which is presupposed in the preaching of Jesus as in the New Testament generally is mythological. . . ." Further, that "this conception of the world we call mythological *because it is different* from the conception . . . which has been formed and developed by science . . . and which has been accepted by all modern men." [60] This statement may be taken to be, and indeed is, the major premise in a syllogism of the unfolding argument.

The minor premise is the following: Jesus the Christ of the "early Christian community" is, in fact, "a mythological figure . . . a pre-existent heavenly being who became man for . . . our redemption and took on himself . . . the suffering of the cross." [61] The conclusion of the syllogism is: "For modern man the mythological conception of the world, . . . of redeemer and of redemption, are over and done with." [62] The syllogism is, in logic, formally valid and is visibly so when reduced to its minimum essentials as follows:

(1) The mythological world-view is unacceptable to modern man.
(2) Christ the Redeemer is a mythological figure.
(3) t. Christ of the *kerygma* is unacceptable to modern man.

The first premise decisively discloses the motivation of Bultmann's new hermeneutic. It is the familiar motive of the earlier liberal apologetic. It seeks to vindicate the claim of the *kerygma* upon modern man's situation, but, in such a form, as not to offend the accepted scientific world-view. On that premise, the premise of the syllogism, the program is mounted and, so far forth, is valid. That is, it is valid insofar as the first premise is true, which, however, remains only *descriptive* and, of course, hypothetical.

The cogency of the syllogism, however, is apparently self-evident to Bultmann and, as it enforces for him the need of a revised theological method, it also precipitates a crisis of faith for those who, standing in the received tradition, are not easily moved from the Johannine *manifesto:* "The Word was made flesh and dwelt among us, full of grace and truth . . ." (John 1:14). Yet, the manifest conclusion of Bultmann's Christological reflections is, it seems, the bleak consequence of the syllogism: "Christ the Redeemer as portrayed in the proclamation of the New Testament" is "over and done with." How, as a Protestant theologian, he arrives at this sundown of the evangelical faith entails the complicated and rather confusing story—in part disclosed—

of Bultmann's own unfolding intellectual pilgrimage. Of this, Karl Barth, his illustrious contemporary, shows keen awareness in his *Rudolph Bultmann: Ein Versuch, ihn zu verstehen.*[63]

Among other things, Barth is aware of a residual inconsequence in Bultmann's statement of the case that culminates in the conclusion of Bultmann's syllogism. In his essay "Demythologizing in Outline," Bultmann earnestly faces the question whether Christian theology is "simply the precursor of existentialism" [64] or whether Heidegger's "existentialist analysis of the ontological structure of human being" is a "secularized version" of the New Testament way of salvation.[65] In his denial he recurrently refers to two things: (1) a "total incapacity of man to release himself from his fallen state"; and (2) the belief that "deliverance can come only by an act of God." Of the latter point—which is reinforced in succeeding pages—Bultmann insists that the New Testament "proclaims the event of redemption which was wrought in Christ." [66] He even states that the "event of Jesus Christ . . . is the revelation of the love of God." [67] In this he finds a "crucial distinction between the New Testament and existentialism, *between the Christian faith and natural understanding of Being. . . .*" This distinction is, namely, that the Christian faith "speaks and faith knows of an act of God through which man becomes . . . capable of faith and love, of his authentic life." [68]

From this it appears that the "syllogism" of the *Shaffer Lectures* may overstate Bultmann's real intention and meaning and that the new hermeneutic does not quite mean that Christ of the *kerygma* is "over and done with," i.e., the Redeemer. In the earlier essay "New Testament and Mythology," Bultmann had separated himself from Harnack, the Czar of early 20th-century post-Ritschlian liberalism, with the charge that with Harnack "the kerygma has ceased to be kerygma." His explanation of this phrase is: "It is no longer the proclamation of the decisive act of God in Christ." [69] One would infer then that Harnack's Christology is deemed to be only a stage above the "natural understanding of Being" of existentialist philosophy. Against both Bultmann affirms "the decisive act of God in Christ." Is he then committed to a defense of the finality of the Christian religion? What then are the limits of demythologizing? Does demythologizing call for the elimination of this "act of God in Christ" or only for some reinterpretation?

That there is here a real problem of apparent self-contradiction is indicated by Bultmann's explicit address to the question in the second programmatic essay, "Demythologizing in Outline." [70] Regarding his assertion of a crucial distinction between "the Christian faith and the natural understanding of Being" and his insistence that "faith knows of an act of God" in Christ, Bultmann asks: "Are we still left with a myth? Further, respecting the new, 'authentic life,' can it be understood otherwise than as an act of God?" [71]

Faced with the apparent contradiction between the espoused program to demythologize the Christ of the *kerygma* in the work of redemption and the claim of kerygmatic faith to an "act of God" in and through Jesus Christ, Bultmann's response is essentially two-fold, and by way of *reinterpretation*. On the one hand, he stresses that the Christian faith looks to "the concrete figure of history—Jesus of Nazareth." [72] It looks to the Cross of Christ as "a permanent historical fact originating in the past historical event. . . ." [73] This is a *datum* adventitious to all observers and, hence, not mythical. On the other hand, this event is, in its "significance" for faith, the event of salvation. [74]

Here, we find Bultmann reverting to his espoused epistemology of history: the proper "subjectivity" is the only assured "objectivity." It is the same insistency we found in the Preface to the early work *Jesus*, now restated with no greater precision. Of the adventitious history *(Historie)* of Jesus of Nazareth—the events of his life—he says: "We can see meaning . . . only when we ask what God is trying to say to each of us through them." [75]

In short, profound, or "ultimate concern" is or may be the catalytic, so to speak, of which faith is the consequent—and, precisely, *in* the Word of God *pro nobis* in Jesus as the Christ. Here the *Historie* is transmuted into *Geschichte*—the history that saves—but relieved of the prescientific cosmology, the "worldly" understanding of the advent of the heavenly Redeemer. It is only the latter which is "over and done with."

But it is not to be missed that Bultmann's vindication of the noncontradiction in his program of demythologizing actually forced his hand in one all-important respect. He was forced to modify his pervasive tendency—the tendency to denigrate *Historie* as superfluous and to conceptualize the saving-event almost exclusively as *Geschichte*. This went so far, his Kantian critical idealism went so far, as to reduce Jesus-Christ to the Christ-event, the *faith* of the early Church. Now he has reaffirmed "historicity" in a more positive sense. He must make such a reaffirmation as the only way to secure or conserve for Christian apologetics the claim of faith that precisely in Jesus Christ God has acted, and not just man, for man's redemption. How else shall we interpret the implied concept of history in the following words: "The real meaning of the cross is that it created a new and permanent situation in history. The preaching of the cross as the event of redemption challenges all who hear it to appropriate this significance for themselves, to be willing to be crucified with Christ." [76] And how else shall we understand the concluding sentences of his controverted essays: "The transcendence of God is not as in myth reduced to immanence. Instead, we have the paradox of a transcendent God present and active in history: 'The Word became flesh.' " [77]

I do not venture to judge whether Bultmann was faithful or deviant from these modulated standpoints that here he evidently adopted. I would only observe that, with the reaffirmation of Jesus' *Historie* as the indispensable given for the referral of "meaning" and "significance," he has subscribed at last to what is indispensable also for the main claim of the *kerygma*, that is, its finality as "act of God," the Incarnation of the Son of God, the Word made flesh. Insofar as the above analysis and exposition are correct, we are relieved of three destructive equivalents in the work of Bultmann: the identification of Jesus-Christ with the "Christ-event" of faith, the reduction of Christology to ecclesiology, and the transmutation of the Word made flesh into a symbol of a universally available passage from inauthentic to authentic existence *coram Deo*. These equivalents fermented powerfully in the earlier philosophy of history of Rudolf Bultmann. Insofar as he checked their hegemony in his later thought he was, to that measure, preserved from following his liberal predecessors in transposing the Christian faith into yet another philosophy of religion.

For those who may be surprised by the outcome of this study, I refer them to certain words preserved to us by John Baillie, written to him by Rudolf Bultmann on occasion of the death of his brother D. M. Baillie. I quote only a line or two from John Baillie's Preface to his brother's posthumous work.[78] Bultmann wrote: "On that occasion he gave me his book *God Was in Christ*, and it is a joy to have that book in my possession as a gift from him. It is the most significant book of our time in the field of Christology." For those who know the argument and position of Baillie's book, Bultmann's personal tribute may be worth pondering—especially in the light of the above findings.

VII. CONCLUSIONS FOR CHRISTOLOGY

In summary, then, what may we conclude respecting the apparent relocation of the miracle from *Historie* to *Geschichte* in Bultmann's theology? Does he finally dislocate the miracle, shifting it from the Redeemer to the redeemed? Does he, therewith, concede to the older liberals what he had censured, that they "eliminate" rather than "interpret" the mythology so that *"the kerygma has ceased to be the kerygma"* and so that the truth of the *kerygma* becomes timeless and eternal? [79] It must, I think, be conceded that he probably hardly meant to allow a total reduction of the *kerygma* to an existential philosophy of religion, although he came near. While his language is often ambiguous, his later mediating position may easily be recognized in *Bultmann Replies to His Critics,* especially the section "The Language of the Act of God." There, while he still retains the basic principle of his epistemology of history (that proper subjectivity yields the truest objectivity), and, while he reaffirms its theological corollary ("to speak of an act of God means to speak at the same time of my existence," i.e., as a believer), he now sets limits to a long-standing and unguarded implication of his "critical idealism." The limitation is sounded in this: "That God cannot be known apart from faith does not mean that he does not exist apart from it." [80] By a parity of reasoning, in what follows he attempts to say that, because of the "meaning and significance" faith attaches to Jesus as the Christ, it does not follow that, in faith, we are deprived of the historical subject of faith's affirmation. While Bultmann continues in this passage to assert that "objective investigation of the historian" cannot confirm that God has acted in Jesus Christ,[81] he can say of that same figure *that just such an event of the past is the once-and-for-all eschatological event, which is continually re-enacted in the word of proclamation."*[82]

At this point Bultmann rests his case. His residual "critical idealism" governing the function and reach of faith, will evidently yield no more in the direction of the Word made flesh in Jesus. Moreover, from these concessions, we cannot harvest one iota more for the *dignity* of the person of Jesus Christ than can be gathered from Melanchthon's famous dictum from the first edition of his *Loci Communes* of 1521, echoed and adopted by Albrecht Ritschl: "This is to know Christ, to know his benefits, not . . . his nature, or the manner of his Incarnation." [83] Yet Bultmann's belated consent to an indispensable reference of faith to the *eschaton* that *was* Jesus Christ retains in some measure the all important continuity in "the name above every name." In doing this much, it does more. It conserves the *kerygma,* from its beginnings, as "proclamation of the decisive act of God in Christ." It perhaps also narrowly preserves Bultmann from reduction of the Redeemer to the redeemed; the reduction of Jesus Christ to the "Christ-event" of faith; and the reduction of Christ to a timeless symbol of the human potential—a passage from inauthentic existence to authentic Being. To have retrieved this much is, perhaps, ground enough for Bultmann's tardy reaffirmation—"The Word was made flesh." [84]

Probably, it would not be fair to ask whether existentialist theology has gotten us no farther than a Ritschlian standpoint in Christology. In Bultmann's version, much of authenticity is recovered from the Reformation tradition. The larger issue that remains is whether the virtual absence of a doctrine of Creation in Protestant theology of the Continental tradition does not deprive it of resources for a doctrine of the Redeemer. While Philip Melanchthon saw fit to withdraw his famous nugatory statement respecting the Incarnation from subsequent editions of his great *Loci Communes,* there was a reason for its original presence, namely, the virtual absence of a basis in 16th-century Protestant thought sufficient to bear the weight of a doctrine of the Word made flesh. Bultmann, steeped in this tradition, may well be only the latest *exemplum*—this time empowered by existentialist philosophy and an idealistic epistemology of history—to perpetuate, in his way, the long-standing *lacuna*. It is the very same *lacuna* that Kant persuasively legitimized for the preponderance of subsequent German Protestant theology and for which Karl Barth supplied but little antidote, indeed, scarcely acknowledged.

THE DOCTRINES OF GOD AND MAN IN THE LIGHT OF BARTH'S PNEUMA-TOLOGY

I

There is some little basis for the claim that 19th- and early 20th-century theology shelved the doctrine of the Holy Spirit. There are reasons for this. One of them is that Christian understanding of the Holy Spirit has usually ben associated with a serious view of the sovereignty of God. This view was weakening by the beginning of the 19th century with the consolidation of the scientific world-view and with its challenge to divine overruling, not only in nature at large, but in human nature in particular. But, concurrently with this development, one would have to mention the pervasively Pelagian character of the vitiated Christianity of the Enlightenment, which had its enormously influential culmination in Kant. Kant fastened upon 19th-century Protestant theology the notion of Christianity as man's moral achievement. Finally, in the third place, Schleiermacher—the so-called "father of modern theology"—tended to absord the doctrine of the Spirit into his own teaching concerning man's native spirituality. Christian life became a species of man's universal capacity for religious experience. The conception of God's movement toward man, in the action of his Spirit, was largely replaced by the movement of man's spirit toward God. These three factors, in combination with others that might be mentioned, conspired to make the Holy Spirit superfluous. This outcome was challenged, mainly in British theology, but not very influentially until Karl Barth created a storm center in contemporary Protestant thinking.

In the theology of Barth, the Holy Spirit is not an addendum; it is integral, inescapable. Theology associated with Barth's name and influence has been variously designated: theology of the Word of God, dialectical theology, theology of crisis. One may be allowed his preference, but the ruling principle, it must be granted, is the "sovereign divine freedom" of God. It is theology of divine sovereignty, not unlike that of Calvin in so far as emphasis falls upon sovereignty of *action* rather than of *being*. It cannot be overstressed that for Barth, God is

Republished with altered title and minor emendations from *Religion in Life*, XXIV, No. 4 (Autumn 1955) with the permission of the Editor.

known only in his gracious *action;* whereas, according to his *nature,* God is inscrutable to man and cannot be unveiled to him.[1] In so far as we speak of God at all, we speak of him *in act* and exclusively in, or in respect to, his act of self-unveiling. His action constitutes the events of revelation. Revelation is the exercise of his sovereign freedom in love, and our apprehension of the revelation in Christ is equally the work of his divine freedom.[2]

This last statement takes us closer to the doctrine of the Holy Spirit, for it is the Holy Spirit which is, to use Barth's language, God's freedom "in us" by which we men are, in turn, made "free *for* God." [3] In this connection it is possible, and I think defensible, to assert that the entirety of Barth's *Kirchliche Dogmatik* exists within an ellipse of two foci: the one is "God's freedom for man," the other, "the freedom of man for God." But the two are really one, namely, the sovereign divine freedom of God; for the freedom of man for God is a "mode" of action of the One God, God the Holy Spirit. "The Holy Spirit is the Lord, wholly and utterly God, the divine Subject. . . ." [4]

Barth maintains that only by reasserting the entire freedom of God in the event of revelation, the event which grasps me, can God's sovereignty be preserved. It is God, not man, who possesses and retains the initiative; for, says Barth: "Were the Spirit, the mediator of revelation to the subject, a creature or a creaturely force, we would be asserting and maintaining, that, in virtue of his presence with God and over against God, man in his own way is also a lord in revelation." [5] This is said specifically against Schleiermacher and his successors. The doctrine of the Holy Spirit affirms "the irreversibility of the Lordship of God in His revelation." [6] This, says Barth, makes the dogma of the Holy Spirit difficult, not so much intellectually, but practically, because men flatly refuse to admit what it implies, that revelation is by grace alone.

In a lecture delivered at Elberfeld in 1929 and given English publication under the title *The Holy Ghost and the Christian Life,* Barth anticipated later utterances and enforced already ruling convictions. "The Holy Ghost," he declared, "is God the Lord in the fulness of Deity, in the total sovereignty and condescension, in the complete hiddenness and revealedness of God." [7] Against 19th-century immanence theology, Barth asserted that the "Holy Spirit is not identical with what we recognize as our own created life of the spirit or the soul." [8] He repudiated Troeltsch's identification of the Holy Ghost with "the individual's immediate putting forth of religion." [9] He rejected Erich Przywara's use of *analogia entis* whereby man, *according to his nature as creature*, is allowed to be "open upwards" toward God.[10] On the contrary, he declared that any "continuity" between God and the created spirit "cannot belong to the creature itself but only to the Creator *in His relation* to the creature." [11] That relation is entirely one of God's grace, his sovereign freedom and is, indeed, realized only in the action of God as the Lord and Spirit. The *relation* is wholly at God's gracious disposal.

Hence, Barth contends that "grace is ever and in all relations God's *deed* and *act,* taking place in this and that moment of time in which God wills to be gracious to us, and is gracious, and makes his grace manifest." [12] So we may conclude, provisionally at least, that the Holy Spirit in Barth's theology is the divine agency by which the two foci, mentioned above, are united: it is the Lord the Spirit who unites "the freedom of God for man" with "the freedom of man for God." The Spirit is God the "Redeemer"; and, in virtue of his working, God remains "all in all"—absolutely sovereign in his freedom—a freedom, however, manifest as Love. It is apparent that Barth can safeguard the first principle of his thought, or shall we say of his system—the sovereign divine freedom—only by profoundly serious use of the doctrine of the Holy Spirit. But there are other reasons to which we must also give attention.

II

In expounding Barth's doctrine of the Holy Spirit we can begin by taking notice of his assertion that in dogmatics we are always speaking of the Holy Spirit (i.e., as a presupposition) because "we are always speaking . . . of the *event* in which the Word of God is not only revealed to man but also believed in by him." [13] The Word of God as revealed is Jesus Christ. The revealed Word of God, as believed in, is the working of the Holy Spirit. God the revealer, God as revealed, and God as revealedness are, respectively, Father, Son, and Holy Spirit.

Barth's pervasive criticism of "liberal theology" is, of course, that, in treating the Holy Spirit, it exchanges the Lordship of the Spirit for "anthropology" or the spirit of man—locating and positing in human nature a faculty of apprehension or "capacity" for revelation. *For Barth, on the contrary, all theological anthropology is treated under the office of the Holy Spirit.*[14] The Holy Spirit in his working assures that God remains Lord in the event of revelation. We may epitomize Barth's treatment of the Holy Spirit in his words to the effect that the Holy Spirit is the Lord through "whose act the openness and readiness of man for the Word of God is true and real." [15] There is no "receptacle of human experience" for receiving the Word of God.[16] "We look in vain for a correspondence with the Word of God on our side. . . ." [17]

The Word of God "is also God's miracle in reaching its goal among men, in the event of man's faith in the Word of God." To be sure faith is undoubtedly "also human experience," but it is human experience "decided" through the working of the Lord the Spirit.[18] Hence, Barth holds that all theology or philosophy of religion that searches for a "method of hearing the Word of God" must be abandoned and yield place to the freedom of the Holy Spirit.[19]

So we reach the point of seeing that for Barth the proper formula under which we comprehend the office of the Holy Spirit is the Psalmist's word: *in tuo lumine videbimus lumen,* "in thy light we see light." [20] Thus the *analogia entis* is entirely replaced by the *analogia fidei.* The "conformity" between man's spirit and the Word of God, necessary for knowledge (viz., "acknowledgment," *Doct.* pp. 234 ff.), exists in the moment of faith; but it rests upon no human capacity for the Word of God, only upon the determination of the Spirit (Cf. *Doct.* pp. 272–73). The "conformity" is loaned for use; it is not to be arrogated to the self and possessed. It remains at God's disposal, subject to his freedom. Thus, the Christian life is not a life of faith, but a moment-to-moment existence-in-faith as man is an object of God's gracious determining action (Cf. *Doct.* p. 381). So Barth declares that, in God's "gifting Himself, He remains free to give Himself afresh or to refuse to, so that it is always His new self-giving that remains man's sole hope. . . ." [21]

As revelation is the eventuating action of grace, correspondingly, the "conformity" obtaining in the faith-moment is *event* rather than *status* or *nature* belonging to men.[22] In this respect, the work of the Holy Spirit is eschatological, viz., we possess our redemption as promise, as something future. "The New Testament speaks eschatologically when it speaks of man's being called, reconciled, justified, sanctified, redeemed." [23] Nevertheless, the Holy Spirit is God, the Redeemer, through whose determination man is opened and made ready to receive the Word of God.[24] So Barth always reiterates that in regard to "the event of hearing the Word of God, we point only to the Holy Spirit." [25]

It is now evident that, for Barth, the Lord the Spirit, in his action, constitutes the whole possibility of man's appropriation of revelation. He adopts as his own what he takes to be the New Testament conception of the Holy Spirit. The Spirit is God in his "revealedness." [26] This is answer to the question: Will the revelation "get at man"? The "possibility of faith does not go automatically with the fact that Jesus takes the stage as revelation of the Father," as the Son or Word of God. The revealed Word of God must become "manifest" to man.[27] The Holy Spirit of God in the "mode" of becoming manifest. The "presupposition of the Church" and of faith "is the possibility of this relation, the knowledge-relation between man and the Word of God." [28] This relation is made good by the office of the Holy Spirit. He is the freedom of God "to be present to the creature, and in virtue of this presence of His to realize [i.e., to eventualize] the relation of the creature towards Himself. . . ." [29] The work of the Spirit is not to add independent content to revelation but to enforce or "manifest" the revelation already perfected in the life, death, and resurrection of the Revealed Word, the Son.[30] It is the Spirit's work to make God, revealed in Christ, revealed also to me.

We are prepared to see, then, that Barth regards Christology and Pneumatology as both correlative and inseparable. The Christian doctrine of Christ is quite impossible without the doctrine of the Spirit. As Jesus Christ is the objective side in the event of revelation, so the Holy Spirit is "the subjective side in the event of revelation." [31] The correlation is fully worked out in *Kirchliche Dogmatik* under the headings, respectively, "God's Freedom for Man" and "The Freedom of Man for God." [32]

The three-in-one God is the persisting subject of revelation. Jesus Christ, the Son, is "the objective actuality of revelation." As God's freedom *for* man, he is the object of revelation. The Holy Spirit is he who effects the revelation as actuality for us and *in us*. We may say, according to Barth, that Jesus Christ and the Holy Spirit are, correlatively, the objective and subjective executors of revelation.[33] "Christology and Pneumatology are consequently one in that they are, respectively, the knowledge *(Erkenntnis)* and the praise *(Lobpreis)* of the grace of God." [34] At this point we are mainly concerned with Barth's view that Jesus Christ, as true God and true man, is "the objective reality of the divine revelation." [35] He is given and adventitious to us, but it is the work of the Holy Spirit through which the given revelation is appropriated by us.

We turn again to the Holy Spirit when we consider the correlative theme, "the freedom of man for God." Here we consider the question "how it comes about that the self-manifestation is revelation for us men." [36] Or, as Barth puts it otherwise: "In what freedom of man is it actual that the revelation of God comes to him?" [37] Barth's answer is, of course, that it cannot be "an original proper freedom of man." [38] Apparently, from Barth's indications, man's proper freedom is only the freedom to resist the grace of God.[39] Nevertheless, Barth cautions that the "freedom of self-withdrawal when faced by the Word of God cannot be limitless and inviolable." [40] Positively considered, "the freedom of man [for God] can only be created by God in the act of his revelation and given to men; it can, in the end, only be God's own proper freedom." [41] The freedom of men for revelation only has its whole "possibility in the action of God." [42]

Hence, Barth extensively illuminates the claim that the Holy Spirit, as the freedom of God for men, is both the "subjective actuality" and the "subjective possibility of revelation." Barth affirms: "Through the outpouring of the Holy Spirit, it will be possible in the freedom of man that the revelation of God can happen to him, because in it, through God's Word, it will have definitively spoken to him so that he has a proper possibility for such an occurrence." [43] The Word of God will be "inescapably master in him." [44] "*Analogia fidei* will be understood as what is here designated *Meister.*" [45] Somewhat earlier Barth had said: "Man acts by believing, but the fact that he believes by acting is God's act. Man is the subject of faith. It is not God but man who believes." [46]

For Barth, what is proposed by the revelation in Christ is enforced by the Lord the Spirit. Historically, the work of the Holy Spirit presupposes the completion of the *kerygma,* that is, "the conclusion and completion of the objective revelation" in Christ.[47] The Pauline statement, "Now the Lord is the Spirit," is not to be taken as "identifying" the Son with the Spirit but, rather, as asserting the Lordship of the Spirit; although Barth regards the Spirit as "qualified" completely by the Son so that the Holy Spirit is equally the Spirit of Christ.[48]

Now, further, the inseparability of Christology and Pneumatology is indicated in this that, if the revelation in Christ is absolute (really God in his freedom for man), then the Spirit, which is the subjective possibility of the appropriation of the revelation, must share equally in the absoluteness. The Word in its "revealedness" must be equal to the Word as "revealed." Thus, the "divinity" of the Spirit's "essence" is required. Apart from this revelation would not be an eventuation of God's sovereign grace alone. Or, furthermore, even if the objective revelation in Christ were a divine event, still it would remain inapprehensible by man. Or, yet again, if it were apprehensible by man apart from the Spirit, then faith would not be of God but of man.[49] Obviously, these alternatives are not acceptable to Barth. On the contrary, it is Barth's view that "faith, the New Testament *pistis,* is rather to be regarded as a possibility coming from a mode of God's existence [Holy Spirit], a mode of existence which is on a level, in essential unity, with Him who in the New Testament is described as Father and Son." [50] Thus we are brought well within the precincts of the doctrine of the Triune God. A serious doctrine of revelation in Christ requires necessarily a doctrine of the equal Lordship of the Holy Spirit.

There are aspects of the office of the Holy Spirit which have been slighted in our treatment. He has a "convicting and reproving office." [51]

Apart from the Spirit's working, man does not know he is a sinner. Furthermore, the Holy Spirit is constitutive both of Scripture and Proclamation. The Spirit is "the only possibility in virtue of which men can so speak of Christ, that their language becomes testimony, therefore that the revelation of God in Christ becomes actual anew by their speaking." [52] Hence, the Holy Spirit is the possibility both of the knowledge of God and the service of God. Accordingly, the Holy Spirit constitutes the existence of the Church in which the Word of God is both heard and proclaimed. The Spirit is constitutive of the Christian life, and through it *homo peccator* becomes *capax verbi divini*, which is also the freedom of the child of God.[53]

III

One does not study Barth without a solid impression of sustained and magnificent effort to revivify the New Testament *kerygma*. This purpose is particularly evident in his treatment of the theme before us. No theologian of modern times has taken up this task more seriously, and none has discharged it with anything like so formidable a result. The result is a revitalized trinitarianism. The *dogma* of the Trinity, Barth admits, is not to be found in the New Testament. Nevertheless, he asserts that it is the proper "exegesis" of the New Testament. But, now, how did he arrive at the Trinity? Manifestly, by reaffirming the biblical and Lutheran principle of absolute sovereignty or divine freedom. In Barth's view, it is this and only this which makes revelation really to be Revelation. The Word in Christ is really God's Word, not man's. The Word as apprehended through the Spirit is assuredly God's Word also, because, as the Spirit's working, it remains with God's freedom and at his disposal. Hence, in one sovereign divine freedom is embraced the threefold mode of the divine action. At the same time, the knowledge of God is lifted above the relativities of historicism, immanentism, and ecclesiastical absolutism (the latter expressed either as Fundamentalism or Romanism).

Some will think that the cost of obviating these evils is too great: it is to make everything of God and all but nothing of man. But how, in the last analysis, is this so different from the clear position of the late William Temple? "All is of God; the only thing of my very own which I can contribute to my own redemption is the sin from which I need to be redeemed." [54] It is true that Temple does not, as Barth, eliminate from human nature every capacity for divine-human encounter. This is a signal difference between them. But it is true that nothing can finally extricate man from the sin that destroys him save the Incarnation of the Word of God. But this Word is appropriated alone through the Holy Spirit.[55] As to human freedom, what do we make of the words: "Nothing can suffice but a redemptive act. Something impinging upon the self from without must deliver it from the freedom which is perfect bondage to the bondage which is its only perfect freedom"?[56]

Glancing again at Barth, can we say that his bold realism with regard to the Holy Spirit is inevitably called for to carry out the import of the sovereignty of God's grace? What else can be done when one is ready to employ the phrase, "all is of God," or when one takes seriously the view that the knowledge of God is God's self-unveiling? Doubtless Barth realizes our discomfort; he has overwhelmed us with God and left us nothing for ourselves except our sin and, therein, nothing wherewith to boast. So we are reduced to apostolic poverty indeed! In this extremity anything more to be said must be *ad hominem*, and so I leave it. But I do not leave it before reminding a few interested readers that Wesley held a very similar view, viz., that "none can trust in the merits of Christ, till he has utterly renounced his own." And with him, quite as much as with Barth, faith is altogether God's gift and in no sense man's achievement.

An evaluation of Barth's doctrine of the Holy Spirit in a large sense entails criticism of his essential theological standpoint, for the whole faith of the church has no basis except in "the freedom of God for man," and that is entirely the work of the Holy Spirit. In 1932 Barth defined theology as *ministerium verbi divini*.[57] About the same time he was asserting that only in the activity of the Holy Spirit is man, as sinner, capable of the divine Word. It follows that in theology we are occupied exclusively with the action of God as manifest to faith. We have nothing to do with the human subject of faith save as he is convicted of sin and redeemed by grace. Indeed, we have nothing to do with man save in his rebellion against God or, alternatively, in his freedom for God. In theology we do not know man except as subject of God's judgment or mercy.

It is this exclusiveness of Barth's theology which offends. It strikes us that, somehow, something is out of focus with this perspective. This relegation of all things human, is it attributable to the "infinite qualitative distinction between time and eternity," which, in 1921, Barth was willing to designate the principle of his "system" if he had any system?[58] This, to be sure, might partly account for his strictures against all theological "anthropology" in so far as, in such inquiry, a point-of-meeting is sought in human nature for the divine-human encounter. However we answer that question, it is, above all, clear that the failure of the Jesus of historicism to "fill the shoes" of the Christ of the Church's faith, and the consequent impoverishment of Christian preaching and witness, impelled Barth to recover a more authentic Word of God for his time. Accordingly, he proceeded to abandon all dependence upon any resources of man's spirituality and to put his confidence in the sovereign freedom of God as "manifested" in the activity of the Holy Spirit.

We can hardly protest his giving God the glory or letting God be God, but we can insist, in the name of New Testament teaching, that, once he has banished the hosts of humanistic immanentism, he find a place for something like "newness of life" in fellowship with the Father of our Lord Jesus Christ. But here is the trouble: so jealous is he for the Lordship of God that Barth will not allow the Holy Ghost to "come to roost" in human life in such a way as that His action and presence is manifest in the texture and shape of historical personality. If it is above all God's business to create reconciliation in place of alienation, *koinonia* in place of rebellion, sanctification in place of sin, then we might expect these to be secured not merely in "promise" but in fact. But, says Barth: "That would be more than God's revelation and reconciliation in time, that would be our existence with him in eternity, in the *regnum gloriae.*" [59] We must regard our redemption as future. "To have the Holy Spirit means to let God be one's confidence, and not one's own possession of God." [60] Our redemption we possess as a promise, "we do not in the least understand it in regard to our present. . . ." [61] And Barth continues: "We believe in our future existence, we believe in an eternal life in the midst of the valley of death. It is thus, in this futurity, that we have and possess it." [62] Everything, says Barth, that is said about man as "driven and filled by the Holy Spirit, is in the New Testament sense an eschatological pronouncement." [63] What he means may be judged from succeeding words: "The New Testament speaks eschatologically, when it speaks of man's being called, reconciled, justified, sanctified, redeemed." [64] Man does not live an eternal life. "That is and remains the predicate of God, the Holy Spirit." [65]

At this point in my copy of *The Doctrine of the Word of God* is a marginal note left by the hand of the late D. C. Macintosh who comments: "This was the one-sided view from which Wesley sought to rescue a moribund Protestantism." I suppose Macintosh had in mind Wesley's insistence upon transformation of life as the normal expectancy in regeneration; in any case, the "one-sidedness" is intentional with Barth, for he says:

Even in receiving the Holy Spirit the man remains a man, the sinner a sinner. And likewise in the outpouring of the Holy Spirit God remains God. *The statements about the operation of the Holy Spirit are statements the Subject of which is God not man,* and under no circumstances could they be transformed into statements about man. They speak of *the relation of God to man*, to his knowledge, will and feeling, to his experience active and passive, to his heart and conscience, to his soul-and-body existence, *but they cannot be reversed and regarded as statements about the existence of man.*[66]

What is the basis of this and what does it come to? The basis is threefold.

1. On the one hand, it accents Barth's uncompromising insistence upon the "infinite qualitative distinction," upon total discontinuity between the Creator's sovereignty and creaturely existence.

2. But this is enforced by Barth's pervasive and dominant view that, because man's existence is in time, the presence of God to him in time is limited to a succession of momentary incidents registered in the events of revelation. God is present to the human creature only *as-in-act* not *as-in-being.* His being remains veiled; his presence is, thus, in a series of momentary eventuations which are best described as recurrences.

3. Furthermore, when Barth says that "statements about the operation of the Holy Spirit are statements the Subject of which is God not man," he is saying that reconciliation, justification, and sanctification are not conditions of the human subject but are, rather, recurrent moments of the divine activity. They are, properly speaking, predicates of the divine operation of the Spirit rather than predicable qualities of a transformed human nature. Barth does not speak of justification and sanctification as constitutive modifications of the human condition; he regularly speaks of men as *justified* or *sanctified*—and so, always only *objects* of divine determination. Hence, even in the work of redemption, Barth reserves the sovereignty of God. So he means what he says when he declares that statements about the operation of the Holy Spirit "cannot be reversed and regarded as statements about the existence of man."

In this way Barth attempts to put the whole content of revelation out of reach of historical, psychological, and philosophical treatment and evaluation. So he insists that even in redemption (the work of the Spirit, the Redeemer) man "remains" man the creature, and God the Holy Spirit "remains" God. Barth does concede that what we experience, "what changes in us in quantity and quality" and "may become the object of an anthropology" is a "human sign of the fact that God has presented Himself to us by His revelation. . . ."[67] Such "signs," he further states, are not to be treated lightly. It would be strange if they did not become visible at all. But here Barth draws back with the Pauline word that "the things which are seen are temporal."[68] This is a plain *non sequitur.*

Elsewhere he rejects Luther's emphasis upon a transformed Chris-

tian man in whom there is assurance, joy, but no want, shortage, sadness
or temptation. *Nein!* says Barth, faith there is, but it is trusting in
the Word that "tells us of the unmerited imputation of His righteousness established as true in our flesh." [69] He adds, "But once more, all
this not in tranquil secured 'givenness' to us, once for all, but in the
act of the divine continual 'giving.'" [70] He specifically labels as heretical
"a divine quality inhering in the soul" attributed to the work of the
Spirit.[71]

In view of such statements, it is difficult to imagine how Barth could
do other than repudiate Luther's word respecting the Christian man:
". . . it is always necessary that the substance or person itself be good
before there can be any good works, and that good works follow and
proceed from the good person. . . ." [72] It is clear that for Barth the
work of the Holy Spirit is more nearly an event or succession of events
in God's action than any transformation of human existence. The Spirit's work is a "process . . . which, in the strictest sense, is first coming
to us and to come, moment by moment. . . ." [73] We live "between
the times" of its incidence. We also live *in* the time of its periodic
occurrence, but even then, what difference it makes for the character
of human existence as Christians is all but impossible to know, and
by Barth's admission.[74]

It is not, I think, possible to square this with the Pauline doctrine
of "newness of life" in Christ and in the Spirit (Rom. 6:4, 7:6). Paul
assumes something like a transformation of existence: "For I through
the law died unto the law, that I might live unto God; . . . and it is
no longer I that live, but Christ liveth in me: and that life which I
now live in the flesh I live in faith . . ." (Gal. 2:19 f.). We do not have
to deny that for Paul also man is *simul justus et peccator.* He is waiting
for his adoption, but he shows forth "the fruits of the spirit" (Gal.
5:22). Man's spirit is nowise identifiable with God's Spirit, but "we
received, not the spirit of the world, but the spirit which is from God"
(1 Cor. 2:12). To be sure, "the natural man receiveth not the things
of the Spirit of God." Yet St. Paul is bold enough to claim, "But we
have the mind of Christ" (2:16).

Such language, even if it is Scripture, must be thoroughly objectionable to Barth. Here community between God and man is rather too
intimate; it robs the Lord of his sovereign freedom and unites man
too readily to his Majesty. St. Paul does what Barth forbids: he predicates of the human subject of redemption what is, for Barth, exclusively
to be predicated of the divine Subject in redemption. This goes too
far in the direction of mingling divine and human existence, and Barth
will not have it, I think, even if it is the divine working. God, the
Holy Spirit, does not so draw near to men as to become the new

ground of their existence; even in his working he "remains" on his side and they on theirs.

Barth's final word seems to be that man, even as subject of the divine operation of the Spirit, "does not live an eternal life. That is and remains the predicate of God, of the Holy Spirit." [75] Even in the work of the Spirit, the Redeemer, new life is conveyed only as a promise, and only in this "futurity" may we be said to have and possess it.[76] Eschatology here is futuristic and in no sense "realized." Barth can have little sympathy for the important results of recent Pauline scholarship, as for example W. D. Davies's solid finding that "the inwardness of the New Covenant of Jeremiah's hope is achieved for Paul through the indwelling Christ, the new Torah 'written in the heart.' " [77] Davies's interpretation of the Spirit in St. Paul's thought requires that, in the life of men, the "new creation" be taken seriously. But Barth seems scarcely more prepared to concede *koinonia* between God and man after the work of the Spirit than before its working. Hence, it is doubtful whether the work of the Holy Spirit achieves any reduction of the hiatus between God and man.

All this suggests that quite possibly Barth has everywhere ontologically divorced the spirit of man from the Spirit of God. It also suggests that he has, despite his disclaimers, been controlled by "the infinite qualitative difference between time and eternity" to the point where a philosophical principle, for such it is, has forcibly subverted or banished the prior reality of Christian experience.

Barth leaves the impression of being overly occupied with a "metaphysical" difference between time and eternity. It is as if the temporal, by its very nature, forbade any abiding place to the Eternal, so that Incarnation must remain highly ambiguous and redemption altogether a trembling hope. The theologian who justly revolted against the 19th-century tendency to settle for God as "religious object" has swung to the opposite extreme and, in making man an object, has tended to rob him of his proper subjectivity—his depth and his freedom. If Schleiermacher put far too great a stress upon man's spirituality, Barth, it may be, has so radically negated it as to make even man's redemption problematic. Can God's Holy Spirit remain so much his own that, in no sense, it can ever become man's portion? Like Elijah, Barth has been "very jealous" for the Lord, the God of hosts. He sees the children of the promise forsaking the covenant, but perhaps there is a point where jealousy for the sovereign freedom of God betrays unseemly mistrust of that all-sufficiency and encourages an excessive division between divine causality and the life of man. Has not Barth, like Luther, presumed upon a complete divorce of Nature and Grace?

ECUMENISM AND SOME CURRENTS OF THEOLOGY TODAY

It will be recalled that the late Archbishop of Canterbury, William Temple, before his death in 1945, expressed the judgment that the advancing ecumenical movement seemed to him "the great new fact of our time." He meant, of course, "the great new fact" *for* Christendom. To this movement William Temple had, for a generation, devoted his great talents as theologian and churchman.

I raise the question whether developments of the past thirty years sustain the measure of promise which Temple entertained regarding both the advance and the achievement of ecumenism. Admittedly the question is many-sided in import and involves a wide range of factors that cannot be explored in one sitting. So let it be understood that our assessment of the evidence must be incomplete, and far more in the nature of an inquiry than of a conclusion—yet I think an inquiry worth making.

It is worth making because, while it is notoriously difficult to assess one's own time—since it is in flux and never quite in focus—it is, nevertheless, necessary to take our bearings for charting our course in a sea of change, especially if we are to try to be responsible churchmen and churchwomen in our generation. Today in theology, furthermore, the question is pressing: responsible to whom—God or man?

I

First, then, I would like to register some impressions respecting the state of recent and present-day ecumenism, and, secondly, to consider some explanations for the impressions I have concerning the state of health of the ecumenical movement today. These explanations will involve reference to the theological climate, especially as this climate affects and finds expression in the "life and work" of the churches. I do not pretend that there are not *other* factors of influence in addition to theological trends, e.g., sociological, economic, and political, that also affect the health of the ecumenical movement. I judge the ecumen-

An address to The Ministerial Association, Cleveland, Ohio, October 1976 and first published in *The Duke Divinity School Review*, XLI, No. 3 (Fall 1976). Reprinted here with permission of the Editor.

ical movement to be, at center, a thrust toward the reunion of Christendom.

As to my impressions, I register the judgment that the thrust of the ecumenical movement in the twenty years between 1945 and 1965 was steadily forward, from the establishment of the World Council of Churches in 1948 and the Lund Conference of 1952 onward to the Montreal Conference of 1963, and that it climaxed in the Second Vatican Council. I judge Vatican II to be an essential outworking of the ecumenical movement and, in fact, a climactic part of it. I also have the impression that since Vatican II the movement, having reached a high plateau, has subsequently suffered a decline of both interest and power. This I judge from many indices such as the failure of the Anglican-Methodist Conversations in England (1973) and the bogged-down, if still hopeful, deliberations that doggedly persist in the circles of our Consultation on Church Union in this country. For this latter project, in the direction of organic union among Protestant churches, I perceive no alleviation of the apathy of the "grass-roots" since 1971 and, partly, because the *rationale* of such union is both unperceived and unconvincing to the generality of church people. Behind this, perhaps, stands the long unfinished business of the Oberlin Conference (1957) that raised but never supplied a clear or cogent answer to the question about "the *nature* of the unity we seek."

Strategically and tactically considered, it is my impression—however unpopular with a now established ecumenical bureaucracy—that moves toward large scale organic union "jump the gun" on the still unsettled issue of the *nature* of the unity for which historically separated churches *can* at this juncture be ready—however needful, even urgent, may be recovery of a more united Christendom. I put the matter this way because I agree heartily with William Temple on the long-range significance of the ecumenical movement. Its emergence in the early 20th century may, in the wisdom of God, yet prove to be the great new promise of World Christianity in its mission of Christ to the world. Meanwhile, today, the ecumenical movement has lost vitality and, for some, is passing, so to speak, under a cloud or has stalled in a climate of some little distraction and confusion, both among and within the churches.

The remainder of this discussion will seek to comment upon one large factor in this confusion, namely, some theological trends and ideological distractions of the day, which, in my view, have had a diversionary influence upon ecumenical thought and enterprise and are international in scope. They bear directly upon both the nature of the church and the conception of both the nature and the way of salvation. In fact, they challenge and notably reject older ways of view-

ing salvation itself. And these trends are represented both within Protestant and Roman Catholic circles at home and abroad.

II

It is my premise, in the following account of some aspects of current
theology, that the ecumenical movement from around 1920 to 1960
was favored by a rising curve of theological or doctrinal consensus,
interdenominational and international in scope. It was undergirded
by a renaissance in biblical studies—first Protestant and then Catholic—
that provided a powerful and constructive background for collaboration at the level of practical churchmanship. If we must, we can "tag"
it, but at the risk of oversimplification, as a revival of classical Christian
theology which some called "neo-orthodoxy." And we can identify
the period, roughly, as the forty years between 1920 and 1960.

My second premise would be that since 1960 the noted undergirding
emergent doctrinal consensus has dwindled and that its place has been
taken by a variety of militant theological platforms both to the "right"
and to the "left." To a great extent both are nonecclesiological in
temper—the "left" of high visibility, vehement sociological awareness,
and sociotherapeutic concern.

As a species, the movements of the "left" may possibly be grouped
together under the general title "renewal theology," whose criterion
of truth is "relevance"; or perhaps, better, they may be described
methodologically as falling under the caption "contextual theology."
By the latter is meant that what is taken to have survival value in
Christian faith is what is required of it, or relevent in it, to meet the
real or avowed needs of mankind in its life in this world, and now.

Let me attempt a sketch of this species of current religious thought
by examining a principal source and some "spinoffs." Of its current
general aspect let this characterization of Melvin Maddocks from the
editorial page of the *Daily American*, published in Rome for September
20, 1975, be introductory:

The very word theology seems to be an embarrassment these days. . . . In
short, theology appears to be of value only as it becomes a partner—and a
junior partner at that—to an ideology of the moment. With an eagerness that
can sometimes be courageous, sometimes plain embarrassing, theology has
hitchhiked on board all the "revolutions" from civil rights to sexual. Almost
apologetically the men and women of God have begged leave from the arbiters
of the time—the psychologists, the sociologists—to contribute a "religious dimension" to whatever the problem in hand.

Having described the apparent syndrome, Maddocks asks: "Do the men and women of God have no options except either to fade into obsolescence. . . . Or else to become a pathetic me-too tag-along of all the new paganisms?"

That I take to be a fair question. Let us review in part the emergence and the development of this "theological" standpoint, that seems to thrive by riding the waves of popular dissent pertaining to some *bona fide* unresolved ills of our time. Let us remember, too, that the viewpoint of these theologies is primarily contextual. The contextual standpoint is a way of thinking. One way to put it is: the world of human affairs is chaotic and needs management; has Christianity anything relevant to offer? Can we use it effectually to meet and resolve the problems of human life today? What this turns out to be is veridical Christian doctrine.

III

Casting one's eye over the spectrum of recent Christian thought, I judge it was Dietrich Bonhoeffer, as rediscovered and interpreted in the mid-fifties, whose *Letters and Papers from Prison* brought the principle of "contextuality" into startling currency as a theological principle. What was done with Bonhoeffer is not necessarily to be identified fully with his own intentions. That will forever be debatable. His final words to his contemporaries were necessarily cryptic, and he was afforded no opportunity for subsequent explication.

It is fairly clear that Bonhoeffer was committed to the view that man finds God and is found of him in the inescapable moral decisions of historical human existence. (His followers have said: *only* in these.) Accordingly, it is clear also that he was impatient with all interpretations of Christian faith that tolerated indifference to the human state of affairs wherein God acts. The theology of the day, in either the Barthian or Bultmannian form, propagated, it seemed to Bonhoeffer, an irresponsible other-worldly eschatology that was really unbiblical.

In the early forties he faced and made a decision for tyrannicide, and this too was in starkest contrast with historic Lutheran Church policy and practice of nonadjudication and/or interference with the affairs of state. But these affairs were in 1940 in the hands of monsters and had reached a level of demonic depravity that, for Bonhoeffer, could no longer go unopposed. He evidently became a coconspirator for assassination of Hitler.

Bonhoeffer's *Letters* covertly explicate and, perhaps, even understandably rationalize his momentous, utterly dedicated, but, to him, morally terrifying decision for this paradoxical Christian vocation. It was the *context* that commanded what was required of Christian discipleship, and it was costly.

Dying a hero in the cause of apparent righteousness, he became, perhaps, by accident of history rather than by intention, the martyred progenitor in modern times of something like Christian revolutionary action and, at least, an implicit ethic of Christian revolution. In addition, as a critic of all self-maintaining and vocationally moribund ecclesiasticism, he seemed to many—stirred by his total dedication—to foster what became the new, and still widely prevailing, dogma of "religionless Christianity." While much was doubtless packed into this phrase by Bonhoeffer, what was unpacked was mainly threefold: (1) a presumed contempt for cloistered worship of the altar; (2) a presumed irrelevancy of justification by faith as the way of salvation; and (3) a conception of Christian mission wholly dedicated to societal renovation as the purpose of God for history and the real meaning of Christian eschatology.

Attending these propositions were corollaries that seemed to commend themselves for serious and questing Christians who came under Bonhoeffer's influence and mystique. One of them of wide acceptance was a budding conception of the Church that flourished first among Dutch theologians. Rightly understood, the Church is wholly and essentially *mission* and not soul-saving in the traditional senses. The emphasis here was captioned later in the title of J. C. Hoekendijk's book, *The Church Inside Out* (1964) and echoed by Colin Williams's *Where in the World?*, that is, where *in* the world is the Church? (1963). The latter study, while not an official publication of the National Council of Churches, was an outgrowth of New Delhi's (1961) call for a long range study of "evangelism and mission" on the premise that "the present form of church life is a major hindrance to . . . evangelism"— a word notoriously undefined! Both these volumes supported the view that the vocation of the Church and of the Christian individual is to be *in* the world—where the action is. To deghettoize the Church came to be viewed as the preeminent task of the day and the justifying rationale for being truly Christian.

A second corollary accompanied these findings with the positive program that the mission of the Chruch is to "let the world provide the agenda." F. D. Davies, writing in his *Dialogue With the World* (London, 1967), understands mission "as the term which describes the activity of God in the world" (p. 10). Mission is the work of reconciliation, he thinks, and is concerned with "overcoming industrial disputes, surmounting class divisions, with the eradication of racial discrimination" (p. 14). Evangelism that is concerned with conversion and "individual salvation" not only creates a "religious enclave" but perpetuates a non-Christian dualism between the sacred and profane—a view which became dogma for many and still is.

A third corollary may be summarily stated. It has to do with the *how* of mission in the megalopolitan society. High in the list of ways and means, according to Harvey Cox, is "the stewardship of power." To this exercise the Church is invited, whether that stewardship take the form of Black Power or, possibly, Gay power, or Women's Lib power. Or, with greater plausibility among some present-day Latin American expositors, stewardship may implement violent revolutionary political power in the cause of justice to the oppressed masses stubbornly deferred. Having attained to this stage, of course, theology may with candor be called, as it now is by some protagonists, "political theology," or more euphemistically, "liberation theology." Allied with these are "third," and lately, "fourth world theology." We now seem to arrive at the point in theology of which Melvin Maddocks, as we noted, both chided and complained, viz., "theology has hitchhiked on board all the 'revolutions' from civil rights to sexual." Nor, perhaps, is it strange, therefore, that the "quota system" applied to theology, has pluralized the theological task very nearly beyond recognition. Indeed, it becomes increasingly doubtful that its full-time practitioners can agree on what it is *about*.

Such in briefest sketch is the course and shape of the so-called "renewal theology," which has wide journalistic billing among us, and which may be said, I believe, to find its inspiration, in part, from Bonhoeffer's somewhat ambiguous apologetic for "religionless Christianity." In his personal and profoundly moral agony, Bonhoeffer, I believe, was obliged to understand organized Christianity not as an end in itself nor, as happens so often in German Lutheran and other orthodoxy, as largely the means of grace for strictly personal salvation; rather, he was obliged to understand its social vocation in action. Granted his irrevocable commitment and his open-eyed expectancy of the maximum and immanent "cost of discipleship" for himself, he could scarcely fail to accent his well-established conviction that the business of the Church and the Christian vocation, in such a world as this, is a call to alliance with God in the spirit of the Hebrew prophets, in the renovation of human history. It was for this that he had left England, returned to his homeland in 1941, and made his ultimate and morally terrifying decision to which the late Bishop Bell of Chichester was privy. He had found Old Testament prophecy replete with the vision of moral vocation under God. Every passage of Old Testament prophecy taught that fidelity to God's will was *always contextual*, had the world of human affairs for its context, and that its demands were both categorical and costly.

So Peter Berger got the message and in the late fifties, in *The Noise of Solemn Assemblies,* could easily fasten, as had the Social Gospel before him, upon Isaiah 1:13 f: "Bring no more vain oblations . . . I cannot away with iniquity *and* the solemn meeting . . . Wash you, make you clean; put away the evil of our doings . . . cease to do evil, learn to do well. . . ." Accordingly, Berger exposed the moral irrelevancy of the churches and justifiably, if with commendable discrimination, urged a deghettoizing of the life and work of the Church. Shortly, Gibson Winter made a by-word of "the suburban captivity of the churches," deplored the case, and asked for speedy remedy. A flood of literature followed supportively—pamphleteering on the same themes. These were to become obsessive and, for many, continue to be so and with a ramifying program, antiintellectual in temper, and usually indifferent to or disdainful of the uses of worship and the intramural life of the Christian community. In the sixties the "parish" was out of bounds for serious ministry.

It is not, perhaps, a needful part of my business in this brief paper to assess critically the substance of "contextual" or "renewal theology" as a theological movement. Our interest is directed rather to the impact of contemporary theological trends upon the now quiescent ecumenical movement. Yet the impact can be better understood if we attempt to summarize the import of this theology and so be better positioned to calculate its implications for that movement.

One thing is quite fundamental, although it is often tacitly presupposed and expounded openly mainly by the European expositors of this viewpoint, among them Metz and Moltmann. What is involved here is an "antimetaphysical" philosophy or theology of history. Bonhoeffer was evidently already moving in this direction. We might say that, with some, history *is* reality and the primary, perhaps solitary, province of the divine-human encounter. For some, history is the scene where man meets God *as* ultimate vocation apart from all questions of a hereafter. From this comes the disposition to retire a difference between the sacred and profane, the worldly and the Transcendent. Renewal theology, therefore, participates deeply in the mood of "Christian secularity" and had as logical outcome the "death of God" theology. The point for us may be that renewal theology tends to repudiate the Augustinian conception of "the city of God" as opposed to "the earthly city," together with any remnants of the view that the Christian Church represents on earth its heavenly prototype or is, in an eschatological sense, the pilgrim people of God for whom heaven is their home, as Cyprian first emphasized.

A second thing to observe is that, in sundry measure and degree, each of the varieties of renewal or contextual theology has a disposition to *reduce theology to ethics,* and, indeed, pretty largely to *social* ethics.

In doctrine of the Church, this has the effect of ignoring 'faith and order' and reducing ecclesiology to 'life and work' or to the world's challenge to responsible Christian vocation. Ecclesiologically, as Hoek-endijk saw, this exhausts the being of the Church in mission, as it also pinpoints its real identity and *raison d'être*.

Thus, for example, in his book *Dialogue with the World,* previously mentioned, F. D. Davies holds that the mission of the Church is to establish "shalom" in the world. He does not say so, but, in the Old Testament, *shalom* means both peace and well-being, or the tranquility of well-being. But, now—watch the language—this *shalom* Davies de-clares to be a "social happening." Presumably he means a desired state of human affairs. It follows that the mission of the Church is a vocation with ethical incentive and, basically, a sociological outcome, named *shalom*—the distinctive mark of the earthly Kingdom of God.

Yet one must comment that in the Old Testament *shalom* also may be equated with personal as well as social salvation, or is the sign of salvation. Yet in the Old Testament this fullness of life or salvation is never simply a positive "social happening." To be sure, it is not without its sociality. It is a communal happening, symbolized by covenant, and one to which a transcendent God is partner. It is, therefore, never "secular," contrary to Davies, but always an eschatological event that invokes the transcendent reference to the Creator. Therefore it is pre-cisely the "sacred" in the midst of time and change and man's resilient profaneness.

Let us examine this thinking a little more closely, since this view of Davies that salvation is a "social happening" is greatly characteristic of renewal theology. If salvation is a "social heppening," then we may infer—and indeed Davies encourages us to do so—that this "social happening" is an obligation of the serious Christian. Leaving aside the question of adequacy of our qualifications for this high calling, must we not suppose that it is something that can be managed or maneuvered by psychological and sociological know-how, provided we marshal the required means? Among the means, then, might be sundry power maneuvers. This was the business of the sixties! Could not these be given a measure of legitimacy by invoking the phrase "stewardship of power"? It has a New Testament ring, and we could prosecute the cause under higher authority and with something of the dignity of a divine calling like Amos.

If we inquire more narrowly into the nature of the "social happen-ing" or salvation which prompts our vocation as Christians, we find a remarkable readiness to equate its substance or content with relief from whatever impairs or obstructs being "truly human," or attaining that fulfillment that belongs to man by nature. At this point, we do not seem to be far from the Jeffersonian principle of the inalienable right of all men and women, and others, "to life, liberty, and the pursuit of happiness" or to their chosen style of life. In short, the *desideratum* that should prompt the Christian vocation in this school of thought is usually the vindication of justice and right to be "truly human." The "social happening" to which our vocation is devoted usually does not, however, embrace the "counsels of perfection" of the Sermon on the Mount!

A third and final characteristic of renewal theology in some of its forms may be mentioned only briefly, however important. I mentioned just now the question of our *qualifications* for this mission and vocation that is laid upon us as Christians. I think it is fair to say that contextual theology as a whole has nothing much to say of sin. That is now left to Karl Menninger! Accordingly, it looks askance at anything like conversion, denigrates what it calls proselytism, neglects preaching, and is all but silent either about the sacraments as means of grace or, likewise, what went under the title "justification by faith" in Pauline, Lutheran, or Wesleyan usage. We can, it then appears, vocate from just where we are on condition of motivation.

This is to say that this "theology"—largely untroubled by sin—is ordinarily very short on the Reformation *theologia crucis,* and, in complete accord with its own logic. The work of Christ in the forgiveness of sins and the Pauline newness of life, that once supplied a dimension of transcendence, is a resource for which the contextualist does not, regularly, experience a pressing need. And, furthermore, one of the reasons is that his view of the context of existence is such that evil has become mostly *externalized.* For him man, or woman, or other, is much more nearly a *victim* of circumstances rather than that he is, himself, the problem. Accordingly, nothing is plainer than that "justification by faith through grace" tends to recede as a legalistic archaism, and the historic means of grace—conceived as in the keeping of the Church—are irrelevant to the real problems and issues of man's life in history, which are taken to be external or environmental.

From all of this it should begin to appear what is meant by contextualism in theology. What it amounts to is a method for sifting out the expendable in the Christian tradition and retaining what is salvageable because it is relevant, by adopted standards of human need, taken from the prevailing psychological, sociological, and ethical consensus of the age.

Without hesitancy we may say that this theology is by method and intent a species of age-old Christian apologetics, the besetting temptation of which has always been, since the first century, to acquire self-

assurance about the Faith by equating it with some *au courant* wisdom
of the world and so be justified.

IV

Now then, if we ask how this line of thinking checks out with the
earlier ecumenical movement, the answers are not hard to come by.

In the first place, the ecumenical movement retained—as Vatican
II explicitly reaffirmed—the New Testament view of the Church as
"the pilgrim people of God"; it retained as axiomatic the polar dialectic
between the wisdom of God in Christ and the wisdom of men; it would
view as apostate dissolving the sacred into the profane, and regard
as heretical the reduction of the theology of the cross to ethics. It
would regard with profound suspicion any conception of Christian
vocation unshaped and unempowered either by justifying faith or the
sacramental means of grace. And Faith and Order at Lund in 1952
or Oberlin in 1957 would have agreed.

In the second place, whereas the ecumenical movement was, at
the center, cutting its teeth and wrestling with problems of "faith
and order" while not leaving "life and work" unattended, contextual
theology is wholly engrossed in "life and work" and largely indifferent
and sometimes contemptuous of most matters relating to "faith and
order." The latter concerns tend to be regarded as irrelevant to real
human problems. Faith is known by its works. Concerns for order—
polity, ministry, and the means of grace—bespeak a ghettoized Christianity preoccupied with itself rather than with human affairs that
cry out for better management and alleviation. Moreover, if the Chruch
is not "the communion of the saints" but, primarily, a handy instrument
of social amelioration and control, then its destiny is not to preserve
its identifiable unity but to make itself unnecessary in whole-souled
identification with the world's renovation. Behind these fascinating
half-truths lies the premise, with the serious expositors, that History
is all the reality there is and that, in its perfecting, God is "aborning"
and, perhaps, that Christians are stewards of "the future of God." In
short, this theology recurrently shows the signs of a "Christianized"
humanism.

One might go on, if time were not finite in its given manifestations.
What it comes to with reference to the earlier ecumenical movement
may be this: in the perspective of renewal or contextual theology, in
some of its current varieties, the faith and order segment of the ecumenical movement is patently rendered banal and superfluous. Practi-

cally all that remains is life and work. But this, in turn, is reduced to the status of an ethical vocation with sociological ends that has hardly any grounding in what either historic Protestantism or Catholicism has understood by Christian faith or its foundation.

If and so far as these things are true and indicate something of the theological climate of this time, then it is so far understandable why it may be true that the earlier ecumenical movement is presently passing under a cloud. Finally, in the light of such theological developments as we have briefly surveyed, the question emerges as to what could justify the older thrust of the ecumenical movement toward the reunion of the churches, i.e., *if* the churches have as their mission to make themselves unnecessary in a world destined to secularize the sacred in that far off divine event—"the future of God"—toward which the whole "creation" presumably moves?

ASPECTS OF CHRISTIAN DOCTRINE

WORSHIP AS ACKNOWLEDGMENT

I. THE ROOTS OF WORSHIP

To speak authentically of worship is always to point beyond man to the Mystery overarching his existence. It is also to say something important concerning man. It is to speak of something that properly does not pertain to the birds of the heaven, to the beasts, or to the lilies of the field. Devoid of option and, therefore, the anxiety of ambivalence, these creatures unresistingly glorify their Maker in the unfolding of the potentialities of their being. Only to man is reserved the option and the freedom to resist the *conatus* of his being by centering his existence in his own will to self-affirmation and so to incur the gnawing anxiety, the guilt of unacknowledged dependency.[1] In his dreadful freedom, which is also his possible glory, man daily confronts and makes his decision. It is a choice between apparent fulfillment through self-assertion or true fulfillment through acknowledgment of responsible dependency.

To speak of worship, then, is to speak of the uniquely human alternative to self-affirmation. It is, to use a phrase of Jonathan Edwards, "consent to Being." But, unlike the "consent" of the other creatures, worship is man's witting and wholly voluntary consent. Without it man's self-consciousness tends toward alienation from Being and the anxiety of self-imposed privacy. Worship is the overcoming of alienation and the establishment of community through consent to Being, first to the Being of God, and, through Him, consent to the being and inherent worth of the creatures.

With some ages and cultures, the integral place accorded to worship was testimony that the whole of man's story is not exhausted in an account of his external relations. It implied that the whole of man's business is not with "the world" but with reality that does not lie-to-hand and is not manageable but must, nevertheless, be reckoned with. In such a context, worship is the implied acknowledgment that, however strenuously man shapes his ends, he is, nevertheless, often mysteriously overruled. Call it *moira*, fate, or *nemesis*, or call it *logos*, man is sensible of a destiny not of his own shaping and an order not of

Here reprinted with permission of The Oxford University Press. An essay from the volume *Worship in Scripture and Tradition*. Essays by members of the Theological Commission on Worship (North American Section 1952–1963) of the Commission on Faith and Order of the World Council of Churches, ed. M. H. Shepherd. (New York: Oxford University Press, 1963).

his own ordering. Worship signifies his acknowledgment that the apparent configuration of things and events, rather than being the powers with which he deals, are manifestations of deeper lying powers or of a Power of decisive moment with which he ultimately deals.

But the powers, or Power, that are half-hidden and half-revealed in the appearances inspire awe and are shrouded in sublimity and evoke both reverence and homage. This acknowledgment, this consent to Being, not simply to beings, inaugurates and sustains new dimensions of experience. On the one hand, it is the dimension of the *noumenous* in so far as all that is immediately given is apprehended as emerging from and dissolving again in mystery worthy of reverence. But it is also the dimension of responsibility, that is, responsibility for something and to something quite other than all that is entailed in man's aboriginal impulse to manage and utilize the immediate appearances in the attainment of sensuous satisfactions. It is responsibility to a good that does not yet appear and to truth that, only half disclosed, remains to be revealed. Herewith is invoked a sense of loyalty to imperatives whose credentials, still bafflingly obscure, are not thereby less commanding. And herewith the hitherto unchallenged and impulsive bent to manage and control the environment for immediate ends is confronted by an imperious counterclaim that serves notice of its authority and lays man under obligation.

Man's consent to the higher sovereignty, though halting and partial, is worship or nascent worship. Its onset is a sign, *semeion*, of man's dawning awareness of a new irrevocable and basic ambiguity within his existence as *humanum*. As a responsible being, he has acquired a transphenomenal reference, that is, by accepting, however partially, answerability to the good that does not yet appear and the truth that is yet to be revealed. For him, time *(chronos)* is no longer the endurance of fulfillment as with the creatures. Time is the interval between his election and the fulfillment of his vocation. It becomes *kairos,* the time for decision. Under claim, he is laid hold of, acquires subjectivity, and so becomes a person. Thenceforth his relations to Being are personal relations. In him, history has supervened upon mere nature, *kairos* upon *chronos,* self-consciousness upon consciousness, conscience upon science.

Worship is the matrix of this transformation. Man may still view himself as of the earth, earthy, but his conversation is somehow in heaven. He can withhold conversation, he can cease to converse; that is always the option of his freedom, but he cannot wholly stifle the presentiment that he has been addressed and that his chief business is to make responsible answers. If he attenuates conversation, if his consent to Being grows to be halting and is withheld, if worship goes cold within him, then he is hung in anxious suspense between the two resident impulses of his personal existence and lives in unresolved inner contrariety, as Socrates described the matter to Callicles.[2] He may continue to traduce and denature his conferred humanity, his responsible personhood, by consenting himself with the management and utilization of the things that lie to hand. Eventually he may become a casual, even a "serene secularist." [3] This is the alternate option open to man's freedom; the other is the fulfillment of worship.

Worship, as consent to Being, defines the way in which man's distinctive nature as personal being is fulfilled. For, in worship, according to biblical language, man hears, heeds, and consents to the divine will and election. On the one hand, election is a summons to action and service; on the other and more fundamentally, it is a summons to enter into a relation best described by the words "I will be their God, and they shall be my people" (Jer. 31:33). Mature worship is acceptance of election which, in turn, constitutes man's fulfillment of being, that is, of being-in-community—fundamentally with God and, derivatively, with men. Worship is responsible existence in which man lives now under the rule of God while yet God's Kingdom remains fully to be revealed. Worship is therefore inherently eschatological in perspective. But true worship is also eschatological existence without constraint, since it is the glad and eager acknowledgment of the claims of the Kingdom. It serves the Lord with fear and yet rejoices with trembling (Ps. 2:11). It cries, "O God, Thou art my God; early will I seek Thee: my soul thirsteth for Thee . . . " (Ps 63:1). The language of worship is prayer; it is a sign of man's apprehension that he stands in the higher Presence and must speak appropriately.

II. THE MODERN ALTERNATIVE TO WORSHIP

Today it must be admitted that worship has dwindling significance for hosts of our contemporaries, even in the churches. For the casual and for the "serene secularist," worship is a word that has dwindling power to impart meaning or to excite interest. Insofar as meaning survives at all, it arouses otiose recollections of archaic churchly usages from which, by some strange alchemy, relevance to actual life has gradually been evacuated. In an age when, it would seem, more respectful heed was given to the affirmation of *The Shorter Catechism*, "the chief end of man is to glorify God and to enjoy him forever," worship might easily possess something like a central place in human culture. But in an age that has rather emphatically adopted the Baconian platform whereby "the kingdom of man founded on the sciences" is reckoned the really plausible end of man,[4] worship will become progressively irrelevant in proportion as the sufficiency of the program and its claims win general acceptance.

One recognizable fact about the recent past is that Bacon's program triumphed. Perhaps the distinguishing fact about the modern world is that the blueprint of human effort sketched in Bacon's *Novum Organum*—along with its method of implementation—has been generally accepted as defining the chief end of man. The "investigation of nature" and the method of "induction" are ways of implementation; and, as Bacon had hoped, they are the principal sources of the fabulous achievements of our present-day technologies.[5]

As Bacon foresaw and urged, technology affords all those "inventions and discoveries" through which man can exercise control over the given world and so exchange his humiliating subserviency for mastery.[6] The "true and lawful goal of the sciences," he declared, "is none other than this: that human life be endowed with new discoveries and powers." [7] Such knowledge is power, and, "by submitting the mind to things," Bacon hoped to "lay more firmly the foundations, and extend more widely the limits of the power and greatness of man." [8] He observed that "blind and immoderate zeal in religion" had long impeded the advance of natural philosophy.[9] But, if, by a proper division of labor, intelligence were directed to God's Work and faith devoted to his Word, no conflict need arise.[10] The range of reason was to be limited by "religion" and all ensuing knowledge was to be "referred to use and action." [11] If it was protested "sense doth discover natural things, but darken and shut up divine," then, in matters of divinity, Bacon is content to rely upon Bible, faith, and religion, thus liberating reason for its proper business.[12] Meanwhile the sciences would assure man's greatest ambition, namely, his "endeavor to establish and extend the power and dominion of the human race itself over the universe." [13] It was a prospect so beneficent in Bacon's eyes as to suggest fulfillment of the promise, "Man is God to man." [14]

Now were opened "horizons unlimited." Herewith humanity was promised emancipation from the fatalities of inscrutable circumstance, relief from the ravages of disease, and some deterrence of the relentless march of time. If, like Bacon, the modern devotee of technological progress does not expressly deny that "the chief end of man is to glorify God," for the most part he is so engrossed with the business that it hardly seems necessary. His denial is practical rather than theoretical. It just does not touch him that the Psalmist exclaims: "Lord, I have no good beyond Thee" (Ps. 16:2) or that another exults: "I will extol Thee, my God, O King; I will bless Thy name forever and ever" (Ps. 145:1). To St. Augustine's entreaty, "Let me know thee, O Lord,

who knowest me: let me know thee as I am known of thee," the Baconian man is a stranger.[15] As a diligent and skillful trafficker in things
visible, Augustine's confession passes him by: "Surely most unhappy
is the man that knows all these things, and is ignorant of thee: but
blessed is he that knows thee, though ignorant of these." [16]

Our age is the latest phase of an epoch which for about three hundred
years has aggressively explored the adequacy of Bacon's program as
the way of human fulfillment and, often unwittingly, as an alternative
to worship. Its chief instrument, technology, is admirably suited to
deal with the manageable, the predictable, and the usable. Its spectacular successes have, in turn, tended to entrench the conviction of both
the ultimacy and the sufficiency of the spatio-temporal order; and,
unexplored, the Transcendent has become progressively unthinkable.
Given this context of existence, human effort is gauged in terms of
efficient utilization of the environment; security is progressive control;
fulfillment is maximum expansion and exploitation. The negations and
limitations incident to physical being are successively overcome. If
man's life continues to be imperiled by the relentlessness of time,
man can at least extend his dominion by expansion, coordination, and
utilization of space. These are the *desiderata* of the Baconian program
for making the most of this world. Utilization has been the shibboleth
and exploitation the prevailing lust. The creatures are admired, but
mainly for use.

Only in an ambiguous sense is it true of this epoch, as St. Paul testified
of his, that men "exchanged the truth of God for a lie, and worshipped
and served the creature rather than the Creator" (Rom. 1:25). The
Baconian spirit may accord to the creature the acknowledgment hitherto reserved for the Creator. It may, as Augustine would have it,
be wholly engrossed with the creatures; but the modern serves them
mainly with a view to their utility. His worship is covertly self-service.
When Western man in the 17th century came to extrude from the
world all divine interposition and resolve providence into laws of nature, thus to make his data wholly predictable, he was contriving the
radical secularization of nature. With respect to nature he ceased to
be husbandman and became entrepreneur. Nature became a thing
for man to exploit. Unlike the ancient idolater, for whom nature was
"full of gods" and worthy of reverence, the modern idolater attends
nature only to serve himself. Thus even in his art he will not consent
to being, that is, to the antecedent structure of nature. The object of
art is dissolved after the imaginations of his own heart and replaced
by the exuberance of his own thirst for self-expression. What he wants
to see in his art is not nature but his reaction to nature. The progressive
nullity of his art is a manifestation of his revolt against being.

Thus the spirit of our time is not consent to antecedent Being but arrogance toward beings, the creatures. The end of man is to be monarch of all he surveys. The world lies to hand to use and to possess. To this extent man accepts as he distorts the divinely conferred "dominion over the fish of the sea, over the birds of the heavens, over the cattle, over the earth, and over every creeping thing . . ." (Gen. 1:26). But, plainly, this is not the biblical dominion. The latter is responsible dominion. It is known to be delegated, and the delegation of authority is acknowledged, first of all, in consent to Being.

The science of efficient utilization has been the undeclared messiah of Baconian secularism—the efficient management of spatial arrangements and resident powers of this world. It is the optimal utilization of space-time within the ineluctable limitation of the one-directional flow of time or biological duration. Whereas unsophisticated man, as Bacon complained,[17] capitulated too soon to the inscrutable and unmanageable restrictions of his existence and uncritically confounded the apparently unmanageable with the ultimately unmanageable, modern man begins by making a careful distinction. To the limits of his ingenuity, his aim is to manage the manageable and let the unmanageable take care of itself, that is, to endure it. This is secularism. It is the disposition to consent to Being only in its manageable appearances, and then to *assume,* rather than to *affirm,* that the appearances exhaust the sum of Being that man can or need know and with reference to which he can be gainfully employed. For these reasons worship is a word that, for the secularist, has become progressively devoid of meaning.

There is almost no way out of the circle of this mentality save through it. The destiny of modern man appears to be yet further exploration of his limited sovereignty until he is starkly and despairingly aware of its limitations. The conquest, the maximal utilization of space, with its reshaping and reorganization, will go on within the unconquerable delimitations of human biological time and private duration. But conquest takes time, more time than is given to any person, to any nation, to any people, to our planet. *Chronos* is our enemy, and, at the *finis,* there is only the ultimate enduring—the travail of the whole creation waiting vainly to be "delivered from the bondage of corruption." The alternative is worship, the consent of the human creature to the Creator. In this context, time may be seen as the indomitable manifestation of absolute Sovereignty with respect to which all human dominion is dependent and derivative. In this perspective, time is not the finality of endurance or the endurance of finality but the interval of God's self-revealing. For time is man's enemy, as the ancient myth has it, unless, as a signature of a more divine sovereignty, it prompts him to acknowledge the Eternal through its incontrovertible notice of the limits of all human duration.

The well-explored alternative to worship is, it may be said, the final endurance of meaninglessness. If the chief end of man is not to glorify God, then for Baconian man—and after all maximal utilization of space—his proper *finis* is the embracement of nothingness as his terminal gesture of resignation to the uncomprehended and uncomprehending enigma of his being anything at all. On the other hand, if St. Paul was right, as Augustine believed, that "the invisible things of him [God] since the creation of the world are clearly seen, being perceived [i.e. perceivable] through the things that are made," then a standpoint does exist wherein the creation prompts to worship rather than simply to exploitation. To recover this standpoint, to subordinate utilization to consent to the being and intrinsic worth of the creatures is, perhaps, once again to stand on the threshold of worship. For, in such a standpoint, there is implicit acknowledgment of the limits of human sovereignty. This, in turn, may issue in man's acceptance of responsibility for the exercise of such sovereignty as he is entrusted with.

God is perhaps first known as the Limit set to man's dominion and his limitless will to dominion. Worship is nascent in the acceptance of limitation. It is maturing in the acceptance of responsibility for the uses of freedom. It is perfected in the constant subordination of self-affirmation to God-affirmation. Therefore, fulfilled worship is perfect obedience. From the standpoint of Christian faith, this is shown forth in the ministry of Jesus Christ; and, from that vantage point, all other worship is participation in that ministry. For the Christian, worship is acknowledgment of God through the mediating vehicle of "the full, perfect, and sufficient Sacrifice."

III. TOWARD FULFILLMENT OF WORSHIP

Worship, as has been summarily affirmed, is "acknowledgment of Transcendence." [18] The cogency of this claim is best seen by contrasting its import with the spirit and program of Baconian secularism in its full-orbed modern expressions. Transcendence, as Karl Heim long since pointed out, is precisely what contemporary man vainly strives to credit and ends by despairing of.[19] Worship, then, is easily the vocation of theonomous man, but he has become a declining species. In his place have arisen varieties of autonomous men who, deprived of transcendent reference and roots, are reduced to the initially exciting, but at length terrifying, destiny of promulgating the Law to themselves and determining the norms of truth, beauty, and goodness.

In the ensuing extremity of relativism and pansubjectivism, the various positivisms of the past century resorted to the expedient of redefining truth as the measurable and the useful, beauty as "significant form" that grasps one, goodness as the greatest good of the greatest number. Objectivity survived only in the sciences of measurement. In the sphere of human relations, morality was negotiable, as the conception of natural law, rooted in the *Logos* structure of Being, was replaced by the positive law of competitive nations. Where balancing of competitive claims proves infeasible, there has been but one appeal, as Plato long ago anticipated, namely, to that of superior power. Baconianism led to secularism and utilitarianism, the latter to positivism; and, all together led to the banishment of the Transcendent reference. So, as we find him today, modern man is struggling in his own power to establish a new positive law of nations, a "world rule of law," resting upon the consent of the governed, but on a world-wide basis. This is man's surviving and desperate hope, deprived as he is of the Transcendent and sentenced to his awful autonomy. The alternative to this may be the recovery of the Transcendent and, therewith, worship, as aknowledgment of the lawful structure of Being.

The Old Testament is replete with instances of man's temptation and overthrow, the fall by which he replaces a theonomous with an autonomous existence, and worships and serves the creature rather than the Creator. The word of the prophets is everywhere an indictment of idolatry and a call to return from the service of multifarious not-gods to responsible acknowledgment of the one God. Everywhere the prophets enforce the view that the first, the commanding, the finally decisive business of man is the acknowledgment of God. However man might traffic with the creatures and exercise his will over them, he profited from them and exercised his authority under the divine dominion. Thus, the first fruits of the earth and the firstlings of the flock were sacred unto the Lord, and man might not appropriate them without first acknowledging both their derivation and his divine authorization to possess and partake of their bounty. Thus sacrifice was overt acknowledgment of the prior ownership and sovereign goodness of God and also man's acceptance of his stewardship of the creatures.

At its heart, therefore, Old Testament worship was dyadic in nature or double-sided. It entailed, on the one hand, consent to God's sovereign being, majesty, and beneficence. It was praise and thanksgiving in reverence and adoration and in confidence, mingled with awe. But, on its other and empircally weaker side, worship was acceptance of responsibility for the uses of the divine benefits. Thus, a great part of the prophetic criticism was that worship was imperfect insofar as men did not adequately praise God by the way in which they administered their portion of the divine largess. True worship was abridged or nullified in those of whom Amos alleged that they "sold the righteous for silver, and the needy for a pair of shoes" (Amos 2:6), or of whom it was charged, they "trample upon the poor, and take exactions from him of wheat . . ." (Amos 5:11).

To the prophetic mind it was all too apparent that sacrifices of "burnt offerings and meal offerings" were but token and calculated obedience, ostentatiously substituting for the whole of it. Accordingly, Amos and Isaiah concur in declaiming against the "multitude of sacrifices" and the pretentious noise of "solemn assemblies" (Isa. 1:11)—which, in making loud protestations to God, presume to distract his attention from the shoddiness of men's common lives. Against this subterfuge, that is mainly self-deception, there is sounded the divine imperative: "Let justice roll down as waters, and righteousness as a mighty stream" (Amos 5:24). Or Isaish admonishes: "Wash you, make you clean, put away the evil of your *doings* from before mine eyes; cease to do evil; learn to do well; seek justice, relieve the oppressed, judge the fatherless, plead for the widow" (Isa. 1:16–17).

Contrary to an earlier mode of interpretation, this message of prophecy is not to be regarded as outright repudiation of sacrifice as such— sacrifice considered as appropriate acknowledgment of the divine favor. It is, rather, radical criticism of sacrifice in as much as it proffers itself as substitute for the whole of worship, namely, for that entire responsibility under God which acknowledges not only the Giver but the Giver's intention for the right use of the gift. Sacrifices were abominations in so far as they were, wittingly or unwittingly, elaborate devices to disguise incomplete acceptance of the total responsibility that God enjoined. So far forth, sacrifice was "phoney" worship, the counterfeit of entire devotion, and Amos might unleash his irony: "Come to Beth-el, and transgress; to Gilgal, and multiply transgression; and bring your sacrifices every morning. . . . for this pleaseth *you*, O ye children of Israel, saith the Lord!" (Amos 4:4, 5). It was plain to Amos that the dust raised by professional worship and intended for God's eyes is actually blinding only to those of the worshippers.

It is, perhaps, from this standpoint that we may see more narrowly into the substance of the *apocalypsis* which overwhelmed Isaiah in the Temple. Only the threefold seraphic *sanctus* could denote the unutterable Holiness which, unveiled to him, disclosed the uncleanness of all things human and shattered every presumption of the adequacy of man to find favor with God in his own strength. Supported by the whole array of the resplendent cultus round about him, neither the prophet nor his people could stand unrefined before the withering

fire of the divine sanctity. Rudolf Otto once described this Presence
of Holiness as the *mysterium tremendum* charged with indefectible
moral rectitude. From Isaiah's own testimony, in the presence of the
Holy Other, the profanity and uncleanness both of the prophet and
of his people were revealed by sharpest contrast. Nothing now, not
even the cultus of the Temple, could obscure the fundamental contrariety and alienation of man's being from the goodness of sanctity by
which he was confronted. The confrontation was negation. Thus, in
the presence of God, man's acknowledgment must first of all take
the form of contrition and repentance. But the Holy One not only
negates, He also reaffirms through cleansing, as fire that destroys also
refines and purifies in refining. And, with cleansing, there is renewal,
and with renewal there is acceptance of responsibility commensurate
with the Holiness that bestows pardon. Thereupon comes the consciousness of election: "Whom shall I send, and who will go for us?
Then I said, Here am I; send me" (Isa. 6:8).

We may be permitted to believe that through Isaiah's shattering
and renewing experience in the Temple, Old Testament worship took
a momentous step toward delocalization, moralization, and dematerial-
ization. Far off down the same road, worship was to be "in spirit and
in truth." Worship was no longer to be gifting of gifts, but entire responsibility based upon a prior acceptance of forgiveness and transformation
of being. Worship was to become the giving up of oneself. Worship
could no longer be a bargaining through which, by acknowledging
primary dependency upon God, men could forestall additional and
unwanted claims. Worship was now the entailment of the whole man,
not the meted out apportionment of his goods in "the nicely calculated
lore of more or less." [20] Worship meant entire obedience or conformity
of life to the sanctity of goodness by which man is confronted. Worship
was on the way to becoming in the words of the Edwardian liturgy,
"the full, perfect, and sufficient sacrifice." It was on the way to becoming what we may call, awkwardly no doubt, *enpersonalized*. This obtains in the measure that man's acknowledgment of God commandeers
his whole life and action. As consent to God's being, it is also consent
to the kind of Being God is. But it is more: worship becomes enpersonalized when the injunction "ye shall be holy as I am holy" has become
a personal aspiration in process of realization. In this emphasis, the
"priestly tradition" perpetuates the meaning of Isaiah's revelation.[21]

Enpersonalization of worship means what is plainly implied in Calvin's words, "true worship consists in obedience alone." [22] But "obedience alone" is fundamental conformity between the will to adore and
the will to conform the life to the Adored. It is assimilation of the
whole life to the likeness of Him who is magnified.

Thus, worship has always two aspects or, as it were, two directions. As, in the case of Isaiah, it exalts the Holiness of God and, then, cleansing following upon repentance, it brings "forth fruits worthy of repentance." [23] It is the inseverable connection between these two moments that constitutes authentic worship. This the prophets saw, and they resisted every separation of the two. With similar understanding, the classic words of the psalmist enforce the point: "For thou delightest not in sacrifice, else would I give it. Thou hast no pleasure in burnt offerings. The sacrifices of God are a broken spirit: A broken and a contrite heart, O God, thou wilt not despise" (Ps. 51:16–17). Worship is the penitential commitment of the whole life. Gone forever is the notion that worship is a certain measure of theonomy through which man reserves a measure of his autonomy. Wherever autonomy is reserved worship is imperfect and, in varying degree, idolatrous. The prophets perceived that the prevailing sacrificial cult, as a substitute for entire obedience, was a device for reserving man's autonomy to himself and, therefore, partook of essential idolatry.

The outcome is, then, that the prophetic invective against sacrifice and the attendant call to righteousness actually rested upon a deeper understanding of sacrifice itself. Sacrifice is the obedience of the whole life, the sacrifice of "a broken and a contrite heart," at once abased and exalted, by an overpowering awareness of the divine Holiness. True worship becomes magnifying God's will by doing it or revering his Holiness in being conformed to his image. Its aspiration is expressed by the prayer of General Thanksgiving: ". . . that we may show forth thy praise, not only with our lips, but *in our lives,* by giving up ourselves to thy service, and walking before thee in holiness and righteousness all our days. . . ." It is the disparity between lip-service and life-service which is the recurring temptation of every established cultus, whereby it earns the displeasure of God and the eventual contempt of men.

Among the reformers, Calvin is notable for his insistence that true worship is obedience to both tables of the Law. While this may have issued in the legalistic excesses of later Puritanism, Calvin's instinct was reliable. Worship is first of all entire obedience or consent to the sovereign Being of God. It is fulfillment of the first commandment, summarized in the *Shema:* "Hear, O Israel, the Lord our God is one Lord: and thou shalt love the Lord thy God with all thy heart, and with all thy soul, and with all thy might" (Deut. 6:4). Since God is one, his proper acknowledgment entails a corresponding unification of the whole life around and upon its divine center. Worship, appropriate to the one God, can tolerate no competitors. But worship possesses a complementary aspect because the one God is a gracious God, which is to say that entire consent to God's sovereignty is also consent to his gracious intention toward the creatures and, among the creatures, other men. Entire obedience, therefore, embraces the second table of the Law and enjoins, as Isaiah perceived, conduct of life in righteousness. This is epitomized in the "second commandment" of our Lord: "Thou shalt love thy neighbor as theyself" (Matt. 22:39). The whole of worship is entire obedience to the two commandments—not complementary, merely, but inseparable.

This is, of course, the plainest import of the emphasis upon the "new commandment" in the Johannine writings. To worship the Father "in spirit and in truth" is almost certainly to unite love of God and love of man in such a fashion as that the one without the other is inconceivable. So to be understood is the startling declaration of the First Epistle: "If a man say, I love God, and hateth his brother, he is a liar" (1 John 4:20). The full exhibition of perfect obedience is reserved for the New Testament. It involves sacrifice, the sacrifice of all reservation of man's autonomy to theonomy.

The aspiring failure of worship under the old covenant is plain to Jeremiah, who looked forward to the fulfillment of true worship under a new covenant that God would yet establish: "But this is the covenant that I will make with the house of Israel after those days, saith Jehovah: *I will put my law in their inward parts, and in their heart will I write it;* and I will be their God, and they shall be my people" (Jer. 31:33). So the prophet looks to the day when the acknowledgment of God is not enjoined upon men but springs naturally from a resident impulse imparted by God's Spirit. He looks to a time when service of God issues from and invokes the whole man in personal response. Herein real community between God and man exists, in the Law written on the heart, in openness to and answerable existence under God. To say that such worship is enpersonalized is to say that worship has become community between man and God—love answering to love.

IV. THE FULFILLMENT OF WORSHIP

Somewhat plainly, the indication of this essay is that there is no radical discontinuity between worship in the Old Testament and that in the New; there is only the incomprehensible "mystery of Godliness" which is the impenetrable mystery of the fulfillment of true worship in Jesus Christ. This, of course, is not to say that there are not all kinds of discontinuity between the prevailing cultic practices of postexilic Judaism and the worship that gradually emerged in Christ's name, the worship of the early church. Enormous differences there were that admit of meticulous delineation by those who make a business of these matters. Mooted may be the question of Jesus' attitude toward the Temple worship and sacrifice. Less questionable is the issue of his disposition toward the scribal refinements of the Law. But one thing is plain in the light of his own ministry: he came not to destroy the Law and the prophets but to fullfill them (Matt. 5:17). If worship is properly understood as to its essence in the Old Testament, namely, as wholly responsible existence under God, as love to God and acceptance of God's will for the neighbor, or, if worship is understood as sacrifice of the self entire to the divine purpose, then it is manifest that, as our Lord fulfilled in his own ministry the two commandments "on which the whole law hangeth and the prophets" (Matt. 22:40), he also fulfilled in his own person the meaning of worship or true service to God. But he did not reject sacrifice; he embodied it so that in him there is the final enpersonalization of worship. The truth in sacrifice he conserved and so fulfilled; its profusion of pretentious objectivities, overlaying and obscuring its essential validity, he rejected without commment. Our Lord perceived what the prophets had adumbrated, that cultus can be substitutional objectification of an act which, properly, can only be a personal commitment, that the sacrifices of God are a broken spirit, and a humble and a contrite heart.

This sublimely lucid but basically simple comprehension of the meaning of man's service to God was to constitute the mastering motive of Jesus' existence. Worship is simply life that, in entire trustfulness, is given back into the hands of Him who gave it. But what is moderately simple to understand becomes thereafter, in the ministry and death of Jesus Christ, the miracle of its being enacted.

As the author of Hebrews so well understood, all surrogates of true sacrifice—the blood of goats and bulls, the altar, the veil, the Temple itself—are outward images of the fulfilled sacrifice of Christ who, once for all, offered up himself (Heb. 7:27). In Christ, sacrifice is enpersonalized. No longer a transaction *without*, in relation to which every man may remain safely a spectator, in Christ sacrifice is enacted all the way from acceptance of Sonship, entire serviceability, in his baptism, through the temptation of the whole wilderness way of his mortal days, to the final commitment of Gethsemane and the death of the Cross. And, with it all, there was a community with the Father and assimilation to his likeness that has left mankind through the ages utterly astonished and hung between incredulity and adoration. Far from being Platonist, the author of Hebrews understands with unexampled clarity that Christ gave sacrifice its personal embodiment and therefore its historical reality by contrast with which all outward sacrifices are but poor and partial images of the true. Henceforth the sacrifice of the altar is but a symbol of the sufficient sacrifice, the sacrifice of human autonomy without reservation.

Viewed in the perspective of Jesus' own proclamation of the Kingdom and his call to men to enter it by way of *metanoia* and acceptance of its rigorous demands (Luke 14:26–27, 33), Jesus' sacrifice may be interpreted as his own unfaltering decision, at every step of the way, to be wholly the Son to the Father. But the historical life of the elect One was existence in continuing temptation, while in every moment, from his baptism to Gethsemane, his victory over temptation was through steady acknowledgment of the Father's sovereign will. Thus, his ministry was service to God through victory in continuing temptation, so that, in the shadow of the Cross, he could say to his disciples, "Ye are they that have continued with me in my temptations" (Luke 22:28). And, in the same moment, he had declared, "but I am in the midst of you as he that serveth" (Luke 22:27).

Refusal to accept "the transvaluation of values" explicit in this passage and that of Mark 10:42 ff., as grounded in the most primitive gospel tradition, is to render the emergence as well as the peculiar offense of Christianity unintelligible. "Whosoever would be great among you shall be your minister *(diakonos)*, and whosoever would be first . . . shall be servant *(doulos)* of all," and "the Son of Man came not to be ministered unto but to minister. . . ." That these words embody the *scandalon* of the Gospel was plain equally to St. Paul and to Nietzsche. That their inherent logic is the Cross is also evident. That Jesus' baptism meant serviceability unto death is still visible in his words," I have a baptism to be baptized with; and how am I straitened till it be accomplished" (Luke 12:50). Thus the meaning of baptism is ministry, and the issue of ministry is sacrifice, that is, if we are to understand our Lord's service in the context of the ancient Hebrew *leitourgia,* and we can hardly avoid it.

As heirs of the Enlightenment and its aftermath, we moderns are virtually incapable of attaining to the realism of Jesus respecting the warfare between God and anti-god as constituting the basic antinomy of human existence. Therefore, we fail to credit Jesus with the lucid realization that, in the showdown with intrenched and acculturated demonic forces, the destiny of unarmed righteousness is death. In this world there is no place for Christ save as the Christ who overcomes the world, and save as a Power greater than that for which the world makes a place. Death can be victory only as it is *self*-sacrifice, offered unto God on behalf of those in bondage to fear of death. Likewise a place is made only through the perfect obedience, the apparent defeat, of the one man Jesus Christ. To the early Church these things signified the establishment of the "new covenant" and included realized community between God and man as the now accomplished *desideratum* of the ages. It was effected through the perfect *latreia* or ministry of Jesus called Christ.

The worship of the early Church was determined and shaped by the impact of this configuration of events upon those who, as witnesses, also received it in faith. If we are permitted to make a somewhat artificial differentiation, it was rather more the fulfilled mission of Jesus than his message which evoked faith. The remembered message more or less adequately, no doubt, illuminated "the mystery of Godliness" that he embodied; but in retrospect it was the total deed-event that evoked faith; and so entirely did his life embody the bearing of his own words that message and mission resolved into an abiding and redemptive unity. For the faith of the early Church, the unity was the ministry of Jesus, an unreserved stewardship of the whole of life. In it the true *latreia* of God was fulfilled, for the Law was fulfilled in its two modal aspects. Here was the ministry of the new covenant, not of the letter but of the Spirit.[24]

The faith that perceives this does so in the perspective of the history of redemption against the background of the imperfect *leitourgia* of the old covenant of which earlier prophecy served continual notice. The public rehearsal of the aberrations of traditional worship made Stephen the first Christian martyr. In his declaration, "Howbeit the Most High dwelleth not in *houses* made with hands," he joins himself not only to the ancient protest of prophecy but, we are bound to believe, gives earliest expression to the emerging Christian understanding that God resists domestication in any house save in the heart of living men.[25] Therefore, in the same letter to the Corinthians in which St. Paul speaks of "epistles" (i.e. testaments) written not in tables of stone "but in tables that are hearts of flesh" (3:3), he also speaks of the new people as "a temple of the living God; even as God said, I will dwell in them, and walk in them; and I will be their God, and they shall be my people." [26]

For Paul, the true *leitourgia* of God is a life of faith, a life indwelt by the Spirit of Christ that shows forth "the fruits of the Spirit" (Gal. 5:22). Accordingly, essential worship is suggested in Paul's entreaty to the Romans: "I beseech you therefore, brethren, by the mercies of God, to present your bodies *a living Sacrifice*, holy, acceptable to God, which *is* your reasonable service" (Rom. 12:1).

How shall we escape the implication that this service is the proper worship of God, since it is participation in the likeness of Christ's ministry of sacrifice? This day-by-day service of living sacrifice—manifesting itself in the righteousness of faith, hope, and love—is to be compared with 1 Peter 2:4–5. Here too Christ is "the *living* stone" to be contrasted with the stones of the earthly Temple. He is rejected of men but elect of God and, in his image, the people of God too are "living stones" who are "built up a spiritual house, to be a holy priesthood, to offer up spiritual sacrifices to God through Jesus Christ" (cf. Heb. 12:28). Herewith the worship of the early Church is seen to be radically enpersonalized. Worship is the service of the whole life.

The outcome seems to be that the worship of the early Church is what it is just exactly through Jesus Christ. It is an image of its original, and its original is none other than the ministry of perfect obedience. Christian worship is participation in the sacrifice of Christ, which supersedes all sacrifices and establishes a new covenantal relationship between God and men.[27] This is the bearing of the Epistle to the Hebrews: "For such a high priest became us, guileless, undefiled, separated from sinners, and made higher than the heavens; who needeth not daily, like those high priests, to offer up sacrifices, first for their own sins, and then for the sins of the people: for this he did once for all, *when he offered up himself*" (Heb. 7:26). St. Paul puts the matter succinctly: "For our passover also hath been sacrificed, even Christ: *wherefore* let us keep the feast, not with old leaven, neither with the leaven of malice and wickedness, but with the unleavened bread of sincerity and truth" (1 Cor. 5:7).

But Christian worship is not simply thanksgiving, although it is never less than that. Nowhere more than in the Johannine writings does it become clear that Christian worship is love answering to love. "We love, because he first loved us" (1 John 4:19). But, further, we cannot love God and fail to love what he loves, namely, the brother (1 John 4:7). Therefore there is the new commandment "that he that loveth God love his brother also" (1 John 4:21). In the new commandment are united the two on which hang the whole Law and the prophets.

But the worship of the early Church contains something more, namely, the *ways* in which the perfect obedience of Christ is appropriated by the believer. If forgiveness of sins and reconciliation to God through Christ are experienced in the early Church, then faith is not simply belief about; it is rather participation in the reconciling and redemptive event itself. This accounts for the centrality both of baptism and of the Lord's Supper in the Church's worship.

In baptism, the one who heeds the Word in repentance is participant in that baptism with reference to which our Lord said he was "straitened till it be accomplished." Thus, St. Paul identifies baptism with the dying of Christ; and in baptism we are united with him in the likeness of his death (Rom. 6:4, 5). While this signifies death to sin, it is at the same time acknowledgment of God in the life. It is intentional recapitulation of Christ's *latreia;* only it is "a living sacrifice."

With the Lord's Supper we also "proclaim the Lord's death till he come" (1 Cor. 11:26). Whatever more the Eucharist may have come to signify, it signified to the early Church the Lord's own invitation, indeed command, to participate with him in his "full, perfect, and sufficient sacrifice." Through such recurrent participation he unites believers to God by the mediation of his own self-offering, and by evoking in them, through his Spirit, the will to self-commitment like to his own. In the Eucharist men are enjoined again and again both to offer up the offering of Christ's perfect obedience and to be themselves wholly conformed to the likeness of his sacrifice.

The worship of the New Testament is celebration of the fullness of sacrifice. It is the unreserved acknowledgment of God accomplished in Jesus Christ and, through him, made possible as the vocation of every man. Worship is living sacrifice, a way of life open to the humble and the contrite heart—but a heart moved to contrition by "the glory of God in the face of Jesus Christ." Christian worship consists of "spiritual sacrifices, acceptable to God through Jesus Christ," that is, acceptable because of his sacrifice and, then, because these sacrifices are images united to his sacrifice. Or, finally, Christian worship is service of God through fellowship *(koinonia)* with, or participation in, Christ's suffering (Phil. 3:8 ff.).

To sum up, in "the full, perfect, and sufficient sacrifice" of Jesus Christ, the whole meaning of the Law is fulfilled, in unfaltering love of God and in unhesitating love of man. This is the enpersonalization of worship; therefore the early Church saw it as God's own deed. God himself set forth this sacrifice to be an "expiation" for sin available to those who received it in faith (Rom. 3:25). The true worshipper is, first, Jesus Christ himself, and true worship is attained for those who, "crucified with Christ," walk in newness of life. This is life in which God's dominion is regnant. It is life in which autonomy is no longer reserved, and in which the stewardship of all of life is acknowledged.

BIBLICAL ELECTION AS SACRED HISTORY

I. THE PARADOX OF ELECTION

As we occupy the vantage point of the New Testament it becomes evident that a "sacred history" of the Bible is inseparably connected with a pervasive paradox that is the substance of the Old Testament itself: the apparent contradiction between Israel's election as the chosen people and the implied universality of God's sovereignty and purpose in world history. The paradox was acknowledged by the late Chief Rabbi of Sweden, Kurt Wilhelm:

Universalism and particularism are . . . inextricably interwoven in Judaism, and it is in the perpetual interpretation of national and religious elements that Judaism itself both consists, and asserts, its own specific God-idea, viz. that the God of Israel is the God of all humanity.[1]

It is noteworthy and significant that no book of the Old Testament surpasses Deuteronomy both in clear acknowledgment and in explicit enforcement of the paradox. As Deuteronomy affirms Israel's election under the Covenant and predicates Israel's life upon obedience to the "ordinances and statutes," it nevertheless propounds openly the paradox throughout its pages, and emphatically, in 4:32–40: since God's creation of man upon the earth, who has heard or when has it happened that the Creator approached and addressed man and he lived? Or took a nation from among the nations for his own—even the Lord God, beside whom there is no other?[2]

This, *in nuce*, is both the core and chief problematic of biblical history. The dynamic inherent in this apparent antithesis has created the mystery of the Hebrew inheritance and the Jewish people to this day. Likewise, however, and perhaps as the resolving fruition of a powerful resident dynamism, it issued in the emergence of the New Testament faith in Jesus Christ that was hailed by St. Paul as "the revelation of the mystery." It is our intention in this study to review the unfolding of this historic dynamism as it at length manifests itself in the preaching witness of the earliest Christian Church. We are proposing to probe the ancient history of what in the 20th century has

Republished here by permission of The Oxford University Press, From *Our Common History as Christians*, Essays in Honor of Albert C. Outler, ed. John Deschner et al. (New York: Oxford University Press, 1975).

been called "ecumenism"—its primordial thrust in the biblical story of man's summons to faithfulness under sovereign grace.

The question about the *Oikoumēne*, as it relates to the Old Testament and to the New, centers on the import of Israel's election as a particular people somehow charged with God's eternal purpose for all mankind. Here if anywhere is the connecting link between Judaism and Christianity. Thus, the Jewish scholar Samuel H. Bergman may be correct:

If what is meant by *Oikoumēne* is the Church of Christ united within itself, then Israel has nothing whatever to say on the subject. If, however, it is to mean "the realm in which the expectation of God obtains" . . . the conception of the *Oikoumēne* becomes a central one for Jewish religious thinking.[3]

II. THE OLD TESTAMENT: ECUMENISM UNFOLDING

Whether, as Bernhard Anderson and Gerhard von Rad have affirmed, the Exodus under Moses definitively marks the election of Israel as Yahweh's own people, or whether it is first signalized, as Martin Buber contends, in the call of Abraham (Gen. 12:1–2),[4] it is with the declaration at Sinai, according to Gerhard von Rad, that Israel remembered corporately Yahweh's choice of her as his "own possession among all peoples" (Exod. 19:3–6).[5] The text singles out Israel as Yahweh's particular possession, while, at the same time, it is the divine universality that accents the singularity—"for all the earth is mine!" Thus, the paradox is illuminated by the implication that the choice of Israel is set within the context of God's sovereignty over all history, with the powerful innuendo that Israel is elect for a role that perhaps a priestly redactor later defined in the words: "And you shall be to me a kingdom of priests and a holy nation" (Exod. 19:6). The immemorial question remains: election for what?

No less a scholar of the Old Testament than H. H. Rowley took the view that "God's choice is never to be understood save in relation to its purpose." [6] But what, according to the Old Testament, is God's purpose? Is it particular or universal? Does it comport with his acknowledged sovereignty over all of history, or is it confined within his special relation to Israel? It is Rowley's view that, even though Israel's election does not exclude privilege, it is fundamentally "election for service." [7] Apparently Von Rad concurs in Rowley's happy phrase that the service in question is "bridging the cleft between God and all mankind." [8]

If this is so, then the apparent contradiction between Israel's election as the chosen people and the implicit universality of God's sovereign purpose is illuminated. Biblical history might then qualify as "sacred history." If election is a divine vocation, then election of a particular people is instrumental to ulterior divine purpose, namely, the sovereignty of God over world history. If, as Bultmann once said of the creation story in Genesis 1, it is "but the first chapter in *history*,"[9] then we may be better prepared to comprehend Paul's teaching about the renovation of the creation in Christ (2 Cor. 5:17) as not discontinuous with the old history, but its long-delayed fulfillment (Rom. 8:22–23).

But, we may ask, does the Old Testament, in its preponderant emphasis, provide for the implementation of God's purpose for the redemption of world history? Repeatedly it is acknowledged that Yahweh is Lord over the nations and may invoke them to discipline his people Israel. Isaiah or a later figure speaks of "the latter days" when "the mountain of the house of the Lord shall be established as the highest of the mountains . . . and all the nations shall flow to it." Zion will be the supreme sacred center of the earth. Moreover, "out of Zion shall go forth the Law, and the word of the Lord from Jerusalem" (Isa. 2:2, 3). But Jerusalem is a *terminus ad quem,* and salvation seems to be by association along a "one-way street." Even with Third Isaiah, it is the prophetic word "that nations shall come to your light, and kings to the brightness of your rising" (Isa. 60:3). From Midian, Sheba, and Lebanon shall treasure be carried: "you shall eat the wealth of nations" (61:3).[10]

Jeremiah's travail over his people, according to John Skinner, had led him to abandon even Isaiah's hope of the "remnant" of Israel, bringing him to the view that "the time had come for State and State-religion to be done away."[11] Hence he looked for a "new covenant" between God and men written on the heart of the individual, although with corporate expression (Jer. 31:31–32). Yet Skinner allows that, in the midst of the desolation of Jerusalem, Jeremiah was yet filled "with a passionate longing and hope for the return of the disinherited." Skinner's subsequent statement in explanation of Jeremiah's residual nationalism is as fair as any I know and has application also to narrowing trends in postexilic Judaism to which we shall turn.

This concentration of interest on the new Israel is due to a limitation in the Old Testament point of view which even Jeremiah was unable to transcend. The limitation springs from a fundamental truth of religion, that religion has a social aspect, and cannot unfold its full powers except in a community; and nationality was the only form of religious community known to men of the Old Testament. The idea of a new community created by the spirit of religion itself and founded on a relation to God common to all its members, was beyond their grasp, because conditions for the formation of such a community did not yet exist. They therefore clung to the traditional idea of Israel as the people in whose history the true God had revealed Himself, and within whose fellowship their personal communion with God was realized. This we must hold true of Jeremiah. . . . Thus while to Jeremiah the nation is no longer the *unit* of religion, it is still the *sphere* of religion. . . .[12]

If we attend to Skinner's discriminating assessment, as I believe we must, it appears that election for service encounters a social introversion that obstructs mission and encourages the chosen people to cherish their given self-identity. Election tends to accent consciousness of claim rather than of vocation and responsibility. So Israel of the Second Temple and of postexilic times seems, indeed, decreasingly aware of a missionary role as the chosen people of God by comparison with the insights of such 8th-century prophets as Micah or Isaiah.[13] Yet it is true that II Isaiah, the prophet of the Exile, with unsurpassed vision proclaimed Israel as Servant of Yahweh: "Behold my servant, whom I uphold, my chosen, in whom my soul delights. I will put my spirit upon him, he will bring forth justice to the nations" (Isa. 42:1). Yahweh formed Israel "from the womb to be his Servant" (49:5), to mediate his salvation: "I will give you as a light to the nations, that my salvation shall reach to the end of the earth" (49:6).

Yet when Israel returned from the Exile it seems to have been under the aegis of the cultic and theocratic exclusivism of Ezekiel (Ezek. 44:9–14). It is sobering to have the careful assessment of Oesterley and Robinson that "the universalistic teaching of Deutero-Isaiah did not bear fruit." [14] The influence of the Servant teaching was, they think, "negligible." It is their judgment that

from now on belief and practice narrowed down, in the main, into nationalistic grooves, and the religion which the greater prophets, and especially Deutero-Isaiah, would have made a world religion, assumed of set purpose a form which excluded non-Jews.[15]

With learning and fairness, W. D. Davies concurs respecting the postexilic drift of Judaism toward "narrow nationalism." The spirit of Ezekiel prevailed "and the postexilic history of Judaism became the history of a 'fenced" community. . . . The Torah, which differentiated the Jew from others, also separated him ["the Jew"] from them." [16] Thus, Davies continues, "by the 1st century B.C., there is almost a complete absence of any expression of universalism." [17] Yet, while the "particularist spirit" prevailed without abatement, Davies perceives an emergent "uneasy conscience" regarding the Gentiles without the law, a mood expressing itself by way of proselytic endeavor as the means of salvation through "naturalization" into the Jewish people.[18]

Joachim Jeremias has interpreted this proselytic activity as intensive in the 1st century B.C., especially in Hellenistic Judaism of the Diaspora. He says that "Jesus thus came upon the scene in the midst of what was *par excellence* the missionary age of Jewish history." [19] The extension of the mission ranged throughout the Roman Empire, yet there remains a question as to the platform of this missionary zeal.

Jeremias concedes that the sources are scanty, and his appeal to the school of Hillel (ca. A.D. 20) for its rationale is unconvincing. For Rabbi Hillel to justify proselytism against the School of Shammai on the supposedly liberal mandate, "love mankind and bring them to the Law," hardly qualifies as mission in the post-Pauline sense.[20] On the contrary, it is exchange, apparently, of the posture of passivity for intensive activity along the "one-way street." Jeremias seems severely to delimit the mission to the Gentiles by his observation that "conversion to the Jewish religion meant nothing less than naturalization, becoming a Jew." [21] Surely, "mission" had to be something more to qualify for the name; at the same time, one is not unmindful of ambiguity attaching to any historically conditioned vehicle of the universal grace of God.

In view, then, of the apparent near-absence in postexilic Judaism of effectual awareness of a missionary role of the chosen people, may we not wonder at the basis upon which H. H. Rowley supported his assessment of Israel's election as "election for service"? Isaiah had, indeed, rejoiced in the prospect of the day when the earth should be "full of the knowledge of the Lord as waters cover the sea" (Isa. 11:9). But this spirit of universal praise hardly prevailed in the ages following the return of the exiles and the building of the second Temple. The centripetal forces of nationalism seemingly became more powerful than the centrifugal forces of universal mission.[22] The individualization of worship envisioned by Jeremiah evidently failed to leave its mark. The spirit of Ezekiel and the priestly tradition dominated the interpretation of the Mosaic Law and the Covenant to the end of securing a separate nation, holy to the Lord, and qualified to inherit the promises fitting to God's chosen people. The deliberate particularism of Deuteronomy tended to prevail, implemented by the ordinances and the statutes of the Law under the surveillance of the Levitical priesthood. Accordingly, perhaps, the Temple cultus and the Law of ordinances, with the synagogue, became the dominating foci of postexilic Jewish piety.

While the main currents of postexilic Judaism seem to move toward heightened national self-consciousness, important eddies of universalistic teaching do find expression in the Wisdom writings and such books as Jonah and Ruth. In general, however, the Servant role of Israel seems to have acquired a muted status in pre-Christian Jewish piety. Nor was it, according to the weighty judgment of Sigmund Mowinckel, in later Judaism associated with the Messiah until post–New Testament times.[23] From Mowinckel's view that the "Messiah is not the central and dominating figure in the future hope of later Judaism," [24] we derive scanty basis for the otherwise feasible inference that in some manner the election of Israel for service was, as it were, transferred to the Messiah and conserved. So we are the more prepared for Mowinckel's eventual finding that "no one in Judaism connected the Servant with the Messiah, the mediator of the kingdom of God, and of the new relation between God and men." [25] And when we add to this his generalization, deriving from the same context, to the effect that "this national and this-worldly element remains the heart of the future hope throughout the entire Old Testament period: God's kingly rule on earth through the world-hegemony of Israel and her Davidic ruler," we may wonder about the grounds of the view that Israel's election was election for service.[26]

Adverting, therefore, to our earlier question, we may be prompted to inquire whether H. H. Rowley's attractive generalization is not largely a reading of the Old Testament in the light of the New. Does he suppose, from the New Testament standpoint, that Judaism of later postexilic times had lost a grasp upon its authentic meaning or drew back from its manifest destiny? And is it perhaps possible that he believes, as it were, with Oesterley and Robinson that "in a very real sense the Cross was the liberation of the eternal truth of Judaism from the casing which protected it but limited its range?" [27] This indeed seems to be the bearing of the final chapter of his important study of election in the Old Testament. In the Cross he finds that Jesus exposed the missionary role of the Suffering Servant and made the Church heir of Israel's election. Through Christ the Church accepts "the obligation of Israel's mission." [28] In Rowley's understanding the leaders of the first-generation church were Jews who regarded themselves as the Remnant of Israel and who had inherited the election.[29]

III. THE NEW TESTAMENT BACKGROUND

However many-sided may be the Old Testament meaning of election as it reflects the self-understanding of Israel and later Judaism, Rowley has doubtless enforced our realization that, with the acceptance by the early Church of "election for service," a decisive transition is made from the Old to the New Testament. In the remainder of this study the intention is to inquire how and in what measure the transition to what we venture to call an "ecumenical"—that is, an inclusive gospel of salvation to the whole inhabited world—was comprehended by the early Church as the import of Jesus' message, ministry, death, and resurrection.[30]

The understanding of election for service is, manifestly, correlative with a certain view of the range and reach of the saving purpose of God. Thus, respecting the early Church, there is question as to what degree universality of grace was in fact consented to by the Church or in what part there was both incomprehension and hesitancy surviving from the Jewish past.[31] For the New Testament, the question is not idle. For the latter recapitulates the Old in large measure even though the *dramatis personae* have changed and the historical variables have been altered. Yet the triumph of the contested Gentile mission in the third quarter of the 1st century A.D. early obscured for posterity the crisis through which first-generation Christianity passed.[32] During that period it was by no means obvious that an "ecumenical" outreach of the new faith would prevail. The measure to which the Lucan author of Acts both obscures and minimizes the dissension within the first-generation church becomes conspicuous when the work is scrutinized from the standpoint of election for mission.[33]

Until perhaps the fall of Jerusalem in A.D. 70, there are strong suggestions that vital elements of Jewish Christianity were largely content to understand the new Way as essentially Judaism if with a momentous difference: namely, that Israel's Messiah had appeared in God's servant, Jesus of Nazareth, who had been crucified, but who had been raised up and exalted to the right hand of God, and "whom the heaven must receive until the time for the establishing of all that God spoke by the mouth of his holy prophets" (Acts 3:21). Repentance and forgiveness are in his name (Acts 3:38).

A powerful segment of Jerusalem Christianity, in the tradition of the Old Testament (cf. Acts 3:17–22), still looked to the age of fulfillment with the chosen people at the center; for was it not written: "I will put salvation in Zion, for Israel my glory" (Isa. 46:13)? Moreover, in that day shall it not still prevail as Isaiah had foretold, that "out of Zion shall go forth the law, and the word of the Lord from Jerusalem" (Isa. 2:3)? This theme is central in Acts. For this fulfillment, and the turning of the Gentiles, early Jerusalem Christianity seems to have awaited the return of the Son of Man and, therewith, perhaps also the proclamation of a new Law of the messianic age to the nations.[34]

Surely, the pressing problem and consequent crisis of the primitive Church was that of an adequate understanding of what had taken place both in and through the ministry of Jesus together with his crucifixion and resurrection, and first of all in the given Old Testament context of "the hope of Israel" (Acts 28:20). The inherited context was limiting, however, for over it presided the ancient paradox of the people of God's own possession. The universality of grace was implied, but through what thematic structure could the universalizing import of the messianic age be applied to the *oikoumēne?*

We get nowhere in understanding the mind of the early Church, or the New Testament as a whole, unless we recognize as the first premise that what had happened in their midst could be comprehended by them only in the tradition of the history of election as disclosed in the saga of the covenanted people of God. To say, in the formula of the Schools, that this entails an eschatological view of history simply encapsules three fundamental standpoints inherited by the earliest Christian believers. The first is the basic Old Testament unanimity about God: "I am the first and I am the last, besides me there is no God" (Isa. 44:6). The second is that Israel's history lies between the beginning and the end of God's gracious purpose of salvation. And third, this history, for the eyes of faith, is more or less transparent to the divine purpose and, thus, the *datum* of any given understanding of God's ways with man in history—which always lies between the beginning and the end.

The early Church, accordingly, somehow must understand the event of Jesus as Messiah within the continuum of God's redemptive purpose, as the paramount moment somewhere between the beginning and the end. It was not until Christianity won a place within the late Hellenistic world that sacred history as the medium of the divine self-manifestation was confronted with the Greek, and specifically the Stoic, alternative of the *Apeiron*—the cosmic Infinite—that challenged the Hebraic view of the beginning *ex nihilo* and proffered in its stead a fate of the world as eternal recurrence. In comprehending the New Testament we do not confront this contrasting worldview. On the contrary, the event of Jesus the Messiah adumbrates the mystery of the divine fulfillment, the perfecting of God's grace in creation. Moreover, as the beginning is *ex nihilo*—that is, of sheer grace—so also is the ending, which has begun in Jesus as the Christ.

IV. THE HOPE OF THE GENTILES IN THE MINISTRY OF JESUS

The ecumenical question was, is, and ever shall be: to what extent and on what grounds is God's grace of salvation open to all mankind? The presupposition of the ecumenical question is the primordial paradox that the Lord of all the world pursues his will through a people of his own "possession" (Gen. 19:5). It is this that makes Israel's history revelatory to the prophetic vision, and all history meaningful or end-directed.

To the ecumenical question St. Paul's answer was that through Jesus Christ there is no limit to the range of God's salvation and that the death and resurrection of Christ have redefined the conditions. He has done so by his deed of the Cross, has become thereby the way of salvation for all who will receive him. This is the Gospel of which Paul is not ashamed: "it is the power of God for salvation to everyone who has faith, to the Jew first and also to the Greek" (Rom. 1:16). With Paul "ecumenism" is grounded in the revelation of God in Jesus Christ and conditional solely upon faith in him who, according to Paul, was "designated Son of God in power according to the Spirit of holiness by his resurrection from the dead" (Rom. 1:4).

The language is loaded and will bear unpacking; for the moment we note two points. The first is that Paul's consciousness of mandate "to bring," as he says, "obedience to faith . . . among all the Gentiles" (Rom. 1:5), is warranted primarily by the deed of the Cross and the deed of God in raising up the Crucified One. The second point is that Christ, "the power of God and the wisdom of God," is good news "to the Jew *first* and also to the Greek." [35] The question occurs as to whether, on this last point, Paul is in touch with the message and ministry of Jesus as it appears in the primitive tradition of the Gospels. Does Paul's stress in Romans upon a certain seemly priority of the Jew as candidate for God's new way of salvation through Christ resound to a note in Jesus' own message and ministry as reported in the Synoptics—namely, his apparent disposition to confine his message to Israel? Matthew verbalizes this into policy, first in Jesus sending forth the Twelve with the injunction: "Go nowhere among the Gentiles, and enter no town of the Samaritans, but go rather to the lost sheep of the house of Israel" (Matt. 10:5–6). Second, there is the rather shocking rebuff of Jesus to the appeal of the Canaanite woman for healing mercies as reported by Matt. 15:24: "I was sent only to the lost sheep of the house of Israel."

In his essay *Jesus' Promise to the Nations,* Joachim Jeremias has confronted the issues of these passages with candor and discernment. He provides support for the view that Jesus expected the incorporation of the Gentiles into the Kingdom of God with its establishment. This, however, Jesus viewed "as God's eschatological act of power, as the greater final manifestation of God's free grace." [36] In this way, God raises up children unto Abraham of the very stones. So, for Jesus, the inclusion of the Gentiles awaits the decisive act of God. Meanwhile, the proclamation of the coming Kingdom to Israel is viewed by Jeremias as the prior responsibility of Jesus' message and work. In support of this view, moreover, he appeals to the rationale provided in Romans 15:7–9 where Paul declares: "For I tell you that Christ became a servant for the circumcised to show God's truthfulness, in order to confirm the promises given to the patriarchs, and in order that the Gentiles might glorify God for his mercy."

It is possible that in this statement, which is also a summation of a portion of his concerns in Romans 9–11, Paul does address himself to the tradition preserved in Matthew 15:24. The phrase "Christ became a servant for the circumcised" may be an oblique acknowledgment of a still widely current word of Jesus, confining his ministry to Israel. It is awkward for Paul, not because his Gospel cannot answer it but because its literal espousal by a segment of contemporary Jewish Christianity constituted resilient opposition to the Gentile mission of the Pauline manner as late as the end of his work at Ephesus.[37] Meanwhile, it is axiomatic with Paul that it is indeed *through* Abraham and his seed, Israel, that the promise derives to all men.[38] But that "seed" comes to mean Jesus Christ, according to Romans and Galatians (Gal. 3:15–16), and for a complex of reasons that must be explored in the remainder of this essay. The heart of it is that, for Paul, in Jesus Christ the election of Israel for service is fulfilled.

For Paul, Jesus' ministry, *katā sarkā*, was a call for Israel to accept in the person of God's Messiah, as incognito in the flesh, the meaning of its own election. It was the ultimate sorrow and perplexity of the Apostle that both prior to the death and resurrection of Jesus the Christ and subsequently thereto, his fellow Jews could not recognize "the glory of God in the face of Jesus Christ" on account of to the "veil" of the Law of Moses that was passing away (2 Cor. 3:12–14). And much of Romans is Paul's labored effort, a generation after the fact, to explain the tragedy, but with clinging hope of "life from the dead" (Rom. 11:15–17). Thus, examination of Romans, chapters 9–11 and 15, shows Paul facing the "mystery" of the "hardening" that has overtaken a "part of Israel" (11:25).

To recur to our original question: it may then be that the Apostle's formula in Romans 1:16, "to the Jew *first* and also to the Greek," is actually an explicit reference to a sharply controverted issue of the early church and one to which Romans as a whole addresses itself in comprehensive answer. Yet Paul's studied *apologia* in Romans is, at the same time and inevitably, an address to adamant Israel as a whole. Eloquently he testifies to his anguish over his own people (Rom. 9:1–3). In the Pauline hermeneutic there was, for those who would receive it, a luminous understanding of Jesus' words "I was sent only to the lost sheep of the house of Israel." In the strength of the plaintive irony of II Isaiah, it went beyond the understanding of late Judaism.[39] Paul championed, though not exclusively, the servant principle in II Isaiah's understanding of Israel's vocation. Rejected by most of Israel, it had for him been fulfilled in Christ and vindicated by God. He could roundly agree that, "according to the flesh," Jesus Christ is of Israel, to which belongs also the sonship, the glory, the covenants, the giving of the law, and the promises (Rom. 9:4, 5), but he could no longer concede that Abraham's children include only those according to the flesh (Rom. 9:7). A half-century later, John the Evangelist could say virtually without fear of contradiction, and by way of intended contrast, "The law was given by Moses; grace and truth came through Jesus Christ" (John 1:17), but he stood on the shoulders of Paul and the embattled missioners of the first age of the Church, and we for the most part have forgotten it.

And so we come face to face with the question, Was St. Paul's interpretation of Jesus Christ, and not just the crucified and risen Lord, closer to the truth than that of contemporary Jewish Christianity? Was this latter not "Christian," too, and proclamation of the faith? Whose *kerygma*, then, is to be credited and honored? The faith of which Church are we to regard as authorized, and by what? [40] We mean only to raise the epistemological question here, neither to argue it nor, much less, settle it, since it has been with us for centuries. Reference to it is, however, implied and becomes critical in face of the virtual certainty that in the first-generation Church there was profound division in respect of *kerygma* and that some historical accidents figured prominently in the eventual victory of the Pauline Gospel. All the more important, therefore, is the question of the norms of adjudication as among the competing early claimants to the truth of the Gospel respecting the message and deed of Jesus.

St. Paul's gospel is undoubtedly an interpretation of a certain history; and, while it presupposes more, it does not presuppose less than the deed of Jesus according to the flesh. So the question presses: in what measure the ministry and message of Jesus comport with the construction placed upon it by the Apostle from his given vantage point of Jesus' death and resurrection. It is, perhaps, precisely against the history of Israel's election as afforded in the Old Testament background that we may hope to avail ourselves of either the problematic or the privileged schema of interpretation essential to comprehension of either Jesus or Paul. On this matter, the stress of Martin Kähler upon the indispensability of the Old Testament background was long ago a permanent gain.[41]

What, then, can be said of the deed of Jesus in the light, not simply of Paul but of the Old Testament background and in reciprocity with the Gospel tradition? We saw earlier that the presiding meaning of election in Exodus, underscored everywhere in Deuteronomy, was the paradox of God's sovereign choice of Israel as his "own possession." Surely, the inherent logic of the paradox calls for some breakthrough, some answer to the question, *For what?* And, to this, weighty Old Testament scholarship answers: *election for service.* And what else is to square the astonishment, noted by the Deuteronomic author, of the unconditional grace of the Creator God allied with the destiny of a particular people? At length the prophet of the Exile proclaims the message of Israel as Servant of Yahweh, but the Word is mostly unheeded in later Judaism; and Sigmund Mowinckel, along with H. H. Rowley and others, agrees that "Jesus was the first to take this prophecy seriously and apply it to himself." [42]

The question is, *Did he?* and what is the New Testament evidence? Plainly the evidence, if available, would not be just a journalist's chronicle of the life of Jesus. As the matter stands, evidence is by way of attention to a variety of episodes and logia (often remembered better than they were understood, as William Manson once discerningly said) with which the Gospels are replete and with a view to sorting and sifting according to modal themes and recurrent motifs, but always against the background of the entire biblical tradition. The end product is not likely to be any sort of demonstration. Rather, it will be interpretation, answerable to the *given* and based upon emergent patterns, which commends itself by shedding maximum illumination over the widest reach of the entire spectrum, and renders some coherence. The criterion of truth in historical judgment, I suggest, is never adequation to brute fact but is rather the measure of light a hypothesis sheds upon the range of our apprehension of the subject matter.

It is perhaps, then, impossible to comprehend the vocation of Jesus save in the light of the ancient election of the chosen people. In fact, the relation between the two is, as it were, isomorphic. As Deuteronomy conceives Israel's calling, it is always either acceptance or evasion of election, with attendant curse or blessing (Deut. 11:26–27). Indeed, Israel is, so to speak, man with options under the constraint of the divine calling; and, in the recurrent prophetic evaluation, Israel's record was often a story of unresolved ambiguity or even faithlessness (Deut. 9:24). Upon this judgment "the beginning of the gospel of Jesus Christ" is surely premised. John's call to repentance is just suited to Israel's existence as faith-in-unfaith, a kind of *infidelis perennis,* somehow painfully inherent in the paradox of election itself (Mark 1:1, 4).

For Jesus, then, to begin his ministry with a proclamation of the imminent advent of the Kingdom of god was indeed to require *metanoia* of his own people as a radical divine imperative (Mark 1:14). The unfolding of the meaning of that *metanoia* runs through the occasional utterances of Jesus, is embodied in his word and work, and is consummated on the Cross. The corollary is rather clear: the primary mission of Jesus was to challenge Israel to comprehend its given vocation and to accept it in view of the imminence of the Kingdom. The Kingdom had been imminent, however delayed for centuries, in the

paradoxical dynamism of the singular election. For Jesus to proclaim
the Kingdom as imminent was, in the language of eschatology, to say
that it was everlastingly implicated as the future of man under God
impounded in the paradox of the chosen people. In the light of this
hypothesis, it is understandable that Jesus should view his mission as
necessarily, and primarily, an urgent challenge to Israel. In view of
the election, salvation is, indeed, *"from* the Jews" if God's declared
way with the covenanted people was to be heeded—and for Jesus it
could hardly be otherwise. So the Johannine Evangelist attributes this
view expressly to Jesus, with intent to answer the Matthean tradition
respecting the limitation of Jesus' message to Israel.[43]

If we look directly to the Matthean injunction that limits the disciples'
mission "to the lost sheep of the house of Israel" (Matt. 10:6), we note
that it is unique in Matthew and without parallel in the Synoptic Gospels. On the other hand, the incident involving the Canaanite woman
in the region of Tyre and Sidon is found in Mark 7:24–30, but with
the absence of the Matthean declaration, "I was sent only to the lost
sheep of the house of Israel." Yet it is more important to note that
in the Markan version, the *injustice* of throwing the "bread of the
children" to the dogs is conspicuously modified by the qualification,
namely, *until* the "children are first fed." Thus, Mark construes the
incident not as restrictive but permissive: it is the *faith* of the Canaanite
woman that triumphs for her petition. "For this saying you may go
your way," says Jesus (7:29). Mark thus notes the passing of salvation
to the Gentiles as part of the mission of Jesus himself.

The Markan account antedates that of Matthew; it is obviously under
the influence of Paul's gospel and in notable contrast with the Matthean
version.[44] The difference between the two may easily be overlooked
and thereby obscure to us markedly contrasting views within the earliest Church respecting the relation of the Gentiles to salvation through
the Messiah. It seems evident that the tradition respecting Jesus' apparent limitation of his message to Israel, retained prominently by Matthew, reflected a crisis of understanding on the part of the first-generation church.

In addition to the ecumenical import of his announcement of the
Kingdom of God, as enforced by the Old Testament Canon, there
are other motifs and themes in the Gospel narratives which are revealing, conspicuously in Jesus' parables. Special attention needs to be
given, likewise, to the Q source, which, as T. W. Manson cogently
remarked, "more than any of the synoptic sources, shows a friendly
attitude to the Gentiles." [45] In this connection, the meaing of the baptism and the temptation of Jesus requires deeper probing. Both are,
I believe, parabolic of the history of the election of Israel for service,
as they are, likewise, more revelatory of Jesus' own self-understanding

and of his identification with Israel in its historical servant-vocation and divine destiny. While Jesus' baptism by John in the Jordan is a fixed point in interpretation of his ministry, it is also, as both Mark and Luke are aware, the paradigm of a continuing travail through which, in identification with Israel, Jesus moves onward toward the fulfillment of the universal divine calling. That travail becomes the more incumbent upon him in the measure that he encounters both incomprehension on the part of his intimate disciples and hostile resistance on the part of scribes, Pharisees, and leaders of the nation.

On this view, hardly any line of the Gospels comes closer to authentic self-disclosure than the isolated saying of Luke: "I have a baptism to be baptized with; and how am I constrained until it is accomplished" (Luke 12:50). His baptism is entire submission to the divine will and purpose in immovable faith and assurance of the sufficiency of God to which Moses called Israel *to stand* in the crossing of the Red Sea (Exod. 14:13–14). To grasp this is to perceive also that Jesus' whole existence, like the existence of Israel itself, was existence in temptation. To be the elect of God is to be under continuing temptation. It signifies the manhood of Man, of Israel, under a divine mandate to be a vehicle of God's eternal purpose. To be tempted is to yield to any contrariety opposed to that mandate. It is to fail to pass beyond the ambiguity of faith-in-unfaith to unambiguous affirmation of the summons of God to body forth His purpose in man's own history. The temptation accounts of the Q source in both Luke and Matthew are eloquent of this meaning (Matt. 4:1–11; Luke 4:1–12).

The inability of the disciples to comprehend the fundamental vocation of the Son of Man is unmistakably evident in the request of the sons of Zebedee as Jesus makes his way to Jerusalem (Mark 10:35 f.). Their private intervention for preferential treatment in the Kingdom to come is, in its opprobrium, matched only by the indignation of the other disciples, who exhibit their own pride of place. So denigrative is this indubitably early tradition to the standing of the leading apostles, James and John, that Matthew makes their "mother" petitioner for their special preferment (Matt. 20:20). As for the first of the apostles, Peter confirms his unknowing in Mark 10:28 by voicing concern for compensations for his fidelity and thereby confirms the substance of his earlier remonstrance at Jesus' announcement of his own forthcoming passion. The severity of Jesus' rebuke is in the measure of his clear recognition in Peter of a veritable Satanic temptation: "Get behind me, Satan! For you are not on the side of God but of Men" (Mark 8:33). The historical authenticity of these traditions is in good part their manifest congruence with the history of election in the Old Testament as we have re-searched its meaning.

Along these lines we are within reach of comprehending the authen-

tic (if aphoristic) sayings of Jesus respecting both his indissoluble relation to Israel and the urgent priority of conveying the message of
the Kingdom, first, to "the lost sheep of the house of Israel" (Matt.
15:23). In this light, if on somewhat different grounds, it is possible to
see the partial truth of Jeremias' view that "the incorporation of the
Gentiles" was consequent to "God's eschatological act of power." [46]
My demurrer would be, however, that the act of God was, in Jesus'
view, inseparable from Israel's fidelity to its divine election as the instrument of God's grace. Jesus partly historicized apocalyptic and mo-
ralized eschatology by recognizing that God's grace of salvation is also
mediated through the elect people. As this mediatorship *is* the paradox
of election, it was inevitably the implication for Jesus' ministry in its
outworking, namely, his passion. Insofar, however, as the chosen people
decline their role in sacred history, they are as salt which has lost its
savor, no longer good for anything except to be thrown out (Matt.
5:13). Or they are a light, a city set on a hill that cannot be hid, which,
nevertheless, perversity may hide rather than put on a stand that it
may give light "to all in the house" (Matt. 5:14).

Against this background may we not come closer to comprehension
of the devastating strictures of Jesus in reference to the scribes and
Pharisees in the Matthean exposé of exclusivistic legalism in religion:
"Woe to you scribes and Pharisees . . . because you shut the kingdom
of heaven against men; for you neither enter yourselves, nor allow
those who would enter to go in?" (Matt. 23:13). And where salt has
lost its savor, why should not Jesus be impatient with those who "tra-
verse sea and land to make a single proselyte?" (Matt. 23:15). What is
accomplished in naturalizing outsiders into a Judaism that has lost hold
upon its reason for being? The call of God to Israel is to embody its
servanthood, to be a light in darkness. What else then but for Jesus
to espouse the election of Israel and undergo the final baptism, the
final exodus and crossing of the everlasting sea? Eschatology is historicized because the election of Israel is *enpersonalized*. The Cross becomes liberation from bondage and, at the same time, emancipation
of the gracious purpose of God for all of history. How this was more
fully understood requires that we look again to the mind of Paul.

V. THE PARADOX FULFILLED AND TRANSCENDED

At bottom, Paul's gospel is proclamation of the revelation of the mystery of election of all men finally unveiled in Jesus Christ.[47] *Its truth
value is indemonstrable and is luminous only against the continuity
of the history of election.* This leaves the revelation as Paul left it, a

matter of faith. Historical "knowledge" is, in the first instance, always hypothetical and, in the last, decisional. We cannot, however, disdain the first because, in the end, we must resort to the last. To do so is either to settle for some species of *fideism* or some *philosophy*, the prevailing expedients of the past half-century in Christian origins and Christology.

In a recent symposium the late Kurt Wilhelm, testifying for current Jewish theological opinion, has said: "Eschatological speculation is unanimous to the effect that at the onset of the messianic kingdom God will bring about a visible miracle analogous to the miracles associated with the creation and revelation." [48] If due regard is given to the qualification "analogous," then it is evidently such an event to which St. Paul testifies respecting the ministry, crucifixion, and resurrection of Jesus of Nazareth. Scandalous as was the claim, it authorized Paul's gospel and impelled his singular mission to the Gentiles. That this is so rests upon grounds as secure as any datum of the New Testament—namely, his own testimony, with time sequences, in Gal. 1–2. There, on the occasion of vigorous defense of his gospel against Judaizing detractors who had disturbed a community of his own founding, Paul set forth the credentials of his claim that "in Christ there is neither Jew nor Greek, there is neither slave nor free, there is neither male nor female; for you are all one in Christ Jesus" (Gal. 3:28).

This epoch-making affirmation is, of course, grounded in what, according to Rom. 16:25–27, Paul, near the end of his Gentile mission, still speaks of as "my gospel and the revelation of the mystery which was kept secret for long ages but is now disclosed." Moreover, it is integral to the mystery and its unveiling that it "is made to all nations." In this summation we are told by Paul that his *kerygma* is directed to the *oikoumēne* and that it transcends geographical and national demarcations.

The explicit use of the phrase "my gospel" refers us at once to the autobiographical chapters of Galatians 1–2, where Paul stresses, and under oath, that his gospel was not received from men, that he was not taught it, presumably by other Apostles or by the mother Church of Jerusalem, but that it came to him "by a revelation of Jesus Christ." As is well known, he proceeds in Galatians to make plain that it entailed these outcomes: (1) that God justifies the Gentiles by faith (3:8); (2) that "no man is justified before God by the law" (2:16); and (3) that, therefore, Jew and Gentile are alike "justified by faith in Christ" (2:16–18; 1 Cor. 1:24).

Forthwith, this not only rendered ambiguous historical Israel as the chosen people and instated children by "adoption" on an equality with native sons (Gal. 4:5), but also denationalized and deëthnicized election to salvation and, in the end, dislocated the place of worship from the Temple in Jerusalem to the temple of the human spirit.[49] In short, it emancipated the Christian faith of particularistic associations by engendering a perspective as unrestricted as the Spirit of the living God. The *oikoumēne* was included within the sovereignty of grace; the centrifugal dynamic prevailed over the centripetal inertia. It was the dethronement of Israel "according to the flesh" (Rom. 10:12), incurring the hostility of contemporary Judaism and the consternation of Jewish Christians and, indubitably, made Paul the most embattled figure of the early Church, by a portion of whom he was, in all probability, done in on his final visit to Jerusalem while bearing alms in the interest of Christian unity.[50]

The revolution in Paul's life must be associated with the completely shattering *apocalypsis* by which he had been discovered an enemy of God in the process of prosecuting what he took to be the righteousness prescribed of God—"the traditions of my fathers" (Gal. 1:14). The mystery unveiled was many-faceted, but, in both Galatians and Romans, it is described as "the righteousness, that has been manifested apart from the law, although the law and the prophets bear witness to it." It is, says Paul, "the righteousness of God through faith for all who believe" (Rom. 3:21–22).

When, however, Paul speaks of a new righteousness through faith, he speaks of the human side of the equation of which Jesus Christ is the correlate. Thus, in the autobiographical account of Galatians, he speaks of his gospel as "a revelation of Jesus Christ" (Gal. 1:12). And by this he means that Jesus Christ is really both its source and its substance. Its substance includes the new righteousness of God. This, again, on the one side is justification by faith; on its other side, however, it is the revelation of the incredible, because absolutely unconditional, mercy of God—namely, his grace through Jesus Christ. So Jesus Christ is both the source and the substance of the revelation which then is likewise the content of Paul's gospel. As such, it is also "the revelation of the mystery," which in Romans and Colossians, as also in 1 Corinthians, has been hidden but now is revealed.

The picture is familiar, but clarification of the import of the revelation for Paul's ecumenical mission is in order. First, it is quite evident that it was the confrontation of Paul with the risen Jesus which compelled him to subjoin to the name "Jesus" the majesty of the title "Messiah." But to leave the matter there would be simplistic, for it neglects the spiritual revolution which was entailed for Paul and of which the appearance of the risen Jesus was catalyst.

The *apocalypsis* can be understood, however, against the historic election of Israel and its inherent paradoxical dynamic, the traditions of the fathers. Fundamental to the revelation was the shattering refutation which echoes through the letters of Paul and, in the Romans passage, is explicative of the new righteousness of God through faith. Paul testifies: "For there is no distinction; since all have sinned and fall short of the glory of God, they are justified by God's grace as a gift, through the redemption which is in Christ Jesus" (Rom. 3:22–24). Likewise to the Galatians Paul says, if "a law had been given which could make alive, then righteousness would indeed be by the law" (Gal. 3:21). But, he adds, in explanation of the new righteousness by faith, "the scriptures consigned all things in sin, that what was promised to faith in Jesus Christ might be *given* to those who believe" (Gal. 3:22).

Adequate exegesis is impossible here; it may suffice to say that Paul is not simply citing Scripture to vindicate his views, such as Hab. 2:4— "He who through faith is righteous shall live" (Gal. 3:11). To be sure, for Paul the word of God is given in Scripture, but the decisive word to Paul now is the *apocalypsis* of Jesus Christ. And it is the Word that, in his zeal to heed Scripture by persecuting "the church" of Christ, he has become guilty of mortal sin. He has, as he saw in a flash, come under the "curse of the law" while persecuting "the church of God violently" in behalf of the law, and while he "tried to destroy it" (Gal. 1:13; 3:12).

The inaugural *apocalypsis,* then, enforced upon Paul the annihilating realization that he himself, a Pharisee of the Pharisees and a zealot for the traditions of his fathers, had come under the condemnation of God. For he, along with his own people "according to the flesh" but in company with the Gentiles also, had, together and alike, been party to the adamant rejection and death of God's own Son. This risen Jesus, in appearance to Paul, confronts him as God's elect Servant but now manifest as God's vindicated and declared Messiah.

The forgiving grace of God veiled in the scandal of the Cross had annihilated Paul the zealot for the law and the traditions of the elders. The annihilation was total. This is what Paul means everywhere as when he explains to the Galatians, "I have been crucified with Christ" (Gal. 2:20); and in Romans 6:4 it is how, after analogy with Jesus' baptismal trial, Paul understands Christian baptism: "We were buried therefore with him by baptism into death." This is first of all a personal testimony. It testifies to Paul's experience of the death of the old man.[51] In this Paul found Scripture fulfilled that "none shall see God and live." Only the mercy of God in Christ had qualified the word to mean *and live as he is!* Paul knew life from the dead, a "new creation" (Gal. 6:15). It was death to sin and new life in Christ, our righteousness (1 Cor. 1:30). This was also the revelation of the mystery; it is new "life from the dead" for all who will receive it. The revelation of the mystery included this also "that as sin reigned in death, grace might abound through righteousness to eternal life through Jesus Christ our Lord" (Rom. 5:21). Paul gave God the glory as a recipient of incomprehensible grace that freed him from "the curse of the law" (Gal. 3:13). "There is therefore now no condemnation for those who are in Christ Jesus" (Rom. 8:1). And Paul saw that, as all had been included under sin, both Jew and Greek, so also all are included under grace (Rom. 3:23). Thus, the *apocalypsis* included also a righteousness of God, not of the law of ordinances which Deuteronomy explicitly makes conditional of grace, but "the righteousness of God through faith in Jesus Christ for all who believe" (Rom. 3:22) and to "the Jew first but also to the Greek" (Rom. 1:16).

Whereas Deuteronomy finds the explanation for unmerited grace by looking backward to God's love of the patriarchs (Deut. 4:37), Paul has lost all confidence in mere continuity of fleshly inheritance as a sufficient reason for God's goodness in perpetuity. Rather than looking to the past or hoping in Torah, Paul lives as a new creature of a new creation (1 Cor. 5:17). He has come to distinguish between the "law of ordinances" and the essence of the Law.[52] The latter is the first commandment heeded by Abraham before Sinai. Abraham "believed God, and it was reckoned to him for righteousness" (Gal. 3:6). For Paul the death of the Cross was the ultimate affirmation of God; it was believing God in perfect obedience (Phil. 2:8). So it was "the end of the Law" in the sense of the perfection of the Law (Rom. 10:4). They are, therefore, sons of Abraham who are united to Christ in the likeness of his death, or his perfect obedience, whether Jew or Gentile (Gal. 3:7–9).

In Christ the ecumenical breakthrough has come to pass. In Colossians it is "the mystery hidden for ages but now manifest," to wit, "how great among the Gentiles are the riches of the glory of this mystery, which is Christ in you the hope of glory" (Col. 1:26–27). The author of Ephesians is a reliable Pauline interpreter if he is not an editor of Paul. He knows that the *mysterion* of the Pauline *kerygma* issues in the view that "the Gentiles are fellow heirs, members of the same body, and partakers of the promise in Jesus Christ through the gospel" (Eph. 3:6).

The revelation of the mystery contains the consequence that, through Jesus Christ, God's grace in redemption becomes commensurate with his sovereignty in creation. It marks a new creation *ex nihilo*.[53] To the Romans Paul had driven home the logic of commensurability. Salvation cannot be by the works of the law: "Or is God the God of the

Jews only? Is he not the God of the Gentiles also?" Paul's answer is the manifesto of the *oikoumēne*, "yes of the Gentiles also, *since God is one*" (Rom. 3:29–30). And to the Colossians the consequence is eloquently summarized in the famous lines:

For he is our peace, who has made us both one, and has broken down the wall of hostility, by abolishing in his flesh the law of ordinances and commandments, that he might create in himself one new man in place of the two. (Col. 3:14–15)

VI. THE PERENNIAL PARADOX

The assumption that the eternal God reveals himself in the history of his elect people is no more at issue in the New Testament than in the Old. For Paul's gospel it is axiomatic, although the precise identity of the elect people becomes permanently ambiguous. This is because election is desecularized, and the vocation of the elect people radically revised. On this matter there was in the early Church far greater diversity of understanding than the Lucan author of Acts has allowed to appear. Paul preached a gospel disturbing to his Christian contemporaries. One must agree, I believe, with Sandmel that it was "revolutionary," but not necessarily so simply because, with it, "the inherited Jewish Law was null and void." [54] Such a view strikes one as simplistic. The oft-used expression, Paul's "universalism," comes closer to the matter; yet is is probable that this Latin word has rather more obscured than illuminated Paul's gospel beamed to the *oikoumēne.*

There is little question that Paul consistently distinguished between the Law of God eternal and laws plural—namely, the "ordinances and statutes" of the covenant of Sinai along with what Paul speaks of as "the traditions of my fathers" (Gal. 1:14). Unlike the Law eternal, the laws plural had from their inception a "fading splendor." The superseding and "permanent" splendor in Christ is the embodiment of the Law eternal—that of "a new covenant, not a written code but in the spirit' (2 Cor. 3:4–11).

Herein, again, is "the revelation of the mystery" in Christ Jesus, who, as he embodies the Law eternal, also emancipates God's redemptive power in history. He transcends the law of ordinances and liberates the promise to Abraham, the primordial meaning of election, "that in Jesus Christ the blessing of Abraham might come upon the Gentiles" (Gal. 3:14). Embodying the unconditional grace of God, Jesus is the Messiah and fulfills the eternal purpose of God—the renovation of world history. It is the paradox of the Cross, in 1 Corinthians 1:18–25, which supplants the ancient paradox of election of Deuteronomy with the inclusiveness of absolute grace, with indiscriminate election of all men through Jesus Christ who believe (Rom. 10:3–4). It is in this sense alone that Paul can allow particularism to be the viator of universal grace. The chosen people was the bearer of God's promise to Abraham: now, however, implemented through Christ and by faith in him (Rom. 4:16–25). The vicarious people have become the vicarious Lord.

Paul's gospel, therefore, was ecumenical not because the Law eternal—i.e., God's righteousness (Rom. 3:21)—had been done away with but because it had been fulfilled. Neither was it ecumenical simply because, as Dodd suggested, justification is by faith apart from the works of the law.[55] Paul's gospel broke the centripetal inertia of Judaism, for in the death and resurrection of Jesus Christ there was the final *Apocalypsis,* the unveiled mystery bodied forth, of the absolutely unconditional grace of God for those who receive it. This was the causal Reality; it was a consequence that justification was by faith and that Paul knew nothing in which to glory save in the Cross and nothing to rejoice in save a new creation *ex nihilo.*

Herewith, the veil of the Temple had been rent from top to bottom, as Mark was to affirm (15:38). The apparent injustice of the owner of the vineyard in Jesus' parable of the hired laborers is vindicated by unconditional grace (Matt. 20:14–15). It becomes evident why "the first may be last and the last first" in the view of Jesus [56] and how it is, as Luke has it, that "men will come from the east and west, and from north and south, and sit at the table in the kingdom of God" (13:29–30). And finally, the unveiled mystery has a bearing upon Jesus' injunction to be mindful of the Father in heaven, who "makes his sun to rise on the evil and the good, and sends rain on the just and the unjust" (Matt. 5:45).

With the dissemination of the Pauline *kerygma,* the hitherto controlling centripetal dynamic of Judaism, resident in early Christianity, gave way to a centrifugal thrust. By the final quarter of the 1st century, attended by historical circumstances, Christianity had become predominantly a Gentile movement in the Mediterranean world. Without this thrust, as Goodspeed judged, the early Church might have remained "just another sect of Judaism" [57]; or it might have been, as B. W. Bacon argued with impressive cogency, a "messianic Judaism." [58] While prognoses are secondary to actualities, it is true that there is little or no extant documentation of the Apostolic Age to demonstrate otherwise, the overwhelming bearing of the Pauline letters to confirm it, and the primitive "Catholicism" of Luke–Acts to mute the conflict of issues of the age itself.

VII. CONCLUSION

From the ancient history of ecumenism many observations and conclusions are possible; only two can be mentioned, and those briefly. The first is that what has been described as the centripetal dynamic of God's election is hardly distinguishable from the "Satanic" temptation, for yielding to which Jesus rebukes Peter in Matt. 16:23. Election carries with it the temptation of Satan. It attended Jesus' own vocation (Luke 22:28) and is represented in his course from the wilderness following his baptism by John, to the agony of Gethsemane.

In this connection it is heartening to have the word of a representative of present-day Judaism affirming that "election is but a means to an end. As, through Abraham, all the peoples of the earth might be blessed," yet it is disappointing to be reminded by yet another spokesmen that the messianic expectation of Judaism entails belief that "the special position of the people Israel never disappears." [59] The issue, however, is not confined to Judeo-Christian ecumenism; rather, it serves to underline the centripetal inertia endemic among the historic branches of Christendom itself. While I do not believe it true, as Sandmel suggests, that for Paul the Church was "but a new particularism," it can hardly be denied that it soon tended to become so, with echoes, perhaps, becoming audible in 1 Peter 2:9–10 and with permutations of the ancient tradition of *primacy* and defensive concerns for *apostolicity* discernible in the New Testament itself. Evidently again we need to hear the twofold testimony of St. Paul, as our second and final observation: "Let him who boasts, boast of the Lord" (1 Cor. 1:31). And there is also his ultimate caution to all heirs of the election in Christ and stewards of the mysteries: "But we have this treasure in earthen vessels, to show that the transcendent power belongs to God and not to us" (2 Cor. 4:7).

In the end, for St. Paul, the only elect One is Jesus Christ. Election resides, as it was fulfilled, in Him. All other election is derivative and is appropriated only by faith as new "life from the dead" (Rom. 11:15). Respecting all precedence, Paul's final word is: "For God has consigned all men to disobedience, that he might have mercy upon all" (Rom. 11:32). For these reasons ecumenism is possible and all particularism irrelevant.

RECONCILIATION, YESTERDAY AND TODAY

1. RECONCILIATION ACCORDING TO PAUL

In this time of mistrust and latent revolt that ferment in our society, the assigned theme, reconciliation, seems both pertinent and improbable. Doubtless, for this very reason Carlyle Marney and his associates at Interpreters' House asked for an airing at this Annual Convocation. In this place, it is hardly necessary to remind anyone that reconciliation is preëminently a New Testament word, a Pauline word, and that it was the Apostle who gave it the meaning and distinctive denotations it has always retained—not alone in Church doctrine but in Christendom, and through Christendom, in Western civilization. For the Apostle, the word *katallagē*, reconciliation, speaks first of God and only thereafter of man. It speaks of what God has done and is doing through Jesus Christ and, therefore, what man must do and may become.

Two classical statements on reconciliation in Paul's Epistles are found, of course, in Romans and in 2 Corinthians. In the Romans passage, Paul writes: "For if while we were enemies we were reconciled to God by the death of his Son, much more, now that we are reconciled, shall we be saved by his life. Not only so, but we also rejoice in God through our Lord Jesus Christ, through whom we have now received our reconciliation" (Rom. 5:10–11).

There are three terms and two contrasting relationships in Paul's understanding of reconciliation. The terms are God, man, and Jesus Christ. Jesus Christ is the mediating term. Of the two contrasting relationships one yields to the other. The first is a relationship of alienation and estrangement—viewed from man's side, not from God's. The second is precisely that of reconciliation. Jesus Christ is the mediating term through whom, as God's reconciling initiative, a transition is made from alienation to reconciliation or communion. It is life in community with God, replacing man's contrariety and remotion. Hence, the Apostle views it as a "new creation," as he declares in the great passage in 2 Corinthians 5:17: "Therefore, if anyone is in Christ, he is a new

This essay is dedicated, with colleagial affection and abiding esteem to the memory of Dr. Carlyle Marney, churchman and prophet in his time, whose ministry was as alert to and as exemplary of St. Paul's understanding of Reconciliation as any I have known. In origin, the essay was an address to the Annual Convocation of Interpreters' House, January 1968, and was published at the initiative of Dr. Marney, Director, with others in *Religion and Life*, XXXVIII, No. 1 (Spring 1969). Republished by permission.

creation." The "therefore" is all-important, that is, the "newness of life" is a concomitant of the reconciliation to God that we participate in, with, and through Jesus Christ. But there is another consequence. In the Romans passage Paul continues: "Not only so, but we also *rejoice* in God through our Lord Jesus Christ, through whom we have now received our reconciliation." Joy is the mark, the tell-tale sign of the new relationship to God the Father, the community of life which replaces existence in alienation. The Apostle understands this reconciliation as veritably a new creation. It is the divine notice that, through Christ, God himself is at work to make all things new, and, first of all, the human world. The Apostle rejoices to have been inducted into a new age, and to be assigned its proclamation as ambassador.

For St. Paul it seems that Christian joy is the overflowing celebration of Christian hope, the hope that through Christ the reconciler, all things will be put in subjection to Christ so "under him, that God may be everything to everyone" (1 Cor. 15:28). This is, indeed, Paul's understanding of the restoration of the Creation. It includes even the vanquishment of death. For, in 1 Cor. 15:25–26, speaking of the reconciling work of Christ, Paul gives reconciliation a cosmic dimension, saying: "For he must reign until he has put all his enemies under his feet. The last enemy to be destroyed is death." This is the consummation of God's work of reconciliation, the abolition of "the mystery of iniquity," the subordination of all principalities and powers—all estrangement from God. This is the substance of Christian hope in Paul's view. It is also the meaning of the kingdom of God. When all powers at enmity with God have been reconciled or rendered subordinate—this is the end, not in the sense of *finis*, but in the sense of *telos* or fulfillment. Then, says Paul, "Christ delivers the kingdom to God the Father" (1 Cor. 15:24). Then God shall be "everything to every one."

Thus, in Pauline teaching on reconciliation, what begins as the overcoming of estrangement between God and individual men progressively takes on scope to include societal structures, such as "every rule and every authority and power" (1 Cor. 15:24), and eventually embraces all cosmic powers, even death itself as the last enemy.

But there is, perhaps, in this extension of the reconciling work of Christ to orders of Creation a temptation for Christians to make a treacherous shift of focus and emphasis. It is indeed, a misplaced emphasis to which Christian people have, I think, succumbed. Christians in all ages have allowed their attention to be focused and their hope of redemption to be fixed upon signs and portents of the cosmic drama of Christ's reign without keeping a tenacious hold upon the core teaching of Paul regarding the nature of reconciliation. In Paul's theology there is an inseverable correlation, even an equation, between reconciliation and what he calls the "new creation" and "newness of life." This is life *in* and empowered *by* the Spirit of Christ. This is what Paul means to signalize then, in the chief passage on reconciliation in Rom. 5:10-11, he says: "For if while we were enemies we were reconciled to God by the *death* of his Son, *much more,* now that we are reconciled, shall we be saved by his *life.*"

What, then, is this life, whence is it, and what is it to Christians, namely, the reconciled ones? If we ask, what is this life, it is first of all the resurrected life of Jesus Christ. It is, moreover, the righteous life of the one who "humbled himself and became obedient unto death, even death on a cross" (Phil. 2:8). The resurrected life of Christ is the servant-life of him who emptied himself of himself that God might be "everything to every one," first of all to him, Jesus. If we now ask, whence is this life, we must answer—in faithfulness to Paul's meaning—that it is given by God and received by the believer. It is, moreover, a life characterized qualitatively by the kind of righteousness that shone forth in the servant-life of Christ and that derives to the faithful man as a gift of God through Christ. Thus, Paul declares in Rom. 5:17, "If, because of one man's trespass [Adam], death reigned . . . , much more will those who receive the abundance of grace and the free gift of righteousness reign in life through the one man Jesus Christ." So the fruit of reconciliation is the new life of the Christian believer as the mark and sacramental sign of reconciliation itself. Thus, also, in the other key passage on reconciliation, 2 Cor. 5:17-18, we have the famous word, as a preface to what is entailed in reconciliation, "Therefore, if any one is in Christ, he *is* a new creation; the old has passed away, behold, the new has come." And then, to give the explanation, Paul adds: "All this is from God, who through Christ reconciled us to himself and gave us the ministry [the *diakonia*] of reconciliation."

The new life of righteousness derives from Christ and is the fruit of reconciliation. In what sense it is simply a gift has precipitated the long history of predestinarian debate and misunderstanding in doctrinal history. We cannot concern ourselves with the vast proliferation of issues here involved; I can only say for myself that the bearing of Paul's words in the sixth chapter of Romans, centering around the meaning of baptism, suffices to indicate that reconciliation involves *participation* with Christ in his self-emptying obedience. Further, there is the indication that only as the believer is crucified with Christ in the likeness of his death can or does he rise with Christ in the likeness of his resurrected life. Thus Paul counsels, "So you also must consider yourselves dead to sin and alive to God in Christ Jesus."

I do not think we do justice to Paul's doctrine of *reconciliation* unless we understand that the death *and* resurrection of Jesus Christ are, together, the vehicles of both reconciliation and *newness of life*. The long-standing difficulty, not to say misdirection, of soteriology of Latin and Western Christianity is that it has not held unambiguously to the normality of "newness of life" as the expected fruit of *participation* in the resurrected life of Christ the Lord. It has stressed forgiveness of sins, sometimes death to sin. In Luther it stressed "justification" as God's wholly unmerited acceptance of the sinner. And, while Luther characteristically and strongly affirmed that good works flow from the justified state as natural outcomes of a new status before God, yet *simul justus et peccator* tended to lower the mood of expectancy relating to what, in Pauline teaching, was the necessary expectation of entire Christian faith. That expectancy in early Christianity was *participation* in the resurrected life of the victorious Lord. Reconciliation was, therefore, not primarily forgiveness of sins but primarily *newness of life* through the indwelling power of the living Spirit of Christ, who is at work in his glorified state to void all enmity against God: *personal, societal,* or *cosmic*. In his earthly ministry Jesus was the proclaimer of the Kingdom; in his death and perfect obedience he won the decisive victory over the powers hostile to God's rule; in his resurrected glory he continues his warfare with the powers of evil and inducts into his ranks and empowers for newness of life those who participate with him in his death to sin and are empowered by his ever-lasting Spirit to assay the life of righteousness as a God-given vocation.

II. DEFICIENT UNDERSTANDING OF RECONCILIATION

By the standard of the Pauline view of reconciliation, traditional Western Christianity has defaulted at a number of points, not by plain omission, but in virtue of perspective and misplaced emphasis.

1. It has stressed forgiveness of sins or justification by fastening too strenuously upon the merits of Christ only. This may become antinomianism

2. This stress has been hardened into a dogmatic perspective by the predominance, in the West, of the penal theory of atonement which views the death of Christ primarily as satisfaction of divine wrath set against human sinfulness. The punitive or penal conception of the work of Christ, while it may have some slight basis in Pauline teaching, is by comparison impoverished since, in Paul, the predominant ground of Christ's espousal of death is *enactment* of God's loving purpose to reconcile the world to himself. Reconciliation is God's act at God's initiative through Christ.

3. In consequence of this misplaced emphasis on the forgiveness of sins through the substitutionary death of Christ (Anselm of Canterbury being the influential leader), Latin Christianity and Reformation theology continued to make justification or forgiveness of sins the accepted common denominator of the Christian life. Catholicism made room for more by allowing "the counsels of perfection" (poverty, chastity, and obedience) to be the "supererogation" expectable of the monastic but hardly to be looked for from seculars, either priests or laity. If the latter need not aspire to Christian perfection, nonetheless, through forgiveness of sins, assured through the devout use of the sacraments and the penetential system, they may at least be confident of eternal acceptance with God even if purgatory, postponed to the next stage of life, must be contemplated in prospect, however successfully evaded in this one. This may not be all that can, perhaps even must, be said for purgatory. I am here only suggesting that it became for popular medieval Catholicism a way of evading or postponing in this life the "counsels of perfection"; more fundamentally, it was a way of ignoring the "newness of life"—as gift and vocation—which Paul regarded as the joyous and viable privilege of faith.

Furthermore, when Luther and the other Reformation doctors rejected the monastic life and, therewith, the disciplined life answerable to "the counsels of perfection," they were still dominated by Latin Catholic soteriology, namely, by one side of the Pauline doctrine of reconciliation. Justification meant forgiveness of sins, i.e., liberation from bondage of sin and release from divine wrath. Not till John Wesley revived a doctrine of "Christian Perfection" (widely labeled in his day "enthusiasm" by Bishops Butler and Warbuton among many others) did anything like the Pauline primary stress upon "newness of life" as an indubitable Christian vocation receive renewal in Protestant Christian teaching. Nevertheless, by the middle of the 19th century in American Methodism Christian Perfection in Methodist preaching and teaching had succumbed to the prevailing Western soteriology of the primacy of justification; and "Perfection" became the emphasis of the Methodist splinter groups and the holiness sects that emerged from them.

4. Perhaps another defect attributable to misreading of the Pauline understanding of reconciliation in such a way as to neglect "newness of life" as integral to existence in Christ is an endemic tendency toward moralism on the part of both Latin Catholicism and post-Reformation Protantism. Where salvation is understood primarily as justification or forgiveness of sin, the vocation of the Christian man is seen to be rather more the avoidance of sins and suppression of temptation than

positive engagement with the living Christ in the reconciliation of the whole creation.

Luther perhaps understood this better than any other reformer. He advised the believer "to sin boldly," by which he meant perhaps that, apart from justifying grace, no amount of scrupulosity in avoiding sin would avail in any case. For Luther, much in medieval monasticism was precisely this. It was negative. Chastity, poverty, obedience were withdrawal in the intent of self-contrived perfection. He found in his own agonized experience that not avoidance of sins but openness to grace availed for justification. Therefore *sola gratia!* This might have emancipated Protestantism from moralism, but history suggests otherwise. Somehow the Protestant persuasion prevailed that a Christian is known by what he does not do after he is once justified. There are no doubt historical and sociological causes, or at least concomitants, for all this, but, in the last analysis, it rests back upon a pervasive misreading of the Pauline teaching on reconciliation and the corresponding dominance of the penal theory of the atonement. In the death of Christ there is forgiveness of sin, but in the resurrection of the victorious Christ are given the grace and ground of "newness of life" and the reconciling vocation of the Christian man. Moralism avoids sinful deeds. Reconciliation in the Pauline sense knows sins forgiven and is constrained to the task of reconciliation through ministry, i.e., *diakonia,* in the power of the Spirit.

Moralism is, then, often a subtle evasion of the full import of reconciliation. It usually substitutes avoidance of personal sins for glad acceptance of partnership in the Spirit with Christ in the reconciliation of "principalities and powers," i.e., "all rule and authority" not submissive to God. It specifically restricts Christ's role as reconciler and is largely content with private redemption. Thus it contrives to maintain and to sanction two diverging lines of one history, namely, the sacred and the profane. It does not see that the profane is precisely the task of the sacred. Thus, in the end moralistic Christianity consents to leave history unrestored and unreconciled, having made a sanctuary for a redemptive transaction between Christ and the individual. The latter is redeemed, but history is left to its own devices.

5. In the fifth place, sacramental Christianity both in the East and West, with its sometimes almost physicalistic conception of sacramental grace in popular comprehension, resulted among other things in the impoverishment and emptying of the Christian life. "Newness of life," in the Pauline sense of character and vocation, ceased to challenge save in the aspiration of monasticism, highlighted in the early 13th century by the sublime primitivism of Francis of Assisi. Instead, salva-

tion was cheapened as the means of grace were more and more domesticated in the sacraments. With reference to baptism, Augustine of Hippo, with all his perceptivity, failed to grasp the Pauline teaching and fastened upon Western Catholicism only the one-sided function of forgiveness of sins, or the purgation of prebaptismal sins, both birth sin and actual sin.

6. Finally, an ambiguity prevails in Christian practice with reference to the reconciling work of Christ. On the one hand, a pervasive tendency is visible throughout Christian history to concentrate upon the cosmic dimension of the reconciling work of Christ, which issues in tendencies to world flight, world denial, and various recurrent forms of millenarianism. In any case, the vocation of "newness of life," as *present* partnership with Christ, tends to suffer eclipse or is ignored as the mark of reconciliation and Christian life in the world.

Correspondingly, a widespread myopia prevails concerning the total range of the reconciling work of Christ which, as we have seen, includes and embraces a subordination of "all rule, authority, and power" (comprising what we would call today the societal structures), to the higher rule and authority of God. As Paul saw it, the risen and exalted Lord is at work on the whole continuum of being to renovate the creation and establish the Kingdom of God entire so that "God may be everything to every one." And the working power bringing all things under the sovereign rule of God is the living Lord, the Spirit of Christ.

In the end, then, it comes to this. The Christian churches, by the standard of Paul's view of reconciliation, have truncated, domesticated, and circumscribed the range of the presently working Spirit of the living Christ, the Reconciler. And here, perhaps, is the pervasive weakness of Latin, indeed of all Western, Christianity. It has lived at least in part with an impoverished and restricted comprehension, not only of the rich meaning of reconciliation in Paul's teaching, but of Paul's understanding of the Holy Spirit, whom he variously styles "the Spirit of Christ," or "the Lord, the Spirit." Accordingly, for Paul, reconciliation is not simply justification, forgiveness of sins; it is rather more (although justification is preliminary), restoration *for* life, that is, for vocation. It is a life *in Christ,* impelled by a love of Christ, and animated by the Spirit of Christ whose temples, Paul declares, are reconciled men (1 Cor. 3:16). Paul says, "For we are the temple of the living God; as God said, 'I will live in them and move among them . . .'" (2 Cor. 6:16). It is fellowship with the risen Christ, Christ the Spirit, which turns the reconciled, not into mere recipients of grace and forgiveness, but into partners of the cosmic Christ in the redemption of the continuum of creation, including, of course, historical existence.

III. RECONCILED TO THE WORLD

So far, we have spoken of reconciliation in its originative expression in Pauline teaching. We have also called attention to perennial deviations of Western Christianity, both Catholic and Protestant, from the Pauline conception. The question now is: How does it stand today with the Christian doctrine of reconciliation? In the face of prevailing winds of doctrine presently buffeting Christendom, honesty compels candor as to whether, in view of these modern developments, a *theological* treatment of reconciliation is either still necessary or even possible. For there is abroad today at least a two-pronged attack upon traditional views as fostered by Western Christianity.

On the one side, the side of *radical theology*, there are representatives of a radical rejection of reconciliation in the whole range of its meanings. These writers are "radical" because for various reasons they see fit to repudiate the presuppositions of any view of reconciliation between man and God. For example, they reject what Martin Buber once described as the essential mark of "the faith of Judaism," namely, that "the whole history of the world, the hidden, real world history, is a dialogue between God and his creature." Buber called it "a dialogue in which man is a true, legitimate partner, who is entitled and empowered to speak his own independent word out of his own being." [1]

The radical theologians reject this "dialogue" situation, which Buber holds to be fundamental to the faith of Judaism and which I think is just as fundamental to the faith of Christianity. Without straining we can say that a coimplication between man and God, perhaps even the "dialogic" one, was likewise a determinative presupposition of Paul's interpretation of the reconciling work of Christ. Paul's most general treatment of this theme is in Rom 1:19 ff. The negativity of the "radical theologians," whatever estimate we may place upon the cogency of their writings, at least alerts us to a violently antitraditionalistic temper that seems to be abroad among us.

If, in the face of this, we suspect that the negativism we perceive about us is in some part a renewal of Kierkegaard's mid-19th-century "attack upon Christendom," we may not wholly miss the point provided we do not fail to see that the current assault upon "Christendom" has different presuppositions. To be sure, the modern radicals hardly attain to the mordant ridicule or trenchant critique to which established folk-Christianity was subjected through Kierkegaard's adroit irony. Christianity does not exist in Protestant Denmark, Kierkegaard chided, if by Christianity we mean that of the New Testament. It was Kierkegaard who in 1854–55 originated the widely held thesis of the church's present-day critics that "Christendom is the betrayal of Christianity." [2] But Kierkegaard's "attack" was prompted by smoldering outrage against a pious cultus and an arthritic creedal orthodoxy, which substituted itself and its established routines for direct encounter with Christ. Christ is the believer's eternal contemporary with whom alone he has to deal. Therefore, outrageously presumptuous is the church to stand in the place of God before the sinner and settle for the sinner's compliant ascription to orthodoxy in place of Christ's justification and reconciliation of the repentant sinner.

With the radical theologians, however, there is no appeal to the New Testament as a norm by which to judge the orthodoxy of "Christendom." Whereas Kierkegaard would distinguish and, indeed, hope to separate the kernel from the husk of acculturated Christianity, the radicals repudiate explicitly Kierkegaard's "assumption that Christendom is simply secularized Christianity," [3] that is, Christianity which has supinely accommodated to culture. Against this, it is the claim of the radical theologians that "Christendom *is* everything that Christianity has become in history." [4] It has become "Christendom." If Kierkegaard's program is to be completed, then, since Christendom *is* all that Christianity has become in history, including its God, the radical rejection of "Christendom" must include God also.

It does not matter that this is a formal logical fallacy, that of "undistributed middle"; the real point is that Altizer does not care to separate the "kernel" from the "husk." He expressly prefers to let God go with the alleged historical disintegration of "Christendom." Indeed, this relinquishment of God is a consequence of the hidden premise of the whole argument. The premise is this: there can be no distinction between God and "Christendom" or between authentic and historical Christianity because of the thinly disguised historical positivism that is assumed initially. The presumption of historical positivism is that *there is no reality transcending history,* for all reality is exhausted in the manifestations of historical development, á là Hegel. To say, then, that God has died in our history is to indulge in unnecessarily mystifying language whose real substance is that, apart from history, there is no transcendent Reality and, if "Christendom" is dying, then, on these terms, the only God that "Christendom" had is also dying with it. Meanwhile, in addition, we are asked to exalt Jesus while we are counseled to empty Christianity of God, even if, without God, it is difficult either to identify Jesus or to determine the basis of any definitive preference for him.

This is not theology at all. It might simply be called naturalistic historicism. Naturalism is the doctrine that there is no reality apart from nature. It is perhaps best, however, to speak of Altizer's view simply as historical positivism. In it, apparently, reconciliation is now quite the reverse of the New Testament view, since reconciliation is the resolute affirmation of history, of the secular, as *itself* the only possible realm of redemption.

William Hamilton strikes me as a more honest and less Promethean type of radical. We seem to locate his working center in the following quotation:

Religion is to be defined as the assumption in theology, preaching, apologetics, evangelism, counseling, that man needs God, and that there are certain things that God alone can do for him. I am denying that religion is necessary and saying that the movement from the church to the world that we [i.e., Hamilton] have taken as definitive of Protestantism not only permits but requires this denial. To assert that we are men moving from cloister to world, church to world, to say that we are secular men, is to say that we do not ask God to do for us what the world is qualified to do. . . . This kind of world-affirmation is the point where I join the death of God movement.[5]

The views here are candid, interesting, and have their identifiable antecedents in theological literature. The definition of Protestantism as "a movement away from the sacred place" to the world [6] would no doubt seem both arbitrary and peripheral, perhaps trivial, to the Reformers who strove valiantly in their time for the sovereignty of God over his grace and the accessibility of it, in Word and Sacrament, independently of ecclesiastical contrivance or control. They demolished the cloister in the interest of the freedom of God over grace and world. Grace could not be cloistered, and the lordship of the Christian man was, indeed, that of exercising his "calling" in the world. But unmistakably it was the Christian's calling *under* God; and, on this latter point, Calvin was, if anything, more emphatic than Luther.

But it is the Bonhoeffer *motif* of man's "coming of age" in the modern world, man's acceptance of the risks of entire faithfulness, that shines through Hamilton's protest against "religion." He revolts against "using God to meet a need or to solve a problem," in short, asking "God to do for us what the world is qualified to do." [7] Elsewhere, it is true, Hamilton makes much of "the absence of the experience of God" as distinguished from "the experience of the absence of God." He does so in such a way as to suggest his own declining, perhaps tenuous, hold upon the "dialogic" character of the Judeo-Christian tradition. It is this which, as we saw, according to Martin Buber, understands the hidden but real history of the world as dialogue between God and man. Hamilton seems to feel that this dialogue has diverted men from their responsibilities in and for the world. His alternative to "religion" seems to be his own somber testimony: "We are not proceeding from God and faith to neighbor and love. . . . We move to our neighbor, to the city and to the world out of a sense of the loss of God." [8]

Here we have something reminiscent of the pathos, the humane agnosticism and humanism of Matthew Arnold's *Dover Beach:*

> Ah, love, let us be true to one another!
> For the world, which seems
> To lie before us like a land of dreams, . . .
> Hath really neither joy, nor love, nor light,
> Nor certitude, nor peace, nor help for pain.

Here reconciliation is reconciliation with our fellowman and resigned acceptance of what "the world" can do to solve our problems.

It is of particular importance to note that in none of the radical theologians is sin taken seriously, in sharp distinction from the theology of a generation ago and, of course, historic Christianity in general. The sinfulness of man is not contemplated either for what glimpse it may give of man's Other Partner in dialogue. Sin perhaps has been psychologized away or understood exhaustively in terms of interpersonal dynamics. In any case, in the absence of any serious consciousness of estrangement, waywardness, or sinfulness of man, both "religion" in general and, presumably, Christianity as a species of religion, are evacuated of relevance. In one way or other, "religion" presumes that "man needs God." Hamilton denies that religion is necessary.[9] This, surely, is to say that reconciliation is unnecessary whether as understood by Western Christianity or by Paul. It means that man does not need God, and that God is not a dialogical partner with man. The alternatives are old ones: In the successive phases of cultural history men seem to vacillate between preference for monologue and for dialogue. Accordingly, the relation between *faith* and *unfaith* is perennially dialectical. With option for the one goes always the possible alternative of the other. "I believe; help my belief!" (Mark 9:24.)

IV. PROTESTANT CRITICS OF DELIMITED RECONCILIATION

I have mentioned a two-pronged attack upon traditional views of reconciliation. The radical one has been easy to identify. The second is more elusive because of the multiplicity both of its aspects and its proponents. Yet this second critique constitutes the burden of the greater part of the theological pamphleteering of our time. Its sources are many, and, above all in this regard, one must not neglect a certain recovery of the Old Testament—its view of history as the vehicle of a divine-human encounter. In this connection, Martin Buber has been recurrently influential in his claim that "redemption must take place in the whole corporeal life. God, the Creator," Buber says, "wills to consummate nothing less than the whole of his creation." [10] This view could also echo that of Paul in 1 Cor. 15:25 ff., as elsewhere.

But, perhaps, we may look to Dietrich Bonhoeffer's *Letters and Papers from Prison* for the immediate and most impelling source of the new perspective on reconciliation—a perspective which is also a stringent criticism of long prevailing notions cherished among the Protestant communions. Perhaps the perspective can be summarized in the well-known phrase "religionless Christianity," but what it signified for Bonhoeffer may be illustrated by some passages from his *Letters* selected somewhat at random.

First, Bonhoeffer had apparently become very conscious of the secularization of modern life and, correspondingly, of the growing divorce between religion and the workaday world. Thus, he complains, "When God was driven out of the world, and from the public side of human life, an attempt was made to retain him at least in the sphere of the 'personal,' the 'inner life,' the private life." [11] To this, Harvey Cox has lately given a positive response: "Today, the Gospel summons man to frame with his neighbor a common life suitable to the secular city." [12] Or this: "The action of God occurs through what theologians have sometimes called 'historical events' but what might better be termed 'social change.' " [13] This is a positive response to Bonhoeffer's complaint: "I should like to speak of God not on the borders of life but at its centre." [14]

Whether we attend to Harvey Cox, Colin Williams, J. C. Hoekendijk, or even the "radical" theologians, there is a common insistence that a long-prevailing separation between the sacred and the profane has resulted in the internalizing of Christian faith, cloistering of the cultus, with consequent irresponsibility toward the arena of history, considered as the sphere of God's action and the object of his redemptive purpose. While the distinctive contribution of Cox's *Secular City* is to specify "urbanization" as providing the peculiar dynamics of the arena of contemporary history in which the kingdom of God is to be advanced, all these current writers are responding positively to Bonhoeffer's call to "secularize" Christianity, that is, to affirm the world, human history, as also candidates for redemption and reconciliation and as the sphere of Christian responsibility when it properly accepts its reconciling and servant function. With varying emphases, much like the social gospel of forty years past, each of these writers receives the gospel of the kingdom of God under the mandate of the redemption of history and repudiates either the medieval or the Lutheran versions of separation between the heavenly and the earthly cities. Above all, they repudiate a view of the church which makes it merely the custodian, gateway, or embassy in this world of the heavenly city. Bonhoeffer said, "The Old Testament speaks of *historical* redemption. . . . Israel is redeemed out of Egypt in order to live before God on earth." [15]

Only one other theme can be referred to in the writings of Bonhoeffer. It comes from "Thoughts on the Baptism of D. W. R.," a nephew. "During these years," he wrote, "the Church has fought for self-preservation as though it were an end in itself, and has thereby lost its chance to speak a word of reconciliation to mankind and the world at large. . . . By the time you are grown up, the form of the Church will have changed beyond recognition." [16]

The positive response to this challenge may be taken conveniently and representatively from the following statements of Professor J. C. Hoekendijk in his important little book *The Church Inside Out.* The title itself conveys its message: the mandate upon the church is to turn from inward concentration upon itself to its apostolate to the world, as servant to the world, for the evangelistic task of the church is not to collect souls to be harbored and nurtured within its enclaves. But Hoekendijk is even more thoroughgoing than that. The body of Christ is not the self-contained community of believers, but "the coming into being of a new mankind." The task of the church is not the harvesting of the reconciled out of the world but the extension of the reconciling task *to* the world. In fact, the church has no place or substantial identity. The church *is* mission, and to the world. She has no other existence than *in actu Christi,* i.e., in the action of Christ. This is her apostolate. She exists in recapitulation of the *diakonia,* the ministry of Christ. "The church," says Hoekendijk, "exists only *in actu. . . . The church is a function of the apostolate.*"[17] In short, we may say that the church is truly the church when she empties herself of herself and becomes, like her Lord, wholly servant.

v. THE RECONCILED ARE RECONCILERS

Plainly, this second line of present-day attack upon Christendom must be heeded. The Word of the gospel is the Word of redemption to the world. That the Word has always tended to become incarcerated within the instrumentalities of its propagation is the somber *leitmotif* of church history, and the successive stirrings of reformation and renewal have regularly emerged against this incarceration of the Word of reconciliation in the interest of emancipation, i.e., its extension to the world. There can hardly be doubt that a perennial tendency of the church has been to immure the gospel of reconciliation as a sacred deposit of which the church tends to view itself as trustee or custodian.

The instinct of the succession of reformers is right; the real safekeeping of the gospel is its *publication* in and through endless service to the world. So that the authentic role of the church in all ages is neither that of sanctuary nor that of custodian, but that of the missioner-servant.

It is not misleading to say that this understanding on the part of John XXIII inspired the Second Vatican Council and precipitated a reformation the outcome of which is not yet fully visible. Ottaviani, Ruffini, and other arch-conservatives of the Roman Church were not misguided in perceiving in the spirit and perspective of John XXIII an attack upon Roman Catholic "Christendom" as it had come to be and was.

A like concern animates the critics of self-maintaining ecclesiastical institutionalism in its Protestant forms. All of them in one way or another are, I think, concerned to extend the reconciling work of Christ to the restoration and redemption of human life in its historical expression. For them the kingdom of God includes history. For some, like the radical theologians, it is *exhausted* by history. But for the moderates, such as Bonhoeffer, the range of the Kingdom extends beyond history and the transcendent dimension of the kingdom of God is retained, if sometimes ambiguously. In all this, what we have is a corrective to a recurrent tendency in Catholic and Protestant Christianity to restrict the function and range of the reconciling work of Christ to a transaction between God and the individual in preparation for the latter's heavenly journey. This is not only to truncate the reconciling work of Christ; it is, in a manner, to forsake the profane and, as it were, to consign the realm of history to permanent dereliction if not perdition.

We can call this "culpable Christian irresponsibility," of which the record of Protestant Christianity in American society is grievously illustrative. Or we can, I believe, say that the consignment of history to insignificance, dereliction, or even to meaninglessness is unfaithfulness to, as well as misunderstanding of, Paul's teaching on the full range of the reconciling work of Christ. Paul not only teaches that "God was in Christ reconciling *the world* to himself," he also declares that the reconciled are precisely reconcilers. That is their explicit role and function. Thus, to them also has been given "the ministry of reconciliation" (2 Cor. 5:18–19). So there is every indication that Paul thinks of the reconciled, like himself, as ambassadors of reconciliation to the world. It is on the strength of this that he looks for the redemption of the creation, which, until the reconciling work of Christ, waited in groaning and travail to be delivered from the bondage of corruption (Rom. 8:20–22).

One may judge, then, that the Christian churches have not and do not adequately credit the Pauline teaching, which, nevertheless keeps reemerging as judgment. It is the message that the reconciliation of our estranged humanity to God through Christ extends to the rule of God in human affairs. It engenders this hope on the finding of the Apostle Paul that, "Therefore, if anyone is in Christ, he is a new creation. . . ." That was the Apostle's epoch-making discovery. Yet it presupposes as its antecedent all that is encapsuled in the "Therefore." The latter refers, first, not to the reconciling work of the redeemed, but to God's gracious initiative that overtook Paul in the grace of the Redeemer. Therefore, and therefrom, derives to the redeemed who receive it, a vocation. "God was in Christ," says Paul, "reconciling the world to himself . . . and entrusting to us the ministry of reconciliation" (2 Cor. 5:18, 19). Had not Jesus said: "By their fruits ye shall know them"? (Matt. 7:20) Hence, we are scarcely responsible to the New Testament witness if we suppose that the Gospel reduces itself to ethics and do not understand that the vocation of the Christian is both authorized and empowered by the Power, "not ourselves which makes for righteousness."

A PROTESTANT UNDERSTANDING OF THE LORD'S SUPPER

To pretend to represent completely the Protestant understanding of Holy Communion of the Lord's Supper in the space of a single essay would be as presumptuous as it is impossible. Historically, lively differences among the 16th-century Reformers were early and influentially manifest in the *Marburg Colloquy* of 1529 between Luther and Zwingli, which became, thereafter, divergent watersheds for Protestant theology of the Sacrament to this day.

Among, as well as within, individual Protestant communions as we now know them, varying interpretations of the meaning and significance of the Lord's Supper often prevail, disclosing a silent alteration of understanding not uninfluenced by intellectual and cultural change but, above all, by altering interpretation, over the years, of the role of Scripture and tradition in the determination of doctrine. Perhaps the facts warrant the judgment that, among mainline American Protestant denominations, less interest has been fixed upon sacramental theology over the past century than upon any other aspect of Christian doctrine. By contrast, in the first age of the Reformation it was a matter of the most lively interest and, indeed, controversy among principal sectors of the reforming movement in Europe and the British Isles.

I

Historically considered, then, one fairly uniform Protestant conception of the Sacrament of Holy Communion is discernible in a common opposition, on the part of reforming communions, to the medieval Roman Catholic doctrine of transubstantiation. This is true whether one turns to the *Marburg Colloquy* or to the treatises of Thomas Cranmer or of N. Ridley on the Lord's Supper. Also there was general consensus at the point of denial that the sacrament of the altar be viewed as offering up to God the sacrifice of Christ's body and blood, and an insistence that living faith was requisite for its proper efficacy to the believer. Accordingly, the reformers tended also to reject the formula *ex opere operato,* or the view that communication of divine

A slightly revised article originally published by The Tidings Press of The United Methodist Church (Nashville, Tenn., 1962).

grace in Holy Communion was effectual independent of human conditions appertaining either to its administration or its reception.

According to the medieval doctrine of transubstantiation—the rudiments of which may perhaps be found in the writings of such early Latin fathers as Cyprian and Ambrose of Milan—the wine and the bread, at the time of elevation and on the occasion of the priestly words of institution, become transformed into the substance of the body and blood of Christ. Their appearance or "accidental" nature is not altered, but they are altered in "substance," or essential nature, so that the communicant actually partakes of the real body and blood of the exalted Saviour.

While Luther, as early as 1520, rejected transubstantiation, he always affirmed the real or bodily presence of Christ in, with, and under the physical elements of bread and wine. And he opposed the views of Zwingli, a fellow reformer, insofar as Zwingli regarded the bread and wine as signs that only signified the body and blood of Christ which was *once* offered up for us. This conception led Zwingli to assert, in controversy with Luther, that the Lord's Supper is primarily "a memorial celebration designed to remind us of the redemption wrought by the death of Christ; and, on the other hand, a profession of adherence to Christ in the presence of the congregation, and thus the assuming of an obligation to lead a Christian life." (See R. Seeberg, *History of Doctrines.*)

The issue here represented has persisted as a basic divergency among Protestant conceptions of the Lord's Supper. In one way or another, the Lutheran and Anglican traditions have insisted upon "the real presence," while the Zwinglian line has tended to find expression, variously modulated, elsewhere as in the "reformed tradition" that has its decisive sources in *The Gallican Confession* (1559) or the Genevan *Catechism* (1541)—both powerfully shaped by the mind of John Calvin. In important contrast with the Zwinglian line, Luther and Lutheranism are represented in Article X of *The Augsburg Confession* (1530) to the effect that, in "the Supper of the Lord . . . the true body and blood of Christ are truly present (under the form of bread and wine), and are (there) communicated to those that eat in the Lord's Supper . . ." (P. Schaff, *Creeds of Christendom.* III, 13). Here are the clear echoes of Luther's concern, and Melanchthon's, for a "real presence" in the sacrament and an emphasis which sometimes takes the name, "consubstantiation."

The issue that split Luther and Zwingli was perhaps this: whether the word "is," in the Dominical words of institution: "This *is* my body," means *"identity"* or *signifies."* For the most part, the Reformed wing of Protestantism settled for "is"—signifies. For Calvin, neither Word nor Sacrament was effectual apart from the present ministry of the Holy Spirit; and, in the sacrament, we have a sure sign of God's promise and covenant, on the one hand, and, on the other, we confess our faith before men.

Attention to the Gallican, or *French Confession of Faith* will immediately indicate a quite variant interpretation of the sacraments, and therewith, of the Lord's Supper, as compared with the Lutheran standpoint in this, that, for Calvin, the work of grace is an *immediate* act of God, equally operative either in the preaching of the Word or in the administration of the sacraments. Moreover, Articles 27 and 28 of the *Confession* make it evident that Calvin assigns a priority to the preached Word as "means of grace" and that he views the sacraments as signs and seals confirming a work of justification and regeneration already accomplished. Accordingly, Article 34 informs us that "the sacraments are added to the Word for more ample confirmation, that they may be to us *pledges* and *seals of the grace of God. . . .*" If, as Article 36 affirms of the Lord's Supper, that by it Jesus Christ "feeds and strengthens us with the substance of his body and of his blood," it is immediately added "that this is done spiritually . . ." (P. Schaff, *Creeds of Christendom,* III, 375, 378, 380). On these views, one may observe only that this semi-Zwinglian standpoint, which finds influential reexpression in *The Westminster Confession* of 1648, has had wide influence in American Protestantism well beyond the confines of the Presbyterian churches.

In one of the influential documents of American Protestantism, the Saybrook *Confession* of 1708, we read: "Our Lord Jesus in the night wherein he was betrayed, instituted the Sacrament of his body and blood called the Lord's Supper, to be observed in his Churches to the end of the world, for the perpetual remembrance, and shewing forth of the sacrifice of himself in his death, the sealing of all benefits thereof unto true believers, their spiritual nourishment and growth in him, their further engagement in and to all duties which they owe unto him, and to be a bond and pledge of their communion with him and with each other" (*A Profession of Faith* [Bridgeport, 1810]). Herein we perceive a remarkable confluence both of the teaching of Zwingli and of Calvin, a splendid amalgam, neither Lutheran nor Anglican.

While American Methodism has come to possess in later days very much in common with the Saybrook Confession of New England Congregationalism, its father, John Wesley, in a very complex way united in himself, both the Anglican insistence upon the real presence of Christ in the Lord's Supper and the Calvinist insistence upon the sacrament as sign and seal of God's covenant and promise. Umphrey

Lee properly stated of Wesley that, for him, "the Lord's Supper is the supreme rite in which the recipient may expect the Grace of God" (*John Wesley and Modern Religion*, p. 252). It is neither merely a rite of memorial nor an oath of allegiance. God *acts* savingly through it so that Wesley recurrently insisted that it is a "converting ordinance." It is, moreover, a celebration of "the one perfect and sufficient sacrifice" in which the believer may himself participate; but he participates by sacrifice of himself, as Dr. Lee said, and of all that he has.

To say that the Lord's Supper is a "converting ordinance" is to acknowledge that, in it and with it, is somehow the redemptive working of Christ. In it the efficacy of his sacrificial death is perpetuated. For Wesley it is a veritable "means of grace" to be neglected at one's peril. Moreover, there is in the *Eucharistic Hymns* of John and Charles Wesley a stress upon the sacrifice of Christ, re-presented in the sacrament of the altar, with which the vital communicant identifies as occasion for a like self-offering. Thus from Hymn 54 we read:

> Saviour, Thou didst the mystery give,
> That I thy nature might partake;
> Thou bidd'st me outward signs receive,
> One with Thyself my soul to make.

Nor is this means of grace optional or subordinate to any other:

> The prayer, the fast, the word conveys,
> When mixed with faith, Thy life to me;
> In all the channels of Thy grace,
> I still have fellowship with Thee;
> But chiefly here my soul is fed
> With fulness of immortal bread.

There is, therefore, a priority of the sacrament of the Lord's Supper as means of grace for the Wesleys. It is not subordinate nor an addendum to the Word preached as in Calvin. Its principal symbol is the sacrifice of Christ made once for all but, in and with the Holy Communion, becomes a vehicle of redemption for those who identify with the divine self-offering (J. E. Rattenbury, *The Eucharistic Hymns of John and Charles Wesley*, [London, 1948]).

Finally it is very evident that the Wesleyan understanding of the Lord's Supper is grounded in, as well as a republication of, Article 25 of *The Thirty-Nine Articles of the Church of England*, 1571. There we read: "Sacraments ordained of Christ are not only badges and tokens of Christian men's profession, but rather *they are certain sure witnesses, and effectual signs of grace*, and God's will towards us, *by which he doth work invisibly in us*, and doth not only quicken, but also strengthen and confirm our faith in Him" (P. Schaff, *Creeds of Christen-*

dom, III, 502). Wesley reasserts the emphasis of the English reformers on "the full perfect and sufficient sacrifice" of Christ in the sacrament of the altar, the sacrament as eminent vehicle of divine grace, and proper reception as participation and identification. There is also not to be missed a certain stress upon the *prevenience of grace in the sacrament* that, in comparison with reformed tradition of the Continent, moves in the direction of restoring the priority of the divine initiative as in *ex opere operato* of the Catholic tradition.

II

Within the Protestant tradition—and we have neglected consideration of other significant representatives—at least two divergent lines of interpretation of Holy Communion become visible.

There is the Zwinglian line which understands the "is" in the phrase "This *is* my body" to mean *signify,* or *stand for.* Such an interpretation tends to make of the Lord's Supper a rite whereby the once-for-all sacrifice of Christ is memorialized and the believer invited to respond with pledge of allegiance.

There is, on the other hand, the line of Lutheranism, Anglicanism, and Wesleyanism which understand the "is" as in some sense a declaration of identity.

The assertion of identity is a striving to assert in one way or another that the redemptive grace which *was* present in the sacrifice of Jesus Christ is *still* effectually present and operative in the sacramental act. It is the effort to affirm that, in the sacrament, God is active and graciously redemptive, not alone on the condition of a man's faith, but as actually engendering that faith.

Thus, it rejects the view that the sacrament is a rite by which *men* are primarily active, either as acknowledging or confessing God's ancient saving deed in Christ or as affirming allegiance in appropriate faith and gratitude.

The "is" of identity in the words of institution, "This *is* my body," strives to convey the truth that in, with, and under the sacrament the saving work of Christ goes on as present reality. This is what is really intended and meant, I think, by the insistence upon "the real presence."

But the phrase "the real presence" is misleading because it is static. It involves what we may call a substantialistic rather than a dynamic and energistic conception of the sacrament and of sacramental grace. It makes the sacrament an objectification of the divine activity rather than a vehicle and medium for it. Instead of conveying the saving activity of God, the elements become, or tend to become, identified with the saving grace.

This objectification of grace is a domestification of it, a localization of it in time and place. Objectification is indicative of the perennial temptation of man, as religious, to house the Deity, to put Him within reach, to get possession of the divine saving power. What is more, it participates in a tendency to forsake the classical and long prevailing, though sometimes wavering, Christian intuition that the sacrament is a *sign* pointing beyond itself and that it never is simply to be identified with the saving grace of which it is, nevertheless, a medium and vehicle.

The Protestant insistency, then, upon "the real presence," wherever made, derives from a proper instinct to recognize that in and with the sacrament of Holy Communion, *God* approaches man for man's redemption. It protests, as deficiently Christian, any notion that in this sacrament *man* is primarily the actor, whether as memorializing Christ's sacrifical death, or confessing his faith, or owning his allegiance.

Yet, on the other hand, emphasis on "the real presence" may go so far in the direction of identifying the sacrament with Christ's saving grace as to approximate the Roman doctrine of transubstantiation, which all the Reformers in fact rejected.

Transubstantiation is the tendency to objectify or substantialize grace come to completion or full realization. It is the domestication of God.

III

How, then, is Protestantism to avoid, on the other hand, the defects of memorialism represented by Zwingli and, on the other, the dangers of substantialistic domestication of grace resident, but not necessarily explicit, in the doctrine of "the real presence"?

The ingredients of the answer are found within both the Protestant and the Roman Catholic traditions and need not be newly fabricated. Most pertinently, they are to be found within the New Testament itself and in long standing commentary upon it.

We are never to forget that the Lord's Supper was instituted by Jesus on the night in which he was betrayed. He knew that he was about to walk into the valley of the shadow of death, for he had come not to be ministered unto, but to minister. He had come to his own, but his own received him not. Now his ministry could be fulfilled only by total obedience to God in the face of, and in full acceptance of, the rejection and hostility of men. To fulfill his ministry meant to suffer rejection in unfaltering obedience.

The Lord's Supper, therefore, looks forward to an absolute fidelity to God in the face of death. But his death is to be the victory of perfect obedience. Therefore, Jesus did not himself partake either of the bread or of the wine on the occasion of his institution of the Supper.

Nothing can be more plain, therefore, than that, when our Lord broke the bread, saying, "Take ye: this is my body" and passed the cup with the words "This is my blood of the covenant which is poured out for many," Jesus signified: (1) that his minstry was to be perfected in his suffering, (2) that his ministry was the victory of perfect obedience, and (3) that his disciples were hereby invited (a) to receive the benefits of his ministry and (b) thereby to participate in the same ministry of victory through obedience.

When both St. Paul (1 Cor. 11:24) and St. Luke (22:19b) add the words: "This do in remembrance of me," *anamnesis,* or "remembrance," is not simply a command to think back upon, but rather enjoins *participation* through recollection. The command to remember is the charge to represent the sacrifice forever through recurrent identification of self with the victory through sacrifice about to be accomplished.

It is from this thought that St. Paul derives his recurring theme that the Christian is one who is united with Christ in the likeness of His death that he too may walk in newness of life. For St. Paul, both baptism and the Lord's Supper signify Christ's victory through death, and the believer *is* such just exactly by way of *participation* in that victory. It is the death of the old man and the creation of the new man in Christ Jesus.

In the sacrament, therefore, Jesus invites his disciples to receive the benefits of his passion, that is, his victory and to appropriate the fruits of his ministry. His ministry is victory over temptation to which all men have succumbed.

The sacrament is a "sign"; it is also a "seal of the covenant," that is, the now established community between God and men that is fulfilled in Jesus' perfect obedience. To eat the bread intentionally is to be made one with Him who reconciles man to God. To drink the cup intentionally is to share with the Lord in His victory through suffering. It is also to pledge allegiance, that is, to take upon oneself the vocation of suffering service. So, as St. Paul declares, to us also is given the ministry of reconciliation (2 Cor. 5:18).

In such a view, mere memorialism is completely transcended in *personal participation.* He who is open to receive the Holy Communion will find in it a "converting ordinance," a vehicle and medium of grace. It will then be to him the instrumentality of the new covenant whereby he is established in renewed community with God the Father. And, inasmuch as the Holy Communion is to him the medium of reconciliation that overcomes alienation, he must declare that Christ's saving work is present to him therein.

But it will be the presence of the restorative Spirit of Christ. Christ will have extended to him, through the sacrament and over the chasm of the intervening ages, the power and redemptive might of His perfect victory through sacrifice.

In his transformed life the believer will inevitably recognize the eternally present and universal power of his Lord. In this way he will testify to "the real presence" of Christ in the Lord's Supper. He will not seek to substantialize it by identifying or locating it in the elements. He will only testify that Christ has been present to him to purify, to cleanse, and to empower as he has received the elements in the strength of the Lord's invitation and promise.

Something like this might be considered the basis of the Protestant conception of Holy Communion.

CONSIDERATIONS BASIC TO REVISED THEOLOGICAL METHOD IN PROTESTANT THEOLOGY

The subject under examination is: "a reconsideration of theological method." After many years of administrative rustication and preoccupation with "controlling reason," I tremble to reenter a controversial theological arena wherein I once flattered myself on being at home. Meanwhile, torrents of unread literature have passed me by and vast shifts in cultural sensibility have contributed to a climatic change in the style of theology for which I can claim but moderate comprehension and about which, consequently no doubt, I entertain immoderate mistrust.

I. SOME GROUNDS OF THEOLOGICAL CONFUSION

From Professor D. C. Macintosh of Yale days, I learned that theological methods are ordinarily prompted by concern for our knowledge of God. It was certainly so in the 19th- and early 20th-century "liberal" period. I am amazed by the late radical "theology of Christian atheism" which solves the knowledge problem precisely by eliminating it, that is, by identifying the sacred with the secular or resolving the Transcendent into historic process. This solves an epistemological problem by a stunning ontological maneuver. So God is said to have died by almost exhaustive identification with cultural history, and the problem of God, or man's knowledge of God, is retired by general demolition. Man is now allowed to "come of age" and attend to his proper business— the effectual management and, no doubt, the redemption of the world by taking his stand beside "the neighbor"!

This naturalistic historicism is, of course, prompted by a radical if wistful humanism, albeit both ambiguous and ambivalent in recent expression. As a theological method, it simply razes the problem like a bulldozer in urban renewal. If this atheistic humanism, like its more sober naturalistic predecessors, is really credible, theology as we have known it has no remaining proper business, and the question of "theological method" has been settled by a *tour de force*, and further meet-

An essay presented to the Duodecim Theological Group, Union Theological Seminary, New York, October 1968.

ings of Duodecim are superfluous. Thus, it will have been our unenviable lot to see our work as a theological society completed in our own time but not, presumably, at our own hands!

If, however, as John Bennett observed to the Union Seminary graduates at the 1968 Commencement, this is a time of "theological confusion" touching the very "substance of faith," it would be both simplistic and unworthy of professional theologians to lay the blame on such flimsy theological sallies as "the death of God theology" when, in fact, the latter, are almost certainly symptomatic more nearly of a deeplying cultural fault than of an intellectual revolution. That is, they are indicative rather more of climatic alterations of *ethos* than assays of intellectually disciplined rigour, and they look more like outcomes of moral depression, failure of nerve, or *accidie* than a spirited rational assault upon a longstanding theological problem in received Protestantism.

Withal, it is the really enormous task of theological, as of philosophical, endeavor to discriminate more exactly what these symptoms are indicative of, not merely by consulting the welter of near unprecedented societal change in sociological perspective, but by unflinching reexamination of the inherited world-structure or structures by which Western man has, more or less adequately, hitherto related the world to God and human existence to destiny. For centuries, since the Renaissance and Reformation, this structure has fallen into both desuetude and disrepair, while it was mainly "bracketed" by the principal theological traditions of Protestantism quite as much (but for different reasons) as by the experimental sciences, which issued from the program of Bacon's *Novum Organum*.

By inattention bred of pervasive indisposition Protestant theology has, I think, for over four hundred years simply shunned encounter with the problem of a viable symbolic structure for relating man to Deity or, conversely, God to the Creation. Consequently, modern man has endeavored to survive intellectually in a broken world with an unresolved dualism, an abyss, between his ordinary world and God. Kant justified both "science" and "religion" but at the cost of sundering the subject-matters of both this side of the life Eternal. If Luther aspired to no ontology, as is certain, Kant made it unnecessary, indeed impossible. Natural science has rejoiced in its liberation, but the living man has found no point of meeting between the God of his "moral consciousness" (important as I take that God to be) and the orders of his work-a-day world. He was forced, therefore, and radically, to live in two worlds that never meet or were not understood as meeting—the secular and the sacred.

With the Lutheran form of *justificatio* as an immediate transaction of grace, between God and the believer, and with Kantian critical idealism to provide the legitimizing philosophical context, it was almost inevitable that Protestant Christianity in the 19th century and onwards should become rootless with respect to Creation, moralistic, and introverted. The 18th-century Evangelical Revival did little to prevent this, and it was clinched by Schleiermacher's formative influence. Premised upon an unacknowledged but pervasive ontological monism, domesticating the divine in human nature, Schleiermacher decisively turned man in upon himself as the privileged and unmediated way to God, bracketing the question of God's relation to the external world. And the succeeding line of German theology, through Ritschl on to Barth, was really postulated upon the irrelevance or the impossibility of any God-and-world ontology.

Only the Hegelian process philosophy assayed to bridge the ontological gap or fill the vacuum. In the interest of the absolute autonomy of faith, it was immediately assaulted by Kierkegaard on the premise that "subjectivity is the truest objectivity" and, so, contrived to dismiss the problem. But, apart from Hegel, the phenomenalism of Kant, on the one hand, and the empiricistic positivism of Auguste Comte, on the other, weighted the scales either in favor of the "dialectical materialism" of Marx or reduced the predicates *(logoi)* Hegel had ascribed to the Absolute to "qualities" (values) invoked by the potentials of the human subject (Feuerbach). So, in either case, left-wing Hegelianism issued in unequivocal phenomenalism, that is, atheism. In the case of Feuerbach, theology was resolved into anthropology and ethics, and is lately showing its face again in species of "renewal theology."

It may be noted in passing that this is, in fact, copied and up-dated by the "death of God theology," especially in Altizer's version. Nevertheless, the point remains that Altizer's *coup* is quite reminiscent of its left-wing Hegelian predecessors. In dissolving the Transcendent through radical identification with cultural-historical process, Altizer and company seek to obviate the unresolved gaping abyss between God and the world and the attendant (if not necessarily consequential) inner directedness or other-worldliness of Christian piety that sits loose to its responsibilities in and for history. Of these, Bonhoeffer's complaints received the powerful certification of a martyr-like death in the cause of tyrannicide.

In short, the hidden logic is like this: if the relation of God to the world, as also to man in the world, remains unintelligibly ambiguous, why not dispense with that relation altogether and distract man's attention from his proper philanthropic business in the world no longer, since also (the undemonstrated premise!) he has now anyway "come of age"? This, too, is simply to espouse Kant's religion of moral responsibility over again while renouncing once-for-all Kant's *Noumenon*, considered as the ontological coimplicate of "the pure practical reason." Christian atheism, then, as I see it is a republication of Feuerbach with assists from Bonhoeffer (unintended!) and Nietzsche, as alleged preeminent spokesman for the prevailing ethos that despairs of the absent God.

But now, in attempting to illuminate, somewhat, the intellectual components that require exhuming for comprehension of the theological confusion of our time, I have wandered, but I hope not aimlessly. In attempting to fathom or, more exactly, diagnose the confusion with its symptoms, I meant to venture an explanatory hypothesis. I would hypothecate that these confusions point to a failure of Western Christianity since the 15th century—a failure more characteristically Protestant than Catholic—to illuminate what I will call, for lack of a more suitable phrase, the God-and-world Structure, and in such a way as to be intelligible to the era of man's astonishing technological mastery of nature and, when man's increasing self-sufficiency in the sphere of "controlling reason" tends to render God expendable. As I see it, the Bishop of Woolwich had really only one point: "the intelligible world" has been breached and broken a long time because it is not possessed of an ontology that can include the God that Christian faith, nevertheless, insists is available in and through the alleged revelation in Jesus Christ.

It may be argued that precisely in this sphere the so-called neo-orthodox resurgence of the second quarter of the 20th century completely failed to speak to the crystallizing dilemma and emergent *Zeitgeist* while it justifiably redressed an imbalance in the long prevailing Schleiermacherian conception of the Word of God, namely, the inherent possibility of human nature as such to give rise to the religious affections. To this, also, Martin Buber addressed his rich researches, but neither he nor Barth, seemingly, were aware that the impending "eclipse of God" was attributable at least as much to a disposition to "make-do" with a world without God as to an indisposition for the divine-human encounter. But the problem was and remains that the vocations to world-mastery (applied science), on the one side, and that of divine-human encounter (neo-orthodox theology) on the other, have no common ground, no intellectual framework which, embracing them both, allows them to comport one with another with intelligible mutuality. Two ways of human salvation—technology and Protestant religion—continue to move as they have moved since the 17th century in opposite directions on the same track.

II. EXHIBITIONS OF THE RESILIENT DUALISM IN RECENT THEOLOGY

While Paul Tillich's theology was a formidable effort to make good the defect of neo-orthodoxy with reference to the unresolved dualism of world-and-God, that is, the cosmological problem; and, while it looked for a time as if he might succeed, Tillich's theological method was basically too dependent upon the "non-objectifying" language of contemporary phenomenological existentialism, I think, to deal significantly either with the *scandalon* of particularity (the Incarnation) or the redemption of the creation i.e., resurrection and newness of life.

In this regard also, of course, Tillich, from the standpoint of Christian tradition, was no better off than Bultmann. Because, in Christology, neither of them could identify the revelatory event "under the conditions of existence," they inevitably circumvented the issue of Creation vis à vis the Creator or the God-and-world Structure. Bultmann, as Bonhoeffer complained, rendered the redemption of history irrelevant because the redemptive event transcended history *as Historie* or had no determinable rootage in it. Likewise, Tillich succeeded in rendering God mainly the vis à vis of man's "ultimate concern" because, like Schleiermacher, he tended towards ontological monism, which had its roots in Benedict Spinoza. This has always admitted of pantheistic inductions that transcend, as Schleiermacher was aware, the stubborn actualities of nature and history, or, conversely, allow for an easy incorporation of God in history (á là Hegel) *or*, admit of the annihilation of Transcendence by atheistic reduction of essence to existence as with Feuerbach or Altizer. This last, of course, Tillich would never countenance, yet it is a perennial option attaching to ontological monism that he, in fact, fostered while standing in the tradition of Lessing and the Enlightenment.

On the whole, it seems evident that Tillich never broke out of Schleiermacher's anthropological starting-point in theology. He could not precisely because he shared Schleiermacher's predilection for monism in ontology. The evident and easiest way to solve the problem of the God-and-world Structure is to circumvent it. Monism does this. Therefore, God is viewed by Schleiermacher as the ontological coimplicate of man's moment of the higher self-conscious—either "absolute dependence" or "ultimate concern." For Schleiermacher, this provided the answer to the vigorous Deistic and Enlightenment debate over "miracle." God in relation to world was thus adequately available through the "God-consciousness." Miracle becomes, therefore, the religious name (i.e., "ecstatic," in Tillich) for an event. The event is perspectival as to quality and, thereby, a diviner immanence assured its efficacy, albeit Transcendence is rendered ambiguous together with all transitive incursions of divine causality.

It is right here that the *scandalon* of the Word made flesh becomes rootless or floorless because the modality of its facticity must remain wholly obscure or ambiguous and only perspectival. What Bultmann could say about it was already explicit in Schleiermacher; it was a faith-event in the province of *Geschichte*. In the same way that the Incarnation is rendered unintelligible as actual event, the God-and-world Structure is circumvented or allowed to remain problematic and unarticulated.

Perhaps it could be allowed that *scandalon* is all that admits of being said of the Incarnation. To be sure Kierkegaard insisted it was so, making it the subject of absolute commitment and leap—a position not unlike Ockham's in the 14th century. There, indeed, is the *fons et origo* of the standpoint, viz., the Incarnation event is properly only the object of *fides acquisita*. Sobeit, the point is not primarily that the revelatory occurence remains a surd; rather, the point turns out to be that the revelatory occurrence is deprived, not only of a determinable locus in nature-history, but is devoid of understandable entrance and access. Nor should it be forgotten that Reformation theology in both Luther and Calvin was premised upon the Ockhamistic demolition of *natura* as understood in the received ontology, either of Augustine or of Thomas Aquinas. In order to provide it entrance into "history," the latter, as with Bultmann and Tillich, had to be redefined as inner history, i.e., *Geschichte*, never *Historie*, so that it came about that neither theologian could avoid a docetic, indeed, a gnostic-tending Christology.

No doubt the problem of the God-and-world Structure is singularly provoked by the Christian tradition. The Christ-event suggests an incursion and, thus, seems to enforce unrelieved Transcendence by intervention in world-history. Augustine spoke of it as adventitious. It is this which incurs the embarrassment that a rigorous Deism might mitigate if not avoid. It was, indeed, on this premise that Francis Bacon conveniently employed the sharp distinction between God's *Word* and his *Work*, contending that the latter was the sphere of experimental methodology while the former was the subject-matter of revelation in which province "experiment" had neither competence nor relevance.

But, with this summary divorcement of the world from God, Bacon's purposes were far better served than those of Christian theology— this for the evident reason that the preeminent revelatory event partakes of both worlds, at least according to the fundamental Christian claim as in the Nicene-Constantinopolitan Creed. And yet post-Reformation Protestant theology has been for centuries unable, as well as indisposed, to fashion or illuminate a viable symbolic structure for the requisite interpenetration of time and Eternity. Its spirit was echoed by Kant's words in the Second Preface of the first *Critique:* he would "destroy dogma to make way for faith."

Accordingly, as I see it, contemporary Christianity does not possess a world-view capable or sufficiently coherent to exhibit tenets of credibility for the prime revelatory Event upon which it, nevertheless, bases its age-old claim that, in Christ, the transcendent God has visited and may yet redeem his people. This circumstance is rendered acutely critical in an age when, by contrast, the Baconian program of scientific exploitation of nature has triumphantly vindicated its capacity to establish "the kingdom of man founded upon the sciences." In turning the Mediator into an "inner history," or an "eschatological" or "faith event," Protestant theology, from the Enlightenment until Bultmann and Knox, has accepted the divorce of God from the world, abandoned nature to science, and offered the "religious consciousness" or some equivalent for those who have interest and the time for it. Accordingly, I am suggesting that the present impasse in theology lies with classical Protestantism's acquiescence in the demise of an ontology of Creation coincident with the emergence of the Lutheran era.

From all of this I do not mean to suggest that knowledge must now replace faith. For me the characteristic of faith remains *acknowledgment.* The truth of the Christ-event remains inaccessible apart from transformation of ethos—of human existence in the direction of God's image. The Holy Spirit and Christian faith are not separable. Furthermore, the ontology for which I plead is not knowledge in the apodictic sense but in the sense of wisdom which must remain optional to the rightly disposed mind. Ontology is, for this Platonist as also for John's Gospel, finally, always decisive knowledge, not apodictic!

Nevertheless, it seems to me a sheer fact that the dominant and formative theology of Protestantism has taken excessive comfort in Tertullian's *absurdum.* This, in part, happened in the estimable interest of restoring priority to the divine initiative respecting both the grace and knowledge of God in reaction to the late medieval era of a shamefully domesticated Deity. Transcendence required to be restored in the 16th century, but its faulty intellectual tool was the *via moderna,* the nominalist philosophy, which demolished any conception of the divine ingression in a day when *sola gratia* seemed a quite sufficient vehicle for reconciliation of God to the world and vice versa. Even for that time, this may have been short-sighted. For the 20th century it seems to me now both "dated" and disastrous.

III. THE PROBLEM FURTHER EXAMPLED

With reference to confusion in theology and possibly failure of nerve today, I would wish to acknowledge the pressing need of community among theologians and of theologians with the Church, as the community of believers. There is plain cogency in the claim that theology cannot flourish in isolation from the Body of Christ and that, when theologians do not work from within the Chruch, the mandate of their "science" is muted, for the wisdom they propound presupposes the living community of faith. It seems to me true that to think coherently about the faith presupposes the *datum* of faith, and that *datum* is regularly received, as it is always nurtured, by the community of faith. To be alive theology must be answerable to the living tradition of faith as nurtured in believing community. I would even go so far as to say that tradition is the vehicle, perhaps the raw material, of Christian theological affirmation and that the community is the vehicle of tradition. Thus, there is small possibility of veridical Christian theological understanding in severance from the Christian community. Yet it is also true that the community is always obscuring the tradition of faith by confounding it with other traditions—as Outler and Skydsgaard made clear at Montreal—and that the sifting process in which theology is called upon to engage will be an occasion of controversy and sometimes confusion.

We are manifestly in such a time of controversy, and yet I do not find the present refining process the primary cause of present-day confusion. The problem goes deeper. It entails, in addition to the current traumatic moral catharsis of Christendom going on, a deep-running fault in the intellectual fabric of Protestant Christianity. It is a lacuna; it is the absence of God to the world or the impenetrability of world history to God and, precisely, in the face of the fundamental Christian claim—namely, the Mediator. Reformed theology has persistently ignored a mandate for a cogent doctrine of God's Creation.

On the one hand, Barth was able to espouse the historic protestant disregard for ontology and to underscore Transcendence by exhibition of the divine priority in the *knowledge of faith*. He accomplished this by means of an impressive theory of the primacy of the divine Subject in the revelatory event based upon the biblical analogy of the "inner witness" of the Spirit. On the other hand, recent existentialist theology (Bultmann and Tillich) was able to make the revelatory event plausible to the modern mind by rendering it an immanent permanent possibility of the human subject. So they could have "Christ without myth," and on the basis of what, long before, Schleiermacher had called "the original perfection of the Creation," namely, the inher-

ent "capacity of human nature to give rise to religious affections."
But the methodological priority of the apperceptive subject rendered
the transcendent reference of "the Word" (i.e., the faith-moment) ambiguous as to its ultimate Referent.

In this impasse, the new radicals have simply cut the Gordian knot
or supplied the *coup de grace* and robustly settled for "this world."
Their motivations were multiple, but, among them, was Bonhoeffer's
daring acceptance of responsibility for world history at the cost of
intended tyrannicide. What the radicals did, actually, was to turn an
epistemological impasse into an ontological *tour de force*—if the Transcendent is inaccessible to the world *in ordine cognoscendi* or, conversely, if the world is impenetrable to the Transcendent *in ordo es-
sendi*, they would retire the Transcendent by its simple identification
with world culture. But the point to be underscored is that both Barth
and the existentialists foundered on the same shoal. Neither succeeded
in facing the unresolved ontological problem as enforced by the Christological one, namely, the problem of the God-and-world Structure.
Barth succeeded in securing the absolute priority of the transcendent
Word but could not secure its *actual ingression*. Indeed, he did not
try. The existentialists secured the immanence of the Word but failed
to assure its transcendence or trans-subjectivity. There they left us.

Closely analyzed, the two outcomes come to the same thing. Neither
theological school is able to provide an understandable footing for
the central claim of the Christian religion; neither has any God-and-
world Structure capable of bearing the weight of the claim that, in
Jesus-Christ, divine reality is *mediated* in or through the fabric of natural history or world history. It is this givenness-in-actuality for which
neither neo-orthodoxy, nor existentialist theology, nor traditional Protestant theology, as a whole, has either aspired to or succeeded in giving
an intelligible account.

The problem of theology today is not merely that this is an era
when the prevailing ethos demands intelligibility as a requisite title
to credibility. This has long been so, indeed since the mid-17th century.
Rather, the intellectual problem becomes a spiritual malaise, perhaps,
and really pinches for a brace of reasons contrary to one another.
On the one hand, science and technology advance the understanding
and control of the world on a purely phenomenalistic premise. On
the other side, the predominant religious tradition of the West fails
to show how divine reality mediates itself to the world at the very
point where an intersection requires to be vindicated if its crucial
message is to deserve respectful hearing. This was the issue pinpointed
by D. M. Baillie in his important work on Christology. If Christianity
had not claimed so much, then perhaps recent Protestant theology

might suffice to assure an *immediate* divine-human encounter. It might again adopt the 19th-century theology of immanence or even the anthropological starting-point with some species of the religious consciousness as the point of departure. Either, both, or some other bridge-head may be found for epistemological head-way to and from Deity, a bridge-head which might still afford sufficient grounding for a philosophical theism and commensurate forms of piety.

Something like this is what, indeed, the British Deistic radicals, from Herbert of Cherbury to John Toland and Matthew Tindal, tried earnestly to settle for and to persuade their Christian contemporaries to agree to. With a kind of theological cunning, they perceived that nominalist philosophy, while it made science free to explore God's work, left historic Christianity enigmatic insofar as it stubbornly insisted on *mediated* revelation and grace "through Jesus Christ our Lord." The tides of controversey in those days, then, ebbed and flowed around the word "miracle."

Protestant theology has, with the help of Schleiermacher, supposed this problem was circumvented. It was by employment of an ontological monism and immanence. Or, Protestant theology has followed the leading of Kant and settled for some version of "religion within the limits of reason alone" with its hidden and unacknowledged (by Kant) doctrine of the ontological reach of the "moral consciousness," which made Ritschlian liberalism possible. But neither of these dominant traditions supplied the basis for *mediated* revelation of God in Jesus Christ but, rather, supplied alternatively only the basis of a post-nominalist philosophical theology or an anthropological starting-point for *unmediated* grace and truth. Then, at last, Barth appeared as the radical denier, the affirmer of the absolute priority of God in the knowledge of God, but he scrupled to permit a conjunction of the Jesus of history with the Christ of faith with such stubbornness, as Donald Baillie saw, that the "historicity" of the Mediator remained ambiguous. It was, I believe, for the old, old reason: Barth not only possessed no God-and-world ontology but, like his nominalist tradition, was contemptuous of any resort to one. *Sola gratia* and *sola fides* suffice.

IV. CONCLUDING OBSERVATIONS

My diagnosis suggests this remedy: we are in need of a viable ontology, a philosophic schema capable of restoring what I have ventured to call the God-and-world Structure. In older language, we are in great need of intelligible cosmological symbolics, which have been neglected since the nominalistic dissolution of the great chain of Being. I believe we have explored by a succession of oscillations all possible resources of Calvin's wisdom in two parts, "the knowledge of God and of ourselves." [1] We have explored to the utmost the issue mooted by Calvin as to which comes first. Whereas Calvin, I believe, tried to hold them in dialectical or elliptical relation, Protestant theology shows a pervasive tendency to view and explore them only alternatively. This has been disastrous. But I am proposing, furthermore, that wisdom has more than two parts, and that it must make place for the mediating term that Calvin only obliquely acknowledged. This is a Christian doctrine of Creation. It must be broad enough in its scope to embrace Creation in both of its modes, that is, nature and history. Among possible existing aids toward this *desideratum* may well be a thorough assessment of resources, resident, perhaps, as some are suggesting, in the thought of A. N. Whitehead, whose up-dated version of the ontology of the later Plato may be useful to the purpose. What is needed is a symbolic system that may complement, not substitute for the fundaments of the Christian faith given and received, and not postulated. There is no inherent necessity that prescribes for Protestant theology that it be mated forever either to nominalistic philosophy, on the one hand, or to Kantian phenomenalism, on the other. [2]

A final word about *theological method* is in order. Since the Enlightenment, theological method has dealt with the source, nature, and validity of religious knowledge. With Schleiermacher, theological method aspired to become "scientific." This involved making its *source* a universal endowment of human nature (the religious consciousness); its *nature*, the God-consciousness of Jesus as its prototype; and its *verification*, the permanent possibility of the recapitulation of this God-consciousness within the Christian community. Thus, Schleiermacher, confronted by Calvin's wisdom in two parts, i.e., the knowledge of God and of ourselves, opted for the priority of self-knowledge as the starting-point. For the most part, this standpoint prevailed in such German theology as aspired to be "scientific" until Karl Barth, taking a cue from Kierkegaard as well as the Reformers, resolutely opted for the other pole—the priority of God in the knowledge of God as the source of religious knowledge. The latter, however, being wholly a gift of grace, took the form of *faith;* and theology became emphatically "confessional" rather than "scientific." Meanwhile, Calvin's polar alternatives were, now, both set against one another and exhausted in their contrariety.

My position, now, would be as follows: first, that theological method cannot be restricted to the epistemological problem but requires, as a presupposition, an ontological context involving "the world" in which any "knowledge" of God is given-and-or-received. Calvin's two-fold wisdom is subject to the charge of "angelism" (or transactions of the Alone vis à vis the alone) in the absence of a theology of the Creation as the *punctum stans* of any knowledge suitable to man as creature of the Creator. Second, I would maintain that theological method must hold the two poles of Calvin's bipartite wisdom in inseverable dialectical or reciprocal polarity. Third, I would suggest that, to do this, entails an open acknowledgment of the *punctum stans* of such knowledge of God as appertains to man's status under the conditions of existence, that is, world history. This, I take to be the mediate term of theological knowledge, neglected by pretty nearly the entire Reformation and post-Reformation German theology. It has ignored the ontological presuppositions of religious "knowledge." Fourth, neither the second nor third point are sustainable without a repristinated doctrine of Creation, without which, in turn, the needed God-and-world Structure remains unprovided. Fifth, if the mediating term is provided, Christian theological method may incorporate the decisive and mediating term of Christian faith-knowledge, Jesus-Christ, who, in the bifurcated world of Calvin's two-fold wisdom, has been assured no determinable status in world history.

In short, the continental shelf on which the long course of post-Reformation Protestant theology was grounded was a pervasive and fundamental indifference to the God-man-and-world context, namely revelation of God suitable to man's creaturely condition. Calvin's bipartite wisdom, without a mediating ontological term, has, on the one hand, led to a "draw" between the defenders of the priority of man or, conversely, of the priority of God in religious knowledge; and the overpowering fideistic standpoint that Calvin (however ambiguously) transmitted to his successors—symbolized by *sola gratia*—intrenched not only the nominalist indifference to ontology but seemed to make the knowledge process *under the conditions of existence* a matter of entire inconsequence.

It has been, among other things, the impasse in recent Christology that highlights, I believe, the stark alternatives presently afflicting us: either of tenacious fideistic supernaturalism or subjectivist humanistic reductionism as instanced by the vagaries of present-day Christian atheism. But from the standpoint of the reigning Protestant theological tradition, devoid as it is of a viable world-view, there is probably no decisive way to mediate these extremes. The "giants" of Protestant theology have now left the field "at a draw" in the contest between Calvin's mooted polarity. What we have, therefore—the evident confusion through which we live enduringly—is a field left vacant save for hectic skirmishes between surviving remnant groups, representing extremes that have resulted from the long conflict between major theological contributors to the post-Reformation era. Their contest in theological method came to a "draw," because, ignoring Creation, they supposed that the issues of theological method were settled with the proper handling of the epistemological question. Ironically, they largely settled for Francis Bacon's bifurcation of the world and of knowing into two compartments, that pertaining to God's Word and that pertaining to God's Work. *Then they argued for four centuries on how God's Word is heard in almost entire indifference to his Work.* This standpoint and its presuppositions, I believe, have proven to be insupportable. If so, a long period of theological reconstruction lies before us at the center of which is a revised doctrine of Creation.

THE ECUMENICAL MOVEMENT:
WITNESS AND REFLECTIONS

THE LUND CONFERENCE: THE DILEMMA OF ECUMENISTS

I

Lund, a small city of about thirty-five thousand souls, is situated a short distance inland from the western coast of Sweden among the gently rolling and fertile wheatlands of the southerly province of Skåne. Very early in the 11th century the town was the center of the archepiscopal see of Scandinavia. The foundation of the cathedral—the great church in which the Conference worship was held—was laid around 1060. The edifice was completed in substantially its present form and consecrated in the year 1149. From the 12th to the 16th century, Lund continued to be an important ecclesiastical center, accumulating during the period twenty-two churches and seven monasteries. After the Reformation the town sank into obscurity until, in the later 17th century (1668), the present University of Lund was established. From the theological faculty of the University, bishops and archbishops of the Church of Sweden have often been recruited. The present primate of Sweden, Archbishop Yngve T. Brilioth—chairman of the Lund Conference on Faith and Order—was formerly of the faculty of Lund. It was in the quaint and delightful town of Lund that delegates to the third World Conference on Faith and Order assembled August 1952.

We had been sent to Lund by our respective churches, commissioned to discuss, in an arranged forum of Christendom, obstacles to fuller unity among the churches. Some of these obstacles had been singled out by the Edinburgh Conference of 1937.[1] In the intervening years they had been made the subject of extensive study by three theological commissions under the Continuation Committee of Faith and Order. The findings of the three commissions, in the form of separate reports, had been in the hands of delegates, together with three source volumes, prior to arrival at Lund. The three reports considered the following basic themes: the nature of the Church, ways of worship, and intercommunion.[2] It was in these areas, especially around the question of the nature of the Church and its ministry, that the problem of fuller unity among the churches had seemed to focus. This, indeed, was the conviction of many seasoned observers. It was asserted by

A lecture on the Third World Conference on Faith and Order to The Divinity School, Duke University, October 1952. Published in *Religion and Life*, xxii, 2, Spring 1953. Here reprinted with the permission of the Editor.

Canon Leonard Hodgson in one of the important opening addresses
to the Lund assembly. Reviewing the work of Faith and Order from
the time of Lausanne in 1927, Canon Hodgson roundly affirmed that
"the differences which divide us in practice are rooted in different
conceptions of the church. . . . Underlying all particular questions is
that of the nature of the church." [3]

II

Turning to the preparatory reports of the three theological commissions, it may be said that each, in its special province, described and
defined existing practice and doctrine relating to its particular subject
more competently, searchingly, and comprehensively than had hitherto been done. The various prevailing doctrines of the Church were
catalogued, the varieties of worship were reviewed, the representative
attitudes toward intercommunion were consulted and recorded, and
the areas of agreement and disagreement were faithfully noted and
observed. The dominant resulting impression was that the ecumenical
movement had finally run upon immovable shoals which had hitherto
been sensed but ignored in earlier enthusiasm for ecumenicity.

In the opinion of Archbishop Brilioth, as stated in his presidential
address, the ecumenical movement had passed through a number of
stages. In its first flush, it tended to ignore differences in order to
find basis for advance by stressing agreements. But having passed
through the stage of "glossing over differences," it had resulted in a
"revival of confessional consciousness." According to Brilioth, the note
of unity still dominated at Edinburgh in 1937. Meanwhile, "the tenacity
of confessional traditions, the different background and temper of the
different churches became realized." [4]

The impression is clear and remains that the prolonged study of
the theological commissions, extending intermittently over a fifteen-
year period, had brought existing differences unambiguously to the
sight of all. It had disclosed that, although there has been hitherto a
large expanse of water for the ecumenical enterprise to maneuver
in, it has at length run upon little reefs which, however little, are
reinforced by the continent in which they lie. The critical nature of
the situation is accentuated by the fact that meanwhile (Amsterdam
1948) the churches had joined together in a World Council. They declared: "We have covenanted together in setting up this World Council
of Churches . . . we intend to stay together." But the question is how
long churches can stay together which are not wholly together, which
by their own respective views of the church, cannot regard one another

as "churches" in the full sense and cannot moreover, in the supreme act of Christian worship, join with one another at the Table of the Lord.

The Lund Conference began, if I may hazard a guess, with full realization on the part of the leaders and some assembled delegates that the ecumenical movement was at a crisis, if not an impasse. Something like this was openly asserted by the principal conference speakers. In a masterly address, Dr. Oliver Tomkins declared that we have come to the end of a period of "mere comparative ecclesiology." He did not assert that the "work of mutual explanation is no longer necessary," but he did say that cataloguing issues no longer seems to be a promising way forward.[5]

In similar vein, Professor Edmund Schlink of Heidelberg declared in one of the most influential of the opening addresses: "I am convinced that we have reached a quite natural limit of the comparative method in our work for Faith and Order, and that on this way alone we can proceed no further." [6] It is safe to assert that this judgment, variously expressed, quickly became a first principle of discussion at Lund; and accordingly, it is found in the first chapter of the Report of the Conference: "We have seen clearly that we can make no real advance towards unity if we only compare our several conceptions of the nature of the church and its traditions in which they are embodied." [7]

III

When the conference was organized for work at Lund, the delegates were divided into five sections: three sections were assigned to deal with the nature of the Church, a fourth to consider ways of worship, and a fifth to treat intercommunion. Each section was entrusted with shaping and drafting its portion of the total Lund Report. Each section was presided over by a previously selected chairman and, usually, two secretaries. These persons were, in every case, full delegates to the conference and were undoubtedly "briefed" beforehand concerning their task. The secretaries participated in discussion and helped to guide it to positive results. Together with the chairman, they acted, in most cases, as drafting committee.

Each theological section was intially charged with producing an "interim report" indicating the general lines which its completed report would likely follow. After these interim reports were received by the plenary session on the third day, each section proceeded to supply a first draft of a report just one week after the opening session of the conference. The first drafts were rather vigorously overhauled in the

plenary session and were remanded to the sections. A second draft
was then prepared in the light of plenary conference criticism and
was submitted after the lapse of a day or two. In the light of plenary
criticism, a third draft was produced for final reception by the conference. The third recension is what stands as the report of the Lund
Conference.

It is worth noting that the reports of the various sections together
with the Preface and Epilogue were "received," not "adopted," by
the conference plenary session. Archbishop Brilioth, the chairman,
ruled that this procedure was in line with precedent set by earlier
Conferences on Faith and Order, and he also stressed the view that
the Lund Report is simply commended to the churches for their earnest
and diligent consideration. At all times it was made emphatic that
Faith and Order decides nothing for the churches; rather, its work is
informative and advisory. This position is underscored in the Lund
Report itself. The Preface states: "Our work is not to formulate schemes
and tell the churches what they ought to do, but to act as the handmaid
of the churches in the preparatory work of clearing away misunderstandings, discussing obstacles to reunion, and issuing reports which
are submitted to the churches for their consideration." [8]

                    IV

In what follows I wish to deal with three of four broad divisions of
the Lund Report and as briefly as is consistent with clarity.

Chapter 2, "Christ and His Church"

Attention has already been called to certain words of Canon Leonard
Hodgson in diagnosing the present situation in the movement toward
unity. In an opening address, he reminded us that, as he had interpreted Lausanne and Edinburgh, "over and over again it became clear
that differences on this or that particular topic were rooted in different
conceptions of the church." Now if one adds to this judgment the
conviction of the Lund planners that "the comparative method" in
ecumenical discussion has quite literally reached the limit of its serviceability and that further mutual self-explanation is a blind alley, some
explication is afforded for the new departure that is actually featured
in chapter 2 of the Lund Report, entitled: "Christ and His Church."
By way of calling attention to this new development, the Preface refers
to the fact that chapter 2 "does not record agreements and disagree-
ments on subjects at present dividing the churches, but seeks to initiate

a theological study of the biblical teaching about the relation between Christ and the Church." [9]

In retrospect, it is quite evident that the conference leaders, perceiving the roadblock incurred by the comparative method, were seeking to outmaneuver a stalemate in ecumenical discussion. Accordingly, Dr. Edmund Schlink of Heidelberg agreed to give a keynote address. In that address, coming from the right kind of conservative quarters, he undertook to press the question of the unity of Christendom. He did so, not by referring us to the historic grounds of division; instead, he put the question of Christian unity in the acceptable context of New Testament eschatology. His striking opening sentence was: "The Church is on her way between the first and second Advent of Christ." He went on to say that in her pilgrimage today she is beset by implacable opposition and persecution—a fact which continental Christians understand better than we. But at the end of her pilgrimage, at the end of this present age, stands the Lord of the Church. He is Victor over the world and over all controversy—both without and within the Church. Referring to the final Judgment, Schlink said: "He will then bring about a separation which will go much deeper than all separations that we men can effect here on earth. In comparison with this division on the Day of Judgment, the divisions of the churches can only be temporal and lack eschatological finality in spite of their seriousness." [10]

The truth of this reminder lies on the surface for all who take the New Testament seriously. Professor Schlink's point was that the crisis in the ecumenical movement is not primarily an impasse in discussion; the real crisis lies in Christ's anticipated judgment and our present disunity. Our present disunity, however historically explicable and however defensible according to partisan rationalization, nevertheless stands under the present and final judgment of Christ. Then, taking a more positive turn and grounding himself upon New Testament teaching, Schlink reminded the delegates that, as in baptism we all die with Christ, are justified, and rise with him to new life, so, despite our historical divisions, we are, if we are redeemed, *already one with Christ*. A clear corollary and one which was to be embodied in the Lund Report is that our unity in Christ is already a present reality, an eschatological reality. Despite our historical divisions, we have, by God's grace in Christ, a common existence together as the "people of God."

In his final exhortation, Professor Schlink pleaded: "Let us tear away our eyes from the visible divisions which we have not yet overcome, and let us look firmly to the One Lord towards whom we are moving. In the view ahead, in the expectation of the Coming Judge of the world and the Redeemer, we shall recognize the temporary character and lack of finality of many things which divide us now." [11]

With this background, we are perhaps in possession of the reasons why the Lund Report turns our attention to New Testament theology and why the chapter on "Christ and His Church" insists that a new and promising way to approach the question of the Church and our present disunity is through the doctrine of Christ and his relation to his Church. The writers of the report believe that the scandalous disunity of the churches cannot forever withstand a searching comprehension of the New Testament proclamation of the unity of the believer with Christ within the Body of Christ, which is his Church.

In chapter 1 of the report the statement is made: "We have seen clearly that we can make no real advance towards unity if we only compare our several conceptions of the nature of the Church and the traditions in which they are embodied." The report goes on to say: "We need therefore, to penetrate behind our divisions to a deeper and richer understanding of the mystery of the God-given union of Christ with his Church." [12] It is in this already existing union of Christ with his Church that Lund finds the hope of a unity which shall replace the historical divisions of the churches. It is interesting to observe in retrospect how the main directions of the Lund Report reflect certain basic emphases its planners had already highlighted. Oliver Tomkins's words, in his statesmanlike address in an early session of the conference, find a rather clear echo in the finished report. He had declared: "I believe that if we took seriously our given unity in Christ it would, in course of time, completely reverse our normal structure of church organization." [13] This, in a nutshell, indicates, I believe, the strategy of Lund.

The first principal section of the report, then, stresses our "given unity in Christ." Our urgent responsibility is to *receive* this God-given unity rather than to *accept* our divisions. If we are, as forgiven sinners, one with Christ, we are also, whatever our "denomination," members of the one Body of Christ. By implication, then, if believers everywhere are one with Christ, they are certainly one with his Church. Furthermore, Christ is the Head of the Church, his Body; it is always in his keeping and in no sense at our human disposal. Consequently, we cannot presume to locate it at any one point or identify it with any single tradition. If these positions are grasped in their full import, there is more powder in the Lund Report than has yet been touched off.

Perhaps the key words of chapter 2, "Christ and His Church," possibly of the entire report, are these: "We seek to penetrate behind the divisions of the Church on earth to our common faith in the one Lord. From the unity of Christ [i.e., the unity of Christ with believers] we seek to understand the unity of the Church on earth . . ." [14] The new approach, then, is twofold: to place our existing divisions under the present and future judgment of Christ, and to assert the eschatological unity already existing among believers in virtue of their present unity in Christ. The problem now before the churches is how to square their eschatological unity in Christ with their historical disunity. That perhaps is the patent and most sobering challenge of Lund. But the report appends a wise and salutory admonition: "We cannot build the one church by cleverly fitting together our divided inheritances. We can grow together towards fulness and unity in Christ only by being conformed to him who is the Head of the Body and Lord of his people." [15]

Chapter 3, "Continuity and Unity"

It is imperative to make at least brief reference to the third principal division of the Report, entitled "Continuity and Unity." Dr. Oliver Tomkins acutely formulated the problem for this portion of conference inquiry: "We claim that we have unity in Christ; we cannot show that we have unity in his Body, the Church. That is the heart of our dilemma." [16] Just so, in chapter 2 the report points our attention to the eschatological union of the church with Christ, but chapter 3, "Continuity and Unity," was not able to find a "roosting place" for the eschatological unity among the divisions of the historical church. This eventuality is frankly conceded in the report. "We affirm that throughout Christendom there is, despite divisions, a unity already given by God in Christ, through whom 'the powers of the age to come' are already in our midst." But the chapter goes on to say: "We differ, however, in our understanding of the relation of our unity in Christ to the visible Holy, Catholic and Apostolic Church." [17] In other words, we cannot locate the eschatological unity anywhere in history, that is, we cannot as an ecumenical company of churchmen *agree* to do so. We may reserve our private judgment that *our* church is the Church upon which the eschatological unity comes to rest, but we are then faced with the embarrassing fact that, by our membership in the World Council of Churches, we have tacitly admitted that other member communions are "churches" in some sense also.

The problem of locating the eschatological unity in history was, I believe, accentuated by certain features of the Lund Report itself in two respects. In the first place, there is a rejection of the concept of the *two* churches: "We are agreed that there are not two churches, one visible and the other invisible." [18] This decision was in line with Professor Schlink's repudiation of a "docetic conception of the church and an unauthorized spiritualism." Schlink had declared: ". . . the Body of Christ is always simultaneously the visible community of its members in Word, Sacrament, and Ministry." [19] In other words, no qualitative distinction between the church *militant* and *triumphant* is permissible which, if it were used, might ease the cleft between the eschatological Church and the historical one.

Rejecting any such procedure, the Lund Report, in the second place, intensifies the problem by laying heavy stress upon the Pauline phrase "Body of Christ." Moreover, it is stated that the "Pauline image of the church as the Body of Christ is no mere metaphor, but expresses a living reality." [20] Whatever ambiguity there may be in the words "living reality," there is no doubt that the authors of the report intend to take the phrase as the definitive New Testament conception of the Church.

We come to the uncomfortable result that no view of the Church is acceptable which detracts from its full historical reality and yet, as churchmen aiming at the unity of Christendom, we cannot agree to identify the Church with any historical actuality. Having found our God-given unity in Christ already eschatologically given, the Lund Conference brings us to a perhaps unanticipated crisis by insisting that, according to the New Testament, the eschatological reality is also historical, but it cannot find the historical counterpart. In Professor Schlink's language, the Church is on pilgrimage "between the first and second Advent of Christ," but we are unable to locate it anywhere on the way.

All this is perhaps only a correlative of the practical and pressing fact that, as ecumenical Christians in the World Council, we are asserting at one and the same time that our sister churches *are* and *are not* "churches." The only way out of our predicament now, is either to deny that they are and reassert a temporarily suppressed opinion that ours is the true church, or to achieve a historical union in which the eschatological reality may find a habitation and a home. To be sure, a less attractive alternative would be to agree either with Rome or with Orthodoxy. But the more promising, as well as the more courageous, way before us seems to be that of adding to our "God-given unity in Christ" full unity with one another in a reunited historical community.

Perhaps, then, one somewhat unexpected but powerful impetus toward unity of the churches provided by Lund is the following: to define so clearly our untenable situation in the "half-way covenant" of the World Council as to drive us toward a full covenant on pain of remaining forever unable to locate a Body of Christ with any semblance of historical actuality. If that is indeed the case, Lund will have done more for the cause of Christian unity than is yet realized or, for the time being, can be.

There will be a good many persons, however, who must doubt that even progress beyond the World Council to organic unity of the member churches will assure an actualization of the Body of Christ in history. To them the rejection of the ancient distinction between the "visible" and "invisible" Church will be tantamount to the error of Rome. While it is a fact that at Lund there was no evident opposition to the denial of the distinction and no outspoken demurrers against the view championed by some German and Scotch theologians that the Body of Christ must be considered historical and not "spiritual," there will be many who will take strenuous exception. To them it will seem evident that any effort to *locate* the Body of Christ in history is indistinguishable from the Roman claim. That is the claim not only to hold the "power of the keys," but the satanic claim to "absolutize the relative." It presumes to domesticate the sovereign grace of God. God does not so bestow himself, not even on the Church. God lends his grace in Christ to the Church, but it remains in God's keeping. The union of Christ with his historical Church never becomes identity.

Chapter 5, "Intercommunion"

With no intention of slighting the searching and constructive chapter 4, dealing with "Ways of Worship," I must hasten on to give a firsthand account of the Section on Intercommunion, for I was privileged to be a participant of that discussion. The preparatory report on intercommunion, produced under the very able leadership of Professor D. M. Baillie, pointed to scandalous disunity among the churches as it is dramatized at the Lord's Table. This scandal provided the problem for section V.

The complexion of the group may be of interest. There was every shade of Anglican opinion represented, from the extreme Anglo-Catholic wing to the equally energetic evangelical Anglicanism of such churchmen as the Bishop of Chelmsford and Canon Greenslade of Durham. Somewhere "right of center" was the eminent and fatherly Bishop A. E. J. Rawlinson of Derby, whose irenic but incisive representation of the main line of English episcopal opinion struck a happy balance between the "highs" and the "lows." We were strongly fortified by German Reformed and Lutheran thought, some of it very conservative in doctrinal matters but, nevertheless, balanced by vocal opposition from within the ranks. Pastor Martin Niemöller was an amiable and constructive member of the group. He frequently translated the speeches of his fellow countrymen and sometimes with a show of good-humored reluctance, for he did not agree with some things that were said. There were two British Methodists. The Reformed Churches of France and Belgium were represented. There was the saintly Metropolitan, Juhanon Mar Thoma of the Mar Thoma Syrian Church of Malabar. There was the brilliant and incisive Rev. D. T. Niles of the Methodist Church of Ceylon, a native Christian leader of great power. There was Dr. Rolla Ram of India, a devoted and truly Christian spirit, who as spokesman for the "younger churches" pleaded ably for the subordination of theological niceties to a larger vision of Christian unity. We had one representative of Orthodoxy and, finally, a number of American churchmen: Episcopalians, Disciples, Congregationalists, and Baptists. There were two American Methodists.

That there was conceived and brought forth any report at all out of the early deliberations of the group has, even yet, not ceased to be something of a wonder to me. To bring together, from all over the world, people with varying backgrounds and traditions and have them produce "from scratch" documents of such quality as were actually produced seemed an astonishing achievement. If our section provided an acceptable report, it was due in the first place to the theological competence of the participating members and their conversancy with the issues. But of equal importance was the skill of our chairman, the Reverend Dr. E. A. Payne, an English Baptist. He, together with our secretaries, succeeded in holding discussion somewhere on the line and in taking the pulse of group sentiment while formulating converging lines of thought into logically arranged sequences. So far as our section is concerned, I can say that the result in printed form is quite literally the product of what Quakers call the "sense of the meeting." As I remember, a vote was taken only once on a crucial issue which gradually came to focus and was forced by the insistence of two German Lutherans. The substance does issue from the actual verbal exchange of the group and represents a corporate judgment.

Turning to the report itself, I have room to stress only a few cardinal points. In the first place, it is recognized that intercommunion becomes a problem only where there is some mutual recognition on the part of churches but where, on the other hand, organic unity does not as yet exist. This, of course, defines the situation in the World Council.

Setting aside an important section on "Terminology" which may well prove to be valuable, I would say that the permanent significance of the report centers in Part III, "The Ordering of the Lord's Table." Certain positive positions are taken which are correctives to narrow ecclesiology wherever found. In the first place, it is declared on principle that the Table is the Lord's. It is not in the keeping of any particular church. Christ is sovereign over his Table. It is not at the disposal of men. Second, it is asserted that "responsibility for the due ordering of the Table in the name of Christ has been committed to the Church." [21] This is a solemn trust, not to be slightingly discharged. Third, there is the following important pronouncement: "We are agreed in recognizing the administration of the Lord's Supper in the divided churches, when controlled by the words of institution, as real means of Grace through which Christ gives Himself to those who in faith receive the appointed elements of bread and wine." [22]

We may, I think, take this pronouncement to be of importance, for it manifestly rests the efficacy of the sacrament upon what the grace of Christ is doing in it. To be sure, there is the condition that its celebration must be controlled by the words of institution; but other conditions, such as "correct" ministerial ordination, are conspicuous by their absence. It is particularly noteworthy that both Anglicans and some rigid Lutherans were party to this statement, yet the statement seems to leave room for the interpretation that the Lord's Supper when celebrated in a Methodist or Congregational church is a *bona fide* means of grace. Either, in this affirmation, ecumenically environed theologians have overstated themselves and will have to "hedge" when they get back home, or they have committed themselves to a less restricted view of what is indispensable to the efficacy of the sacrament and, just possibly, to the "essence" of the Church.

Here, then, is one observer's report and reflections upon what happened at Lund. A delegate to a World Conference on Faith and Order learns, if he did not know before, that to be a witness and an on-the-spot observer of a great historic event does not by any means assure him of comprehending what he sees. He is easily outdistanced by the pace of events which swirl about him. He is overwhelmed by the cataract of words that pours over him. Mimeographed materials flood upon the delegate in such volume that powers of intellectual digestion are overtaxed, and even to be in possession of the content does not assure understanding at the moment. In point of fact, I have found it indispensable to read and reread the conference material since Lund in order to begin to piece together the puzzle. I have had no opportunity to refer to the conference services of corporate worship in the cathedral, the great communion service to which all delegates were invited by the Church of Sweden. I have not mentioned the daily services of morning and evening prayer which did so much to make our fellowship at Lund a *communio sanctorum,* and give to all a consciousness of being for awhile, at least, in something closer to the One Holy Catholic Church. I have not referred to the truly gracious, as well as commanding, leadership of the great Archbishop of the Church of Sweden, Yngve Brilioth, who was, with every justification, the President of the Conference and was by its action made chairman of the Commission on Faith and Order.

Nothing has been indicated concerning the complexion of conference leadership; but on this point it is sufficiently evident that personnel of "established" as distinct from "free" churches seemed to hold leadership positions. This is in part attributable, of course, to the geographical centrality of Western Europe in the ecumenical movement and to the fact that European churchmen and theologians have for a somewhat longer period been revitalized in their interest in doctrinal, and especially ecclesiological, issues. It is, however, quite apparent that the majority of European churchmen simply do not grasp the fact that, in America, the chief bearers of ecclesiastical leadership are and have been the "free" evangelical churches. This is understandable: for example, in modern Germany Methodism is a very small minority church of only about sixty thousand souls. Nevertheless, the misconception of the complexion of American Christianity apparently causes European churchmen to misplace the centers of gravity in the American church scene. On the other side, however, it may be said that the American evangelical churches have not always been represented at world conferences with the best theological talent available. Thus there are two sides of the story; both require consideration.

Some people will ask, somewhat impatiently and with some condescension, what definite advance toward church unity was accomplished at Lund? In answer, they should be reminded that church unity is the work of the churches, not the work of Faith and Order or even of the World Council. The function of Faith and Order is to supply the churches with the kind of thinking and incentives, the kind of theological understanding by assistance of which they will be supported in their efforts toward fuller unity with one another. The function of Faith and Order is to point out where real barriers exist and to dissipate imaginary ones.

But if I were to hazard a judgment as to the main contribution of Lund to the cause of Christian unity, then I would point again to what was suggested earlier. The great contribution of Lund will be seen to consist in forcing upon the consciousness of the churches, especially those in the World Council, an honest recognition that, while we claim to have a God-given unity in Christ, "we cannot," in the words of Oliver Tomkins, "show that we have a unity in His Body, the Church." The influence of Lund will consist in so pressing the reality of the "eternal" union we have in Christ, that we shall not be able to rest complacently in historical disunity.

REFLECTIONS ON VATICAN II, THE SECOND SESSION

I. THE SCENE

In the basilica of St. Peter's on December 2, 1963, slightly before noon, the elegantly bearded Eugene Tisserant—Cardinal Dean of the Sacred College and chief presiding officer of the Holy Synod—arose at the President's table in front of the Bernini baldaquino to dismiss the seventy-ninth General Congregation of the Second Vatican Council. As he had done on each previous day, Tisserant read the Angelus in Latin so fluent and clipped that the assembled fathers could only join him by floundering after him. When they had trailed him to the 'Amen,' the business of the Council's second session was terminated, and the purple-gowned throng, passing through the pillared atrium, spilled forth into the great circular piazza of St. Peter's.

In the second session there had been forty-three General Congregations devoted to business. In addition (on September 29), there had been the opening ceremony with its much anticipated inaugural allocution by the new Pope. This had not been disappointing. Not again until December 3 was the Pope publicly visible at the Council. That day he presided at the celebration of the Fourth centenary of the consummation of the Council of Trent. The event was marked by an important address by Cardinal Urbani, Archbishop of Venice. On the following and final day, December 4, the Pope again presided with a fair show of papal splendor. There was mass, as on every other day, and the enthronement of the Gospel. There was the final voting, the papal promulgation of the two perfected decrees of the Council— that on the Sacred Liturgy and that on Media of Communication. Finally, there was the summarizing address of Paul VI into which he inserted the surpise announcement of his proposed pilgrimage to the Holy Land. There was the papal benediction and withdrawal. Then, for the last time, cardinals and bishops—white-coped for the day— poured out of the basilica into St. Peter's square. Throughout the entire Council the observers, who had been accorded unbounded courtesy in all things, had witnessed all proceedings from the best seats in the house.

With what measure of satisfaction the Council fathers turned home-

Published as "Report to the Church on the Second Vatican Council," in *World Parish*, World Methodist Council, Lake Junaluska, N.C., April 1964.

ward a second time can only be a matter of surmise. It is fairly plain that all were weary, chastened, and yet hopeful. In two sessions, totaling seventy-nine General Congregations, only two schema of the originally prepared seventeen had been perfected. During the second session three others of central importance had been extensively debated. The fathers had listened to 596 speeches on the part of colleagues. They had heard approximately 24 reports from Council commissioners, charged with preparation, emendation, and redrafting of decrees. Collectively, they had written thousands of proposed emendations for schemata which in turn had to be reviewed, assessed, and incorporated or rejected by the appropriate drafting committees.

Eighty-nine secret ballots had been taken respecting the substance of decrees, not counting nine votes of cloture on further discussion. Each morning at 8:30 the Council fathers had celebrated mass. They had prayed together, endured together, hoped together, jostled one another in the press of the coffee bars—"Bar-rabbas" or "Bar Jonah." Now they would go home, some together, others singly to remote corners of the earth. They would resume their essential role in far-flung places as pastors of pastors and shepherds of souls. And most, I think, would face with renewed spirit and devotion the varying exigencies which the Catholic Church confronts in widely differing parts of the world.

There is no doubt in my mind that the devout and compassionate concern of John XXIII for the inner renewal of the Catholic Church has both inspired and released a latent and ripening response on the part of the Church's episcopal leadership, and that from widely differing areas of the world. Not unanimously but predominantly the mood of the Council is one of self-searching. Pastoral concern for the salvation of mankind seems to have replaced dogmatic arrogance or fearful self-defensiveness. There is a leaven of openness at work in the midst and a growing and devout concern for the recovery of essential Christian community, first among brethren within the Church and, secondly, with brethren outside the Catholic fold. It is this leaven and this predominant but not uncontested mood and spirit which, I believe, promises to make the Second Vatican Council, in the end, a fruitful as well as fateful milestone in the history of ecumenical Christianity.

It must, however, be fully admitted that the clear and explicit meaning, import, and character of the event called the Second Vatican Council is only adumbrated and, at the moment, is far from manifest. Signs and signposts there are—admitting one must confess of varying interpretation—but the fact is the Council is not over, and until its final decree is promulgated and the 2400 fathers have dispersed to implement in their several places both the positive and permissive legislation of the Council, we shall scarcely be possessed of either the data or the historical perspective required to apprehend, much less to evaluate, the meaning and significance of the Council for present-day Christendom or even for the Catholic Church. In a certain sense Archbishop Leo Binz of St. Paul, in a pastoral letter to his people, is right in suggesting that the meaning and significance of the Council rests with the young who "will live the Council in the coming years."

In any case, the Council will reconvene September 14, 1964, and very much is in flux concerning the substantive content of decrees yet to be perfected or discussed. At this juncture no one, not even the Pope, can foretell what will finally prevail as the thrust and growing edge of this enormous conciliar effort. I say this not alone on the ground that John XXIII, in his concern for bringing the Church up-to-date, intentionally called a Council as a way of breaking the Church open to the renewing and reforming influence of the Holy Spirit. I say it because, as a Protestant, I believe that the Holy Spirit has unpredictable surprises for those who really submit themselves to His working. And unless I am deceived there is impressive evidence in the Roman Church today of uncommon openness to the Holy Spirit's working. In addition, there is a very threatening secularized world confronting the Roman Church, as it confronts all churches. In a stagnant condition, no church can fulfill its mission to this world, or perhaps even survive.

Fully sensible of this and other perils, John XXIII, with uncommon insight and courage, declared for *aggiornamento,* not as accommodation to the modern world but as renewal for mission. He knew that what brings the church "up-to-date" is never conformism or face-lifting but recovery of the Church's own inner meaning and essential life. Animated more by pastoral concern and love of men and less by considerations of dogmatic and scholastic refinement, he was able to perceive and declare that renewal might entail alteration, not of the substance of the Church's teaching and life, but the form and mode of its historic expression. Explicitly, John XXIII had declared in his opening address to the Second Vatican Council: "The substance of the ancient doctrine, of the *depositum fidei,* is one thing; the way in which it is expressed is another."

The full import of this unprecedented papal declaration may long be debated. It confirmed the tradition-bound conservatives of the Curia in their suspicions of Pope John and hardened them in resistance that continues today. Nevertheless, Pope John's declarations broke open a dam of self-defensive conservatism behind which the living waters of faith were artificially impounded and becoming stagnant. It was stagnation which so oppressed the Pope. More than any modern Pope he had seen and experienced the restless material and spiritual agonies of the modern world. More than any he could see the sterile impotence and irrelevance of arthritic ecclesiasticism to the perplexed and tortured human situation all about him. From Saint John the Evangelist he had learned that "perfect love casteth out fear"; so he opened windows. He opened the sluice-gates and let the waters flow. The situation remains fluid with the Council today because the waters that were unloosed as yet remain incompletely channeled. This is what gives such keepers of the impounded waters as Cardinals Ottaviani, Ruffini, Siri, and Marella the awful sense of being swept away in the flood. Their instinct is to close the sluice-gates or shore up the bursted dam. And, I have no doubt they sincerely believe they'll be damned if they don't!

Doubtless we shall be well advised to treat this metaphor of the flood, like other metaphors, with proper caution. It is only a manner of generalizing a state of affairs of which there is sundry cumulative evidence for those who attentively followed the speeches of the Council. Granting to the metaphor, however, some measure of truth-value, I think it possible to understand better not only the forward movement and subsequent impasse of Vatican's second session, just concluded, but also the extremely dynamic, fateful and difficult assignment inherited by Paul VI from his daring, beloved, and evocative predecessor.

II. SOME NONTHEOLOGICAL FACTORS

As I read the situation, linear and interlinear, Paul VI is a man called to guide unleashed waters into new and serviceable channels that do not too much alter the received dogmatic and ecclesiastical structure of the Roman church. Serviceable channels are those capable of conserving essential Roman Christianity while better fitting, at the same time, its doctrinal, pastoral, and liturgical expressions for fulfillment of its mission to the modern world. This calls for statesmanship of the first magnitude in the reigning Pope, assuming, as I do, that he has the will and the purpose to pursue the end in view. For the Pope is caught between insurgent extremes at either end of the continuum. His eventual success will depend upon obtaining the articulate support of the moderate and preponderant center.

During the second session of the Vatican Council, Paul VI discharged with magnificent self-discipline the enormously difficult role of being the Supreme Pontiff while carrying out under the shadow of his highly revered predecessor the program of his predecessor. With something like filial piety, he restated in his inaugural address to the second session, and with the beauty of intellectual clarity, his own version of the program of John XXIII. The re-affirmed objectives he named as: the Church's self-awareness or self-knowledge; her renewal; the coming together of all Chirstians in unity; and the dialogue of the Church with the modern world. The controlling motif of the address was its Christo-centricity: "Let no other light illumine this Council," the Pope urged, "than Christ the light of the world."

As I listened to his messages and carefully watched his face and manner, I was assured of the authenticity of his piety and the integrity of his mind and word. I was aware that he carried his conferred eminence with something like embarrassed modesty but, nevertheless, with resolution to represent in his person, word, and deed the Supreme Pontificate. But it was a burden for him that called for more than human resources. It was not that he said so, but his face said so as he steeled himself for the requisite repose in the midst of pretentious ceremonial splendors.

Everything indicated that Paul VI is a man of disciplined intelligence whose avowed platform followed closely upon that of his beloved predecessor but who with a scholar's temperament and without the transparent personal magnetism of John XXIII or his extraordinary prestige inherited the tough and treacherous task of seeing the program through. He was destined to see it through, I believe, as the focal point of powerful contending forces both from within and without the Church.

As to forces within the Church, it is quite likely that the reactionary and conservative group within the Curia did succeed, by sundry maneuvers in obstructing progress at the second session, especially in its closing weeks and days. After the historic vote of October 30, establishing by a strong majority the principle of "collegiality," the "freeze," perhaps, was on. It was commonly acknowledged that Ottaviani, chairman of the Theological Commission that was charged with indispensable business for the Council, called few meetings, and, when ordered to get the Commission to work by the Pope, consumed valuable time interposing an array of procedural questions that prevented attention to substantive business relating to the emendation of the schema *On the Church*. When the Holy Office was publicly indicted by Cardinal Frings of Cologne for scandalous procedures, Ottaviani's reply in the Council was unconcealed exhibition of anger and veiled threat, embarrassing for its unseemliness in Council.

Respecting the slowing down of Council action, it is true that the moderators of the Council, whose good faith can scarcely be doubted, did not put to vote the question of including for formal debate chapters 4 and 5 of the schema *On Ecumenism*, which deal with the Jews and "religious liberty." In fairness to the facts, however, it is not to be overlooked that the Council was running out of time and that both pace and procedure would probably not have allowed unhurried deliberation and decision on these critically important issues. This, indeed, Cardinal Bea admitted on the final day of business. While he confessed to disappointment that a vote was not taken to make the chapters a basis of discussion, he conceded to the moderators a wisdom in giving full rein to debate on the first three chapters. At the same time, most adroitly, he served notice to any subversionists that the Secretariat would persist in its proposals regarding chapters 4 and 5 and quoted the proverb: "What is put off is not put away."

Nevertheless, these and other circumstances have occasioned expressions of disappointment and criticism on the part of some observers and publicists. I cannot agree with the reasoning of the Catholic writer of the *Time* article for December 6, caricaturing the second session of the Council as "a parliament of stalemate, compromise, and delay." There was delay, but not stalemate; and, as for compromise, only the disappointed idealist anticipates that his reforming program should have received *carte blanche*. Also, I would regard it as naïve for any Protestant observer to go to the Vatican Council with "buoyant optimism." The history of Councils affords slight basis for such expectancy, and I would think that both the writer of the *Time* article and the erstwhile "buoyant optimist"—both of whom I knew at the Council— exhibit scant understanding of ecclesiastical power structures and the hard realities of political and administrative maneuver. These are unavoidable in the accomplishment even of the Lord's business when confronted by built-in forces of resistance within the Church. As I see it, there was moderate and commendable progress at the second session of the Vatican Council together with the decisive exposure of vectors of future development that are unfulfilled but promising.

In the midst of it all, the new Pope was faced with the hard task of establishing his leadership of Church and Council without objectionable exercise of authority. He had the delicate job of deferring to his predecessor and his predecessor's program of Church renewal—both of which he conscientiously desired to do—while at the same time, he passed out from under the shadow of his predecessor and acquired stature, the right to leadership, and created his own image as Supreme Pontiff. All this had to be done quickly and in the limelight of the assembly of the world's Catholic hierarchy. In that context, he could neither attempt too much nor too little. Furthermore, he had to establish his leadership while confronted with the embarrassment of Curial obstructionism which got into the open in the Council, but could not openly be man-handled in the presence of the Council. Indeed, it could not, I believe, be immediately handled at all because of serious problems in and formidable pressures from the external political arena. On this I will only say that Italy has recently been and is still passing through a precarious political crisis of gravity for the Vatican State and also for Western Europe.

I am suggesting, then, that the great ecclesiastical and spiritual impulse in the Catholic Church represented by the II Vatican Council cannot now be viewed in isolation from the environing political context and that, accordingly, its accomplishments to date cannot be measured or evaluated simply in terms of the potency or impotency of resident ecclesiastical impulses within the Church itself. The program of renewal to which the majority of the Council recurrently shows itself committed by its voting, and to which Paul VI is conscientiously pledged by avowed declaration, encounters not only the adept and entrenched resistance of some powerful curial forces but also the ingenious capacity of those reactionary forces to contrive to marshal more than their own weight of resistance. And this weight is brought to bear most directly upon the Papacy.

III. COUNCIL INTERMISSION AND PAPAL TASK

It is against this background, as I interpret the matter, that we heard the surprise announcement from Pope Paul, on the final day of the Council, of his intended pilgrimage to the Holy Land. Some things that I surmised then have been subsequently verified by actual events. Most obviously, the Holy Land, particularly the sacred scenes of Christ's sacrificial death, would afford the likeliest spot in all the world for a meeting with high representatives of Eastern Orthodoxy. One immediately surmised that there would be a meeting necessarily with the Orthodox Patriarch of Jerusalem. As it turned out, the Pope's journey to Gethsemane and the Mount of Olives would be rewarded by a meeting with the Ecumenical Patriarch of Constantinople, the spiritual primate of the Orthodox Church. The Pope, in his pilgrimage to Jerusalem, went to the one place in all the world where neither he nor his Orthodox peer would need condescend to the other in going and in meeting. Orthodoxy could not go to Rome to a Council and had not gone. But both Rome and Orthodoxy could accept the humiliation of meeting the other in the place of the Lord's humiliation. This meeting is of the highest historic significance and Paul VI has proved that he could contrive what no Pope has been moved to contrive in a thousand years. This I submit is uncommon Christian statesmanship with promise of fruits unknown.

Secondly, it was plain that a pilgrimage to the land of Jesus Christ

was an affirmation of the primacy and lordship of Christ and the dependent subordination of Peter as the "servant of servants." No Pope
had gone to the place of Christ's life, death, and resurrection. Through
the centuries the Roman Church had asserted the primacy of the See
of Peter. In asserting its primacy, it had often assumed its self-sufficiency. In its claim to the "keys" it had often succumbed to what Bishop
DeSmedt of Bruges, in the first session of the II Vatican Council, deprecated as "triumphalism." At Nazareth the Pope did not fail to extol
Mary and sacredness of family life, but he gave the greatest part of
his time and energy, as on the Via Dolorosa, to scenes of Christ's ministry, his teaching, and sacrifice. I leave you to match these facts with
subsequent pronouncements, but do not forget two things. Do not
forget the Christo-centricity of the Pope's inaugural allocution and
do not forget that, by a somewhat slender majority on October 29,
the Council fathers voted to include a statement on Mary, the mother
of the Church, within the schema *De Ecclesia* rather than constitute
a separate schema on Mariology. The Pope did not ignore Mary, but
in his trip to the Holy Land it was Christ he honored centrally.

Thirdly, in order to visit the sacred places of Jesus' life and ministry,
it was necessary to go to the Jews and then to the Moslems and, among
them, to Arab Christians. It was necessary to cross and recross the
bitterly disputed boundaries which none are allowed to cross. But the
Pope was allowed to cross and recross. From both warring sides he
recieved gracious greetings and returned them in kind. From the Holy
Land he sent personal messages to the heads of those confessional
groups from which observers to the Vatican Council had come. It
was a greeting from the Pope on pilgrimage in the land of our common
faith. In that land the Pope is a common debtor with all Christian
believers, Protestant or Orthodox alike.

But let us, in the fourth place, not obscure another main point. The
Pope was warmly received by Arabs and then by Jews. In this connection, let us remember that chapter 4 of *De Oecumenismo* is an exculpa-
tion of the Jewish people in reference to Christ's death, the first such
official pronouncement by any part of Christendom. In Council debate,
it was openly opposed by certain fathers representing the Eastern
rite churches in communion with Rome as having danger for Arab
Christians in Moslem lands. Perhaps we should consider whether the
Pope, in going to both Jews and Moslems, was preparing the way
for a right interpretation of this momentarily delayed conciliar pronouncement. I think so, and by visit to the Jews he was doing what
he could in the face of persecutions still alive and seemingly reactivated
in Russia.

But, fifth, there is still another implication of this papal pilgrimage.

From another standpoint, the pilgrimage was a spectacular reminder to Latin, and especially to conservative Italian Catholicism, that Catholic Christianity is not exclusively or primarily Roman at all, that it rests upon Jesus Christ, not upon the See of Peter, and that it had its origin far away on soil made sacred by the Son of God. I venture to offer the surmise, which only the future can confirm or refute, that, basically and fundamentally, Paul VI went to the Holy Land to enforce the internationalization of Catholicism, the Papacy, and the Curia. He went to further advance what John XXIII strove to do, namely, to emancipate the Church from the ingrown and inbuilt domination of the Latin curial mentality and its oppressive control. To do this Paul VI must become more than the Roman primate and partiarch. He must become independent enough of the Vatican to properly claim leadership of the world Catholic Church. For it is a Church whose episcopal leadership will not much longer accept unresistingly the hegemony of a group of unreformed, socially unenlightened, and outdated Italian provincials.

This, I think, is what the Pope also knows. He knows that this is part of the meaning of the overwhelmingly favorable vote for the "collegiality" of the episcopate. He knows also that curial reactionaries tried to steal and subvert the import and fact of this vote after its adoption October 30, 1963. He knows that this will not be tolerated by the majority of the Fathers.

The Pope has work to do in the next few months before the reconvening of the Council September 14. He went abroad to strengthen his hand and clarify his pontifical image with his own Roman People to ready himself for the showdown. We are in point of fact, on these hypotheses, at a turning point in the history of Roman Catholicism.

Finally, the Pope knows, I think, that ecumenical discussion between Roman Catholicism and Protestantism or Orthodoxy cannot become serious so long as the authority and authenticity of the Roman See is compromised by a Latin or Italian regional bureaucracy. Catholic Christianity can no longer endure such provincialism. Inevitably, the renewal of the Church means its *de facto* internationalization as the pre-condition of *bona fide* ecumenicity. Just prior to the second session Paul VI had made important policy statements in this direction. But to accomplish these things is the work of a master statesman who must also be a Christian. It remains to be seen whether Paul VI will be able to enlist the resources of the II Vatican Council that he distinctly needs. It remains to be seen whether the Council fathers, in their turn, will be pliant and answerable to the leadings of the Holy Spirit. I do believe the signs of the Spirit's working are visible and that they are signs of promise.

iv. ECUMENICAL ACHIEVEMENT AND PROSPECT

The author of the controversial volume *Letters from Vatican City* nar-
rates a widely circulated story about Pope John's explanation, to a
visiting cardinal, of his call for a Council. The Pope simply went to
the nearest window, opened it wide, and let in fresh air. There is
hardly any doubt of a new circulation of air in the Roman Church
and, further, that unprecedented gusts of ecumenical wind are blowing. Evidences of this are various. At the Montreal Conference on
Faith and Order this past summer, on an epoch-making evening, Paul
Emile Cardinal Leger was host to an interfaith convocation of common
praise, prayer and ecumenical address that left some of the sophisti-
cated gasping. After the meeting, the High Commissioner of Canada's
Salvation Army told me that the icy cold of Roman priests toward
the persons and work of his people had perceptibly thawed in recent
months.

It is this widely recognized atmospheric change, replacing a long
prevailing cold front, that has fostered the somewhat inaccurate notion
among non-Catholics that the main purpose of Vatican II is Christian
unity. The primary purpose is, more exactly, the "renewal" and even
"reformation" of the Catholic Church to the end of fulfilling more
perfectly her pastoral and redemptive ministry to a demoralized and
unchristianized modern world. On one occasion Pope John is reported
to have commented: "If after this is accomplished, our separated brethren wish to realize a common desire for unity, they will find the way
open to a meeting and a return to the Church." The word "return"
may not indicate the whole of Pope John's ecumenical thinking, but
the stress upon "renewal" does indicate his understanding of the order
of priorities. The Catholic Church must set its own house in order
first, and, in point of fact, this principle finds emphatic statement in
the schema *On Ecumenism,* where even the word "conversion" is
mentioned as preliminary to honest search for unity by Catholics. In
his inaugural allocution Paul VI underscored the point: "Only . . .
after the Church has perfected the work of inner renewal, will she
be able to show herself to the whole world and say: 'He who sees
me sees also the Father.'"

Without trying to measure or expound the range of Pope John's
ecumenical understanding, which, in him, rooted in Christian charity
and experienced-ripened Christian fraternity that crossed denominational lines, two things he did to promote ecumenicity must be noted.
He created the Secretariat for the Promotion of Christian Unity and
placed the German theologian Augustine Cardinal Bea at its head and,
secondly, through the Secretariat, he invited non-Catholic Christians

to participate in the Holy Synod. They were to come not as participants in official debate nor with voting privileges but as fraternal delegates or observers. They were to be privy to all the public events of the Council and recipients of all documents received *sub secreto* by the Council fathers. And they were to be invited to make commentary, through the Secretariat, on any and all subject matter submitted for deliberation and debate in the Holy Synod.

It is no doubt out of place here to enumerate endless courtesies and most thoughtful provisions afforded the observers by the able staff of the Secretariat under the direction of its notable chief officer, Monsignor J. Willebrands. Common courtesy, however, not only requires public acknowledgment but also serves to point out two important ecumenical facts about the Council. They are that, on the one hand, Vatican II itself became the context of vital and authentic ecumenical interchange and fellowship; and, on the other hand, the regular and continuing attendance of the observers had a galvanizing and, I believe, curative effect upon the Council itself. Both of these outcomes, I well believe, were anticipated by Pope John and his counselors.

If the windows of the Catholic Church needed opening for circulation of fresh air, it would be even better if fresh air could be imported. If there were mentally air-tight curialists who abhorred and feared Protestants, what was better than to bring the stereotyped dreadful creatures where they could be seen and, possibly, spoken to in passing? It might be worth seeing whether contempt and disdain for non-Catholics, who had the effrontery to call themselves Christians, could survive continuous observation of them across the main aisle of the aula and recurring casual meetings and greetings in the to and fro of daily encounter.

As for the galvanizing and curative effect of the continuing presence of the observers, just imagine what would be the effect upon the meeting of an Annual or General Conference if a body of fraternal delegates of several denominations, including Catholics, were corporately provided a box and invited to observe and audit the discussion and debate of Methodist churchmen dealing with the most fundamental questions of church, ministry, worship, and social concerns, with each auditor fully equipped to hear and evaluate critically every utterance!

I give you the answer briefly: old shibboleths become clanging symbols, clichés are palpably thread-bare, sectarian animosities are restrained or silently rebuffed. Provincialisms are better seen for what they are even by their protagonists, and irresponsible partisanship somehow stands revealed for what it is. The result is something like candor, self-imposed restraint, self-critical awareness and probity. Enforced is the necessity of being cogent rather than noisy, persuasive rather than emotive, and coherent rather than grandly unctuous. The case is argued on its merits, and where there is profound difference and disagreement, tactful but honest dissent is openly acknowledged rather than covertly rationalized.

I suggest that in very fact, not uniformly, perhaps, but in quite a perceptible measure, this was a consequence of the continuing presence of the observers within the Council precincts. It was a kind of silent encounter whose fruits, while they may never be measured, will surely figure causatively in whatever ecumenical advances are made by Vatican II. John XXIII had done the most that he could to simulate, if not fully to realize, the conditions of a truly ecumenical Council of Christendom. This of itself, as I perceive it, is among the important ecumenical facts of our time.

v. *DE OECUMENISMO* AND CURRENT CATHOLIC ECUMENICITY

The schema *On Ecumenism* was laid open for Council discussion by Cardinal Cicognani and Archbishop Martin of Rouen, November 18. Therewith, the emphasis on Christian unity, inaugurated by John XXIII and reaffirmed by Paul VI, was given articulate voice and, at least, a preliminary substantial form. *De Oecumenismo* had been prepared by the Secretariat for Christian Unity, and some members of the Secretariat, by their own testimony, had anticipated rigorous criticism in the forum of the Council. However, save for the outcries and somber warnings of a few die-hards, it was adopted for discussion by what Cardinal Bea interpreted as moral unanimity, that is, the first three chapters dealing with the principles and practice of Catholic ecumenism and a chapter on separated Christians.

The chapter on the Jewish people in relation to Christ's death and that on "religious liberty" were not formally adopted for discussion, as we have seen. While that on "religious liberty" may regarded, at least by non-Catholics, as a necessary and integral part of any significant platform of Catholic ecumenicity, nevertheless the first three chapters set forth the basic principles and chart the ecumenical course. In passing, it is worthy of record that the American and British hierarchies solidly, even fervently, supported the chapter on "religious liberty." Its language, I might say, is often strikingly and, to me, amusingly like that of the 17th-century Puritans.

What little I can say about *De Oecumenismo* should, in all fairness, be qualified by the warning that it does not embrace in fact all the fruitage of the Council which contributes to Christian unity or promotes that cause. Achievements to date, conducive to Christian unity, would properly include important advances in liturgical reform, already promulgated, together with developments in the doctrine of the church, bearing upon both "collegiality" and Mariology. These cannot helpfully be discussed here, although they are verily integral to the total ecumenical thrust within the Roman Church. However, it remains true that the schema on ecumenism must carry the heavy responsibility of articulating the rationale of Christian unity as currently understood and expressed by the Catholic Church.

This is a real chore and a heavy burden and a tricky assignment for the Secretariat for the Promotion of Christian Unity. For it is only recently created and without the status and prestige of far more venerable offices of the Roman Curia. It is a new-comer, charged with implementing the fervent vision of Christian unity unveiled by John XXIII, but forced to plot an uncharted way between the Scylla of intrenched traditionalism and the Charybdis of fermenting enthusiasm. Thus, whatever we conclude about the schema in its present form, and it is under revision now, we must acknowledge the hazards attending its composition. It was prepared for the highest Council of the Church at a time when the ecumenical impulse within the Roman Church was nascent and but recently released and could not be counted upon to have invaded the consciousness of the whole episcopate as an urgent claim much less to have permeated the constituency.

I am, therefore, not surprised that the chapter on principles is, from the Protestant standpoint, disappointingly conservative or that the chapter on Catholic practice of ecumenicity is encouragingly progressive. It is, further, no occasion of real surprise that, in the third chapter, the Roman Church reveals its consciousness of greater historic, doctrinal, and liturgical affinity with Eastern Orthodoxy than with the Protestant West. Both the schema and the Pope's recent pilgrimage rather plainly indicate that Roman efforts toward Christian unity in the immediate future will be forthright attempts at *rapprochement* with Orthodoxy. To this end, I would say that the solid and definitive establishment of the "collegiality" of the episcopate, correcting the imbalance of papal absolutism—permitted by Vatican I and fostered by the Curia—is simply indispensable as a condition *sine qua non* of any reconciliation with the East.

In the long thoughts of John XXIII, there had to be Vatican II to complement and modify Vatican I. Collegiality is the core issue; and I see in Paul VI's word and action nothing to countermand and almost everything to vindicate and confirm this movement. Reconciliation with Orthodoxy is most probably the immediate objective, or one might say, the "big push" of Roman ecumenicity. Great, then, was the disap-

pointment when only Protestant confessional or independent Eastern
rite churches patronized the Council, and when the Orthodox appeared belatedly only in the persons of two observers from the Russian
Orthodox Church.

This interpretation may not be confirmable by the testimony of any
Roman ecclesiastic. The American hierarchy would be the last to know
or to confirm it. It is a proffered hypothesis which only events will
confirm or confute, and it need not in any way suggest that the Roman
Church is indifferent to unity as related to the Protestant West. It
only suggests that Rome understands quite well the range of probabilities in things ecumenical and, quite understandably, designs to puruse
the likliest. In this interpretation of the situation, there is, obviously,
import of moment for the structure and strategy of the World Council
of Churches. The powerful ecumenical thrust of Catholicism toward
the East, if even half successful, could easily upset the balance of forces
in the current World Ecumenical Movement as we have known it.

As we find them stated in *De Oecumenismo,* the principles of Catholic
ecumenism are fairly plain. Ecumenism is the end-product of the love
of God whereby he sent his Son into the world for the redemption
of human kind. Out of the redemptive ministry, death, and resurrection
of the Son was raised up the Church, the people of God of the New
Covenant and possessed of "One Lord, one faith, one baptism." Christ's
Holy Church was built upon the foundation of the apostles. The universal mandate of teaching, governing, and sanctifying was accorded to
the "college" of the twelve over which Peter was chosen to preside,
confirming them in faith, and feeding the entire flock in perfect unity.
In short, ecumenicity is wholeness and unity of the historic and undi-
vided Catholic Church.

Christ prayed for the unity of his Church, "That they all may be
one." But there have been schisms or separations that deface the unity
of Christ's Church. Those separated are deprived of the plenitude of
grace and truth that has been entrusted to the Catholic Church. Therefore, the ecumenical mandate is to cleanse the Church of all that im-
pedes the adherence of the separated brethren in order to share more
fully the treasures of truth and grace entrusted to her by Christ. The
ecumenical task is imperative and a mandate upon all clergy, laity,
and religious. Ecumenicity defines the *telos* of the Church. It is the
unity of all the faithful in the Holy Catholic Church, considered as
fulfillment of the purpose and redemptive love of God. Accordingly,
exclusiveness, polemic, and defensiveness must be replaced by inclusiveness, inner renewal, and openness.

There is not any doubt that John XXIII and his dedicated followers
have, in great part, accomplished this revolution already and that,

within the compass of these principles, the Roman Church is already ecumenically on a great offensive push. Obviously, this is not quite what we have understood by ecumenicity in circles of the World Council or Faith and Order, at least it is not what the Protestant participants have understood. We have thought of unity against the background of a different conception of disunity. We have thought of our present dividedness as just that, namely, separation *among* something like equals. But not so *De Oecumenismo:* it conceives dividedness as separation from the authentic parent body—the Catholic Church—full of the plenitude of grace and truth. And a part of her dis-grace is that her rightful children are separated from her. And this is now admitted to be, in some part, her own fault and a fault that needs and is in process of removal by the II Vatican Council. Thus, it is also a basic principle that renewal is preliminary and indispensable to reunion or unity.

Before referring to Catholic practice of ecumenism, one further salient principle needs mention. It is that duly baptized separated brethren, while they may not enjoy perfect communion with the Church, are bound to her by *some kind of communion.* This halfway bond is, moreover, a fraternal bond. It justifies the recognition of many signs of the Spirit's working outside the Church. It justifies also, perhaps, the following recommended ecumenical practices, viz.: study of the religious life, culture and doctrine of non-Catholics; theological dialogue; ecumenical instruction for priests, missionaries and religious; common prayer in company with the separated brethren; cooperation with them in social amelioration and humanitarian action.

As one morning Gustave Weigel, now of blessed memory, translated these passages for some observers at the Pensione Castel San Angelo, someone—I think it was Albert Outler—expressed disappointment. To this Father Weigel replied, "There is progress here all the same!" There is progress when we compare this openness with former Roman exclusiveness. But I am disposed to wonder whether the composers of the schema ventured too little and too timidly. In the forum of the Council few voices were raised in warning against the dangers of such a modest measure of community with non-Catholics. True, the voice of Cardinal Ruffini was raised again and a few others, but the strenuous criticism anticipated did not materialize in reference to ecumenical practices allowed or commended. Voices were raised, sometimes, urging recognition of greater dignity for the churches of the separated brethren.

In conclusion, I propose the following alternative hypotheses, the respective merit or truth of which only time can verify or correct: on the one hand, what we find in the first recension of the schema on ecumenism may be a tentative probing maneuver to discover what latitude of movement there is within the episcopate for positive ecumenical advances, what are the pockets of resistance, and the maximum leeway or expectancy. In short, we have a trial balloon from which the Secretariat may receive guidance for a more constructive and daring venture. This is a likely possibility in view of the great sagacity of the Secretariat's leadership.

On the other hand, it simply may be true that the existing Roman Catholic vision of ecumenicity is no wider or longer than the timeworn thesis that Christian unity is union *with* the Roman Church as disunity is separation *from* the Roman Church. It may be that the ecumenical effort of Rome is a general house-cleaning as a needful inducement to come home. This is really all the schema in its present form holds out. And this, it may be, will prove enough to initiate stages of reconciliation with Eastern Orthodoxy, provided that, in the schema on the Church, the full import of episcopal "collegiality" is confirmed and sharpened to the point that the Papacy becomes only the chief *praesidium* and focus of unity in the Church. At least theoretically, reconciliation with Orthodoxy may be possible when the Pope is conceded to be *primus inter pares,* first among equals.

I do not venture to declare whether the principle of "collegiality" has in it such potentiality. I am sure that to understand and follow the present ecumenical drift of the Council requires keeping "collegiality" and the expressed principles of ecumenism in complementary relationship. If these can be made to dovetail, then reconciliation with Eastern Orthodoxy will be the direct and practical outworking and program of the aftermath of the Council and of Pope John's revolution of modern Catholicism.

ECUMENISM—A CRISIS OF DECISION: VATICAN II, THE THIRD SESSION

I. INTIMATIONS FROM PAUL VI

The rays of a late afternoon September sun slanted through the high windows of the Sistine Chapel and warmed the bluish tones of Michelangelo's great masterpiece, the Last Judgment. From where I sat, the man contemplating eternal damnation was discomfitingly visible, as was also the sovereign Divider of the sheep from the goats. The great fresco left no room for doubt that human life is always in crisis that calls for decision. And, in a real sense, the fact of our being there at all as non-Catholic observers was evidence that momentous decisions are called for in the face of the revolution within Catholicism precipitated by a Pope, now gone to his reward, himself having faced the formidable issues of his moment of leadership of the Catholic Church.

That afternoon, as the observers to the Second Vatican Council sat in a rectangle awaiting the entrance of Paul VI, it was easy to imagine the scaffolding and the titan of artistic genius, centuries earlier, plying his colors in a colossal effort to discharge his lay apostolate to Pope, to Church, and to the glory of God. Now, centuries later, strangers and pilgrims, we entered into the immortal inheritance of Michelangelo's stewardship of faith in the course of pursuing our own stewardship of larger ecumenical understanding.

It was hardly possible to conceive a more majestic and solemn setting for a climactic moment in modern church history. It was to be the third meeting of the observers during the period of the Council with

This is a revised and updated version of Lecture V of the James A. Gray Lectures on "The Second Vatican Council" by Father Godfrey L. Diekmann, O.S.B., and myself. It was first published in the *Duke Divinity School Review*, XXX, No. 1 (Winter 1965). Preparing this essay for the present volume I am very mindful of the high privilege of colleagueship with my eminent and cherished friend, Father Diekmann, in presenting with him the Gray Lectures of 1964—both of us fresh from the third session of the Council. It was an added and memorable privilege for my wife and me to be his associates at The Institute for Advanced Ecumenical Studies, Jerusalem, in its first year, 1971–72—an experience of ecumenical community in common life and worship in the Holy Land no participants will ever forget.

I also wish to refer the reader to the "Prolegomena to the Gray Lectures, 1964" penned by my esteemed colleague of many years at Duke, the late James T. Cleland, chairman of the lecture committee. Dr. Cleland's words tellingly indicate the excitement abroad in those days incident to an emancipative influence of the unfolding Council. It was sensed by non-Catholics, and experienced vitally by Catholics—clerical, lay, and religious—in our Southern region, as elsewhere, and at the grass roots.

the reigning Pope—a privilege not regularly afforded the generality of Catholic bishops. The first meeting was in the fall of 1962, when John XXIII asked the observers not to ponder his words merely, but to try to penetrate his mind and heart and comprehend the measure of his rejoicing in their presence, the warmth of his welcome, and the fervor of his hopes.

Now, this meeting would be the second with John's successor. The Secretariat for the Promotion of Christian Unity, under Augustine Cardinal Bea, had made the arrangements with customary unostentatious competence. Its chief director, second in command to Bea, the newly elevated Bishop Willebrands, was the attentive and unfailingly gracious presiding host. Monsignor Arrighi bustled pleasantly, as usual, securing every detail of protocol, and Monsignor Dupré, Father Stransky, and others of the Secretariat staff hovered in the wings.

Cardinal Bea himself entered, stooped, as it were, with the weight of benign sagacity but devoid of all pretense, and took his seat to the right of the papal chair.

At length, Paul VI entered without announcement: restrained, composed but masterful, and smiling somewhat shyly or sadly, I thought, followed by his attendants. When he had motioned us to be seated, Cardinal Bea arose to give the observers both welcome and introduction. Thereafter, the Very Reverend Archimandrite Panteleimon Rodopoloulos, the rather youthful emissary of Athenagoras, Ecumenical Patriarch of Istanbul, addressed the Pope on behalf of the observers in irenic but somewhat reserved, if hopeful, generalities. To this Paul VI responded, reading slowly in French with directness, evident earnestness, and disciplined warmth.

What the reigning Pope had to say on the ecumenical front, activated as it was by the Second Vatican Council in its third session, cannot be passed unnoticed.[1] He expressed "spiritual joy" in the renewed meeting with the observers. In the fact itself he found renewed evidence of mutual satisfaction unmarred by signs of fatigue or disappointment but, on the contrary, of increasing liveliness and trust. An "abyss of diffidence and scepticism" had been "mostly bridged over," he declared, and, in physical nearness, there had been much conducive to "a spiritual drawing-together" formerly unknown. "A friendship has been born," he said. "A new method has been affirmed." You may note, said the Pope, "how the Catholic Church is disposed towards honourable and serene dialogue. She is not in haste, but desires only to begin it, leaving it to divine goodness to bring it to a conclusion, in the manner and time God pleases." While the Catholic Church is "unable to abandon certain doctrinal exigencies to which she has the duty in Christ to remain faithful," she is nevertheless "disposed to study how difficulties can be removed, misunderstandings dissipated, and the authentic treasures of truth and spirituality which *you* possess be respected. . . ." Paul VI went on to say, that the Catholic Church is ready to study "how certain canonical forms can be enlarged and adapted." All this, he affirmed to the end of facilitating "a *recomposition in unity* of the great and, by now, centuries-old Christian communities still separated from us. It is love, not egoism, which inspires us: 'For the love of Christ impels us' (1 Cor. 5:14)."

As the Pope spoke, the setting sun accented the colors of Michelangelo's Last Judgment. The sincerity of his spoken words was unmistakable and compelling. So also was their tact, their candor and integrity. Together we joined in the *Pater Noster,* each in his own language, and before departing, we recited together the *Gloria in excelcis Deo.* Such was the common prayer of the observers with the Pope as lector.

Observers of the Second Vatican Council cannot easily dismiss the Pope's expression of spiritual satisfaction in their continuing presence. It is true, not merely at the Council but elsewhere, that chasms of diffidence and pervasive distrust have been greatly replaced by emergent friendships and unprecedented fraternity. From the side of the observers, I can corroborate the Pope's impression that relations between us, the Council fathers, and the theological consultants became, especially in the third session, matters of mutual acceptance, one might say almost of expectant normality. Manifest everywhere down to the level of the Vatican guards was an atmosphere of enhancing trust and enlarging respect. In informal discussion, at receptions, and private dinners, lively dialogue replaced hesitancy and protocol. Conversation became increasingly unstudied, free, and eager and even probing. Amusing, perhaps, but significant was a tendency of many observers to identify themselves almost unconsciously with liberalizing tendencies and spokesmen thereof.

The fact is that "dialogue" became the fashionable word at the third session of the Council. It found a new place in both official language and official function. In the interim between sessions, it had received not only papal sanction but also development and elucidation. The Pope's strongest and clearest utterance in his recent encyclical *Ecclesiam Suam* set forth the nature and advanced the desirability of enlarging and continued dialogue with non-Catholics. Moreover, it was recognized that, by its nature, dialogue presupposes a certain mutuality of respect between partners of dialogue, a spirit of openness and inquiry with the prospect of enlarging mutual understanding.

This sustained and quite forthright invitation to dialogue on the part of the Roman Pontiff is a remarkable departure from the defensiveness of late 19th-century papal pronouncements that warned of the menace and required abstention of the faithful from intercourse with non-Catholics. At the same time, Paul VI has been candid. In *Ecclesiam*

Suam he has said that "it is not in our power to compromise with the integrity of the faith." [2] So also in his words to the observers he spoke openly of inability to abandon "certain doctrinal exigencies" as the price of fruitful conversation. Nevertheless, now that the Catholic Church has entered into conversations and taken "the initiative toward reunion," it is prepared to study how obstacles may be overcome to facilitate "a recomposition in unity."

This is a new phrase and worthy of most careful attention. Offered in the newly enunciated context of "dialogue," it proposes, I think, to find a way of advance toward unity that avoids and may supersede the offensive and, certainly, naive notion of *return* to the Catholic fold. "Recomposition" is not simple "return." It acknowledges "the authentic treasures of truth and spirituality" possessed by non-Catholic Christian communions. No longer is Catholic truth peremptorily juxtaposed to non-Catholic error with no prerogative left to the erring but recantation and return. Tokens, signs, and marks of authentic Christianity are conceded, however incomplete. Moreover, if only truth has rights, then partial truth has also the right to some acknowledgment.

Having granted, then, elements of truth and godliness, some signs of the Spirit's working, in non-Roman communions, there is, I believe, in the Pope's recent statements discreet announcement of a willingness to enter by "serene dialogue" into an era of doctrinal discussion and theological negotiation looking toward "a recomposition in unity" of the separated communions with the Catholic Church. The consummation may be late or soon, but its declared vehicle is dialogue and negotiation, however protracted. It is not individual conversion but communal *rapprochement* and recomposition based upon an open forum of free give-and-take and not only in conversation but also in fellowship of common prayer and common social action. The new approach was so plainly set forth by Archbishop J. C. Heenan of England at the second session of Vatican II that it bears quoting: "The ecumenical dialogue," he said, "is not undertaken with individual souls in mind, nor in order to gain the better of an argument. The dialogue has to be a sincere attempt to understand the beliefs of our separated brethren. It must also present and explain Catholic teaching to them. It is a coming together of brothers, not an encounter of enemies. It takes place mainly between communities, that is, between the Catholic Church and non-Catholic Christian churches or communities. It is rooted in mutual trust and complete charity."

From these things I believe we may perceive that, in his conception and authorization of dialogue, Paul VI has provided a recognizable method and vehicle of ecumenical endeavor for the Catholic Church in its thrust toward the reunification of Christendom. Not to be over-looked, either, are many open doors for larger development of Catholic thought and action in almost every conciliar document of the Second Vatican Council. Through these open doors, with the instrumentality of dialogue—and providing the present temper continues—the Catholic Church is mounting an ecumenical offensive of very great potential influence and power. The Church manifests an increasing determination, from its side, to change radically the climate of interconfessional relations. Surely, in the days and years ahead, it will require unforeseen varieties of positive, theologically informed and forthright response on the part of the member churches of the World Council. They can hardly ignore the challenge to encounter through continuing dialogue. They were less vulnerable with Rome in self-imposed isolation.

II. THE CONCILIAR DECREE ON ECUMENISM

Turning now to the Council documents, what is their import for the development of Catholic ecumenism? The limit of time forces me to be very selective. The ecumenical import of the already promulgated Constitution on the Sacred Liturgy has been illuminated by Father Diekmann, whose role, not only in its composition but in its postconciliar implementation, has been and continues to be deservedly large. From the Protestant perspective, I would underscore only the importance of its pervasive stress upon congregational participation in worship, the centrality of the Bible in liturgey as a teaching instrument, and the indispensability of the preached Word to illuminate the Church's celebration of the Word in sacrament. The introduction of the vernacular will do more to demystify and, correspondingly, instruct Catholic worshippers than the majority of the Council fathers, who voted for it, may admit publicly. Obviously, the attendant adoption of the Revised Standard Version of the New Testament by the American hierarchy, making it the common text of American Christians, has enormous significance and will be the basis of unprecedented communication at all levels. The express recommendation of the schema "On Divine Revelation" that the Scriptures be read by clergy and laity is, especially with reference to the latter, an unlocked door, capable of swinging, one would judge, both ways.[3]

Catholic Principles of Ecumenism

Turning attention directly upon *De Oecumenismo* and the work of the Secretariat, let me say with studied reserve that the work leading to the preliminary adoption of this conciliar document October 8, 1964, was discharged with fidelity to a great insight, genius of administration, and epoch-making and adroit determination. The Secretariat itself has been a remarkable working team. When some day the story can and will be told about the Second Vatican Council, it will center around two very old men and a somewhat younger man, the last of whom, in the face of formidable complexities and age-encrusted tradition managed somehow to keep faith with the larger vision he had received.

John XXIII well knew that to open the Catholic Church to both the opportunity and challenge of Christian unity and the recovery of initiative, already completely lost to the World Council of Churches, required new and radical vision, extraordinary sagacity, and a totally new instrument within the Church itself. Thus, there came into being, as the pivotal and nucleating vehicle, the Secretariat headed by the learned biblical scholar, Jesuit educator, and papal counselor, Cardinal Bea. As confessor to Pius XII, Bea knew more about the captivity of the Papacy to the Curia than most living men. Affinity there was between his authoritative learning and understanding and the spirit of John XXIII.

From that affinity the thrust of the Council toward up-dating world Catholicism emerged. It emerged against the resolute opposition of a majority of the inner ruling circle of the Curia, whose mentality was largely unrevised "counter-Reformation" but implemented by the antimodernistic decrees of the 19th-century popes, *Syllabus of Errors* of 1864, and the unrestricted absolutism of the First Vatican Council. If Pius IX and Leo XIII had denied the right of error, freedom of conscience, and religious liberty, for the conservatives of the Curia this was infallible truth and the only available platform of Catholic relations with non-Catholic Christians. Christian unity could mean only one thing, recantation and allegiance to the Pope. In politics, Latin Catholicism had never really emerged from feudalism; and, in ecclesiology, it acknowledged no effectually saving action of God outside the Roman Church. Had not the *Syllabus of Errors* condemned even the moderate and humane surmise: "We may entertain at least a well-founded hope for the eternal salvation of all those who are in no manner in the true Church of Christ"? [4] Ecumenism could mean nothing but "return" to Rome, the only course held open by the *Dogmatic Decrees* of the First Vatican Council.[5] What to Rome, then, was the significance of the 20th-century ecumenical movement? From the perspective of Vatican I, nothing at all.

The story of the loosening of this mental straight-jacket would be a long one. Its outcome and eventuation is, perhaps, formulated for the first time in "De Oecumenismo" of Vatican II and reverberates in the schema "On the Church." From the former a few crucial principles may be noted. First, interest in the restoration of unity is in some measure "a manifestation of a fraternal bond existing among all Christians." Second, "the spirit of compunction and longing for unity" manifested among Christians separated from the Catholic Church is a work of divine grace. Third, separations from full communion with the Catholic Church issued "not without the fault of people on both sides." Fourth, the validly baptized are possessed of a kind of communion, though not perfect, with the Catholic Church. Fifth, the Holy Spirit is the Church's principle of unity. This is to be noted in conjunction with the sixth point, namely, the life of grace, faith, hope, charity, and other internal gifts of the Holy Spirit are found outside the visible Church among the separated Christians. All these things, it is said, proceed from Christ and lead to Him; all of them belong rightly to the one Church of Christ. And, in the schema "De Ecclesia," a certain real connection with the Holy Spirit is affirmed of non-Catholic Christians. The Holy Spirit is "active even among them with his sanctifying power." [6]

This is a long way from the theory and practice of counter-Reformation popes: that dissent from the doctrine of the Church is deserving of death. Its presiding principle is that separated Christians may be participant also, though deficiently, in the gifts of the Holy Spirit, the Spirit of Christ. They are invited to consider the benefits of the perfect dispensation of grace afforded through the one divinely authorized and truly apostolic Church. Yet it is allowed that, among the separated communions, "sacred actions" are celebrated that "can without doubt really generate the life of grace." In this we may see the victory of empiricism over dogmatic idealism. Dialogue is now the medium of communicating the excellency of the fullness of grace of which non-Catholics can appropriate but a portion. Irenics supersede polemics, but it is not a deceptive or "false irenicism," for behind these new and truly advanced positions lies the limitation of "doctrinal exigencies" which Paul VI warns the Church has not the power to modify. Christ entrusted his Church and, therewith, the authorized dispensation of his saving grace to the keeping of Peter and the apostles and their divinely empowered successors. The question before us now as before, perhaps, is that of custodianship. It is the long-standing ecumenical question of the *ministry* and the *means of grace.*

Of Religious Liberty

The declaration on religious liberty or, as its subtitle reads, "the right of individuals and communities to freedom in matters of religion" appeared as "Declaration One" appended to the schema "On Ecumenism." This was a modification adopted by the Secretariat in response to criticism that it was not integral to a statement of the principles and practice of Catholic ecumenism. In the 1963 recension it had appeared as a fifth chapter. Revised by the Secretariat between the second and third sessions of the Council, it was introduced on September 23, 1964, by Bishop Joseph DeSmedt of Bruges, who had also presented it in its initial form, and for the first time, November 19, 1963.

Summarizing a central theme of the declaration, DeSmedt asserted that "the basic foundation of religious liberty is the nature of the human person as created by God. The right to religious liberty rests in the fact, that, under the guidance of his conscience, every human person must obey God's call and will."

In his initial introduction of the text November 19, 1963, Bishop DeSmedt had presented four reasons why many Council fathers had insistently demanded that the Sacred Synod should proclaim the right of man to religious liberty. First, the Church must teach and defend the right to religious liberty because *truth* is committed to her care. Second, the Church cannot remain silent when half of mankind is deprived of religious liberty by atheistic materialism. Third, today in all nations men of differing religious faith or no faith must live together in the same human society at peace. Fourth, many non-Catholics suspect the Church of duplicity in seeming to demand religious liberty when Catholics are in the minority but refusing it when Catholics are in the majority.

Prefacing his remarks with this compelling candor, DeSmedt went on to define religious liberty as "the right of the human person to the free exercise of religion according to the dictates of his conscience." The words have a familiar ring, as if the Pilgrim Fathers were *redivivus* in Rome or Roger Williams had returned to receive plenary indulgence from unlikely quarters. Religious liberty, negatively considered, DeSmedt declared, "is immunity from all external force in man's personal relations with God. . . ." DeSmedt's *relatio* was received with applause. So also was the clipped and cogent intervention of Archbishop Heenan, now a cardinal, on behalf of the hierarchy of England and Wales. "We praise and unreservedly approve," he said, "the proposals of this schema on religious liberty." He cited the statement of Pius XII that "the common good might impose a moral obligation in what are described as Catholic countries to respect the freedom of other religions." The world is small today, Heenan continued, "and the internal events of one nation have consequences over all the world." For the sake of the common good freedom of religion must flourish in every nation of the world.

The offensive had been adroitly mounted. An effort to persuade and to allay the reaction of conservative prelates from Catholic countries of southern Europe was evident. At that juncture the groundswell of support that actually emerged was not by any means presumed upon by the Secretariat. Plausible as might be DeSmedt's persuasive view that religious liberty is implied in the very act of faith as unenforceable response to a supernatural gift, there was pervasive suspense and uncertainty. The *Syllabus of Errors* of 1864, in condemning "indifferentism," had condemned the proposition that "every man is free to embrace and profess the religion he shall believe true, guided by the light of reason." True, the declaration states he shall now properly be guided by "conscience," and a quite different conception of man is envisioned. But religious liberty has no standing in Catholic countries, and the Latins did not easily forget that Leo XIII had condemned "liberty of worship" as "no liberty, but its degradation" unless it is worship which God has plainly revealed and entrusted to the Catholic Church.[7] Furthermore, the dogma of Vatican I, "that the Roman Pontiff, when he speaks *ex cathedra*, that is, when in discharge of the office of pastor and doctor of all Christians, by virtue of his supreme apostolic authority, he defines a doctrine regarding faith or morals to be held by the universal Church, . . ."[8] is possessed of infallibility, complicated the situation. Religious liberty as "the right of the human person to the free exercise of religion according to the dictates of his conscience" did not immediately appear to square with the prevailing understanding of what the Church had taught generally and some pontiffs of the Church in particular.

It is not surprising, therefore, that the redoubtable and eloquent Cardinal Ruffini, archbishop of Palermo, Sicily, was first to speak to "vindicate the protection of the common law of our holy religion." He supposed it gratuitous to exhort Catholics not to use force in effecting conversions. But we should not, he declared, confuse *freedom*, which appertains to those possessed of truth, with *tolerance*, which must certainly be patient and kind. "Only truth has rights, and truth is one." And, recalling Leo XIII, it was not hard to see that the tradition was on his side. Here was a living survivor, flesh and blood, of the counter-Reformation, in the afternoon of the 20th century.

Such a view as this, which justified the Inquisition, has no doubt served well to repress religious liberty of conscience for centuries in what its spokesmen blandly call "Catholic countries." It was echoed by prominent representatives of Italian and Spanish Catholicism such as Cardinal Monreal of Seville, Cardinal Ottaviani, the archconservative Dominican, Cardinal Michael Browne, and Bishops J. Abasolo of India, Nicodemo of Bari, Granados of Toledo.

The declaration was declared a novelty in its substance and in contradiction with alleged assertions of Pius XII. Ignored was the printed documentation of the decree which, in support, claimed the authority of John XXIII, who in *Pacem in Terris* had declared: "Among the rights of men this too is to be reckoned, that he can venerate God according to the right rule of his conscience, and profess his religion privately and publicly; to this right corresponds the duty of recognizing it and cultivating it; which duty is incumbent upon all other men, especially upon those in charge of the public weal." John's infallibility was, it seems, not as palatable as Leo's. Even more emphatically than Ruffini, Granados of Toledo declared that our traditional doctrine has always been that only truth has rights while error is treated with tolerance if this is required in the interest of the common good. That this is indeed the traditional doctrine of Spanish Catholicism few will doubt. It is significant that important representatives of Latin American Catholicism did not, in speaking, support this inquisitorial line.

The bishops of the United States stood firmly together in defense of the declaration on religious liberty. They had come to the third session prepared so to do. Leadership was given by both Cardinals Meyer and Cushing. The colorful oratory and unfettered stance of the Cardinal from Boston won him a restrained ovation in the Aula. He rejoiced that at long last there was opportunity for full and free discussion of the important topic. The Catholic and non-Catholic worlds, he said, are waiting for this declaration. Taking his text from the Preamble of the *Declaration of Independence* he said of this declaration on religious liberty: "It aims to safeguard what has well been called 'decent respect for the opinion of mankind.'" The question of religious liberty, regarded by some as complicated, is in fact simple. It has a twofold aspect: it is first the assertion of the freedom of the Church, that is, her divine right to achieve her spiritual end, and secondly insistence by the Church on this right for every human being. John XXIII, delcared Cushing, has outlined the more cogent reasons demanding this declaration on religious liberty. Without impugning for a moment the Cardinal's sincerity, one may say that it was a politic speech both politically and ecclesiastically.

With care and cogency Cardinal Meyer defended the declaration as conforming to the teaching of modern popes, especially of John XXIII. Moreover it is "necessary" to assist freedom of religion where it is repressed, to insure fruitful ecumenical dialogue, to assure to others what we claim for ourselves. True religion is the voluntary acceptance of the will of God apart from all external constraint. Experience testifies that where the state dominates religion, civic welfare is harmed, whereas civil welfare flourishes where religious freedom is enjoyed.

The last point reflects opinion widely shared by the American hierarchy. Among the American bishops one may also often hear the view expressed that where religion is disestablished, religion thrives; where it has the patronage of the state, it languishes.

The implication of disestablishment is plain; it is religious liberty for all. Thus, the issue is joined within world Catholicism between southern European Latin Catholicism, still committed to the figment of "Catholic countries," and world Catholicism long accustomed to exist and propagate itself amidst religious and cultural pluralism. To the latter group, the Leonine articles on "liberty of worship" are theoretically untenable and anachronistic. For the American hierarchy, the Church, as the schema "On Ecumenism" declares, is a "pilgrim" in an alien world and better for the challenge this entails. Latin Catholicism, nestling in the false security of state establishment, still seeks, as Cardinal Rufini proposed, to "vindicate the protection of common law for our holy religion."

Here again is a basic rift in contemporary Catholicism between those who have learned that Christ does not need the protection of the state, and those, who with the outlook of the Middle Ages, would commandeer the succor of the "civil arm." If Catholicism enjoys and requires state protection, then religious liberty remains a matter of toleration under law. If it does not, then the Church must risk its temporal fortunes on the cogency and verity of its message and life in a pluralistic society. We may well believe that to enter such a society, defenseless save for "the sword of the Spirit" and "the breastplate of righteousness," is a part of what John XXIII envisioned in his program both of inner renewal of the Church and the bringing of it up-to-date in the modern world.

We may perhaps perceive that John XXIII was the first Pope to break decisively with the Constantinian establishment which made Christianity the official religion of the Empire and which has controlled the mind of Roman Catholicism for fifteen hundred years. If so, he created a new era and deserves the title of first modern Pope. The question before the Second Vatican Council concerning religious liberty is, therefore, fateful above all others. Small as is the document, it embodies the answer to the question posed by the 16th-century Reformation whether the Church, in discharging its evangel to the world, shall walk by faith only in the power of the Holy Spirit of Christ or by connivance with and support of secular power. Although the 16th-century Reformers did not always perceive it clearly, the import of *sola fide* was equally appropriate to the Church corporately as to the believer individually.

To some within the Catholic Church who sincerely believe that Peter still holds the power of the keys, it has become painfully clear that this power can be enforced in the modern world only by the "sword of the Spirit." This is the underlying theological issue in the continuing struggle within Vatican Council II. A powerful and stubborn minority continue to resist. It is very evident that the attempted subversion of the declaration through the office of the Secretary General of the Council over the week-end of October 10-12, 1964, was a well calculated maneuver of desperation, presuming to circumvent normal conciliar process.

The temper of the Council had plainly indicated that reactionary Latin Catholicism of the "Catholic countries" was in imminent danger of being overwhelmed by a majority of the Council fathers. On September 25, after three days' debate on the declaration, Cardinal Suenens, the Moderator, proposed a standing vote on the opportuneness of closing off debate. A "vast majority of the Council fathers," according to the official record, "declared themselves favorable." This vote remanded the document to the Secretariat for emendation and revision. Fifteen days later the move was made, through the Secretary General, to take the declaration out of the Secretariat's hands, placing it elsewhere for emendation and for some suitable disposition not wholly clear. It was then that a group of cardinals in company with the dauntless Cardinal Frings of Cologne interposed and were sustained by Paul VI in their insistence upon due conciliar process.

The final effort at obstruction was adroitly timed for the next to last general congregation of the third session. On November 19 came the vote on the complete text of the epoch-making schema "De Ecclesia," for which 2,134 favorable votes were cast against 10 *non placets*. The announcement was received with recurring applause by the fathers. Thereafter, announcement of the final vote on the morrow "On Ecumenism" was made by the Secretary General as the schema had been amended and revised by the Secretariat for Christian Unity, including the altered version of the declaration on religious liberty. Thereafter the most dramatic moment of the Council's third session occurred.

Cardinal President of the Council, Tisserant, having publicly consulted his colleagues at the presidential table, announced that several members of the Council had asked for further time to formulate mature judgments before being called upon to vote, that the new text of the declaration was substantially different from the previous text discussed in the Council Hall, that this was admitted by the Secretariat. Accordingly, it had been felt that extra time should be granted and that the concession of this time was not a question that could be decided by a vote of the Council. Consequently, after the presentation of the report on the document in that morning's General Congregation, there would be no vote of the Council on the declaration on religious liberty.

A perceptible sag in the spirit of the Council issued in general consternation and erupted into a conventicle that first centered around the dismayed Cardinal Meyer and then Father Godfrey Diekmann, O.S.B. in the south transept of St. Peter's as Dean W. R. Cannon of Emory joined the group. Cardinal Ritter entered the discussion. A crowd of bishops and *periti* gathered. Within a short space of time a petition to overrule the Council Presidency was circulating and gained under a thousand signatures. The response of Pope Paul VI to the representation made by Cardinal Meyer, Ritter, and Leger is common knowledge. He decided, and probably in accord with due conciliar process, to sustain the majority decision of the Presidents—however close it doubtless was—to postpone until the fourth session of Vatican II the vote on religious liberty. It was a critical and tough decision to make, but, in fidelity to conciliar process and, indeed, to the principle of collegial responsibility and rights the Pope's decision was unavoidable. On the succeeding day, the 127th and final General Congregation, Cardinal Tisserant took notice of the great disappointment of a number of Council fathers, and in the name of His Holiness, informed the Council that the Council Presidency had agreed to the request of postponement advanced by certain Council fathers, that "this request had to be honored and conformably according to the Council's procedural rules." He assured the Council that the declaration on religious liberty would come up for discussion and vote in the next session of the Council and, if possible, would have priority on the agenda.

III. ECUMENICAL PROSPECTS IN SUMMARY

In May 1964 the Secretariat on Religious Liberty of the World Council of Churches issued a memorandum evaluating the declaration on religious liberty as revised for presentation to the fourth session of Vatican II. It concluded that in spite of some shortcomings regarding the criterion of limiting religious liberty the new draft is "satisfactory." It was added that, if approved by the Council without major changes, "it will notably improve the ecumenical climate and the relationship between the Roman Catholic Church and other Christians." This last judgment hardly needs reinforcement. The Secretariat for the Promotion of Christian Unity early came to a like conviction. It was, as we have seen, openly stated by DeSmedt on occasion of the declaration's initial public presentation to the Council in November 1963. Subsequently, the ecumenical import of the declaration was echoed and

reechoed in conciliar discussion. This in part accounts for the consternation of many Council fathers over further delay in vote and promulgation.

Meanwhile, the final approval of the schema "On Ecumenism" was
given at the 127th General Congregation of the Second Vatican Council
and the final one of the third session. Of the 2,129 votes cast, 2,054
were affirmative, 64 negative, 6 approved with proposed changes, and
5 were null. This was a momentous victory attained over a long, thorny,
arduous way, conceived in the spirit of John XXIII and executed with
imperturbable moral fidelity, wisdom, and Christian understanding
by the Secretariat under Augustine Cardinal Bea.

After the successful vote on the fourteen sections of the three principal chapters of the schema "On Ecumenism," continuing October 5
through 8, 1964, the Secretariat gave a reception for the observers.
It was in many ways a celebration. And nothing could be more appropriate than celebration among those who had, in this sphere, become
by now colleagues. There was cause for mutual rejoicing and no more
felicitous way could have been found, nor one of greater ecumenical
and Christian tact, than for the Secretariat to share its rejoicing with
the "separated brethren," for a deeper unity with whom it had valiantly
labored.

In sharing his reflections with the assembled company, Cardinal Bea
said ". . . the very fact that the vote was, one can say, morally unanimous is a motive for deep joy and great hope. In effect, more than
98% of the conciliar Fathers who were present and voted approved
the schema. . . . This result surpassed by far even the most optimistic
hopes which we could have imagined little more than a decade ago.
This unanimity gives evidence that for the future the Roman Catholic
Church, through its highest and most qualified representatives, is completely engaged in fostering, with all its strength the unity of all those
who believe in Christ and are baptized in Him." Then alluding to
"the inevitable difficulties" the further work of the Secretariat "will
undoubtedly encounter," he gave utterance to what one may well
believe is the unfailing source of his greatness as the leading Catholic
ecumenical statesman of his day: "God's manner of proceeding in the
work of Redemption consists precisely in being triumphant *by means*
of difficulties and despite the insufficiency of his instruments and their
weakness, 'in order to show that the transcendent power belongs to
God and not to us.' " If I may venture a surmise it is just this transcendent power of God, which Bea honors above the defensive tendency
to domesticate it, that has made him the chief architect of Catholic
ecumenism and launched the Catholic Church upon a way whose outcome is not known to men.

Whatever else might be said, would, I think, only and manifestly come to this: it is now time for non-Catholic Christianity to awake to the challenge which has issued from the Second Vatican Council. It is not a challenge that can be ignored. It requires searching and thoughtful response. The "Catholic principles of ecumenism" will have to be faced, not alone by the World Council of Churches, but by the member bodies. The Catholic Church is now surely on the ecumenical offensive, and in defining how it stands with reference to us, it will force us to define with greater precision than has been our wont how we stand with reference to it.

After four centuries of mutual distrust, remoteness, and the virtual nonexistence of communication between Catholicism and the Protestant Churches of the West, the Catholic Church has broken the silence as well as the ice, and taken the initiative. It addresses us with an invitation to friendly dialogue in the atmosphere of restored Christian fellowship and without obscuring the differences between us. Sooner or later even in this citadel of Protestantism, the American South, we shall have to acknowledge that we are spoken to and that a new situation in World Christianity requires responsible answers.

We shall be faced with some decisions, and what decisions we make will be for us an occasion of judgment. It is just barely possible, or so it seemed to me, that this was the reason that prompted someone to decide to hold the meeting of the observers with the Pope in the Sistine Chapel that late September afternoon. We are always confronted by the divine judgment, for judgment is incident to the decisions we make in life, in the history of church and of nations. Michelangelo's fresco sets before the eyes this inescapable truth of existence in matchless line and unforgettable color. What we must not fail to realize is that today we are faced with the beginnings of a new era in Christian history. When I returned to Rome in September 1964, I was prepared for disappointment with reference to the Council's fidelity to the vision of John XXIII. I returned from the Council with the conviction that, despite great obstacles, the Council had been able to lay the groundwork for a renewal of Catholicism and, therewith, the beginnings of a new era of ecumenism that will inevitably implicate us all.

IV. A POSTSCRIPT

As is suggested in these last two chapters, I was not unaware in the days of the Council that the new "ecumenism" of Vatican II might subsequently foster what may be termed "latitudinarianism" among some Catholic theologians and laity toward still unrevised positions of the Church on faith and morals. This was almost inevitable as a concomitant of John XXIII's revolution of openness, and the tendency and bearing, as well as implications, of the Council documents themselves. Remarkable daring in theological reformulation—however guarded and refined—already had precedent in the constitutions and decrees of Vatican II. Innovation, however, is one thing for the Church's fully authorized Holy Synod or *magisterium*. Independent theological creativity, however, is quite another thing in the Canon Law and tradition of the Roman Church. Such independent theological creativity, if it claims to be truly Catholic, must square with the prevailing *consensus fidelium* as authoritatively interpreted, and requires certification by acknowledged authorities.

It is this to which Pope Paul VI was referring in his *Discourse* to the Observers at the Third Session (see Appendix), namely, how it is that the Catholic Church is "unable to abandon certain doctrinal exigencies to which she has the duty in Christ to remain faithful. . . ." The theological "creativity" of certain Roman Catholic theologians in the years following the Council may well be understood as variant interpretations of what, in fact, "duty in Christ" does require of faithful believers. It is this variance over which Paul VI found it burdensome to preside while declining, for the most part, either to exercise overmuch his pontifical authority, through channels, or to invoke head-on synodical review of variant teaching within the Church.

What, then, we may perceive in the troubled waters of present-day Catholicism on the theological front is a delicate and unresolved problem. It is at least two-sided. On the one hand, it is the hermeneutical problem: what in fact is required for dutifulness in and to Christ, as the issue was framed by Paul VI? On the other, who is or are the decisive interpreters? For the Roman Church the answer to the second question remains unchanged. The Church is interpreter. Nothing in Vatican II altered this *fundamentum*. The issue, then, comes to be how, without discouraging theological creativity, and, while nurturing it, to enlist its services and employ its findings selectively. By Canon Law and by the principles of Vatican II's "Dogmatic Constitution on the Church" provision for judicious selectivity may well be available. But selection is unavoidable on existing premises.

But let us not suppose that these issues confronting the Roman Church today are confined to Catholicism, or that Protestantism has long since found the answer to the question about "doctrinal exigencies" implied by our "duty in Christ." Rather, it seems, Protestant Christianity in its main-line American expressions has for long been waiving the question. This, insofar as it has declined to consider seriously the presumptive role of doctrinal standards if a church, so-called, is to be the Church, that is, the Church of Jesus Christ. Likewise it remains a problem if there is to be a "Church-theology" at all. If so, who then is the judge or where do we look for authorized adjudication as among multifarious claims to Christian truth?

Here is the inescapable problem of ecclesial coherence in the absence of decisive authority. The Church is not the university as, conversely, the university cannot be itself and be the Church. At the same time, it seems unfortunate that the Roman Church, in exercising the proper authority of the *magesterium*—the supreme teaching office—and by long tradition, has failed to distinguish between the *esse* of faith and the *bene esse* of order and of *mores*. In treating all alike it imposes upon itself a range of responsibility exceeding, perhaps, both the demands of the gospel and the need of the faithful. So doing, it may tend to revert to the Jewish Christianity from which St. Paul's gospel set the Gentiles free in the first age of the Church.

v. APPENDIX

DISCOURSE OF THE HOLY FATHER TO THE OBSERVERS AT THE THIRD SESSION OF THE II VATICAN COUNCIL (SEPTEMBER 29, 1964)

Gentlemen, beloved and venerable brothers!

(1) This new meeting of your group with the Bishop of Rome, successor of the Apostle Peter, on the occasion of the Third Session of the Second Ecumenical Vatican Council, is a new motive for spiritual joy, which We like to believe to be reciprocal. We are made happy and honoured by your presence; and the words just now addressed to Us give assurance that your feelings resemble Ours. We feel the necessity of expressing Our gratitude to you for the favourable reception accorded Our invitation, and for your attendance, with such dignity and edification, at the conciliar Congregations. The fact that our mutual satisfaction over these repeated meetings of ours shows no signs of fatigue or disappointment, but is now more lively and trusting than ever, seems to Us to be already an excellent result; this is a historic fact; and its value cannot be other than positive in regard to the supreme common aim, that of full and true unity in Jesus Christ. An abyss, of diffidence and scepticism, has been mostly bridged over; this our physical nearness manifests and favours a spiritual drawing-together, which was formerly unknown to us. A new method has been

affirmed. A friendship has been born. A hope has been kindled. A movement is under way. Praise be to God Who, We like to believe, "has given His Holy Spirit to us" (1 Thess. 4:3).

(2) Here we are, then, once again seeking, on one side and on the other, the definition of our respective positions. As to Our position, you already know it quite well.

(a) You will have noted that the Council has had only words of respect and of joy for your presence, and that of the Christian communities which you represent. Nay more, words of honour, of charity and of hope in your regard. This is no small matter, if we think of the polemics of the past, and if we observe also that this changed attitude of ours is sincere and cordial, pious and profound.

(b) Moreover, you can note how the Catholic Church is disposed towards honourable and serene dialogue. She is not in haste, but desires only to begin it, leaving it to divine goodness to bring it to a conclusion, in the manner and time God pleases. We still cherish the memory of the proposal you made to Us last year, on an occasion similar to this; that of founding an institute of studies on the history of salvation, to be carried on in a common collaboration; and We hope to bring this initiative to reality, as a memorial of our journey to the Holy Land last January; We are now studying the possibility of this.

(c) This shows you, Gentlemen and brothers, that the Catholic Church, while unable to abandon certain doctrinal exigencies to which she has the duty in Christ to remain faithful, is nevertheless disposed to study how difficulties can be removed, misunderstanding dissipated, and the authentic treasures of truth and spirituality which you possess be respected; how certain canonical forms can be enlarged and adapted, to facilitate a recomposition in unity of the great and, by now, centuries-old Christian communities still separated from Us. It is love, not egoism, which inspires Us: "For the love of Christ impels us" (2 Cor. 5:14).

(d) In this order of ideas, We are happy and grateful that Our Secretariat for Unity has been invited, on various occasions, to send observers to the conferences and meetings of your Churches and your organizations. We will gladly continue to do this, so that Our Catholic organizations and Our representatives may, on their side, acquire a knowledge, corresponding to truth and to charity, which are a prerequisite of a deeper union in the Lord.

(3) As for you, Gentlemen and brothers, We ask you kindly to continue in your functions as sincere and amiable observers; and to this end, not to content yourselves with a simple passive presence, but kindly to try to understand and to pray with Us, so that you can then communicate to your respective communities the best and most exact

news of this Council, thereby favouring a progressive drawing-together of minds in Christ Our Lord.

In this regard, We would ask you now to bring to your communities and to your institutions Our thanks, Our greetings, Our wishes of every good and perfect gift in the Lord.

All this, you can see, is only a beginning; but, in order that it may be correct in its inspiration, and fruitful one day in its results, We invite you to conclude this meeting of ours by the common recitation of the prayer which Jesus taught us: the "Our Father."

ROMAN CATHOLIC RENEWAL AND VATICAN COUNCIL II: A PROTESTANT OBSERVER'S VIEW

Vitacan Council II is now an event of the past. As the writer stood with perhaps seventy other observers before the massive facade of St. Peter's Basilica on the last day of splendid ceremonial, the 8th day of December 1965, he was deeply conscious of high privilege. So were his colleagues beside him. They had been witnesses and participants in one of the epoch-making events of modern church history. The Council had begun under the inspired leadership of the aged and beloved Pope, John XXIII. It was the writer's good fortune to begin observership in the second session of 1963 and to return to the third and fourth, or final sessions. Close, even intimate were the associations and friendships that had been formed, not only with fellow observers but with the hosts, the Roman Catholic brethren. The unfailing courtesies and consideration shown to the observers by the staff of the Secretariat for the Promotion of Christian Unity, under the presidency of Augustine Cardinal Bea and the executive direction of Bishop J. Willebrands, will remain a lifetime of pleasant heart-warming memory.

How shall we forget the many vivid hours spent in travels, conversation, and dining together? Together we shared the hospitality of monasteries and their monastic brotherhoods. Ancient precedents were set aside, and our wives accompanied us. They dined at tables in refectories where women had never set foot. It was so at the Franciscan Monastery of Assisi, at Subiaco, at Montecassino, at Florence, and most memorable of all, at Casa Mari, a Cistercian Abbey to the south of Rome, where we were feasted and serenaded by a most engaging band of young monks—for all the world reminiscent of my own seminary students.

As the observers returned session after session, the friendships and interchange with their Catholic hosts became warm, vital, and ever more fruitful. In the final discussions of the fourth session, we were marvelously engaged with emancipation of mind and spirit in candid discussion in which Catholics often held variant views among themselves, Methodists sided with Orthodox against Calvinists, and Lutherans were quite as likely to gainsay an Anglican as they were a Roman.

A lecture presented to faculty and students of Duke Divinity School, first published in its *Review*, 1966. In its present form published by *The Review and Expositor*, XLII, No. 2 (Spring 1967). Reprinted with permission of the Editor.

In the closing session of the Council we were really "mixing it up" with candor and unembarrassed good will that was the fruit of mutual trust and personal understanding nurtured by prolonged association.

So, at the Council's closing, December 8, 1965, it seemed to the observers, and probably to most Council Fathers, that John XXIII's courageous risk in inviting non-Catholic observers had paid off. Quite apart from the indirect influence on Council debate, quite apart from formal and informal conversations with committees of Catholic bishops interested in observer judgment and opinion, quite apart also from actual, if indirect, contribution to the shape and emphasis of some conciliar documents of first importance, the presence of the observers had created a new ecumenical reality. It was the reality of living personal exchange, abiding friendships, and the heartening experience of Christian fellowship that had grown to ripeness over and above acknowledged doctrinal differences. It was a fellowship that asserted its reality and vouched for itself and for its own possibility despite ancient misunderstandings and predisposing suspicions and hostilities. These things, bred of a long past, were somewhat transcended. They were transcended in being together, in worship at St. Peter's, in debate, in informal gatherings, in the sheer momentum of a common concern for the truth of Christ and the advancement of his Kingdom in a secular world, and perhaps above all, in common prayer. In Vatican Council II, Catholics and non-Catholics learned that they could pray together, indeed that they could hardly avoid praying together because it had become almost embarrassingly plain that they owned a common Lord.

So, the self-conscious approach of the first session of the Council, the earlier rather circumspect attention to protocol and nicety, gave way in the later sessions to the *openness* that had come to be the new spirit of the Council itself. Whereas the observers were known at first as the "separated brethren," it is quite important to note that Pope Paul VI, in his last and farewell audience with the observers addressed them as "Brothers, brothers and friends in Christ."

So it came about in those prolonged and sustained interrelationships of Christian with Christian, of man with man, in the Council days that the question before us was and remains how to grasp our divinely given unity in Christ so as to overcome our actual historical disunity. Too long it has been a disunity in which Christians have been not only content but stubbornly resolved to live. For many years, one may suppose, Christians shall be occupied with "the nature of the unity we seek."

Christians will be probing this question. But there are things in particular to note: first, Vatican Council II actually marks a radical change of course in world Catholicism. Present-day Catholicism not only now seeks but has come to acknowledge at least in foretaste not simply the possibility but the actuality of Christian community above and beyond ancient ecclesiastical divisions and long intrenched divisive suspicion and hostility.

Second, with the historic service of common prayer held in the sanctuary of St. Paul's Without the Walls December 4, 1965, the highest possible official authorization was given to the practice of common worship short of sacramental communion. Thus was implemented by papal action and precedent the permissive legislation of the Council's "Decree on Ecumenism." Over obstacles and obstruction, opposition and maneuver, this decree eventually passed. In peril and often in doubt as to its outcome, it was finally adopted to the profound relief of the observers and the deep satisfaction of Cardinal Bea and his staff in the third session of the Council in 1964. With the service of common prayer at St. Paul's (at which this writer was privileged to be present), the "word" of the "Decree on Ecumenism" "was made flesh" by the Pope himself.

So, John XXIII's revolution of openness has in this respect prevailed. It has prevailed in others, such as religious liberty, the "collegiality" of the bishops, the reconstruction of the sacred liturgy, the *Constitution on the Church*, the enlarged place and responsibility of the laity, and many others. But the writer's concern here is to mark the revolution of openness which now replaces the withdrawal and introversion that, on the whole, characterized post-Tridentine Roman Catholicism in theory, spirit, and practice until these recent days.

The Catholics, one might say, have joined the common Christian world. They will give it leadership. One can expect the pace of this leadership to accelerate. One may even see shortly a revitalization of the old-line Protestant churches in America. They will need a renewal of their witness and their life. If they have a distinctive message, it will behoove them to possess it, to know it, and to publish it. The well-worn ruts and the time-honored routines will hardly suffice in the days ahead, for former times have passed away.

If asked what is the consequence and outcome of Vatican Council II, the writer would first point out that it symbolizes and prophesies a new day in world Christianity. It signifies, at least in its beginnings, the passing away of the post-Reformation and counter-Reformation eras. The most palpable effect of Vatican Council II is a new readiness and openness for Christian community and common Christian effort, on the part of world Catholicism. Just as Methodists or Lutherans do not expect forthwith to become Anglicans by having fellowship or common worship, so neither a Methodist nor a Roman Catholic shall cease to be such by mutually acknowledging the common Christian commitment of the other and sharing with him in the measure that doctrine and conscience allow.

Accordingly, contemporary Christians are about to live in a different Christian world. It will not be one of complete unity in the foreseeable future, but it will be increasingly a world of enlarged understanding, enhanced good will, fellowship, and common effort and purpose. Its effect on Protestantism will, this writer believes, be, among other things, renewed theological awakening and renewed vitality of doctrinal discussion and inquiry. This will have its effect both upon the conception of ecclesiastical and institutional structures and upon worship or liturgical practice. It will also have an effect upon the social concern and action of the churches in the world and bring about a deepening of their consciousness of responsibility for the world.

II

If, with this background, one asks more narrowly what is the import of Vatican Council II for Protestant Christianity, for the several Protestant communions, the first answer would be this: Protestant Christians of all denominations should mark well the new and unprecedented openness of Catholicism toward other Christian communions. It is of utmost importance to recognize that the Roman Catholic Church has officially decided to enter into dialogue with the world: first of all, with non-Catholic Christians; second, with non-Christian religions, and third, with the whole of the modern world in its agonies, defeats, and triumphs. This seems to me to be a revolution when compared with the Catholicism of Vatican Council I or even with the pontificate of Pius XII. It is a reversal of the standpoint of censure, defensiveness, and withdrawal that marked the prevailing tone and temper of 19th-century official Catholic teaching and ecclesiological policy.

The journeys of Paul VI to India in 1964 and to New York in the fall of 1965, his address to the United Nations, his urgent and deliberate effort to mount a peace offensive in the face of the Vietnam crisis, and, most recently, his encyclical letter on peace and supportive of the United Nations (September 19, 1966) are indications of the new dialogue with the world. Also the *Declaration on the Relationship of the Church to Non-Christian Religions* (1965), contains not only the long controverted "Declaration on the Jews" but also statements of appreciation for the values of non-Christian religions through which men (no longer depreciated as unbelievers) seek to discover and to relate themselves to the Supreme Being. "The Catholic Church," it declares, "rejects nothing that is true and holy in these religions. She regards with sincere reverence those ways of action and of life, those precepts and teachings which, though differing in many aspects from the ones she holds and sets forth, nonetheless often reflect a ray of the Truth which enlightens all men."

But, above all, the dialogue is commended with respect to non-Catholic Christians. It is plain that Roman Catholicism finds its closest affinity, on doctrinal and ecclesiological grounds, with Eastern Orthodoxy. A central aim of Paul VI's trip to the Holy Land in January, 1964, was to find the proper place of meeting with the spiritual leaders of Orthodoxy. The mutual and simultaneous lifting of the ban of excommunication by Pope Paul VI and Patriarch Athenagoras of Istanbul on December 7, 1965, was at once a fruit of the Palestinian journey and a further important step toward reconciliation of Eastern and Latin Christianity. The ban had been mutually imposed above 900 years ago in A.D. 1054. It was lifted by a mutual exchange of letters on the final day of official business of Vatican Council II in St. Peter's Basilica. As the next day, December 8, this writer walked to the closing ceremonies with Bishop Aimilianos, representative of the Patriarch to the Council, he was assured that this was a most important beginning which could, in the providence of God, lead to eventual reestablishment of communion between Eastern and Latin Christianity. The way may be long, but the two ancient churches are presently on the march in the direction of one another.

But what of dialogue with Protestant Christians? Indeed it has begun already in the four years of Vatican II. It will be attended by increasing occasions of common prayer or worship, short of sacramental intercommunion. The signs of this are numerous. Since the close of the Council, reaction on the part of conservative Catholics has been in the press. But the Father DePauws cannot subvert the spirit and the declaration of Vatican Council II. Catholic ecumenism is here to stay, at least until it is rescinded by another Council. Uncritical and excessive Catholic enthusiasm for the recent ecumenical emancipation may embarrass constituted authorities in the Church responsible for conservation of authentic tradition. There is bound to be internal stress, but the new ecumenical outreach has conciliar authorization and its deliberate advancement may be expected.

III

Now, then, what are some achievements of Vatican Council II that both make dialogue possible with Protestant Christians and also constitute some of its important presuppositions? What, in other words, are some of the things affirmed or sanctioned by the Council which Protestants ought to bear in mind as they contemplate both dialogue and closer association with their Roman Catholic brethren? What are the things they must regard as altered and changing within the mind of Roman Catholic Christianity that, as it seems, markedly distinguishes it from the 400-year-old defensive posture of the counter-Reformation era? What are Protestants to understand if they are not erroneously to hold and be guided by clichés and consequent animosities and suspicions of the past?

Here are a few such changes and emergent positions, officially adopted by the Council, that require the notice of Protestants if they are not, like Don Quixote, to fight windmills or confound ancient hostilities with real and important issues and differences:

In the first place, Protestants must bear in mind that Vatican Council II was conceived and aimed for, and now has succeeded in, turning the searchlight of self-criticism upon the ancient Roman church. Protestants cannot escape the fact that Vatican Council II represents the most thorough, searching, and sustained self-examination to which any branch of Christianity has subjected itself since the 16th-century Reformation and counter-Reformation. The 18th-century Wesleyan self-examination was long and sustained; but it was neither heeded nor shared by the Anglican establishment, and by confluence of historical circumstances it became a schism. This Roman self-scrutiny and self-criticism is also marked by a monumental and theologically informed intellectual output probably unequalled in modern ecclesiastical history. Protestants, in undertaking dialogue with Catholics today and tomorrow, must understand not merely that some Catholics have really done their homework but also that it has been honestly and remarkably self-critical.

Second, Protestants should realize that Vatican Council II, again and again, has adopted the principle that the Chruch is perpetually in need of self-renewal and reformation, that the unfaithfulness of men clouds and obstructs the redemptive mission of Christ through his Church. Cognate to this was and is the rejection of what Archbishop de Smedt of Belgium in the first session of the Council denominated "triumphalism" in the Church. Triumphalism is not simply the disposition to pomp and vainglory. It is not simply pride of mind and ecclesiastical snobbery or complacency. Basically, "triumphalism" was deprecated as a tendency to identify the Church on earth, the Church militant or the embattled Church, with the Kingdom of God itself. In its place a new sobriety is accepted about the Church. It is the "pilgrim people of God." It is the people of Mission. It is the servant Church, not one asserting its claim or affirming its prerogatives but one accepting anew its responsibility for service in Christ's name to the world. This is a central acknowledgement of *The Dogmatic Constitution on the Church.* Vatican Council II rejects "triumphalism." It is a fair question, the writer thinks, whether American Protestantism has yet fully recognized its own need to do so.

In the third place, Protestants must recognize that a new understanding of the nature and role of the Church has been strenuously debated and defined by the Council. The Church is viewed more nearly in biblical, Pauline, and Augustinian terms. It is, first of all, "the People of God." It is the body of Christ. It is no longer the hierarchy. It includes *all* believers, among whom the laity have an integral and indispensable "apostolate." Correspondingly, "clericalism" has been officially checked and disapproved. The distinctive role of the ordained clergy is reaffirmed but always in company with the laity, who are also servants of Christ in mission, word, and deed. The sacramental ministry as a distinctive service of bishops and priests is affirmed but with the understanding that even in sacramental worship the congregation and the laity have an integral and active part.

Fourth, the doctrine of the Church has been altered by greater clarification of the function of the episcopate. The absolute sovereignty of the See of Rome, affirmed in the decrees of Vatican Council I, has in this writer's judgment been modified in practice and precedent and, perhaps, in constitution. First, in the "collegiality" of all bishops as (1) holding the highest order or ordination and as (2) conjointly *with* the Pope exercising the supreme governing and teaching role in the Roman Church. The limited autonomy of national and regional conferences of bishops has received formal authorization. Provision for a Synod of Bishops, world-wide in composition (and with ordinary and extraordinary convocation and business), has been made by Paul VI. Thus, the absolute or almost absolute power of the Roman See and, more particularly, its administrative and adjunctive arm, the Curia, has been, both in principle and in fact, limited and modified. A far more pluralistic world Catholicism is to be looked for in the future, even though it will not be attained without struggle. The monolithic absolutism of Vatican Council I has, as this writer sees it, been breached. Finally, while the doctrine of Papal "infallibility" (adopted over weighty protest from within its own membership by Vatican Council I) remains, the writer will hazard the opinion that it has been modified by Vatican Council II *in fact* rather than *in theory.* This seems indicated on two scores: first, it has been *broadened to include* conciliar declarations and, secondly, it, accordingly, has been explicitly shared with an ecumenical council such as Vatican Council II.

A fifth reality which Protestants must come to understand is a newly established centrality of the Bible and of biblical authority as normative for the determination of faith and practice, doctrine and worship. The mainspring and source of the liturgical reform and renewal represented by the Council's *Constitution on the Sacred Liturgy*, adopted in 1963, is undoubtedly a renewal of biblical study, exegesis, and theology among Roman Catholic theologians over the past half century. Catholic biblical scholarship is rapidly catching up with and overtaking this prominent achievement of Protestant scholarship. But Protestant interest centers in the fact that the new definitions of Church, ministry, worship, revelation, and Catholic ecumenism (represented by several important Council documents) are the result of the somewhat recent vital thrust of biblical research and understanding among the generality of Catholic scholars, theologians, and clergy. It is of great significance that the *Pastoral Constitution on the Church and the Modern World* says that the Church in its life and faith is always subject to the judgment of the Gospel. This is to acknowledge the stone of stumbling which made Luther's break with Rome inevitable in the unequal balance of forces of the 16th-century. The centrality of the Scripture is both a cause and the fruit of Vatican Council II.

Cognate to this, and in the sixth place, Protestants must study carefully the long controverted and finely chiseled *Dogmatic Constitution on Divine Revelation*, adopted almost at the end of the Council after four years of constant debate, amendment, and review. So nicely juxtaposed are the complementary authorities of Tradition and Scripture that the knowledgeable modern Protestant will find very much to commend in the balance of Scripture with tradition that is attained. The relation is one of dialectical tension, so that the crude superiority of tradition over Scripture, characteristic of post-Reformation Catholicism, is greatly modified. The position attained is, the writer thinks, not far removed from that of many contemporary New Testament scholars of Protestant origin.

Quite apart from what this suggests by way of reconciliation of longstanding Protestant-Catholic differences and even hostilities, it must now be recognized that Vatican Council II has quite definitely adopted a biblical basis as fundamental in restructuring its life and doctrine as a Church. This is official; it is no longer the aspiration of liberalizing Catholic scholars or theolgians. It is, with Vatican II, the acknowledged position of the Roman Catholic Church. In September 1966, addressing a group of eminent Catholic theologians, Paul VI stressed the Scriptural foundation of Christian doctrine, reminding the assembled group of "the great importance the Council always attached to Sacred Scripture in doctrinal explanation."

In the seventh place, it is now official policy and doctrine of the

Roman Catholic Church that it participate in the ecumenical movement of modern times. Whatever uncertainties attach to regional implementation, and there are many, Catholic ecumenism is policy. It
is more fully and thoroughly defined and avowed than among many
of the churches of the Reformation. Now, the aim and effort toward
Christian unity is a mandate upon all Catholics, not just clergy but
the whole of the laity, and is a real part of "the lay apostolate." The
division and disunity of Christendom is declared contrary to the will
of Christ for his Church, and while it is affirmed that the Roman
Catholic Church is the authentic church of Christ, it is by no means
supposed or declared that the reunion of Christendom is to be understood simply as return to Rome. The writer would venture to say that
in his words to the observers in the fall of 1964, the Pope plainly intended something else. The words he used, "recomposition in unity"
suggest, this writer believes, a new conception of the nature and way
to the unity we seek.

In this connection it is of importance for non-Catholic Christians
to notice carefully a phrase which appears in the Council documents.
It is the proposition that "the one true religion *subsists* in the Catholic
and apostolic Church." One should mark it well that: (a) the true Christian religion is not exhaustively identified with the Roman Catholic
Church but *subsists* in it, and (b) that "the Catholic and apostolic
Church" is *not* exhaustively identified with the Roman Catholic
Church. From these seemingly small distinctions an unforeseeable harvest of ecumenism may grow, for what is evidently allowed for is the
possibility that true Christian faith or religion may *"subsist"* in some
measure also in other churches of Christendom. And just this, in fact,
is what is allowed and affirmed in the "Decree on Ecumenism."

These distinctions may seem insignificant. The phrase of Paul VI,
"recomposition in unity," may give small satisfaction to those impatient
for immediate and unambiguous solutions to long controverted issues.
This is understandable, yet it should be realized that in the solemn
context in which the words were uttered, as a direct address to the
observers and by the supreme reigning authority of the Roman Church,
such words are not to be taken as casual but as deliberate and finely
chiseled vehicles, not merely of ideas agonizing to be born, but as
usable instruments for the "easement" of eventual policy and action.
The present writer became conscious of three things in the context
of discussion and deliberation: the profound sense of inescapable responsibility entertained by Catholic officialdom, and preeminently by
the Pope, to be faithful to the venerable *consensus* of Catholic doctrine;
the long, long look ahead and readiness to discover vehicles for the
future emerging in the conjunction of ancient truth with present ur-

gencies; and, consonant with John Henry Newman's theory of the development of doctrine, but added to it, was a remarkable disposition to open small "growing edges" into the future with confidence in the leading of the Holy Spirit to find pathways into larger truth, aspired after, but not yet visible. Nowhere is this more apparent than in the "Decree on Ecumenism"; but it is worthy of notice that this perspective, fostered and nurtured by Cardinal Bea and the staff of the Secretariat for the Promotion of Christian Unity, was not only a presiding rationale in the formation of this document but gradually created a pervasive spirit of acceptance among the Fathers of the Council that made its adoption possible.

There is (in the eighth place) one other and last matter to be mentioned, which Protestant Christians should have in mind as dialogue and fellowship between Catholics and Protestants develop. Protestants should understand that, however belatedly in their view it has come to pass, it is now true that after a most interesting and vigorous contest very full of suspense, Vatican Council II did adopt—against the lag and drag of centuries of contrary theory and precedent—the principle of religious freedom for both individuals and communities. The dignity of man, according to natural and revealed law, supports the right of conscientious worship. Men can be constrained neither by ecclesiastical nor political power to assent or dissent in matters religious. The inviolability of conscience and man's vocation before God are affirmed against all coercion whatsoever.

The importance of this reaffirmation of historic Reformation and, one may say Separatist Puritan, principles, is great in this period of 20th century. In and with it is contained a most wholesome corrective against forces in our time that have mocked and traduced the essential dignity of man. Man's dignity is once again grounded upon his responsibility and calling under God.

But over and beyond this laudable emphasis is the implied acceptance of the disestablishment of religion as a protectorate of the state. The medieval doctrine of the "two swords" which made the state the servant of the Church is silently relinquished. But it is also relinquished in principle, in the explicit affirmation that religion, and Christian faith in particular, are matters transcending the power of man or institutions to establish or dissolve. Religious liberty is a corollary of the basic Christian tenet that religious faith is a transaction between God and the individual person, that it cannot be enforced or coerced, and that the truth of the Christian religion must convict and persuade by the transparency of its own light. Accordingly, the primary work of the Church and its ministry and laity is witness, mission, proclamation in word and deed. One can reasonably say that, with this standpoint, Roman Catholicism and Evangelical Christianity are again standing more nearly upon the same New Testament and apostolic ground.

These, then, are some of the things that are results of Vatican Council II. They have obvious implication for all Protestant or non-Roman Catholic Christians. Collectively, they compose an astonishingly different and unprecedented standpoint from which quite unexpected but promising conversations and *koinonia* between Catholics and non-Catholics may unfold in the years ahead. If so, *Deo gratias.*

DOCTRINAL STANDARDS AND THE ECUMENICAL TASK TODAY

With a few exceptions to the contrary, notwithstanding, it is rather evident that the mainline Protestant Churches of the United States are at sea with reference to either the relevancy or the manifest role of doctrinal standards for effectual functioning in present-day society. In some ways, this is anomalous, since it was a keen awareness of doctrinal differences which greatly accounts for their being and differentiations, first in Europe and, subsequently, in America. In Methodism the concept of doctrinal standards is as old as John Wesley himself and, in the church organized in America in 1784, has as old an official status as the First Restrictive Rule of *The Doctrines and Discipline* of 1808: "The General Conference shall not revoke, alter or change our Articles of Religion or establish any new standards or rules of doctrine contrary to our present existing and established standards of doctrine." [1]

Coincident with unification of the Methodist Church with the Evangelical United Brethren, the General Conference of 1968 established a Commission on Doctrine and Doctrinal Standards for study and report. The Commission undertook a quadrennial task and in 1972 submitted its unanimous findings for legislative action to the General Conference, with the stipulation of the chairman that "we do not regard it [the document moved for adoption] as in violation of the First, Second, or Fifth restrictive rules." In accord with the motion, the report was adopted in place of its disciplinary antecedent (1968) and was published as Part II of *The Book of Discipline*, 1972. The stipulation, on presentation to the General Conference, that the legislation before the supreme law-making body did not invoke or infringe upon the Restrictive Rules was sustained by Decision No. 358 of the church's Judicial Council.

Of Part II of *The Book of Discipline* there are three sections: (1) "Historical Background," (2) "Landmark Documents," and (3) "Our Theological Task." In principle and fact, Section 2 republishes undoubted historic doctrinal standards of the former churches, now The United Methodist Church. These include the Twenty-five Articles of Religion (1784), the Confession of Faith of the former EUB Church (1962), and the General Rules (1784).

When, in these times, a major Protestant church not only aspires

Published in abridged form, *Religion and Life*, XLIV, No. 4 (Winter 1975). Here republished with permission of the Editor with original substance partly restored.

but ventures to risk reexamination of its doctrinal heritage with a view to assessing where indeed it stands with reference to historic norms, present internal uncertainties, and relentless worldly metamorphosis, the result should command the attention of serious churchmen almost anywhere. Not only what is essayed but also what is accomplished may be revealing, or at least symptomatic, of what mainline Protestant Christianity in general may undergo in attempting to give an account of itself doctrinally in an era almost incomparably secularized and markedly pluralized. Nor can we deny that the climate of the age so invades some Protestant communions as that an intramural *consensus fidelium* is hardly to be looked for.

It is primarily the want of this consensus, however, which constitutes, at one and the same time, both the risk of such an undertaking and also its imperative. Herewith the churches confront an agonizing dilemma not unlike that of Pope John XXIII in proclaiming *aggiornamento*. Moreover, derivative of this situation is an inherent, attendant twofold problem: (1) on the one hand, how can a secularized church arrive at a *consensus fidelium,* i.e., viable doctrinal unanimity faithful to the tradition? (2) and conversely, how can practicing theologians function if the churches are doctrinally incoherent or unable for want of consensus to clarify doctrinal standards, either by reaffirmation or by reformulation? With whom or what lies the norm?

I. UNITED METHODIST CONCILIARISM AND PROCESS THEOLOGY

As I study Part II, one feature fully merits our attention. It is everywhere implicit and recurrently explicit that doctrinal standards and, indeed, Christian theologizing are taken to be a proper task and responsibility of the whole church, and there is conspicuous absence of any mention of theologians. Thus, a frankly conciliar conception of the source of doctrinal standards is affirmed while, at the same time and somewhat shockingly, it is also affirmed that "in this task of reappraising and applying the gospel, theological pluralism should be recognized as a principle." [2]

In Section 3 this conciliar stress is emphatic in such words as: "The United Methodist Church expects all its members to accept the challenge of responsible theological reflection." [3] If this expectancy is exorbitant, the risk is somewhat curtailed by the definition of "doctrinal guidelines" (i.e. the norms of Scripture, tradition, experience, and reason) [4] and by explicit delimitation of theological initiatives according to a twofold rule, viz., "careful regard to our heritage and fourfold guidelines, and the double test of acceptability and edification in corporate worship and common life." [5]

In sum, Part II, Section 3 commits itself to something very close to corporate ecclesial responsibility for the authorization and development of doctrinal standards. The move seems to be in the direction of a kind of collegial *magisterium*, of which there are no elders or bishops as guardians of the faith once delivered to the saints. Indeed, it is denied that doctrinal statements are the special province of "any single body, board, or agency," and none others are dignified by so much as mention.

We have, then, I would think, a most emphatic commitment to a species of intramural conciliarism as the source and authorization of doctrinal standards. Procedurally this may not entirely accord with the tradition of historic Methodism, which, in fact, early made the Conference the prime judicatory for both faith and order. To this, Section 1, "Historical Background," itself gives prominence without, however, noting that Wesley's Conference was composed of preachers and was itself something of a catechetical school.[6] Yet it is now daringly proposed that the whole church become, as it were, a catechetical school writ large for the crossing of what are called "theological frontiers" and in "new directions." Then, rather distinguishing the church from its pilgrim people, it is declared: "The Church's role in this tenuous process is to provide a stable and sustaining environment in which theological conflict can be constructive and productive."

From such a statement a question emerges as to what stability may be expected of a church possessed, for doctrinal standards, of little more than "landmark documents" and for whose pilgrim people doctrine is spoken of most nearly as a continuing process of "informed theological experimentation" and "our never-ending tasks of theologizing." This conception of doctrine as process is to be sure not unchecked by the already noted twofold condition: "careful regard for our heritage and fourfold guidelines." We shall, then, have to examine more closely what is allowed respecting the normativeness of our acknowledged doctrinal heritage.

II. OUR DOCTRINAL HERITAGE: STATUS AND FUNCTION

The authors of Part II are aware that they are faced with the question "as to the status and function of 'doctrinal standards' in The United Methodist Church" as an inherited issue. Both Sections 1 and 3 manifest conspicuous effort to attain firm dialectical balance between the norm of tradition with loyalty to our heritage, on the one side, and to make way for timely doctrinal restatement on the other. I would wish to acknowledge the earnestness with which our document faces the treacherous task of attempting to balance the reciprocal counterclaims of loyalty and freedom. We can consider only briefly these contraries in tension, the principle of freedom first.

One has the impression that operative in favor of the principle of freedom are certain prepossessions of thought as various as: Wesley's important sermon, "The Catholic Spirit"; John Henry Newman's theory of the development of dogma; the *aggiornamento* of Vatican II; American process theology; and a wee bit of existential openness for the future. All these leave their mark, but preeminently does Wesley's denigration of what he called "opinion" in matters religious—a concept popularly misunderstood but not, I think, misused in our document.[7]

Disregarding these presumed prepossessions, certain working principles favoring flexibility in doctrinal standards and hospitable to "yet further unfoldings of history" in continuing doctrinal developments are worth noting. They fall into the following groups: (1) judgments of historical fact as interpreted, (2) principles of historical interpretation, (3) axiomatical theological postulates, and (4) pragmatic-prudential considerations.

Among a dozen historical judgments precedential for the principle of freedom and development are such debatable assertions as: that among the fathers of Methodism "doctrinal pluralism" already was acknowledged; that they declined to adopt the "classical forms of the confessional principle"; that a conciliar principle in "collegial formula" was manifest in the Model Deed; that the role of the Articles was ambiguous early in nineteenth-century Methodism. It is judged that the collegial formula "committed the Methodist people to the biblical revelation as primary without proposing a literal summary of that revelation in any propositional form." [8] This last seems right-headed enough save for the objectionable confusion of creedal symbol with a literal proposition.

Finally, and of large import, is the dubious historical judgment rendered upon the longstanding Articles and the Confession that they "are not to be regarded as positive, juridical norms of doctrine," although it is not clear whether this is meant to characterize their past status by alleged longstanding consensus or their future standing. In response to this judgment, one is disposed to inquire earnestly by what rationale the First Restrictive Rule was first instituted in 1808 and with what purpose it has survived in the intervening wisdom of the church. What was the function of such a rule if indeed the confessional principle was as much a matter of indifference to the mind of the church as is represented?

As to principles of historical interpretation, three can be mentioned here. Emphatically conciliar in import is the hermeneutical principle that "Scripture is rightly read and understood *within* the believing community." This also is anticipated and affirmed in Wesley's way of interpreting biblical language—another question of fact. Secondly, the "new historical consciousness" justifies the historical interpretation of all historical documents and thus also the Methodist Articles or Confession—meaning that they are relative to their given context and so without finality. On this ground there emerges the third and decisive principle that all doctrinal standards of the past, present, or future are "landmark documents." They may be pointers to the truth, never finalities. And, finally, the infinite qualitative difference between time and eternity is illustrated in the self-evident proposition that "God's eternal Word never has been, nor can be exhaustively expressed in any single form of words." In consequence, it is perhaps in order to be informed, as historical *fact*, that the founding fathers did not invest "summaries of Christian truth . . . with final authority or set them apart as absolute standards for doctrinal truth and error."

One outcome of this hermeneutic is surely expressed in the following summation: "But, since they are not accorded any status of finality, either in content or rhetoric, there is no objection in principle to the continued development of still other doctrinal summaries and liturgical creeds that may gain acceptance and use in the Church—without displacing those we already have. This principle of the historical interpretation of all doctrinal statements, past and present, is crucial." [9]

The express denial of any status of finality, of course, imperils the very conception of doctrinal standards and would seem to require positive attention to the question of such surviving normativeness they might yet command. The final quoted sentence strikes me as a remarkable understatement. Depending on how it is hereafter to be used, it is momentous in implication for all doctrinal standards whatsoever (i.e., norms)—and not only those past or present, but, on the same principle of historical interpretation, *those of any conceivable future.* Accordingly, it is not out of keeping that Section 3, whether intentionally or not, tends to replace *all* past, present, or future doctrine or dogma with an unlimited *process* of "theologizing." [10]

In this perspective, is it something like the case that the Church is now to live perpetually on theological credit? In reflection one is inclined to wonder whether the authors of this document either did not fully understand their own logic as a committee, or that some did, and because they had relinquished any possibility of standards had resort to collective "theologizing" as a permanent substitute for doctrine. Yet this seems to be the outcome of the logic employed, however awkward the new day in which the church is obliged to rely mainly for truths to live by upon the ever-receding promise of the future.

III. PRIMARY THEOLOGICAL POSTULATES AND THE CORE OF DOCTRINE

By examining some theological postulates of our document—mainly set forth in Section 3, "Our Theological Task"—we may be better informed respecting the unanswered question as to what normativeness the "landmark documents" may yet possess, deprived, as they are said to be, of any status of finality. At the same time, we may be better positioned to judge the success of our document in achieving a balance between loyalty and freedom toward the heritage of doctrinal standards. That Part II aspires to such a balance is a note variously sounded, as, for example, with reference to emerging ecumenical theology which seeks to "provide a constructive alternative" to the confessional tradition or in the expressed view, in retrospect, that Part II has been seeking to chart "a course between doctrinal dogmatism on the one hand and doctrinal indifferentism on the other." [11]

Methodologically speaking, this disavowal of indifferentism in doctrine does operate as a theological postulate whether vindicated or not. It has explicit antecedence in Wesley's pervasive teaching on "the catholic spirit," which rejects speculative or practical latitudinarianism and excludes, therefore, indifferentism in either doctrine or ecclesiology.[12] Whether the contrasting phrase "doctrinal dogmatism" is unduly denigrative of "doctrinal standards" we leave unattended. It suffices here to note that on its face our document allies itself with Wesley in rejecting indifferentism and sets aside as erroneous "the notion that there are no essential doctrines and that differences in theology, when sincerely held, need no further discussion." To this extent, then, we must acknowledge that theological pluralism considered as a principle suffers some modification.

A second primary postulate prefaces Section 3: "Both our heritage in doctrine and our present theological task share common aims: the continuously renewed grasp of the gospel of God's love in Christ and its application in the ceaseless crises of human existence." Herewith, it is plainly indicated that the doctrinal process proceeds both with a core inheritance and is undertaken in context. Our theological task, then, is always contextual and, for that reason, must appropriately take the form of an answering process if it is to be living or relevant. This undergirds the postulate of theological development as an inescapable requirement, which is yet a third.[13]

But let us consider the postulate of the "core" of Christian truth as a fourth postulate, although it deserves to be regarded, and does function, as primary in Section 3. I think it is not misleading to say that the core of any surviving doctrinal standard is intended to be encapsuled in the already quoted phrase, "the gospel of God's love in Christ." The key paragraph is the first under the heading "United Methodists and the Christian Tradition." There it is said that Methodist theologizing does not begin *de novo,* but shares a "common heritage with all other Christians everywhere and in all ages." It is affirmed that there "is a core of doctrine which informs in greater or less degree our widely divergent interpretations." It is not clear whether "divergent interpretations" refers to the *oikoumene* or to Methodists themselves, but we may safely assume to both.

But here one thing becomes very clear: the well-known scene of ecumenical diversity is being applied by analogy to a single denomination—the Methodist—and that, partly on this analogy, the factual diversity *without*—as among denominations *inter alia*—is affirmed to obtain *within* Methodism as a fact *but also as a norm.* This is, I think, misuse of analogy, but it becomes another basic and unexamined postulate which contributes its unannounced support for the presiding thesis of "theological pluralism as a principle." An appropriate rejoinder may well be the question, *With what right is factual doctrinal diversity among a plurality of separate churches taken to be a standard model in assessing the role and status of doctrinal standards in any one denomination?* To assume that it is or may be modular or normative begs the question on an issue of maximum importance.

What, then, is "core of doctrine," and what is its status for "doctrinal standards" in The United Methodist Church? It is at this point that the assessment of the issue of loyalty will have to be played down to the wire. The core in our document is delineated under two aspects. The first succinctly relates the principal doctrinal content of the universally shared Christian tradition on pages 71–72. This is the "common faith in the mystery of salvation in and through Jesus Christ," which includes overcoming our willful alienation through God's pardoning love in Christ and states that through faith, enabled by the Holy Spirit, we receive "the gift of reconciliation and justification." The second aspect of the core of doctrine, presuming the common Christian tradition as above, singles out distinctive emphases or particular traditions of the Methodist heritage. These, with right, may be viewed as truly embedded in that tradition and as rooted in both the *Standard Sermons* of John Wesley and in the liturgy and hymnody, and exemplified in the Social Creed of American Methodism. Since they are readily available, and for economy of space, I pass over their substance.

Such, then, is the "common," together with the "distinctive," core of the doctrinal heritage by which it is indicated our loyalty ought rightly to be claimed as a wholesome guide and check upon freedom in theologizing. *This doctrinal core is, then, a norm claiming our respect, but evidently not our adherence.* However, as we scrutinize the language of our document respecting the normativeness of the core of doctrine, a resilient ambiguity persists.

IV. FOUR SUCCESSIVE POSTULATES AND THEOLOGICAL PLURALISM

On further examination, the ambiguity appears to rest upon a succession of mutually supportive unexplicated theological postulates that, collectively, reinforce the thesis of "theological pluralism . . . as a principle." This may indicate that the ambiguity is intentional or at least unavoidable in view of the premises.

The first postulate takes the form of a tacit definition of the nature and the status of the doctrinal heritage represented by the core in the following proposition: "From our response in faith to the wondrous mystery of God's love in Jesus Christ as recorded in Scripture, all valid Christian doctrine is born." Doctrine, then, is always faith's response to the mystery. Its nature and status are that it is *our response.* Such a status is also that of the traditions of doctrine which are later described as "the residue of corporate evidence of earlier Christian communities." Actually, the postulate simply reiterates the earlier declaration of Section 1: "that God's eternal Word never has been, nor can be, exhaustively expressed in any single form of words." Here, then, the limit to finality—and now with respect, not simply to the Confessions but to the core of tradition—is not the historical relativity of any response of faith; it is, rather, the ineffability of the eternal Word or the wondrous mystery that is symbolized.[14]

The seconding postulate occurs earlier in our document and is used to retire the older "confessional tradition" in favor of "our newer experiments in ecumenical theology." Apparently, there is here further unargued dependency on the analogy earlier noted. Thereafter, the passing of the confessional tradition in favor of the ecumenical method in doctrine is justified by the seconding postulate: "The transcendent mystery of divine truth allows us in good conscience to acknowledge the positive virtues of doctrinal pluralism even within the same community of believers, not merely because such an attitude is realistic."[15] Immediately thereafter, it is stated: "The invitation to theological reflection is open to all."

The third consummating postulate is, then, invoked in the paragraph just mentioned, although carried over from its earlier formulation "as the principle of the historical interpretation of all doctrinal statements"—self-styled as crucial, as already discussed. It is this hermeneutical principle that banishes any status of finality for standards and opens the door to horizons unlimited in theological development. And it is this that justifies not only the thesis of theological pluralism as a principle but does so by way of the final postulate.

The fourth postulate functions as the conclusion of the series. It first appeared and offered itself as a judgment of alleged historical fact, viz., that the Methodist fathers "declined to adopt the classical forms of the confessional principle." It now appears in the succession of scantily supported theological postulates as the conclusion: "No creed or doctrinal summary can adequately serve the needs and intentions of United Methodists in confessing their faith or in celebrating their Christian experience" (p. 79). This is, indeed, far reaching in import and amply supplies the rationale for the view that our doctrinal standards are merely landmark documents. It also appropriately justifies the exordium, viz., "The United Methodist Church expects all its members to accept the challenge of responsible theological reflection." If there is no finally reliable past in standards, perhaps hope may yet make a future! So be it, but the concluding postulate, standing as an unsupported *ipse dixit*, smacks rather more of academic sophistication than of the living piety of generations of Christians who have found in the venerable language of the Liturgy and the Creed more than enough light to illumine their darkness, indeed more than they used.

v. A BRIEF PROVISIONAL ASSESSMENT

This critical analysis must be abruptly terminated without further needed scrutiny of certain of the working postulates, consideration of the role of "experience" in the Wesleyan tradition, or perhaps adequate attention to a defined method for doctrinal development which does set some bounds to conciliar "theologizing" that is otherwise enthusiastically enthroned. This methodology is developed under the heading "Doctrinal Guidelines in The United Methodist Church."

The treatment of guidelines is knowledgeable and skillfully executed. It invokes a fourfold reference to Scripture, tradition, experience, and reason as guidelines in theological reflection. It finds them in Wesley and attributes their centrality to the founding fathers. The method is briefly stated very early in Section 1. There it is allowed that the fathers did acknowledge a marrow of true doctrine, and states: "This living core, as they believed, stands revealed in Scripture, illumined by tradition, vivified in personal experience, and confirmed by reason." [16]

In this viewpoint, attributed to the Methodist fathers, we seem to be within reach of some yardstick to measure loyalty to doctrinal standards. It may be inadvertent as it is, I believe, unfortunate that the later, more expansive treatment of "guidelines" does not recapture the centrality of Scripture or vindicate its primacy. On the contrary, it vitiates the greater decisiveness of the earlier passage in which tradition, experience, and reason are recognized, in that order, *and are subsumed to the primacy of Scripture.* Such a viewpoint might well have clarified the dialectic balance of loyalty and freedom, and likewise qualified the outcome, by way of appropriating faith, to be what Wesley did describe, among his sermons, as "Scriptural Christianity." Yet under "Doctrinal Guidelines," faith, though possibly presupposed, has no mention as requisite for operation of the guidelines. In fact, justifying faith has scant treatment in the entire document and is scarcely conceived as the presupposition of Christian theology.

This, too, contributes to the vitiation of the standpoint justly attributed to the fathers respecting the primacy of Scripture, but of course for faith. But the decisive vitiation of the admirable earlier statement quoted above and the resurgence of ambiguity ensues again with the following two sentences in summation of the guidelines: "There is a primacy that goes with Scripture, as the constitutive witness to biblical wellsprings of our faith. In practice, however, theological reflection may find its point of departure in tradition, 'experience,' or rational analysis."

This statement takes back, it seems, with the left hand what it gives with the right. Moreover, the extraordinary second sentence in this binary formulation quite evidently gives covey to every species of theological partridge except one bred in the Reformation tradition or cognizant of the Pauline Gospel. Allowing for whatever the qualifier, "in practice," may mean to the authors, the latter sentence allows to Scripture only par value with the other three norms. But, altogether astonishing, it gives back all that Part II has striven to deny, namely, the confessional principle or tradition, as a starting point in doctrinal formulation. Finally, it is an understatement to observe that *Christian* doctrine, of whatever provenance, has not often found its starting point in "rational analysis." This is a fatal sentence, but perhaps it illustrates a pervasive claim of the document that all theological reflection is historically conditioned.

So far as this analysis has taken us, ambiguity respecting the status of doctrinal standards remains largely unrelieved and the vindication of a true dialectical balance of loyalty with freedom seems unattained.

Among things accomplished is a rather fervent postulation of fully liberated conciliarism conceived in virtual equivalence with 20th-century ongoing interchurch ecumenical dialogue. Without adequate representation of the case, this is unhesitatingly proposed as the timely model for intramural doctrinal standards, both in *status* and in *function*. In addition to installing intramural theological pluralism on principle, Part II is correspondingly bent upon the eradication of what it recognizes as "classical forms of the confessional principle." Perhaps it has won favor because in The United Methodist Church, as doubtless elsewhere, theological "indifferentism" has for long been nurturing a favorable climate.

One question that emerges may be, What is the import that tendencies herein assessed may entail regarding the ecumenical movement towards the reunion of Christendom? For example, how may *intramural* conciliarism, as the denominational font of unlimited doctrinal reformulation comport with, let us say, a Roman Catholic understanding of the *magisterium*—the teaching office of the Church? Manifestly, the two are worlds away. Who speaks for the Church, not alone in Methodism, but in much of American Protestantism? If any one, or no one, or none with assurance, what then is the real feasibility of fruitful *extra-mural* conciliarism? It does not yet appear in fact that doctrinal amorphism is an auspicious platform for hopeful or responsible ecumenism. This seems to be the case unless, perchance, the viable outcome of recent ecumenics is, horticulturally speaking, potential merely of hybrids.

A CASE-STUDY IN ECUMENISM: FIFTY YEARS OF THEOLOGY AT DUKE

If we are to speak of theology at Duke, what may we mean by "theology"? Nowadays, this is not an idle question. The fact is that it has been in dispute for so long that there is today no little controversy among practitioners and, understandably, no little confusion among bystanders. In this situation I might show my colors and invite you to join me in taking our cue from John Wesley's *Plain Account of Genuine Christianity* (1749), except that, to my knowledge, hardly any Methodist theologian ever had the good sense to set us a precedent for doing so. We might ponder the subject by reference to the first paragraph of Calvin's *Institutes*. This might well be helpful, especially if we were also interested in going on to show how Schleiermacher laid the foundations of so-called "modern theology" by seizing upon one horn of the dilemma Calvin, there, seemingly propounds. But we have no time for elaborate historical recollections, and I will come quickly to the conception that, for me, alike describes both theology and the role of theological education.

It is that saying of Anselm's already quoted: *fides quaerens intellectum*. For me, whatever more it is, at rock bottom, Christian theology is "faith seeking understanding." And the *scandalon* is—as the Apostle Paul first saw and enforced upon the attention of the Corinthians— that appropriating faith in "the glory of God in the face of Jesus Christ," however alien to the wisdom of the world, is just exactly the kind of response suited to that unspeakable gift which passes all human understanding. For the apostle faith is acceptance of the incomprehensible grace of God in Christ. Accordingly, St. Paul saw that it was indeed a God-given starting-point, *from* which, not *to* which, enlightenment proceeds.

This, too, is what John Wesley, at length, arrived at by way of a personal ordeal he found resolved under the auspices of the longstanding Pauline formula, then, lately rejuvenated: "justification by grace through faith." But what had been a tenet of doctrine among both the Continental and Anglican reformers became alive and recapitulated itself in Wesley's own experience, and the 18th-century Evangelical Revival was born. For Wesley, as it were, the doctrinal map had

An abridgment of a Fiftieth Anniversary address presented to Fall Convocation 1976 entitled: "Fifty Years of Theology and Theological Education at Duke," *The Divinity School Review*, XLII, No. 1 (Winter 1977). Reprinted by permission of the Editor.

all the while lain open before him, but it was a "dead letter" until Wesley himself actually made his own way over the road. This is what he conveys in his *Plain Account of Genuine Christianity.* Then, for him also, theology became "faith seeking understanding." And this meant new comprehension of the whole range of human experience— its depravity without Christ, its radical promise of renovation through Christ—and this, both for the individual and for societal renewal.

I. FAITH SEEKING UNDERSTANDING—A CORPORATE ENDEAVOR

With this background we are, perhaps, in better position to understand the meaning of "theology" within the institutional context—that of the theological school, including this one. If indeed, theology—as also theological education—is, at bottom, "faith seeking understanding" as chief witnesses of the faith declare, then, plainly, the indispensable prerequisite of any Christian theology is Christian faith. And this is more nearly a gift than a good work. It follows that this puts theology in a somewhat different position from other human inquiry, although not so different as is usually supposed in one respect, since all human inquiry starts, at last, either from naturally assumed premises or expressly formulated hypothetical ones. In any case, Christian theology, in so far as it is candid and not primarily apologetics, openly acknowledges its faith-premise as its reason for being and proceeds to inquire what this premise means, that is, *how it illuminates the totality of human life in the world.* This is interpretation and reaffirmation of the *given* Christian faith.

The exploration of this import through successive generations in changing contexts—which history always thrusts upon us—is, perhaps, a major differentia of systematic theology as distinguished from historical studies, whether biblical or doctrinal. Yet we can hardly speak of theology in the institutional setting—that of a Divinity School—without acknowledging that this same theology is a corporate endeavor of the whole faculty, and, furthermore, in the context of serious faculty-student dialogue.

Space forbids discussion of the distinctive contribution of the several disciplines to the theological climate and standpoint of the school. It is apparent, however, that the curriculum of biblical studies, the application of historical method to the Scriptures, to the interpretation of Christian origins and to the apostolic and postapostolic witness, adopts standpoints having implicit doctrinal import. Yet, for all of these inquiries, it is still faith seeking understanding. Likewise church history, at-

tending as it does to the unfolding of the tradition catholic—as the
Church discharges its vocation in the world and in interchange with
it, for better or worse—is nerved also by faith pursuing enlarging self-
understanding. Nor can pastoral theology and professional studies be
excluded from this comprehensive inquiry, since the meaning and
verity of Christian faith comes better into relief precisely in the granu-
lating exchange which attends its communication and interaction with
the resistant and resilient mind of the world. All of these disciplines,
premised upon faith, pursue, in their several provinces, enlarging understanding.

When, therefore, we seek to take the measure of theology at Duke
over the half-century since 1926 and ascertain its character and directions, we are immediately confronted by the fact that theology, here
as elsewhere, is the many-sided *resultant* of a corporate endeavor of
a company of teacher-scholars manning their distinctive disciplinary
tasks in their own time and place. But there are, in addition, other
very influential factors that have shaped theological emphasis and
standpoints during the half-century of Duke Divinity School. These
can be mentioned and some of them considered briefly.

II. THE POLICY OF THE FOUNDERS: A DIALECTIC OF OP-POSITES

Let us, then, attend first of all to the intention of the founders. When
we do so, we shall, I think, be persuaded that the presiding influence
has been the inherited religious motivation and theological frame of
reference of the founders, firmly rooted in the Methodist tradition.
Yet it would be over-simple not to perceive that, granted this foundational commitment of the founders, their ends and aspirations for the
school also reflected perspectives and a certain selectivity from the
given tradition which seemed to them of central importance in setting
forth the objectives of a university school of ministerial education.
These objectives were, in fact, quickly implemented in the gathering
and subsequent further staffing of the faculty. And, in this whole matter,
William Preston Few was undoubtedly the original architect and
builder as also, for many years, he continued to shepherd at close-
hand the fledgling enterprise.

The twofold principle that embraces *both* the received religious
tradition of the founders *and* yet freedom to accent those essentials
deemed suited to advance theological understanding in a university
context is simply and candidly set forth under the title "School of
Religion" in the first *Bulletin* or catalogue for 1926–27. It reappears

largely unaltered for several years and, in revised language, has persisted substantively to this time. Because of its formative significance I shall quote the concluding paragraph entire:

Duke University retains the same close relationship which Trinity College always held to the Conferences in North Carolina of the Methodist Episcopal Church, South. This legal relationship has always been broadly interpreted. Members of all other Christian denominations, as well as Methodist, will be made to feel welcome in the School of Religion and may be assured that the basis on which the work is conducted is broadly catholic and not narrowly denominational.[1]

No little exegesis and commentary upon the facets of this statement—which must, I believe, be referred to President Few himself primarily—might well occupy us. On the one hand, the status of the new school—as that of its parent institution, Duke University—stands in close, derivative, and even legal relationship with the then Methodist Episcopal Church, South; but, on the other hand, instruction in the theological disciplines is to be "broadly catholic and not narrowly denominational." On this latter basis, it is affirmed that "all other Christian denominations" are welcome. And on this basis, and from the very start, theological education at Duke was grounded on the ecumenical premise. This was immediately implemented by recruitment of an interdenominational faculty and, likewise, little by little, an interdenominational student enrollment. In the first two decades it was mainly Congregationalist and Baptist students who swelled the predominatingly Methodist core of the student body. Meanwhile, the second dean of the school was Elbert Russell, a Quaker. In late years we have been enriched by the appointment and contributions of two Roman Catholic members of the faculty.

The history of developments cannot here detain us. Yet the import of this candid and daring policy—combining in single amalgam Methodist derivation and grounding with ecumenical or "broadly catholic" commitment—not only makes the status of the Divinity School, from its origin, all but unique among university divinity schools in this country but also, without much question, was the formative influence in predetermining the tone and character of the theological enterprise at Duke during the past half-century.

This deliberate and clear-headed espousal by President Few—in collaboration, we may reasonably suppose, with Edmund D. Soper, the first dean—of a *dialectic of opposites* as foundational policy must be seen for what it was and still remains. On the one hand, it expressly grounded theological endeavor at Duke in one particular historical tradition of Reformation Christianity as channelled through the Wesleyan evangelical heritage. On the other hand, it explicitly claimed a place for the riches of the whole range of "catholic" Christian tradition as the rightful domain of responsible scholarship and unfettered theological teaching. But in this, too, it is not amiss to note that it was scarcely at variance with Wesley's notable sermon on *The Catholic Spirit* or with his equally famous *Letter to a Roman Catholic.*

III. COROLLARIES OF THE FOUNDING POLICY

There are two or three corollaries deriving, I believe, from this dialectic of opposites, which I should like to mention for the record. The first is that the founders did not suppose that legitimate theological reflection or teaching could proceed without reference either to a particular living church or to the Church universal. Theology without grounding in a living *consensus fidelium* would be, in the absence of this, rootless. The founders did not, therefore, confuse the scientific study of religion as a phenomenon of human culture, with the distinctive tasks of Christian theology. Such study, together with philosophy of religion, might well have place in the total university curriculum, but it was not the galvanizing center of Christian theological studies devoted to the Church's ministry.

Secondly, resident in the phrase "broadly catholic and not narrowly denominational" was the clear reaffirmation of both "the freedom of the Christian man" under God (Luther) or "the liberty of prophesying" (Jeremy Taylor). To both of these John Wesley, long since, had already consented. And here was the minimal statement of the "liberal creed" which the founders invoked. By this they meant to say that, however rootless theology is in abstraction from a living church, yet it can never be in bondage to any one dogmatic rendering of the Christian Tradition. From these two corollaries in tandem a third quite properly followed: the founders were standing in the truly "catholic" tradition— whether of Augustine in the 5th or Wesley in the 18th century—namely, that theology if it is to be *Christian* theology is at the core "faith seeking understanding."

If we put the outcome of these three corollaries together, they come to this: there is to be, as an integral part of the university, a faculty of theology which—with the school it represents and whose defined tasks it discharges—relates itself positively to the *consensus fidelium* of the living Church as its primary and constant point of reference. From that reference, the standpoint of living faith, it proceeds to enlarging understanding of the on-going tradition and to the communication thereof as its reason for being. But it does so with liberty to explore the entirety of the Tradition and, furthermore, in the confidence that the tradition of faith itself is a *living* reality with, as we say, a growing edge or an expanding frontier. And, indeed, this frontier must expand if it is to be commensurate with its proper subject-matter. And that is God, the Creator and Redeemer, in his dialogue with man in history.

IV. FIFTY YEARS OF THEOLOGY AT DUKE IN RÉSUMÉ

Now, having insisted upon these fundamental considerations and principles as basic to the unfolding shape of theology at Duke, how, then, would one characterize the outcome over these fifty years? This is to raise the theological question head-on or, more exactly, the question of doctrine in the theological curriculum. This question is no longer concerned simply with what *has been witnessed*, historically considered, but what *must* be reaffirmed in fidelity to the essential Gospel as it bears upon human life in the world. But this, to be sure, is always being done according to the light and understanding of its delegated professors at a given time in history. Here always there is risk. So we ask, what is the doctrinal profile of the school during these years? Can we, or ought we, label it, and with what tag or tags? Or are tags both dangerous and superfluous in evaluating the doctrinal contribution of the School to its students, the Church, or the world?

To address myself to this latter question requires, it would seem, the naming of names of justly revered teachers and the omission of others, both living and departed, whose express and implied Christian witness has been doctrinally formative through these years. This puts me in a peculiarly delicate not to say treacherous position. Accordingly, I must avoid at all costs a course which John Henry Newman—and however laudable in his case—found unavoidable, namely, an *apologia pro vita mea!*

Fortunately, these hazards can be circumvented in some measure if we may take careful note of the conception of systematic or doctrinal theology referred to already. The latest mention was the implied definition of this kind of theology as what must be or *ought to be reaffirmed* in fidelity to the essential Gospel as the latter bears upon human life in the world in the considered judgment of its delegated professors. Here I use the word "professor" in its classical as well as in its etymological meaning. But, more importantly, I intend to differentiate systematic from other theological disciplines by two considerations: first, it takes explicit responsibility for what *ought to be reaffirmed* of the received catholic tradition, and, second, it does so, in part, by reference to the pressing issues enforced upon it by sundry problems of man's life in the world as currently understood, and, in turn, as these reflect back upon the Christian message itself.

Do not confuse this description of the doctrinal task with the late Paul Tillich's much patronized "method of correlation" in theology. Rather, is the description I give, as it were, the more general case of which his, in my view, is a very dubious derivative. The intentions here are very nearly the reverse of one another. Tillich would find what is still luminous in the faith by submitting it to the "spotlight," as it were, of the world's ultimate concern. Mine would be to illuminate the human world with the light of the Gospel and, in the process, recover and further discover the inherent luminosity of the faith itself. In this way faith not only seeks but finds understanding, indeed, acquires enriching discoveries respecting its own essence.

But, now, this conception of the task of theology is useful for deciphering the character of theology at Duke these fifty years. In short, one may get significant leads respecting Duke theology (or any Protestant theology of the recent past) by taking one's bearings—much as the sextant serves the sea captain—by reference to the prevailing "problematics" acknowledged and faced by theologians at given periods.

Accordingly, in fifty years of theological reaffirmation at Duke there have been, I judge, at least three quite distinguishable periods of doctrinal response to the circumambient environment punctuated, at intervals, by World War II, the civil rights movement, and the prolonged and adversely influential Viet Nam national debacle. It is this surrounding environment of issues—as understood, of course, by theologians—that stimulates the response of faith and greatly contributes to the shape of theology or doctrinal expression anywhere. This has most surely been the case at Duke. Here, this generalization applies provided we do not forget that theology is a corporate product and that, at Duke, it has developed under the aegis of what has been described as the "dialectic of opposites."

The three periods to which I refer—each distinguishable by presiding concerns, problems, and diagnoses—are the following: There is, first, the liberation of preaching and doctrine from both Scriptural fundamentalism and provincial and denominational traditionalism. There is, second, the powerful thrust of the world ecumenical movement toward recovery of a united Christendom—attended, at the same time, by a truly vast reassessment and critical reappropriation of doctrinal riches of the Church universal. There is, third, the current period—world-wide in scope and presupposing, likewise, the so-called "third-world"—which, taken at large, is bewilderingly diversified in concerns and aspirations. It manifests a reactionary temper toward the previous period in persistent ambivalence toward confessional theology and the Church catholic. Its prevailing standpoint is "contextual," which means *either* that it measures the truth of Christian faith by its *relevance* to the ubiquitous human problem, *or* that it lays the churches under judgment—in some few instances, truly, the judgment of God in Christ. About each of these eras and how they are reflected in theology at Duke only a few words can be said in the allotted space.

Concerning the first era: when Gilbert T. Rowe accepted appointment at Duke for the fall of 1928, the catalogue had already for two years carried six hours of "Christian Doctrine" as required work but with no surname in the space prefixed by the word "professor." When Dr. Rowe—whose colleagueship I was privileged to share for three years prior to 1948—took up teaching duties, he was already a pastor and noted preacher of the Western North Carolina Conference with a record of rather meteoric rise to church-wide recognition and veteran experience. Furthermore, he had come to Duke from the important position of Book Editor for the Methodist Episcopal Church, South, and was the highly admired if somewhat controversial editor of the *Methodist Quarterly Review.* The persistence with which he was courted by Drs. Few and Soper, albeit with near failure, to occupy the chair of Christian Doctrine has now been revealed by Reverend O. Lester Brown in his valuable biography of Dr. Rowe.[2]

Among the interesting statements of the reported correspondence is Dr. Rowe's written comment to Dr. Soper, which gives us a glimpse both of the context for doctrinal revision as Dr. Rowe conceived it then, and of the message he deemed suitable to the hour. In 1927 he wrote: "It seems to me that Duke has a very great opportunity and responsibility in the matter of helping the preachers get in touch with the last [latest?] thought and life of the age and at the same time to be genuinely evangelical in their ministry. . . ."[3] In his subsequent teaching of Christian theology he recurrently used as textbook D. C. Macintosh's *Theology as an Empirical Science.* This he commented upon with extensive elaborations of his own in a style inimitable, picturesque, whimsical, but also trenchant. As one who studied under Professor Macintosh I believe I understand something of Dr. Rowe's theological interests and prepossessions. Both men—Rowe and Macintosh—were, in their distinctive ways, spokesmen for an "evangelical liberalism" that accepted the findings of biblical criticism and the import of the biological and physical sciences as these related to God's work in creation, and yet strongly affirmed both the experiential basis of Christian faith and its consequential compelling and lofty moral vocation.

Much, much more there is to say were there space to say it, and as it should be said. The *Resolution* of the faculty on the occasion of Dr. Rowe's retirement in 1948—written by very knowledgeable colleagues—underscores the point of special bearing upon the question before us. Among other things, it states: ". . . the South owes him much for the transition which he assisted it to make from an older uncritical orthodoxy to a more *timely* grasp upon the eternal gospel." [4] As one studies Dr. Rowe's articles on "Present Tendencies in Religious Thought" in *The Divinity School Bulletin* of 1936, one has clear glimpses into the theological premises from which he worked.[5] His final word on the work of the new school, after just over two decades, was this: "Without pressure from any source all the members of the faculty were gradually drawn together into an essential unity, and Duke Divinity School is now well known as an institution characterized by evangelical liberalism." [6] Although we have but scratched the surface, this general characterization of theology at Duke in the earlier days, I am content to leave standing, coming as it does from a chief expositor.

Chronologically, the second period at Duke overlaps with the first, extending, let us say, from 1940—or prior to the Second World War—into the mid-sixties. I take, for objective reference, the close of the Second Vatican Council (1965) as the approximate terminus as, likewise, it was the summit point of the world ecumenical movement. This movement, together with its accompanying theological renaissance, undoubtedly provided the living *milieu* for theological endeavor and doctrinal reformulation at Duke as elsewhere during this second period. Not merely regional but even national boundaries of earlier American theological preoccupation, animus, and debate acquired a span, certainly as wide as the Western Christian world.

The theological faculty began to re-think long-standing impasses between conflicting confessional viewpoints as refracted by species of Protestant "liberalism"—either historicism, on the one hand, or ethicism on the other. It did so in the enlarging consciousness, sometimes half-articulate, that Christian faith and devotion, after all, do antedate the 16th-century Reformation. Especially at Duke did trends in biblical study as well as in Church history both reflect and contribute to the emergence of an expanding context for doctrinal restructuring and emphasis.

The marks of this change of perspective at Duke cannot all be enumerated here. One such mark was the manuscript and textual researches of Kenneth Clark, that made him a respected and trusted New Testament scholar of the West with leading representatives of Orthodoxy in the eastern Mediterranean world and led to unprecedented textual studies and findings at St. Catherine's monastery, Sinai, at Athos, in Palestine, and elsewhere. One of them was Ray C. Petry's extraordinary unfolding of the rich medieval inheritance. Another, surely, the flowering of studies in the hitherto obscure and neglected but rich heritage of our own American Christianity in the notable work of H. Shelton Smith. Still another sign is the enormous undertaking represented by the Wesley Works Editorial Project, now incorporated. Begun in 1959—and still far, too far, from completion—it is committed to the publication of the *Oxford Edition* of the works of John Wesley. The collaboration required has been international. In this enterprise the Divinity School has been principal investor and so continues. Other marks there are of the thrust toward recapture of the great tradition. One would miss the main point, however, unless he sees that the ecumenical movement not only fostered unprecedented international theological exchange across long and rather firmly closed denominational frontiers but also nurtured exploration and recovery of the entire range of the Christian tradition in depth.

It is in *this* perspective, primarily, that Karl Barth's or Emil Brunner's resurgent neo-Reformation theology received the attention it in fact commanded in those days. Today, it is doubtful that such system-building is possible, were it in all respects desirable. A principal reason, I believe, is that there is today no comparable "rising curve of Christian affirmation" in the churches to support it. The emerging but unfinished *consensus fidelium* that attended the high-tide of the ecumenical movement has fallen silent—not so much exhausted, I think, as overwhelmed by other insistent cares in an era of world-wide and profoundly resident anxiety. In our time the word salvation, therefore, has largely been redefined by the twin-concept: security and social mobility.

If, then, I am to characterize the second period of doctrinal ferment at Duke, I might venture to describe it as the inaugural era of exploratory ecumenical theology—as yet unfinished—and based upon a very considerable recovery of the tradition catholic as contrasted with the traditions, plural, and featuring the twofold theme of the Third World Conference on Faith and Order, namely, "Christ and his Church."

In the second period of the Divinity School's theological creativity, professional theology assayed its tasks in a consciousness of growing colleagueship with practicing churchmen and the larger fellowship of believers. In addition to enhancing general ecumenical vision, the now near-forgotten liturgical revival of the same period offered a common ground of the Spirit for both theological revision and common worship in a developing interdenominational forum. For historical reasons of baffling complexity and enormous scope, the succeeding third period of theological endeavor at Duke reflects more than a decade of widespread societal disassociation if not disintegration, although signs of healing may be appearing in the wings. As, perhaps, the dis-union of Christendom was the central "problematic" of theology in the second period, so, in the third, the self-conscious disunity of man-kind becomes the focus.

A mark of this trend is that, viewed as a whole, theology in America has become predominantly either "free-lance" or emphatically "aca-demic," and tends to be as remote from "church dogmatics," in self-understanding and method, as the previous period was well advanced on the way towards it.[7] This is true especially of the American scene, and more emphatically, perhaps, than in Europe. American provincial-ity in theology, therefore, is already fully resurgent but in pluralized and multifarious shapes and platforms too numerous even for mention here. Meanwhile, the so-called "third world" viewpoints—representing more nearly socioeconomic and ethnic concerns than geographic ones—are belatedly clamorous for their share in Christian doctrinal revision, especially as this bears upon *both* the social application of acknowledged Christian ethical norms to the plight of the oppressed of the earth and, also, the fidelity of the Church to its calling in the world.

Of the several species of so-called "renewal theology," which came forward with some very understandable incentives in the late sixties, two mottos in particular may sample aspects of the theological program of the time. As you may recall, one of them was: "Let the world provide the agenda." This was exhortation to the churches. The other was its complement, namely, J. C. Hoekendijk's injunction for the times: "The Church Inside Out." The corrective included the thesis that the whole business of Christianity *is* mission—indeed, it seems, is quite exhausted in mission. Explicit was the exhortation to "de-ghettoize" the church—which is, to be sure, always timely—but in particular Hoekendijk with others enjoined the need to quit making of the Church a refuge for private salvation and all cloistered virtues. For some representatives of the viewpoint, justification by faith considered as private salvation was totally expendable. Accordingly, a new evangelicalism was in the making! But it is not clear that it had a firm grasp upon the whole Gospel. In all of this, of course, one hears echoes of Dietrich Bonhoeffer who, probably, more than any other, gave leadership in the period.

Further accounting of recent theological tendencies is excluded. On the whole—and taking a purview of the rather humorless, tactless, and joyless voices in "professional" theology of the immediate pres-ent—the preponderance of utterance seems to derive from three sources: the applied-ethics bureaucracy of the churches, religious journalism of many stamps, and the faculties of university departments of religion. Meantime, it is a good while since churchmen of the stature of Francis J. McConnell, Henry Sloan Coffin, William Temple, or a Gilbert T. Rowe of the South have entered the lists for anything like serious theological leadership.

Taken together, these circumstances are, I think, indicative of a pressing issue today respecting the sources and norms of Christian doctrine, namely: "Who speaks for the Church"—*anymore?* Shall the word spoken be primarily that of its critics, or, if its thoughtful communicants speak, will they have the currency of "paper-back" appeal and, hence, find a publisher? Here at the Divinity School, as elsewhere, the disciplined theologian experiences as his regular diet something not unlike a Sahara of sand in the midst of which he is intermittently buffeted by squalls of special interest, often abrasive, coming from the twelve points of the theological compass. What shall he do? Where shall he begin, and how shall he speak?

Under such circumstances it does get to be rather a matter of nicely calculated priorities, as Professor Herzog has quite lately urged, namely, as to which of the winds—and from what point of the compass—one faces into. Yet facing into the winds is quite as any seagull, I have noticed, regularly does on the rock-bound coast of Maine.

In his frequently misunderstood "liberation theology"—yet, I think, with a proven evangelical concern—Herzog has faced into winds blowing, probably, ever since the Barmen Declaration of the confessing Evangelical Church of Germany—with solitary courage in 1934—acknowledged in the face of the ill-wind of Hitler's National Socialism a treacherous temptation of the churches and reaffirmed the sovereignty of God over man's history and the fidelity of the church to its calling before God in the world. Karl Barth later declared himself on this head in his *Rechtfertigung und Recht* (*Justification and Justice*, 1939), and one will not really understand "liberation theology" in Herzog's version, I believe, unless one sees that—in line with Barth, his teacher, before him—Herzog is urging that to take "justification by faith" seriously and to comprehend its full import requires the acknowledgment that salvation is not only a private transaction between Christ and the individual, but a public commitment of the justified community, the Church, to the purpose of God in the affairs of mankind.

I think I am not far afield in judging that "liberation theology" is a call to the Church and church people really to affirm their liberation, through Christ, from conformity and bondage to "the mind of the world." In addition to recalling the Apostle Paul to our attention in this way, Professor Herzog is underscoring what Luther was saying in the 16th century: Let God be God in the church! In Herzog's view this is an urgently needed word for the hour among the established churches of the South. On this point, although I think we can be somewhat more inclusive, he can scarcely be wrong. Yet the insistence is as old as Amos' exhortation against "ease in Zion" and as recent as H. Richard Niebuhr's stress in the forties on the pressing need of Christians to be converted to Christianity.

Anyone who has read even moderately in the writings of Wesley knows that the conversion of nominal Christians to Christianity was what Wesley's preaching and indefatigable labors of more than a half a century were all about, and, furthermore, that in contrast with very nearly the whole Continental Lutheran and Reformed theology, Wesley made "Christian perfection"—with social outreach—the undoubted test of any private salvation worth mentioning. It does not follow, of course, that Wesley's succession has continued to hear him. It is, therefore, reassuring to know that the voice of authentic Wesleyan evangelicalism is timely among us! I believe it has promise of recovery of the great tradition. It is always healthy for Methodists, in particular, to be reminded of Wesley's later life *Thoughts Upon Methodism*, where he says: "I am not afraid that the people called Methodists should ever cease to exist either in Europe or America. But I am afriad, lest they should only exist as a dead sect, having the form of religion without the power." [8]

What this means for us today Dr. W. P. Stephens touched upon in his first Gray Lecture in the stress that "conversion is political and social as well as personal." [9] Unpopular as this has been among many evangelicals, it is plain enough that Wesley would be no stranger to the thought that authentic Christianity cannot be passed off for private fence-mending between God and the sinner. He was, of course, clear about man the sinner. But, in the hotly controverted *Conference Minutes* of 1770, Wesley scandalized the Calvinists of his day by declaring that "works meet for repentance" are the inescapable obligation and outcome of justification and, further, if absent, absent too is the "condition" of salvation. [10] This let loose probably the most formidable doctrinal debate of the 18th century, between John Fletcher, against antinomianism, and Augustus Toplady and others. In plain words, Wesley had flown in the face of Reformed theology simply to stand firm with the words of our Lord: "By their fruits ye shall know them." With Wesley "Christian perfection" was not optional. It was part of the doctrine with which the Methodists began and heedlessness to which might incur the sectarian deadness he feared most.

V. CONCLUSIONS

My account of theology at Duke these fifty years is now done. I have attempted, in brief compass, to recount and to interpret the story as faithfully as I am able. It cannot escape our notice how vastly expanded is the context and how multiplied the issues by reference to which doctrinal reaffirmation today must be undertaken as compared with the twenties and the thirties of this century. Nevertheless, I must register the judgment that any and all responsible theological reflection of the future at Duke will be well advised to keep before it the foundational guidelines embraced in the founders' conception that I have named "the dialectic of opposites." Authentic Christian theology must recognize that, from *faith*, it may *hope* to move onward to understanding—also that its primary point-of-reference is the faith of a living Church. Coordinately, on the other hand, this same theology is under mandate to go on probing the Scripture and the tradition of the Church catholic, always with a view to illuminating the darkness of the human world with the "light of the world," even Jesus Christ. For the Psalmist has the final word for the past as also for any future in theology: "In thy light shall we see light."

VI. EPILOGUE

While this essay intrudes seemingly parochial concerns that might trespass upon either ecumenical vision or fully academic theological discourse, I have opted, after much reflection, on inclusion of this Fiftieth Anniversary address primarily because I believe its conception of the inescapable task of a Christian theology transcends its accidental and partial but illustrative instance at Duke University Divinity School. My students will not be unfamiliar with the thesis that Christian theology does not fulfill its vocation or even legitimately exist in careless independence of a living community of faith—a Church. It is the living Church that underwrites its mandate if it is indeed to be Christian rather than merely philosophical theology. Accordingly, however much in our time the vision of "the coming great Church" may enlist the aspiration of all, the latter has, so far, provided the actuating rootage and nurture of none.

I am not embarrassed by the invariable fact that the Christian faith is "traditioned" but, only, that it is often quite content merely to be so. Christian theology, I believe, rightly exists precisely in the antithesis between what is livingly traditioned and the coming Kingdom of God. Likewise, it is safe only as it endures creatively the attendant divided loyalties of the truly faithful. If, therefore, much recent Protestant theology tends to expire in the pure air of the coming Kingdom of God, the long-standing Catholic *faux pas* has been the contrary—to look for the Kingdom as a *depositum* in the midst. As I see it, the truth is neither, alone, but both together in insoluable dialectical tension. This, too, may yet be an eventual discovery of faith seeking understanding.

NOTES

FAITH AND REASON IN THE THOUGHT OF ST. AUGUSTINE

1. *Enchiridion*, V. Except for the *Confessions*, references to the literature of Augustine and quoted matter are from the *Nicene and Post-Nicene Fathers*, ed. Philip Schaff (New York, 1900). The Loeb edition of the *Confessions* is constantly employed: *St. Augustine's Confessions*, 2 vols. (London, 1931). For a Latin text I have depended on Perrone, *Œuvres complètes de St. Augustin* (Paris, 1872).

2. *De civitate Dei*, VIII. 5; X. 29.

3. *Confessions*, VII. 9; cf. *Epistulae*, LXXXII. 13.

4. *De Trinitate*, XII. 14. 21; XII. 14. 25; cf. *Enchiridion*, II; *In Ioannis evangelium*, XCVII. 7; *De Trinitate*, XII. 11. 16; XII. 13. 20.

5. *De Trinitate*, I. 8. 17; cf. *Enarrationes in Psal.*, XL. 20; *De Trinitate*, I. 2. 4.

6. It is difficult to understand what Harnack meant (*History of dogma*, trans. N. Buchanan [Boston, 1899], V, 126) by saying that Augustine "never advanced to history." It is true that, unlike the neo-Kantians, Augustine never regarded history as the sole source of divine revelation, viz., Ritschlianism, but it is beyond dispute that the revelatory value of history is precisely that which he regards as distinguishing him from the Platonists. Cf. C. N. Cochrane, *Christianity and Classical Culture* (New York, 1944), p. 416.

7. C. C. J. Webb, *Studies in the History of Natural Theology* (Oxford, 1915), pp. 30, 136.

8. See *De civitate Dei*, VI; VII; VIII.

9. Ibid., VIII. 10 and 12.

10. Ibid., X. 6.

11. *Confessions*, IV. 3; IV. 4.

12. *De civitate Dei*, X. 18.

13. Ibid., VIII. 5.

14. *De doctrina christiana*, II. 40; II. 60.

15. *De civitate Dei*, VIII. 4; cf. VIII. 1 and 9.

16. Ibid., XI. 25.

17. Ibid., IX. 16.

18. *In Ioannis evangelium*, XV. 19.

19. *De Trinitate*, II. 5. 8.

20. *Confessions*, VII. 9. 13; cf. *De civitate Dei*, VIII. 5.

21. *De civitate Dei*, X. 28 and 29; cf. *Confessions*, VII. 9; VII. 14; VII. 21. 27.

22. *Soliloquia*, I. 7; cf. *De gratia et libero arbitrio*, II. 6. 13; *De Trinitate*, III. 3. 8.

23. *De gratia et libero arbitrio*, II. 4. 13; cf. *De Trinitate*, XII. 7. 10.

24. *De Trinitate*, XIV. 8. 11; XI. 5. 8; XIV. 12. 15.

25. *De civitate Dei*, VIII. 9.

26. Ibid., VIII. 7.

27. *Soliloquia*. I. 12.

28. *De gratia et libero arbitrio*, II. 12. 34.

29. *Confessions*, X. 12; X. 19.

30. Ibid., X. 10. 7. A variant rendering to William Watt's graphic translation of *haurimus* is we "draw in" or "drink in."

31. *De civitate Dei*, VIII. 6; *De Trinitate*, XII. 14. 22; XI. 8. 14; XII. 14. 23.

32. Ibid., XII. 2. 2.

33. Cf. *Confessions*, X. 6; X. 9: *In Ioannis evangelium*, XIII. 5; XV. 19; *De Trinitate*, IV. 2. 3; XI. 8. 14.

34. *De civitate Dei*, VIII. 6; X. 14; *Confessions*, VII. 17; VII. 24; X. 6; X. 10.

35. Ibid., X. 6; X. 9.

36. Ibid., III. 6; III. 10; cf. *In Ioannis evangelium*, XV. 25.

37. *De civitate Dei*, VIII. 6; cf. *Confessions*, XI. 5; XI. 13; *De Trinitate*, VIII. 3. 4.
38. *Confessions*, VII. 17; VII. 23; cf. *De Trinitate*, VIII. 6. 9.
39. *De Trinitate*, IX. 6. 10; cf. *In Ioannis evangelium*, I. 7.
40. *De Trinitate*, IX. 7. 12; cf. *De civitate Dei*, VII. 6; IX. 16; X. 2.
41. See *De Trinitate*, VIII. 6. 9; VIII. 9. 13; IX. 6. 9; XV. 4. 6.
42. *Confessions*, XIII. 38; XIII. 53.
43. Ibid., VII. 9; VII. 13.
44. *Enchiridion*, V; cf. *De Trinitate*, I. 1. 1; 2. 4; IV. 3. 5.
45. *De Trinitate*, V. 11. 12.
46. *In Ioannis evangelium*, III. 5.
47. *Enarrationes in Psalmos*, VI. 8.
48. *Confessions*, VII. 9; VII. 14; X. 24; X. 35 sqq.
49. Ibid., X. 17; X. 26; cf. *De Trinitate*, XIV. 12. 16.
50. *De Trinitate*, XIV. 4. 6; cf. XIV. 8. 11.
51. *Confessions*, X. 23; X. 33.
52. *Enarrationes in Psalmos*, VIII. 5.
53. *Confessions*, VI. 4; VI. 5 and 7.
54. *Epistulae*, LXXXII. 5. In this instructive correspondence with Jerome, Augustine's concern is lest Jerome's form of "higher criticism" of *Gal.* 2–4 impugn the reliability and infallibility of Scripture.
55. *Contra epistolam quam vocant fundamenti*, V. 6.
56. *Contra Faustum Manichaeum*, XXXIII. 6; XXXIII. 9; cf. *De utilitate credendi*, XIII.
57. *De spiritu et littera*, XI. 18.
58. For this mode of argument see *De utilitate credendi*, XXXI–XXXII; *Contra epistolam quam vocant fundamenti*, IV. 5.
59. *Contra Faustum Manichaeum*, XXXIII. 9.
60. *Enchiridion*, V; cf. *De doctrina christiana*, I. 14; I. 13.
61. *Enchiridion*, IV.
62. *De civitate Dei*, VIII. 3; cf. *De Trinitate*, I. 2. 4.
63. *De utilitate credendi*, XXIII.
64. *De doctrina christiana*, II. 7; II. 11; *De fide et symbolo*, IX. 20; *Enarrationes in Psalmos*, XXXVI. 13. XLIII. 4; LXXXVI. 20; XC. 15; *In Ioannis evangelium*, I. 8; I. 19; III. 18; XIX. 16; XX. 11; CXI. 3.
65. *Enarrationes in Psalmos*, XL. 20.
66. *De Trinitate*, IX. 1. 1.
67. *De civitate Dei*, X. 28.
68. *De Trinitate*, I. 2. 4.
69. *Confessions*, VI. 4; VI. 6.
70. *De Trinitate*, VIII. 10. 14.
71. *De utilitate credendi*, I and II.
72. *Confessions*, VII. 21; VII. 27.
73. *De Trinitate*, III. 4. 10.
74. Ibid., XI. 1. 1.
75. Ibid., XI. 3. 6; XI. 5. 8.
76. *De civitate Dei*, VIII. 10.
77. Ibid.
78. *De civitate Dei*, XIV. 13.
79. *De Trinitate*, VIII. 7. 11.
80. *Confessions*, VIII. 10; VIII. 22; cf. VII. 16; VII. 22; VIII. 7; VIII. 17; X. 6; X. 8.
81. *De Trinitate*, IX. 12. 18.
82. Cf. John Burnet, "Aristotle," *Proceedings of the British Academy* (London, 1924), XI, 15–16.
83. *De Anima*, 432b 7 sqq.
84. See *De Anima*, 431a 11 and *Metaphysics*, 1072a 30.
85. *De Anima*, 433b 28; cf. 434a 17.
86. Ibid., 433a 15 sqq.

87. *In Ioannis evangelium*, XXVI. 4.
88. *De Anima*, 427b 17 sqq.
89. *De Trinitate*, IX. 12. 18.
90. Ibid., VIII. 9. 13.
91. Ibid., XV. 27. 50; cf. *De civitate Dei*, XIV. 7 where Augustine defines a right will and a wrong will as *bonus amor* and *malus amor* respectively.
92. *De Trinitate*, XV. 20. 38.
93. *In Ioannis evangelium*, XXV. 15.
94. *De civitate Dei*, XIV. 11.
95. *De Trinitate*, XII. 11.16.
96. Ibid., XIV. 15. 21.
97. *De civitate Dei*, X. 29; cf. X. 32; *Confessions*, V. 3; V. 4; *In Ioannis evangelium*, XXXIV. 9; *De Trinitate*, IV. 15. 20; XIII. 19. 24.
98. *De civitate Dei*, X. 24. The italics are mine.
99. *De Trinitate*, XII. 11. 16.
100. Ibid. Cf. XII. 11. 16.
101. Ibid.
102. Ibid.
103. Ibid. Cf. *De Trinitate*, XII. 12. 17.
104. *Enarrationes in Psalmos*, VIII. 8.
105. *Confessions*, VII. 18; VII. 24.
106. *De Trinitate*, IV. 18. 24; cf. *In epistolam Ioannis I*, III. 1.
107. *De civitate Dei*, X. 24.
108. See *De Trinitate*, I. 6. 11; II. 17. 28. *In Ioannis evangelium*, XIII. 3; XIV. 12; XVII. 3; XXXIV. 6; LXXV. 2.
109. *Enarrationes in Psalmos*, XXXIV. 1.
110. See *De civitate Dei*, X. 29; *Confessions*, IV. 1; VII. 18; VII. 24; *In Ioannis evangelium*, XVIII. 1; XX. 5.
111. *Enarrationes in Psalmos*, XXXVI. 15.
112. *Confessions*, XII. 10.
113. Ibid., XI. 2; XI. 4.
114. *In Ioannis evangelium*, XXIII. 6. ". . . he has made a passage, as it were, from the region of unbelief to the region of faith, by motion of the heart. . . ."
115. *De Trinitate*, I. 13. 60.
116. *In epistolam Ioannis I*, III. 1.
117. *De Trinitate*, XIV. 8. 11; cf. XV. 27. 49.
118. Ibid., XIII. 19. 24.
119. Ibid., VIII. 3. 4. cf. *Confessions*, X. 19.
120. *Confessions*, XIII. 12; XIII. 13.

GREEK AND CHRISTIAN VIEWS OF TIME

1. *Republic*, 493b, 615a; *Philebus*, 38e; *Laws*, 891a.
2. *Protagoras*, 345b; *Cratylus*, 419d.
3. *Timaeus*, 27d. Cf. *Phaedo*, 79a; *Phaedrus*, 247d; *Republic*, 585c.
4. *Republic*, 477a–479d; *Philebus*, 23c ff.
5. *Phaedo*, 75b. Cf. *Symposium*, 208a–b.
6. *Metaphysics*, 987b 5. Cf. *Republic*, 476e; *Theaetetus*, 157a ff.
7. J. E. Harrison, *Themis* (Cambridge, 1927), p. 186.
8. *Republic*, 546a.
9. *Timaeus*, 49d ff., 51b.
10. For Aristotle's most extended treatment of time, see *Physics*, IX. 10–14.
11. *Physics*, 223a 30 ff., 223b 9.
12. Ibid., 221b 3, 223a 33; *De caelo*, 279a 15.
13. *Timaeus*, 39d.

14. *De caelo,* 279a 18.
15. *Physics,* 218b 1 ff.
16. Ibid., 218b 13.
17. Ibid., 218b 16–18.
18. Ibid., 223b 18 ff.
19. Ibid., 219b 16, 220 b 6.
20. Ibid., 219b 5.
21. Ibid., 221a 29–30.
22. Ibid., 219a 2.
23. Ibid., 219a 6.
24. Ibid., 219a 22, 219b 16.
25. Ibid., 219a 19.
26. Ibid., 219a 28 ff.
27. Ibid., 219b 24.
28. Ibid., 220b 15–17.
29. Ibid., 218b 28.
30. Ibid., 223a 22 ff.
31. Ibid., 221b 1.
32. References are to the "Loeb Classical Library" edition (London, 1931). For convenience, most references are inserted in the text.
33. *Confessions,* XI. 15. This analysis virtually repeats the observations of Aristotle, *Physics,* IV. 10. 1–2.
34. *Confessions,* XI. 15.
35. *De civitate Dei,* II. 3.
36. Ibid., I. 6; II. 14; II. 18; II. 22; IV. 6.
37. Ibid., II. 18.
38. Ibid., IV. 11.
39. Ibid., IV. 1. CF. I. 6 *rerum gestarum* or *res gestae.*
40. Ibid., II. 7.
41. Ibid., IV. 1. 7. Cf. II. 18; II. 24; II. 29.
42. Ibid., I. 1.
43. *Phaedo* 96a ff. The phrase is *peri physeus historia.* As the chief occupation of Ionian pre-Socratic philosophy, see, for example, J. Burnet, *Early Greek Philosophy* (London, 1920), p. 12.
44. *De civitate Dei,* II. 19; II. 28; II. 29; IV. 3.
45. Ibid., II. 21.

HUMANISM SECULAR AND CHRISTIAN

1. Francis Bacon, *Novum Organum, Works,* ed. Spedding, Ellis, and Heath, 15 vols. (Boston, 1863), VIII, 99.
2. Ibid., p. 67. Cf. pp. 113, 162, 206.
3. Ibid., pp. 147, 104.
4. Paul Kurtz, "Humanist Manifesto II," *New York Times,* August 26, 1973.
5. John A. Symonds, *The Revival of Learning* (New York, 1960), p. 51.
6. Ibid., p. 52.
7. Plato, *Republic,* 518b–521c, 586a–c, 603d, 611b–612a.
8. M. T. Cicero, *De Natura Deorum,* ed. Loeb, trans. H. Rackham (London, 1967), Bk. III. 35. 371 f.
9. Ibid., I. 6. 123; II. 88.
10. Symonds, *Learning,* pp. 17 f.
11. Cf. R. E. Cushman, *Therapeia: Plato's Conception of Philosophy* (Westport, Conn., 1976), pp. xx, 42.
12. Plato, *Theatetus,* 152a Cf. R. E. Cushman, *Therapeia,* pp. 38–44.
13. Religious or "ecclesiastical humanism" in the early decades of the 20th century

is comprehensively discussed in *Humanism—Another Battleline*, ed. W. P. King (Nashville, 1931).

14. Kathleen Freeman, *The Pre-Socratic Philosophers* (Oxford, 1949), p. 347.

15. Plato, *Protagoras*, 319a.

16. J. B. Bury, *The Idea of Progress* (New York, 1932), p. 4.

17. Ibid., p. 5.

18. Bacon, *Of the Proficience and Advancement of Learning, Works*, II, 96.

19. Bacon, *Novum Organum, Works*, VIII, 99.

20. David Hartley, *Observations on Man* (London, 1749). The work was translated into French and published at Reims in 1755. J. Priestly published a volume, *Hartley's Theory of the Human Mind, On the Principle of the Association of Ideas* (London, 1755). A second edition of Hartley's *Observations* was published in London in 1791 and, most recently, by the University of Florida Press, 1966. For a critical interpretation of Hartley's system, reference may be made to an unpublished doctoral dissertation at Duke University: John W. Chandler, *An Examination of David Hartley's Thought and Its Influence on Philosophical Radicalism*, 1954.

21. Joseph Priestly, *An Essay on the First Principles of Government* (London, 1768). It is true that Priestly interpreted the possibility of reconditioning the affections and, thereby, the intellectual powers of humanity, by socially controlled means at the disposal of government, to be a general providence of the Creator, p. 6. His secular humanism was, therefore, reserved. He was a Deist and a Unitarian.

22. Sylvia Benians, *From Renaissance to Revolution* (London, 1923), p. 129.

23. Ibid., p. 102.

24. Bacon, *Of the Interpretation of Nature, Works*, VI, 28, 37; and *Advancement of Learning*, pp. 94–97.

25. M. Jean Antoine de Condorcet, *Outlines of an Historical View of the Progress of the Human Mind* (London, 1795), p. 4.

26. Baroness Stael de Holstein, *On the Influence of the Passions Upon Happiness* (London, 1798), p. 31.

27. The quotation is fixed in the memory of the author as from Thomas Hobbes's *Leviathan*. Diligent search has not located the precise passage.

28. Frederic Seebohm, *The Oxford Reformers* (New York, 1913).

29. P. Schaff, *Creeds of Christendom* (New York, 1877), III, 676.

30. Cf. Hans J. Hillerbrand, *Erasmus and His Age* (New York, 1970), pp. xv–xix.

31. Symonds, *Learning*, p. 52.

32. Robert Browning, *The Poetical Works* (New York, 1896), I, 524.

THEOLOGICAL LANDMARKS OF THE WESLEYAN REVIVAL

1. Thomas Coke and Henry Moore, *The Life of the Reverend John Wesley* (Philadelphia, 1793), p. v.

2. Ibid.

3. Nathaniel Curnock, ed., *Journal of the Reverend John Wesley* (London, 1938), II, 274 f.

4. *A Plain Account of Christian Perfection. Works of the Reverend John Wesley*, ed. J. Emory (New York, 1832), VI, 488.

5. *A Short History of Methodism* (1764), *Works*, V, 246.

6. *Divine Inspiration of the Holy Scriptures, Works*, VI, 554; and *The Character of a Methodist, Works*, V, 240.

7. *The Principles of a Methodist* (1740), *Works*, V, 256.

8. Ibid., 256–57.

9. *Sermons on Several Occasions*, ed. T. Jackson, 2 vols. (New York, 1847), Sermon CXXXII, ii, 17. Here appears the overworked sentence: "Whosoever thou art, whose heart is herein as my heart, give me thine hand." Wesley also affirms the early fidelity of the Methodists to the *Articles* and *Homilies* of the Church of England, and declares:

"Methodism, so-called, is the old religion, the religion of the Bible, the religion of the primitive church, the religion of the Church of England" (ii, I).

10. *The Character of a Methodist, Works,* V, 240.

11. *Sermons,* "On the Trinity," LV, 1. See *Journal,* II, 411, on right opinion as profitless in the absence of the "Christian temper."

12. *Sermons,* "On the Church," LXXIV, 11.

13. *Journal,* III, 20.

14. *A Plain Account of Christian Perfection, Works,* VI, 484.

15. Ibid., p. 530.

16. *Sermons,* "The Circumcision of the Heart," XVII, 3.

17. Ibid., i, 11.

18. *Plain Account of Christian Perfection, Works,* VI, 484.

19. Ibid., p. 530.

20. Ibid., p. 531. Cf. *Minutes of Some Late Conversations,* I (1744), *Works,* V, 197.

21. *Journal,* I, 418.

22. Ibid., p. 442.

23. Ibid., p. 454. Cf. *Minutes,* I (1744), *Works,* V, 194 f.

24. Ibid., iii, 3. See the similarity between this declaration and that of the Moravian, Michael Linner, *Journal,* II, 27, upon Wesley's visit to Herrnhut, August 1738.

25. *Journal,* I, 455–56.

26. Ibid., p. 419.

27. *Minutes,* I (1744), *Works,* V, 201. Cf. *Sermons,* "Spirit of Bondage and Adoption," IX, ii, 1–7. The denial of "free-will" means the denial of ability to love God completely and man as neighbor. It is denial of the power, apart from justifying grace, to attain Christian perfection. It is denial of freedom *for* "the righteousness of faith"; there is still freedom *to* evil. Ibid., ii, 7.

28. *Sermons,* "Justification by Faith," V, iii, 1–5; "Salvation by Faith," I, ii, 4.

29. Cf. *Sermons,* "Spirit of Bondage and Adoption," IX, iii, 5; "On Sin Believers," XIII, iii, 10.

30. Cf. *Journal,* I, 462, John Gambold's letter.

31. Ibid., pp. 441 f.

32. Ibid., II, 362.

33. Ibid., I, 470.

34. Ibid., p. 471.

35. *Sermons,* "Justification by Faith," V, iii, 1.

36. Ibid., 5. Wesley's italics.

37. Ibid., "On the Death of George Whitefield," LIII, iii, 2.

38. Ibid., "Justification by Faith," V, iii, 5.

39. Ibid., "The New Birth," LXV, ii, 5.

40. Ibid., iii, 1.

41. *Minutes* (1746), *Works,* VI, 205.

42. *The Whole Duty of Man* was published anonymously in 1658 and went through, perhaps, ten editions to 1748, with more to follow. Attributed to Richard Allestree (1619–1681), Regius Professor of Divinity, Oxford, 1660, and included in the *Works* of Richard Allestree (London, 1687–95).

43. *Sermons,* "Spirit of Bondage and Adoption," IX, ii, 7. There is, of course, no doubt at all of Wesley's recurrent if largely silent reference to Martin Luther's famed *Commentary on Galatians.*

44. *Journal,* I, 454.

SALVATION FOR ALL—JOHN WESLEY AND CALVINISM

1. Nathaniel Curnock, ed. *Journal of the Reverend John Wesley* (London, 1938), II, 184.

2. Maximin Piette, *John Wesley in the Evolution of Protestantism* (New York, 1938), p. 362.

3. *Journal*, II, 71.
4. Ibid., II, 177.
5. Ibid., II, 176, 223.
6. Ibid., II, 203.
7. See *Thoughts on Salvation by Faith, Works of the Reverend John Wesley*, 7 vols., ed. J. Emory (New York, 1831), VI, 560.
8. *Journal*, II, 289. See entry May 2, 1739, whence it is evident that opposition on this ground was already crystallizing.
9. *Works*, V, 282.
10. *Journal*, II, 427 ff.
11. Ibid., p. 421.
12. Ibid., p. 422. Obviously, the debate was not limited to Kingswood.
13. Ibid., p. 439.
14. See *Long Minutes, Works*, V, 238. By 1770, in retrospect, Wesley was clear on this point.
15. Letter to Whitefield, *Journal*, II, 428.
16. *Sermons on Several Occasions*, 2 vols., ed. T. Jackson (New York, 1847), Sermon I, iii, 3.
17. *Works*, VI, 560.
18. *A Treatise on Justification, Works*, VI, 122.
19. Sermon LIV, 21–23. Cf. Sermon LXXXIX, iii, 2. The importance of the above is seen in Wesley's understanding of the essence of religion: "It lies in one single point: it is nothing more or less than love, . . . the love of God and our neighbors." But we cannot love God except He first love us (Sermon X, i, 8). Therefore, the Calvinist God makes religion, i.e., Christianity, impossible, inherently a contradiction.
20. *Works*, VI, 60.
21. Sermon XLIII, iii, 8.
22. Sermon I, iii, 3.
23. Sermon CXI, ii, 4.
24. Sermon XC, iii, 15.
25. Ibid. Italics mine.
26. *Journal*, III, 85. August 1743, in the *Doctrinal Eirenicon*, Wesley declares that while "most believers may remember some time when God did irresistibly convince them of sin, . . . yet I believe that the grace of God, hath before and after those moments, may be, and hath been resisted; and that in general, it does not act irresistibly; but we may comply therewith, or may not." Cf. Sermon LXVIII, 12. But Wesley never meant that we may of ourselves, voluntarily comply with it or not.
27. William R. Cannon, *The Theology of John Wesley* (New York, 1946), p. 115.
28. *Formula of Concord*, Art. II, neg. ii, iii, in P. Schaff, *Creeds of Christendom*, (New York, 1877), III, 107–109.
29. Sermon XLVIII, i, 4.
30. *The Theology of John Wesley*, p. 114. Nevertheless Dr. Cannon persists in alluding to this freedom as a positive ability to a measure of goodness.
31. *Journal*, III, 85.
32. Ibid., II, 428.
33. Umphrey Lee, *John Wesley and Modern Religion* (Nashville, 1936), p. 124.
34. Sermon XLIV, iii, 1.
35. Sermon XVII, i, 3.
36. Sermon XVII, 1.
37. Ibid.; cf. Sermon LXVII, i. 8.
38. *Works*, V, 201. Cf. Sermon VII, ii, 1; IX, i, 7; IX, iii, 8; LIII, iii, 2.
39. *Works*, VI, 156. The final sentence refers probably to the prejustification state, but note that insofar as man's will is free to good, it is of grace. See the taunt to "learned men" (Sermon IX, i, 4).
40. Sermon XC, iii, 3, 4.
41. Sermons LXVIII, i, 11; CX, i, 1, 11. Here is the point where Wesley departs from the *Thirty-Nine Articles* which, though they employ the concept of preventing grace (Art. X), yet continue to contemplate a natural state devoid of grace (Art. XIII).

42. Sermon XC, ii, 1.
43. Sermon XC, iii, 4.
44. Sermon CX, i, 5.
45. *Journal*, I, 239.
46. Sermon XLIII, i, 2. This teaching, integral to Wesley's whole thought about man, distinguishes him from Calvinism. It is Wesley's explanation of Augustine's ontologism; how man is made to be unsatisfied until he rests in God. It is not nature but grace. It belongs to all in virtue of their humanity (as in Plato). It may be obscured by willful resistance or desuetude culminating in final and invincible ignorance like the Platonic *amathia*, or double ignorance.
47. Sermon CXXXV, i, 1.
48. *Works*, VI, 560–61.
49. Ibid.
50. Cf. Sermon XCVI, ii, 3–6 for full explanation. Cf. Art. XII, *Thirty-Nine Articles.*
51. U. Lee, *John Wesley and Modern Religion*, pp. 166 f.
52. *Works*, V, 238.
53. Cf. Sermons XCVI, LXXVII.
54. *Journal*, V, 397.
55. Sermon LIII, ii, 2–3.
56. *The Theology of John Wesley*, p. 113.
57. Sermon IX, ii, 1.
58. Cf. Sermons CXXVIII, i, 1; IX, iv, 2.
59. Sermon IX, iii, 8.
60. *Journal*, II, 278. See the description of his own experience, *Journal*, I, 423, 470.
61. Sermon LXV, iii, 1. Cf. I, iii, 5; V, iv, 6; CXXXVIII, iii, 1.
62. Sermon IX, ii, 7–8.
63. *Journal*, I, 470.
64. Ibid., II, 362.
65. Sermon XX, ii, 11.
66. Sermon XIV, iii, 4.

A STUDY OF FREEDOM AND GRACE IN RESPONSE TO RECENT INTERPRE-
TATION OF THE GOSPEL ETHIC

1. R. Niebuhr, *An Interpretation of Christian Ethics* (New York, 1935), p. 65.
2. Ibid., p. 67. For a most telling exposition of the source of this primary thesis in the thought of Luther, see A. Nygren's *Agape and Eros*, Part 2 (London, 1939), I, 463–73.
3. Ibid.
4. Ibid., p. 56.
5. Ibid., p. 58; cf. p. 31. Elsewhere Niebuhr discloses his own stand with reference to the strife between the counsels of perfection of Jesus and the counterpunctual realities of essential humanity. He says: "The measure of Christianity's success in gauging the full dimension of human life is given in its love perfectionism, on the one hand, and its moral realism and pessimism, on the other" (p. 65).
6. *The Nature and Destiny of Man* (New York, 1941), I, 299.
7. Ibid., p. 16.
8. J. Wesley, *Sermons on Several Occasions*, ed. T. Jackson (New York, 1847), II, 90, 237.
9. Cf. K. E. Kirk, *The Vision of God* (London, 1937), pp. 55 ff.
10. T. W. Manson, *The Teaching of Jesus* (Cambridge, 1943), pp. 154–60.
11. 2 Cor. 2:12–16.
12. *Religion within the Limits of Reason Alone*, ed. T. M. Greene and H. H. Hudson (Chicago, 1934), p. 17.
13. *Critique of Practical Reason*, ed. T. K. Abbot (New York, 1923), p. 175.

14. Manifestly, the object is viewed, existentially speaking, quite differently by Spinoza and Jesus. For Spinoza it is nonteleological and immanent; for Jesus, teleological and transcendent.

15. *The Teaching of Jesus*, p. 301.

16. *Metaphysic of Morals*, ed. T. K. Abbot (New York, 1923), p. 29.

17. Ibid., p. 30.

18. Ibid., p. 2.

19. Ibid., p. 30. Cf. F. E. England, *Kant's Conception of God* (London, 1929), pp. 169–72.

20. Ibid., p. 4. Says Kant: "The basis of obligation must not be sought in the nature of man, or in the circumstances in the world in which he is placed, but *a priori* simply in the conceptions of pure reason. . . ."

21. Ibid., p. 43.

22. Ibid., p. 45; see also ibid., pp. 45–46. Here a subjectivist theory of value, not unlike Spinoza's, is distinctly set forth. All objects of desire are "subjective ends" as distinguished from "objective ends," the latter being furnished by pure practical reason.

23. Ibid., p. 15.

24. Ibid., p. 12.

25. *Critique of Practical Reason*, pp. 171, 173.

26. *Metaphysics of Morals*, p. 33. Hypothetical imperatives belong merely to an ethic in which the will is materially determined to ends which are relative to individual preferences or valuation.

27. Ibid., p. 65.

28. Ibid., p. 31.

29. *Religion within the Limits of Reason Alone*, p. 17.

30. *Metaphysic of Morals*, p. 58.

31. Cf. *Critique of Practical Reason*, pp. 220 f.

32. W. L. Davidson, *The Stoic Creed* (Edinburgh, 1907).

33. *Ethics*, Bk, III, Defs. 2 and 3 in *Spinoza Selections*, ed. J. Wilde and trans. W. H. White (New York, 1930). An *affectus* is a modification of the body so as either to increase or to decrease its power of acting, viz., its reality or perfection. Further, affects are of two kinds: products of the mind's *passivity* or *activity*.

34. Of the primary affects, see *Ethics*, Bks. III and II, *Schol.*

35. Ibid., Bk. III, Defs. 8, 9.

36. Bk. II, Def. 49.

37. Ibid., Def. 35. Cf. Bk. I, app.

38. Ibid., Def. 9, *Schol.* "We neither strive for, wish, seek nor desire anything because we think it to be good, but on the contrary, we adjudge a thing to be good because we strive for, wish, seek or desire it."

40. Cf. *On the Improvement of the Understanding* (New York, n.d.), p. 5; cf. *Ethics*, Bk. IV, app. 32.

41. Ibid., Defs. 3, 4.

42. See the opening pages of *On the Improvement of the Understanding*. The modern world has wagered everything on the validity of the first method.

43. *Short Treatise*, etc., trans. A. Wolf (London, 1910), chap. 5. General providence is Spinoza's equivalent for God or Nature—the *Deus sive Natura* of the Stoics. Those who are acquainted with Schleiermacher's "ethical analysis of the religious self-consciousness will recognize interesting dependencies upon Spinoza. Cf. *The Christian Faith* (Edinburgh, 1928), pp. 3–5.

44. Ibid.

45. Bk. V, Def. 42. For passages of similar import see *Short Treatise*, etc., chap. 26, and *Ethics*, Bk. IV, Def. 37.

46. Cf. *Ethics*, Bk. IV, app. 4; also ibid., Bk. III, Def. 2; Bk. IV, Def. 61; Bk. V. Def. 36, *Corol.*

47. Mark 10:27.

48. *An Interpretation of Christian Ethics*, p. 56.

49. I am indebted to Amos N. Wilder for his comment on my remarks: "Thus the

rigor is for the nonbeliever." This exactly states the case as I see it. For the nonbeliever the words of Jesus must remain commands from without upon a will which is in no sense assimilated to the Will which the commands describe.

50. Luke 6:45 = Matt. 12:35.

51. *The Teaching of Jesus*, p. 305.

52. Ibid., p. 103.

53. *Ethics*, Bk. IV, Def. 68.

54. George Santayana, *Egotism in German Philosophy* (London, 1916), p. 62.

55. *Critique of Practical Reason*, pp. 229 f.

56. Aristotle, *Metaphysics* 1059a 36; *Nicomachean Ethics*, II, i, 1; VI, ii, 3–6; vii, 6–7.

57. Cf. Plato, *Crito*, 49d; *Apology*, 40a ff; *Phaedo*, 83b, 85b, 99a–c; *Phaedrus*, 230a.

58. Aristotle, *Metaphysics*, 1074b 34 f.; *Nicomachean Ethics*, VIII, vii, 5.

59. Ritschl, *Justification and Reconciliation* (Edinburgh, 1900), p. 17.

60. *Kant Selections*, ed. T. M. Greene (New York, 1929), p. 21.

61. *Critique of Practical Reason*, p. 218.

62. Niebuhr, *An Interpretation of Christian Ethics*, p. 56. Cf. ibid., pp. 39, 48, 55–57, 121, 209, 213.

63. Ibid., p. 56.

64. Ritschl, *Justification and Reconciliation*, p. 58.

65. Niebuhr, *An Interpretation of Christian Ethics*, p. 58.

66. *Critique of Practical Reason*, p. 175.

67. Ibid., p. 176; see *Metaphysic of Morals*, pp. 15–16.

68. *An Interpretation of Christian Ethics*, p. 209.

69. Ibid., p. 56. Cf. Ernst Troeltsch, *The Social Teachings of the Christian Churches* (New York, 1931), I, who also views the ethics of Jesus from within the Kantian mold as radical demands made upon the will: "The will is given to God in absolute obedience, in order that it may attain the real and true life . . ." (p. 52). This exactly reverses the true sequence. Then there is the reference to eschatology for for explanation: "This message of the Kingdom was primarily the vision of an ideal ethical and religious situation, of the world entirely controlled by God . . ." (p. 40). Again, "faced by the extreme tension of these demands, we must also remember that they were formulated in the expectation of the final judgment of the immanent end of the world" (p. 55). Here are the same Kantian assumptions. In Troeltsch's version of liberal Christianity, the cleavage of nature and grace is, as with Kant, complete.

70. *An Interpretation of Christian Ethics*, p. 209.

71. *Critique of Practical Reason*, p. 176.

72. *Niebuhr, Christianity and Power Politics* (New York, 1940), pp. 3, 18.

73. Ibid.

74. *An Interpretation of Christian Ethics*, p. 217.

75. Ibid., p. 209.

76. *Critique of Practical Reason*, p. 146.

77. Ibid., p. 221.

78. Cf. *On the Improvement of the Understanding* from *Spinoza Selections*, p. 5.

79. *Ethics*, Bk. II, Def. 6, *Realitas et perfectio*. This is, of course, a corollary of the Stoic, *Deus sive Natura*. To equate "What-Is" with God is usually spoken of as pantheism. To equate God with "What-Is" (Nature) is to hold "reality and perfection one and the same thing." Existence is already Essence. This essentialism Niebuhr denies whole and part, as also Kant.

80. Ibid., Bk. I, Def. 16; cf. Preface to Bk. IV.

81. Ibid., Def. 17, *Schol.*

82. Ibid., app., p. 143. Plotinus, in his employment of the *principle of plenitude*, holds precisely the contradictory of Spinoza's Stoic pantheism. He is the progenitor of modern Existentialism in holding that all existence is *fallen* or deficient being, not Essence, but not-being. Spinoza's use of the principle is reminiscent of Aquinas's recurring use in the *Summa Contra Gentiles*, Bk. II, to treat the problem of theodicy.

83. Baron von Hugel, *The Mystical Element of Religion* (London, 1923), I, 41–42, who appreciates the fundamental religious cast of Spinoza's thought, remarks the incom-

patibility of Spinoza's rigorous determinism with the emphasis upon the need for conversion—interior purification and beatitude.

84. *Ethics,* Bk. V, Def. 52, *Demonst.*

85. Ibid.

86. Luke 6:45 = Matt. 12:35. The source is the Q document.

87. Luke 18:18 = Matt. 19:17.

88. The Revised Version seems to me correctly to translate μεριμνάω (Matt. 6:25, 27, 28, 31, 34) as "to be anxious." This is ἡ μέριμνα τοῦ αἰῶνος, "the anxiety of the age," which makes hearers of the word to be unfruitful (cf. Matt. 13:22).

89. Luke 18:17. Of course, there is a genuine sense in which the Kingdom is also future.

90. Mark 10:15 = Luke 18:17.

BARTH'S ATTACK UPON CARTESIANISM AND THE FUTURE IN THEOLOGY

1. *Systematic Theology* (Chicago, 1951), I, 41.

2. *The Doctrine of the Word of God,* trans. G. T. Thomson (Edinburgh, 1936), pp. 209, 82, 83, 156 (=*Die Kirchliche Dogmatik,* I, 1 or the English translation, *Church Dogmatics,* I, 1). Hereinafter cited as *Doctrine* (*Doct.* in the text). Succeeding volumes of the corpus are cited *KD* in the notes.

3. Tillich's statement to the Graduate Seminar in Religion, Duke University, March 13, 1955. Cf. Tillich, *Systematic Theology,* I, 94–95, on "the reintegration of reason."

4. Emil Brunner, *The Mediator* (London, 1934), p. 90.

5. Cf. Friedrich Schleiermacher, *The Christian Faith,* trans. H. R. Macintosh (Edinburgh, 1948): "And thus, however far our consciousness extends, we find nothing the origin of which cannot be brought under the concept of Preservation, so that the doctrine of Creation is completely absorbed in the doctrine of Preservation" (p. 146). Apply this to Jesus Christ and add the following: "But notwithstanding, it must be asserted that even the most rigorous view of the difference between Him and all other men does not hinder us from saying that His appearance, even regarded as the incarnation of the Son of God, is a natural fact" (p. 64).

6. Tillich's statement concerning the validation of religious symbols illustrates the point ("Religious Symbols and Our Knowledge of God," *Christian Scholar,* XXXVIII, No. 3 [September 1955], 196): "Symbols are independent of any empirical criticism. You cannot kill a symbol by criticism in terms of natural sciences or in terms of historical research. . . . Symbols are not on a level on which empirical criticism can dismiss them." The claim has merit, but it should be recognized that, as employed by Tillich, the theory is calculated to evade, by transcending, all questions concerning the "historicity" of New Testament kerygmatic events.

7. Karl Barth, *Die Kirchliche Dogmatik* (Zurich, 1948), pp. 34–35, hereinafter *KD.* Where references to the *Dogmatik* appear in parentheses within the text, I have simply referred to the volume number, etc.

8. Cf. *Doctrine,* p. 223.

9. Cf. John Calvin, *Institutes of the Christian Religion,* trans. Henry Beveridge (London, 1949), I, i, 1.

10. Cf. *KD,* III. 2. 50, 51, and I. 2. 253.

11. *Doctrine,* p. 148. In *KD,* III. 1. 225, it becomes clear that Barth's preceding treatment of the *analogia relationis* makes superfluous the Reformation doctrine of an actual historical *status integritatis.* Not only is the God-likeness of man, viz., the mutual for-ness of man for woman, not lost by the Fall, but also the text of Genesis, chapter 1, has no place for such "an original ideal man." The *status integritatis* is only visible in Jesus Christ and cannot be spoken of apart from him in faith (III. 2. 262). It is in fact the ontological definition of man as "being together with God" (III. 2. 167).

12. For the conception of *analogia fidei,* see *Doctrine,* pp. 275–79; cf. *KD,* I. 2. 266–69. Barth recognizes that knowledge entails conformity between knower and known.

This is secured, however, not by "analogy of being," which would condition the freedom of God, but by the direct activity of God the Holy Spirit (*Doctrine*, pp. 208–9). "In faith man is in conformity with God, i.e. capable of apprehending the Word of God" (*Doctrine*, p. 275).

13. Cf. *Doctrine*, p. 232, and *KD*, III. 1. 208.

14. For this quite central insistence, see *Doctrine*, p. 176, and *KD*, II. 2. 358.

15. Cf. D. C. Macintosh, *The Problem of Religious Knowledge* (New York, 1940), pp. 336–37.

16. Cf. *Doctrine*, pp. 168 ff.; *KD*, II. 1. 54, 58, 143. The incognito of the Word in the flesh is axiomatic with Barth. It is the "worldliness" of the Word; but in faith, through the Holy Spirit, "the divine content of the Word" is discernible to us (Doctrine, p. 201).

17. Cf. *Doctrine*, pp. 214, 226.

18. *KD*, III. 1. 400–401; III. 2. 23.

19. William Temple, *Nature, Man and God* (New York, 1949), p. 57.

20. Ibid., p. 73.

21. *Doctrine*, p. 222; cf. *KD*, III. 2. 23.

22. Cf. *Doctrine*, pp. 220–21.

23. Cf. Karl Barth, *Die Theologie und die Kirche* Zurich, n.d.), essay on "Ludwig Feuerbach" (1926), pp. 212–39. Barth fully intends a counterattack upon Feuerbach's humanism which, by the latter's admission, "elevates anthropology to theology" and "subordinates God to man" (p. 219). In Feuerbach's psychological idealism Barth saw the extreme outworking of Cartesianism; but Feuerbach impressed upon Barth the realization that the only way out of the human circle is the divine break-through from without. Cf. *Doctrine*, p. 241.

24. Cf. *Doctrine*, p. 217 (Barth's reply to Traub).

25. Cf. *Doctrine*, p. pp. 178 ff.; *KD*, I. 2. 1; II. 1. 21.

26. Cf. *Doctrine*, pp. 228, 237.

27. Cf. *KD*, II. 1. 142, 148, 150, 158.

28. *KD*, II. 1. 86–87.

29. *KD*, III. 2. 23. Cf. *Doctrine*, pp. 219–20, for a representative critique of Schleiermacher, and ibid., pp. 111–12, for a critique of Augustine's Cartesianism.

30. *KD*, II. 1. 156; III. 1. 213; III. 2. 391.

31. See *KD*, III. 1. 400. Cf. *Doctrine*, pp. 148, 159, 183, and *The Knowledge of God and the Service of God* (London, 1938), pp. 46–59, 61.

32. *Doctrine*, p. 148. Pages 137–49, the important excursus on anthropology, supplies, perhaps the most instructive *entrée* to Barth's thought.

33. *KD*, III. 2. 50; cf. II, 1. 166.

34. *KD*, III. 2. 161–62, 261, 270–71.

35. *KD*, III. 2. 261, 266; III. 1. 213.

36. *Systematic Theology*, I, 14.

CHRISTOLOGY OR ECCLESIOLOGY? A CRITICAL EXAMINATION OF THE CHRISTOLOGY OF JOHN KNOX

1. The works referred to are the following: *The Man Christ Jesus* (Chicago, 1941); *Christ the Lord* (Chicago, 1945); *On the Meaning of Christ* (New York, 1947); *Criticism and Faith* (New York, 1955); *The Death of Christ* (New York, 1958).

2. *Criticism and Faith*, p. 21.

3. Cf. *On the Meaning of Christ*, pp. 18–25, and *The Early Church*, pp. 66–67.

4. *Criticism and Faith*, pp. 47, 49, 55. Cf. *On the Meaning of Christ*, p. 64.

5. Cf. *The Man Christ Jesus*, pp. 39–40; *Criticism and Faith*, pp. 29, 31, 41; *The Death of Christ*, p. 128 et al.

6. This formula is consistently employed; cf. *Criticism and Faith*, p. 41; *The Early Church*, pp. 52, 65, 68; *The Death of Christ*, p. 109.

7. Cf. *On the Meaning of Christ*, p. 103; *Criticism and Faith*, pp. 32, 52–53; *The Death of Christ*, p. 128.

8. *The Man Christ Jesus*, p. 69; *On the Meaning of Christ*, p. 59; *The Early Church*, p. 75.

9. *On the Meaning of Christ*, p. 44.

10. Ibid., p. 26; cf. *The Death of Christ*, p. 109.

11. *Christ the Lord*, pp. 88–89.

12. *The Death of Christ*, p. 129.

13. *The Early Church*, p. 67. Italics are mine.

14. *The Early Church*, pp. 70–71.

15. Ibid., p. 81.

16. Ibid., p. 73.

17. Ibid., p. 74.

18. *On the Meaning of Christ*, pp. 19–20.

19. *The Early Church*, p. 66.

20. *The Man Christ Jesus*, p. 68.

21. Ibid., p. 15.

22. Ibid., p. 65. Cf. *Christ the Lord*, pp. 39–41; *The Death of Christ*, Chap. 3.

23. *The Man Christ Jesus*, p. 66.

24. Ibid., p. 67.

25. Ibid.

26. Ibid., p. 68.

27. Ibid.

28. Ibid.

29. Cf. *On the Meaning of Christ*, pp. 6, 67, 85; *Criticism and Faith*, pp. 30, 33, 38, 40.

30. *The Man Christ Jesus*, p. 73. Cf. p. 93 and *Criticism and Faith*, p. 32.

31. *Christ the Lord*, p. 3. Cf. *Criticism and Faith*, pp. 42, 49, 52.

32. *Christ the Lord*, p. 5.

33. Ibid., pp. 7, 59. The structure of the book is determined by these three principal themes.

34. Ibid., p. 67.

35. Ibid., p. 66.

36. *The Man Christ Jesus*, p. 69.

37. *On the Meaning of Christ*, p. 19.

38. Ibid., pp. 25–27.

39. Cf. ibid., pp. 65–67.

40. *Criticism and Faith*, p. 31. Cf. *On the Meaning of Christ*, p. 34.

41. Cf. ibid., p. 40, and *Criticism and Faith*, pp. 59 f.

42. *On the Meaning of Christ*, p. 66. Cf. *Criticism and Faith*, pp. 33, 59, 82, 86.

43. *On the Meaning of Christ*, p. 67. Italics and brackets are mine.

44. *Criticism and Faith*, p. 33.

45. Cf. *History and the Gospel* (London, 1952), pp. 28, 36.

46. *The Early Church*, p. 45. Cf. *Criticism and Faith*, pp. 32, 59–61.

47. *Criticism and Faith*, p. 60.

48. *On the Meaning of Christ*, pp. 17–19 ff.; also *The Early Church*, pp. 74–76.

49. Cf. ibid., p. 61; also *The Death of Christ*, pp. 109, 120–21.

50. *Criticism and Faith*, p. 54.

51. Cf. ibid., pp. 49, 52; *On the Meaning of Christ*, pp. 14, 28, 33.

52. *The Early Church*, pp. 70, 73; *The Death of Christ*, p. 159.

53. *The Early Church*, p. 73.

54. Cf. *Criticism and Faith*, pp. 30, 36, 106; *On the Meaning of Christ*, pp. 28, 33.

55. Ibid., pp. 26–27.

56. Cf. ibid., p. 22.

57. Ibid., p. 41.

58. Ibid., p. 65.

59. *Criticism and Faith*, p. 82.

60. *The Early Church*, p. 65.
61. *On the Meaning of Christ*, p. 40.

THE INCARNATION—A SYMBOL OF WHAT? AN INQUIRY INTO THE CHRIST-
OLOGY OF RUDOLF BULTMANN

1. H. W. Bartsch, ed., *Kerygma and Myth*, trans. R. H. Fuller (London, 1953), p. 209, n. 1.
2. Ibid., p. 196; also cf. p. 199.
3. Ibid., p. 198. Cf. *Essays Philosophical and Theological* (London, 1955), pp. 17–19, 78–85.
4. *Kerygma and Myth*, pp. 200–201.
5. *The Study of the Synoptic Gospels* (1930), trans. F. C. Grant, in *Form Criticism* (Chicago, 1934) pp. 22 f. The historiographical principles here stated explicitly are represented and widely illustrated in Bultmann's formative early work, *The History of the Synoptic Tradition*, trans. J. Marsh (Oxford, 1963). The First German edition, 1921.
6. Ibid., pp. 17–20. This sharp differentiation survives and confidently prevails in Bultmann's mature writing. See *Theology of the New Testament* (New York, 1951), I, 35, 51, 121–33, et passim. There are signs that John Knox entertains a comparable viewpoint in his *Christ the Lord* (Chicago, 1945), Chap. 6. With Knox, however, the *present* knowledge of the living Christ was the decisive beginning of the Palestinian community and also the "culmination" of the Christ-event. Cf. *History of the Synoptic Tradition*, p. 374.
7. Cf. *Jesus and Mythology* (New York, 1958), p. 13.
8. *Jesus and the Word*, trans. L. P. Smith and H. Lantero (New York, 1934), p. 141.
9. *The Communion of the Christian with God*, trans. J. S. Stanyon (New York, 1909), p. 70 f.
10. Ibid., p. 71.
11. Ibid., pp. 77–78. Cf. *Kerygma and Myth*, pp. 199–201.
12. *Kerygma and Myth*, p. 199.
13. Ibid.
14. *Jesus and the Word*, p. 8. Cf. *Essays*, pp. 134–35.
15. *Kerygma and Myth*, p. 37.
16. Ibid. Cf. *Essays*, p. 284.
17. Cf. *Jesus and the Word*, pp. 51–52.
18. *Kerygma and Myth*, p. 203.
19. *Jesus and the Word*, p. 14.
20. *Theology of the New Testament*, I, 26.
21. "The Problem of Hermeneutics" in *Essays Philosophical and Theological* (London, 1955), pp. 251 f. The Phrase "understanding of history" employs the word *Verständnis* which has, in the usage of the German philosophical tradition, a technical denotation that derives from Kant and is plainly related to Kant's "transcendental deduction of the pure concepts of the understanding." So far as I presently ascertain, it is this that comes nearest to unpacking the meaning of Heidegger's so-called "ontological analysis of being." It is, namely, something analogous to a "transcendental deduction" of the new category of *Geschichte*.
22. J. Macquarrie, *An Existentialist Theology* (London, 1955), p. 35.
23. Cf. *Jesus and the Word* (New York, 1958), pp. 206–9. Cf. pp. 77, 195.
24. Buber's phenomenological analytic of human experience in two dimensions is definitive in his famous *Ich und Du (I and Thou)*, trans. R. G. Smith (Edinburgh, 1950). Its import for religious knowledge and philosophy of history has explicit development in *Israel and the World* (New York, 1948). The importance of the following for Bultmann is apparent: "The events that occur to human beings are great and small, untranslatable and unmistakable signs that they are being addressed; what they do and fail to do can be an answer or failure to answer. Thus the whole history of the world, the hidden

real world history, is a dialogue between God and his creature; a dialogue in which man is a true, legitimate partner, who is entitled and empowered to speak his own independent word out of his own being." For the views of Karl Heim, see *God Transcendent*, trans. Dickie and Bevan (New York, 1936).

25. *Jesus and the Word*, pp. 208–9.

26. Ibid., p. 211. This transcendent reach of *Geschichte*, I surmise, is the "king-pin" of Bultmann's latent philosophy of religion which, however, Bultmann has not, so far as I am aware, seen fit to advance as competitor to the *kerygma*. The I-Thou dimension in its transcendental reach also provides for Bultmann a useful vehicle for a demythologized version of the *eschaton*. Cf. *Jesus*, p. 211.

27. *Kerygma and Myth*, p. 199.

28. The pervasive and heightened individualism of Bultmann's conception of Christianity is implied in the "decisive" and "existential" character of faith. Cf. *Essays*, pp. 15, 76–78, 83 passim.

29. *Kerygma and Myth*, p. 199.

30. Cf. *Jesus and the Word*, p. 210.

31. Cf. *Essays*, pp. 100–102, 286.

32. Ibid., pp. 106 f.

33. Ibid., p. 107. With such language Bultmann seems to be identifying with Lutheran and Reformation orthodoxy. All that is missing is an explicit appeal—always conspicuously lacking—to the *testimonium internum Spiritus Sancti*.

34. *Jesus and the Word*, pp. 41, 47.

35. Ibid., p. 51.

36. Ibid., pp. 51–52. Italics are mine. The inescapable "necessity of decision" doubtless refers us to Kierkegaard's formative role in the thought of Bultmann. At the same time, Bultmann plainly belongs in the post-Kantian tradition of German theology which has been overwhelmingly controlled by Kant's insistence upon the "primacy of the practical reason" that here registers itself in the proposition "this necessity of decision constitutes *the essential* part of . . . human nature."

37. *Kerygma and Myth*, p. 19. Cf. Essays, p. 112.

38. *Kergyma and Myth*, p. 22.

39. Ibid., p. 36.

40. Ibid.

41. Ibid., p. 38.

42. *Essays*, p. 286. Again, the received influence of Kant is echoed in the absence of any "moral" or "theological" import by way of an empirical employment of the theoretical reason restricted to *phenomena* or the external world. Cf. Barth's statement: "As a choice taking place, the Word of God in the humanity of Christ, in the Bible and in the proclamation is also a human act and therefore a temporal event." *Doctrine of the Word of God* (Edinburgh, 1936), p. 179. Or this: "The Word of God is not reality . . . in the way of an experienceable state of affairs" (p. 179). But is it a world event?

43. Ibid., p. 154.

44. *Kerygma and Myth*, pp. 208–9.

45. Ibid., p. 209.

46. Ibid., p. 209, n. 1.

47. Ibid.

48. F. Schleiermacher, *The Christian Faith* (Edinburgh 1928), secs. 59–61. "Religious experience, however, consists precisely in this, that we are aware of this tendency to God-consciousness as a living impulse, . . . so we account it a part of the original perfection of man that in our clear and working life a continuous God-consciousness as such is possible" (pp. 244, 245).

49. References are to Hans W. Bartsch, *Kerygma and Myth*, Vol. 1. The essays *New Testament and Mythology* seem to have been first published in German in 1941.

50. *Jesus and the Word*, pp. 3–5. Cf. *Essays*, p. 254. "If the concept of objective knowledge is taken from natural science . . . then it is not valid for the comprehension of historical phenomena; for these are of a different kind from those of nature." Further: "The 'most subjective' interpretation is in this case the 'most objective,' that is, only

those who are stirred by the question of their own existence can hear the claim which the text makes" (p. 256). Bultmann's reference in quotes is to Kierkegaard.

51. Ibid., p. 4. Cf. n. 49 above.
52. Cf. n. 49 passim.
53. Cf. bibliographical reference above, n. 48.
54. *Kerygma and Myth*, p. 12.
55. *Jesus Christ and Mythology*, Shaffer Lectures, 1951 (New York, 1958), pp. 2–3.
56. *Kerygma and Myth*, p. 6.
57. Ibid., p. 3.
58. *Jesus Christ and Mythology*, p. 18.
59. Ibid., p. 19.
60. Ibid., p. 15. Italics are mine.
61. Ibid., pp. 16, 17.
62. Ibid., p. 17.
63. K. Barth, *Ein Versuch, ihn zu verstehen*, Theologische Studien, XXXIV (Zurich, 1952).
64. *Kerygma and Myth*, p. 23.
65. Ibid., p. 24.
66. Ibid., p. 27.
67. Ibid., p. 32.
68. Ibid., p. 33.
69. Ibid., p. 13. I quote Bultmann's summation: "Here then is the crucial distinction between the New Testament and existentialism, between the Christian faith and the natural understanding of Being. The New Testament speaks and faith knows of an act of God through which man becomes capable . . . of his authentic life" (p. 33).
70. Ibid., pp. 33 f.
71. Ibid.
72. Ibid., p. 34.
73. Ibid., p. 37.
74. Ibid., p. 35.
75. Ibid., p. 35.
76. Ibid., p. 44.
77. Ibid.
78. D. M. Baillie, *The Theology of the Sacraments* (New York, 1957), p. 35, n. 1.
79. *Kerygma and Myth*, p. 13.
80. Ibid., p. 200.
81. Ibid., p. 207.
82. Ibid., p. 209.
83. Cf. A. Ritschl, *Justification and Reconciliation* (Edinburgh, 1900), p. 396.
84. *Kerygma and Myth*, p. 44.

THE DOCTRINES OF GOD AND MAN IN THE LIGHT OF BARTH'S PNEUMA-TOLOGY

1. *The Doctrine of the Word of God*, trans. Q. T. Thompson (Edinburgh, 1936), p. 369. This is the English translation of the first half of the first volume of Barth's *Kirchliche Dogmatik*. It is the first of eight quarto volumes so far published, and the work is still unfinished. Henceforth, it is to be referred to as *Doctrine* (Doct.).
2. *Die Kirchliche Dogmatik*, I. 2 (Zurich, 1945), p. 1. We have here, undoubtedly, something close to a restatement of Luther's distinction between the hidden God, *Deus absconditus*, and *Deus revelatus*, the God who reveals himself through Christ for man's redemption.
3. Ibid., p. 3.
4. *Doctrine*, p. 535.
5. Ibid.

6. Ibid., p. 536.

7. *The Holy Ghost and the Christian Life*, trans. R. B. Hoyle (London, 1938), p. 11.

8. Ibid.

9. Ibid., p. 12.

10. Ibid., p. 15.

11. Ibid., p. 14

12. Ibid., p. 12

13. *Doctrine*, p. 207.

14. Ibid., p. 208.

15. Ibid.

16. Ibid., p. 210.

17. Ibid., p. 209.

18. Ibid.

19. Ibid., p. 210. This, of course, dispenses with all reliance either on Schleiermacher's "God-consciousness" or Ritschl's moral or value-consciousness. It, thus, sets aside every philosophy of religion, or philosophical theology.

20. Cf. *Doctrine*, p. 532, and *The Knowledge of God and the Service of God*, Gifford Lectures (London, 1938), p. 115.

21. *Doctrine*, p. 372. In this statement, Calvin's teaching on the inscrutability of divine sovereignty is approximated, placing Barth, therewith, in the tradition of both Duns Scotus and Ockham. There is, indeed, no question that Barth has placed himself in the tradition of late medieval Ockhamism despite his avowal to forsake all philosophy.

22. Ibid., p. 274. This "eventualism" or "actualism" precisely echoes the Calvinist understanding of the status of the entire creation and is consequent upon the nominalist dissolution of substantialistic ontology of the Greek tradition.

23. *Doctrine*, p. 531. Cf. *The Holy Ghost and the Christian Life*, pp. 69, 72.

24. *Doctrine*, p. 516.

25. Ibid., p. 212.

26. Ibid., pp. 513 f.

27. Cf. *Doctrine*, pp. 317, 515.

28. Ibid., p. 215.

29. Ibid., p. 516.

30. Ibid., p. 518.

31. Ibid., p. 515.

32. *Kirchliche Dogmatik*, I. 2. secs. 13 and 16.

33. Ibid., p. I.

34. Ibid., p. 3.

35. Ibid., p. 28.

36. Ibid., p. 223.

37. Ibid.

38. Ibid., p. 223. Cf. p. 289.

39. Cf. *Holy Ghost and the Christian Life*, p. 28. In this freedom of resistance to the grace of God, it is to be noted that Barth separates himself from both Luther and Calvin at a crucial point, which, indeed, qualifies the divine sovereignty.

40. *Doctrine*, p. 215.

41. *Kirchliche Dogmatik*, I. 2. 224.

42. Ibid.

43. Ibid., p. 280. The statement is paradoxical. It is also ingeniously circular and ambiguous.

44. Ibid., p. 289.

45. Ibid., p. 294.

46. *Doctrine*, p. 281.

47. Ibid., p. 517.

48. Ibid., p. 518.

49. Cf. *Doctrine*, p. 526.

50. Ibid., p. 528.

51. *Holy Ghost and the Christian Life*, pp. 43, 44.

52. *Doctrine*, p. 520.
53. Ibid., pp. 523–24.
54. *Nature, Man and God* (New York, 1949), p. 401.
55. Cf. *Christus Veritas* (London, 1949), pp. 162, 168.
56. *Nature, Man and God*, p. 397.
57. *The Epistle to the Romans*, trans. E. C. Hoskyns (London, 1932). Author's Preface to the English edition, p. x.
58. Ibid., Preface to the second German edition, p. 10.
59. *Doctrine*, p. 529.
60. Ibid.
61. Ibid., p. 530.
62. Ibid.
63. Ibid.
64. Ibid., p. 531.
65. Ibid.
66. *Doctrine*, p. 528. Italics are mine.
67. Ibid., p. 531.
68. Ibid., p. 532.
69. *Holy Ghost and the Christian Life*, p. 49.
70. Ibid.
71. Ibid., p. 35.
72. M. Luther, *Treatise on Christian Liberty* (Philadelphia, 1947), p. 271.
73. *Holy Ghost and the Christian Life*, p. 16.
74. Ibid., pp. 69–71.
75. *Doctrine*, p. 531.
76. Ibid., p. 530.
77. W. D. Davies, *Paul and Rabbinic Judaism* (London, 1948), p. 226.

WORSHIP AS ACKNOWLEDGMENT

1. *Conatus* is here used as thrust toward fulfillment or completion of being. Employed by Spinoza, it signifies the endeavor of each thing to persevere in its being and as such is identical with the "essence" of the thing (*Ethics*, Bk. III, props. vi–viii). The distinctive *conatus* of man is constant "intellectual love of the mind toward God" (Bk. V, prop. xxxvi). Spinoza recognized, however, a disparity between reality and perfection in the case of man, but it was rather in his bondage to the "passions" than to self-will, as in the Christian Fathers.
2. Plato's *Gorgias*, 482a–c.
3. A phrase borrowed from Karl Heim in *Christian Faith and Natural Science* (London, 1953), pp. 20 f.
4. Francis Bacon, *Novum Organum, Works*, ed. J. Spedding, Ellis, and Heath (Boston, 1863), VIII, 99.
5. Cf. *Novum Organum*, p. 138.
6. Ibid., pp. 67, 206.
7. Ibid., p. 113.
8. Ibid., pp. 144, 145.
9. Ibid., p. 124.
10. *The Interpretation of Nature, Works*, VI, p. 29.
11. Ibid., p. 28.
12. Ibid., p. 29.
13. *Novum Organum*, p. 162.
14. Ibid.
15. *St. Augustine's Confessions*, X. 1.
16. Ibid., V. 4.
17. *Novum Organum*, p. 125.

18. Evelyn Underhill, *Worship* (New York, 1937), p. 3; cf. Calvin, *Institutes of the Christian Religion*, 1. iii. 1.

19. Cf. *God Transcendent* (New York, 1936), pp. 35–40.

20. Wordsworth's line in the sonnet "On Trinity College Chapel."

21. Lev. 11:44; cf. 1 Pet. 1:15.

22. *Institutes*, II. viii. 5.

23. Luke 3:8; cf. Eph. 5:9.

24. Cf. II Cor. 3:3 ff. and Heb. 8:6 ff.

25. Cf. Heb. 9:11–15.

26. II Cor. 6:16; cf. I Cor. 3:16–17.

27. In his famous sermon "The Circumcision of the Heart" (1733), John Wesley declared: "Other sacrifices from us he would not; but the living sacrifice of the heart he hath chosen. Let it be continually offered up to God through Christ." *Sermons*, XVII, *Works*, ed. T. Jackson (London, 1872) V, 202 f.

BIBLICAL ELECTION AS SACRED HISTORY

1. Kurt Wilhelm, "The Idea of Humanity in Judaism," in *Studies in Rationalism, Judaism, and Universalism*, ed. Raphael Loewe (London, 1966), p. 292. Cf. Samuel Sandmel, *The Genius of Paul* (New York, 1970), p. 20. That pure universalism "did not exist in Jewish thought, not even in the heights of the Exilic period," is Sandmel's view in acknowledgment of the paradox.

2. Df. Deut. 6:4–7; 7:6–9; 9:5; 10:14–15; 26:5–9; 28:1–5.

3. Samuel H. Bergman, "Israel and the *Oikoumēne*," in Raphael Loewe, ed., *Studies*, p. 47. See also note 30 below.

4. Anderson, *Creation Versus Chaos* (New York, 1967), p. 37: "From the Exodus, Israel looked back to the creation, confessing that the God who was active at the beginning of her history was likewise active at the beginning of the world's history"; Buber, *The Prophetic Faith*, trans. C. Witton-Davies (New York, 1960), pp. 31–36.

5. Deut. 7:6. Cf. Gerhard von Rad, *Genesis: A Commentary* (London, 1961), pp. 16–18. The Abraham tradition is joined to the Exodus-Sinai tradition in Israel's "corporate confession of faith" of Deut. 26:5–9. Von Rad also sees the Yahwist editor as interpreting the "primeval history" (i.e., Creation) in terms of the Exodus "creation" of Israel as a people. The Yahwist becomes a true prophet, "for he proclaims the distant goal of the sacred history effected by God in Israel to be the bridging of the cleft between God and all mankind" (p. 23). Anderson, *Creation*, p. 37, speaks of the Exodus as Israel's creation *ex nihilo*.

6. H. H. Rowley, *The Biblical Doctrine of Election* (London, 1952), p. 44.

7. Ibid., p. 45.

8. Gerhard von Rad, *Genesis*; see note 5 above.

9. Rudolf Bultmann, *Primitive Christianity*, trans. R. H. Fuller (London, 1956), p. 21.

10. Wilhelm, "Idea of Humanity," pp. 298–300, holds that indeed Isa. 60:3 means, "Jerusalem will be the metropolis of all humanity; but the idea that the Gentiles will then find it possible to profess Judaism plays no crucial part in this picture." He entertains the view of Maimonides, viz., "mankind coming to the light, and not the light to Mankind." Evidently, then, the revelation of God does not necessarily entail the unity of the people of God in Wilhelm's view. Israel seems to remain an "intermediary."

11. John Skinner, *Prophecy and Religion* (Cambridge, U.K., 1926), p. 268.

12. Ibid., p. 309.

13. Compare Mic. 5:4 and 4:1–4 with Isa. 2:2–5; 11:2–9.

14. W. O. E. Oesterley and T. H. Robinson, *Hebrew Religion* (New York, 1937), p. 316. Cf. Ferdinand Hahn, *Mission in the New Testament*, trans. Frank Clarke (Naperville, Ill., 1963), pp. 19–20. Hahn believes of II Isaiah that there is "absence of any idea of going out to the nations. Israel is God's witness solely by reason of its existence and of

God's salvation which is given to it." He concludes: "We may therefore say that in the Old Testament there is no mission in the real sense." He notes that while Israel's role is "entirely passive," there is the universalistic view of God's salvation and lordship over the nations.

15. Oesterly and Robinson, *Hebrew Religion*, p. 316.

16. W. D. Davies, *Paul and Rabbinic Judaism* (London, 1948), pp. 61, 62. Cf. the consensus in the following authors: G. F. Moore, *Judaism in the First Centuries of the Christian Era* (Cambridge, Mass., 1962), pp. 326 ff.; Charles Guignebert, *The Jewish World in the Time of Jesus* (London, 1951), p. 154; R. H. Pfeiffer, *History of New Testament Times* (London, 1949), pp. 51 f.

17. Davies, *Paul and Rabbinic Judaism*, p. 62.

18. Ibid., p. 63. Cf. Matt. 23:16. Pfeiffer observes that the monotheism of II Isaiah implies the universal worship of Yahweh, but that the accentuation of the Temple cultus in postexilic times together with the ascendency of Torah served to divide Jews from Gentiles (. . . *New Testament Times*, pp. 7, 46, 51).

19. Joachim Jeremias, *Jesus' Promise to the Nations*, trans. S. H. Hooke (London, 1958), p. 12.

20. Ibid., p. 17.

21. Ibid.

22. It is remarkable that Bergman recognizes even today "the centripetal force which, directed inward, emphasizes what is particular and divisive" as antithetical to "the centrifugal force, directed outward and universalistic" in bearing, but urges that "neither of the two contrasting tendencies may be repressed without what is characteristically peculiar to the Jewish religion being lost." ("Israel and the Oikoumēne," p. 48.)

23. Cf. *He that Cometh*, trans. G. W. Anderson (New York, 1954), pp. 280 f. As Mowinckel says, "Even in Deutero-Isaiah, universalism is limited by Jewish nationalism" (p. 148).

24. Ibid., p. 4.

25. Ibid., p. 449.

26. Ibid., pp. 148–49. Cf. Rabbi Wilhelm's belief ("Idea of Humanity," p. 292) that "traditional" and "modern Jewish messianic" views look to a divinely instituted kingdom "of this world," of justice and moral order; yet 'with this aspect of the messianic expectation, belief in the special position of the people of Israel never disappears."

27. Oesterley and Robinson, *Hebrew Religion*, p. 417.

28. H. H. Rowley, *Biblical Election*, p. 161.

29. Ibid., p. 149.

30. Cf. James Hope Moulton and George Milligan, *Vocabulary of the Greek New Testament* (London, 1963). *Oikoumēne* appears fifteen times in the New Testament and in every case signifies the world of mankind as distinguished from the natural world or cosmos. The primary meaning is the "inhabited world" and may denote also the Roman Empire. Important instances include Matt. 24:14, Mark 14:9, Luke 4:5 and 21:26, Acts 11:28 and 24:5, Rev. 16:14. The adjective *oikoumenikôs* does not occur in the New Testament.

31. Cf. Acts 2:22–39.

32. Cf. J. A. Robinson, *Epistle to the Ephesians* (London, 1955), p. 11, and Johannes Weiss, *History of Primitive Christianity*, trans. and ed. Frederick G. Grant (New York, 1937), II, 661.

33. Cf. M. S. Enslin, *Reapproaching Paul* (Philadelphia, 1972), pp. 97–98, and C. K. Barrett, *Luke the Historian in Recent Study* (London, 1961), pp. 61–63.

34. See W. D. Davies, *The Setting of the Sermon on the Mount* (Cambridge, U.K., 1966). That the early Christians would be concerned with the role of Torah in the messianic age, as Davies urges, cannot be denied on his wholly cogent premise that the early "Christians believed that Jesus of Nazareth was the messiah of Jewish expectations" (p. 109). Important for understanding the lively presence of Judaistic Christianity is Davies's analogy drawn from the Exodus-Sinai background: that "the event [Exodus] was an act of grace, but it is accompanied in the Old Testament by a demand, the Law" (p. 119).

35. Rom. 1:16, Cf. Rom. 2:9–10, where the recompense falls first upon the Jew as, likewise, the reward of righteousness. For Acts the priority of the Jews as candidates for reception of the Gospel has acquired dogmatic status. In 1 Cor. 1:24 no priority is accorded; parity prevails.

36. Jeremias, *Jesus' Promise*, p. 70.

37. Enslin (*Reapproaching Paul*, pp. 108–11) convincingly presents the view that Romans was composed en route to Jerusalem as Paul's *confessio fidei* in face of impending uncertainties attaching to his personal visit. See Rom. 15:30–32. See also T. W. Manson, "St. Paul's Letter to the Romans—and Others," *Bulletin of John Rylands Library*, XXXI, (1948), 224–40.

38. Gal. 3:6–18; Rom. 4:13–18. Cf. John 4:22.

39. Isa. 49:6. In the context of Rom. 15:7–9, Paul finds Old Testament support for the indecision of the Gentiles from Pss. 18:49; 117:1; Deut. 32:43, and Isa. 11:10. Isaiah is referred to by Paul twenty times in Romans, and there are an additional eight references to the Servant passages.

40. Cf. the author's "Christology or Ecclesiology? A Critical Examination of the Christology of John Knox," chap. 8, this volume, and John Knox's reply in *The Church and the Reality of Christ* (New York, 1962), pp. 29–31.

41. M. Kähler, *The So-Called Historical Jesus and the Historical Biblical Christ*, trans. and ed. Carl E. Braaten (Philadelphia, 1964), pp. 84–86.

42. Mowinckel, *He that Cometh*, p. 449.

43. John 4:22. John's use of the preposition "from" in the words ὅτι ἡ σωτηρία ἐν τῶν Ιουδαίων ἐστίν is fully intended. There is little doubt that John has reason for making this Jesus' own word and that the entire incident confronts, as it seeks to interpret, the long-debated issue in the early Church.

44. See Benjamin W. Bacon, *The Gospel of Mark* (New Haven, 1925), p. 262. Bacon's main thesis still prevails, and Vincent Taylor's demurrers, however carefully based, are not decisive in my view, since he retains those factors that vindicate the general correctness of Bacon's claim. See Taylor's *The Gospel According to Mark* (London, 1953), pp. 126–29.

45. T. W. Manson, *The Sayings of Jesus* (London, 1950), p. 20.

46. Jeremias, *Jesus' Promise*, p. 39.

47. Cf. 2 Cor. 3:7–18 as of primary importance.

48. Wilhelm, "Idea of Humanity," p. 291.

49. 1 Cor. 3:16–17, 6:19; 2 Cor. 6:16 and John 4:21–22.

50. Acts 21:17–36 is to be consulted and confirms the judgment of Enslin, *Reapproaching Paul*, p. 113. The Lucan author takes no notice of Paul's gifts for the poor of the Jerusalem church. Cf. Rom. 15:30–31 and Acts 20:17–38.

51. Cf. Gal. 2:20; 2 Cor. 5:14; Rom. 6:2–8.

52. Cf. C. H. Dodd, *Epistle of Paul to the Romans* (London, 1932), pp. 64–65, in regard to the "double meaning" of the law in Paul's thought. Cf. Col. 2:15.

53. For Paul, Christ inaugurates the new Exodus and the new covenant *ex nihilo*.

54. S. Sandmel, *The Genius of Paul*, p. 159.

55. Dodd, *Epistle of Paul*, p. 63.

56. Cf. Matt. 20:16, 19:30; Mark 9:35, 10:31; Luke 13:30.

57. Edgar S. Goodspeed, *Paul* (Philadelphia, 1947), p. 56.

58. B. W. Bacon, *The Story of St. Paul* (Boston, 1904), p. 4. Cf. A. D. Nock, *St. Paul* (New York, 1963), p. 19.

59. S. H. Bergman, "Israel and the Oikoumēne," p. 51, and respectively, Wilhelm, "The Idea of Humanity in Judaism," p. 292 in Loewe (ed.), *Studies*.

RECONCILIATION, YESTERDAY AND TODAY

1. Buber, *Israel and the World* (New York, 1948), p. 16.
2. *Attack upon Christendom* (Boston, 1966), p. 33.

3. Thomas J. J. Altizer and William Hamilton, *Radical Theology and the Death of God* (Indianapolis, 1966), p. 13.
4. Ibid.
5. Ibid., pp. 40, 41.
6. Ibid., p. 36.
7. Ibid., pp. 40, 41.
8. Ibid., p. 48.
9. Ibid., p. 40.
10. *Israel and the World*, p. 27.
11. *Letters and Papers from Prison*, p. 165.
12. *The Secular City* (New York, 1965), p. 121.
13. Ibid., p. 105.
14. *Letters and Papers from Prison*, p. 165.
15. Ibid., p. 205.
16. Ibid., pp. 187–88.
17. *The Church Inside Out* (Philadelphia, 1966), p. 43.

CONSIDERATIONS BASIC TO REVISED THEOLOGICAL METHOD IN PROTESTANT THEOLOGY

1. John Calvin, *Institutes of the Christian Religion*, trans. J. Allen (Philadelphia, 1935), I, i, 46. "True and substantial wisdom principally consists of two parts, the knowledge of God, and the knowledge of ourselves. But, while these two branches of knowledge are so intimately connected, which of them precedes and produces the other, is not easy to discover."
2. After the lapse of a decade, I judge that these last two sentences come close to summing up the positive alternative to the critique, running throughout the essay, of the historic Protestant theology of the reformed Continental tradition. It is time that the long and costly bifurcation of reason and faith, Nature and Grace—as well as tradition and Scripture or, lately, history *versus* "hermeneutic"—be transcended. All of this is consequential to the trifurcation of Being in 14th-century nominalism—the loss of continuity as between God, man, and world. This William Temple sought valiantly to mend in his *Nature, Man, and God*. Cartesianism, as *rationale* of the discontinuity, was a principal philosophical vehicle from the 17th century onwards. With the loss of the above-mentioned continuity, it was inevitable, as with Luther or Calvin, that the relation of God to world must be by inscrutable Decrees, since the concept of *natura* had been destroyed by nominalism.

THE LUND CONFERENCE: THE DILEMMA OF ECUMENISTS

1. Leonard Hodgson, ed., *The Second World Conference on Faith and Order* (London, 1938), Part 2, The Report, pp. 220–76.
2. See reports of Continuation Committees of the World Conference on Faith and Order (Edinburgh, 1937): *The Nature of the Church*, Report of the American Theological Committee, G. W. Richard and F. W. Loetscher, eds. (Chicago, 1945); and *The Nature of the Church*. European Theological Commission, R. Newton Flew, ed. (London, 1952); *Ways of Worship*, P. Edwall, E. Hayman and W. D. Maxwell, eds. (London, 1951). Also *Intercommunion*, ed. D. M. Baillie and J. Marsh (London, 1952).
3. See Leonard Hodgson's address: "The Task of the Third World Conference," etc. in *The Third World Conference on Faith and Order*, ed. O. S. Tomkins (London, 1953), pp. 111 f.
4. Presidential Address, see ibid., p. 101–2.
5. Ibid., pp. 165 f. "Implications of The Ecumenical Movement."

6. Ibid., pp. 156–57. Some variation between the quotation, taken from immediate documents to delegates, and final edited copy is here acknowledged. E. Schlink's address was entitled "The Pilgrim People of God."
7. Ibid., p. 15. The Report to the Churches, I.
8. Ibid., p. 11. Preface.
9. Ibid., p. 12. Preface.
10. Ibid., "The Pilgrim People of God," p. 152.
11. Ibid., p. 161.
12. Ibid., p. 15, Report II.
13. Ibid., p. 169, Tomkins.
14. Ibid., p. 18, Report II.
15. Ibid., p. 20.
16. Ibid., p. 172, Tomkins.
17. Ibid., p. 33, Report III.
18. Ibid., p. 33.
19. Ibid., pp. 159 f. Schlink.
20. Ibid., pp. 24 f. Report III.
21. Ibid., p. 53, Report V.
22. Ibid.

ECUMENISM—A CRISIS OF DECISION: VATICAN II, THE THIRD SESSION

1. See Appendix for the verbation address of Pope Paul VI in English translation.
2. *Ecclesiam Suam*, English trans. (Huntington, Ind., 1964), p. 37.
3. *De Divina Revelatione*, Council Document, III, 25, 1964.
4. *The Vatican Decrees*, ed. P. Schaff (New York, 1875), p. 113.
5. Ibid., p. 135.
6. *De Ecclesia*, Council Document, II, 13, 1964.
7. *Libertas Praestantissimum* 1888 in *The Church Speaks to the Modern World*, ed. E. Gilson (New York, 1954).
8. Schaff, *The Vatican Decrees*, p. 167.

DOCTRINAL STANDARDS AND THE ECUMENICAL TASK TODAY

1. The "Articles" referred to in the First Restrictive Rule are Wesley's abridgment of the *Thirty-Nine Articles of the Church of England* for the prospective new church in America, transmitted and adopted in 1784. In 1968 the doctrinal statements of the uniting churches were "deemed congruent if not identical in their doctrinal perspectives and not in conflict."
2. *The Book of Discipline*, 1972, p. 69.
3. Ibid., p. 79.
4. Ibid., pp. 75–79. This remarkable summation may, perhaps, itself be regarded as a landmark in Methodist hermeneutic of doctrine, almost destined to acquire formative influence upon doctrinal development in the Methodist tradition if preserved.
5. Ibid., p. 81. Cf. the final paragraph of p. 80.
6. The measure and manner in which the Conference under Wesley was made to serve a catechetical purpose and to the end of clarifying, for both proclamation and confession, the substance of doctrinal standpoints to which both the lay preachers and the Societies were expected to adhere is highly relevant to, as it contrasts with, the species of conciliarism unfolded in Section 3. It is, therefore, surely tendentious, in exegeting the import of the Model Deed, to suggest that by its provisions laymen were made participant in the formation of doctrinal standards. They were provided doctrinal standards by the Conference wherewith it might adjudge the orthodoxy of the traveling preachers.

7. In "The Catholic Spirit," Wesley adopts the principle that while "every man neces-sarily believes that every particular opinion which he holds is true . . . yet no man can be sure that *all* his own opinions, taken together, are true." This principle is then generalized with reference to doctrines singular and plural, demanding reserve about the verity of the whole sum of doctrine.

8. *The Book of Discipline*, p. 41. Cf. p. 42.

9. Ibid., p. 48.

10. Ibid., p. 69. "Theologizing" is used recurrently in Section 3 and is jargon for "theo-logical reflection," used alternately with it. It is a loaded word comparable to "philoso-phizing"—also with comparable nonconfessional connotations.

11. Ibid., p. 79. Cf. the discussion on p. 70.

12. "The Catholic Spirit" stood among the forty-four *Standard Sermons* of Wesley and therefore among received early Methodist "doctrinal standards."

13. *The Book of Discipline*, pp. 49, 80. Theological development, regarded as both an attribute of doctrinal standards and their viability, is another ground for the recurrent judgment that existing standards are *not* "positive juridical norms of doctrine" (Cf. pp. 48, 79).

14. Cf. ibid., pp. 40, 42. Unaccountable, I find, is a pervasive presumption that, in the history of the church, creeds and confessions ordinarily had the standing of "absolute standards" and "literal propositions" or that they have in Protestantism normally so functioned.

15. Ibid., p. 70.

16. Ibid., p. 40. The phrase "confirmed by reason" if applied to Wesley can be in error. Faith, for Wesley, is a "divine *elenchos*, evidence or conviction," specifically a work of grace in the heart. Cf. his sermons, "Scriptural Christianity" and "Salvation by Faith." Living faith is rationally defensible but not rationally derivable.

A CASE-STUDY IN ECUMENISM: FIFTY YEARS OF THEOLOGY AT DUKE

1. *School of Religion—Duke University*, 1926–27, Announcements for 1927–28 (Dur-ham, N.C., 1927), p. 18.

2. *Gilbert T. Rowe: Churchman Extraordinary* (Greensboro, N.C., 1971), pp. 74–90.

3. Ibid., p. 78.

4. *Divinity School Bulletin*, XIV, No. 2 (May 1949), 20. Italics are mine.

5. Ibid., I, No. 2 (May 1936), 29–35.

6. Ibid., XIV, No. 2 (May 1949), 19.

7. The word "academic" denotes more than institutional setting. As Dean James Laney makes clear in his Convocation address, it denotes a "guild" mentality among academi-cians who are more disposed to find their "identity" by reference to their "peer group" than to any fellowship of the community of believers, the Church.

8. *Thoughts Upon Methodism, Works.* ed. J. Emory (New York, 1831), VII, 315.

9. W. P. Stephens, Gray Lectures for 1976 Convocation.

10. *Minutes of Several Conversations Between Mr. John Wesley* etc. (Leeds, 1803), pp. 66–67.

INDEX

of, 71, 73, 89–90, 97, 167, 196; righteousness of God through faith, 214, 215
Jewish Christianity, 204, 205, 207, 208, 210,
214

Kahler, Martin, 146, 208
Kant, Immanuel: xiv, 75–99, 132, 139, 140,
145, 147, 246, 252; theoretical reason, 79,
90, 105, 145; Copernican revolution, 79,
113, 114; divorce of nature and grace, 80,
88, 99; theoretical agnosticism, 85, 87,
88, 94; moral argument, 86, 87–88, 92,
95; practical reason, 86, 87; phenomenal-
·ism of, 88, 111; bifurcation of experience,
105; dualism, 132, 152
Kantian ethic: 78–81; moral consciousness,
76, 86, 87; autonomy, 78, 79, 80, 86, 87,
89, 90; morality, 78, 80, 84, 93; human
freedom, 80, 81, 84, 87; holiness, 81, 90,
91; divorce of nature and morality (the
is and the *ought*), 85, 90, 93; heteronomy, 88
Kantianism, 145, 147, 152, 156, 244, 246, 253
Kerygmatic theology, 148–55
Kierkegaard, Soren, 109, 116, 140, 146, 227,
228, 248
Kingdom of God: 48, 50, 141, 175, 233; according to Jesus, 98, 208–12; according
to Paul, 206–7, 226; condition of entrance, 209; relation to Israel's election,
218
Knox, John, 123–33

Law, William, 56
Laws of nature, 44–45, 46
Lee, Umphrey, 71, 238
Léger, Card. Paul E., 280, 299
Lessing, G. E., 82, 247
Liberal theology, 75, 99, 145, 151–54, 156–
57, 325–27, 336
Liturgy of life, 192–97
Lord's Supper, the, 196–97, 235–42
Lund Conference on Faith and Order, 169,
259–70
Luther, Martin (Lutheranism), xii, 48, 62,
75, 91, 133–34, 165–66, 170, 223, 225, 235,
236, 244, 245, 249, 313, 340

Macintosh, Douglas C., 106, 111, 164, 243,
335
Macquarrie, John, 139
Maddocks, Melvin, 170
Man (theological anthropology): fall of, 7,
9, 16–17, 19, 117, 186–87, 188; liberation
of, 9–10, 17, 72–74, 77, 84, 89, 96, 98, 162;
as natural man, 9, 69, 72, 75, 94, 160;
alienation (sin) of, 14, 42, 48, 60, 76, 88,

98, 181; as autonomous, 16, 21, 38, 44–46,
78, 84, 88, 89, 107, 118, 186–87, 188; as
the onomous, 38, 86, 89–90, 118, 181, 190;
dignity of, 42–43, 49, 50, 88, 116–20, 158;
freedom of, 42, 70, 80–81, 89, 181; end
of, 48, 50, 56–57, 80, 117; redemption of,
53, 60, 98, 146, 164, 166; bondage of, 60,
68, 71, 73, 82–83, 86, 186; Christ the norm
of, 109, 110, 117, 119. *See also* Image of God
Manson, T. W., 79, 85, 86, 97, 210
Manson, William, 209
Marburg Colloquy (1559), 235
Maridogy, 283
Martin, Card. Joseph M., 282
Marx, Karl, 43, 46, 47, 245
Means of grace, 237, 269. *See also* Sacra-
ments
Melanchthon, Philip, 154, 155, 236
Menninger, Carl, 176
Messiah, 202–3; Christian view, 205, 215
Metanoia, 194, 209, 289
Metaphysics, 4, 6–7; antimetaphysical, 87–
88, 124, 244, 245; substantialistic, 140
Methodism: doctrinal standards, 317–27;
doctrinal guidelines, 318, 325–26; plural-
ism, 318, 320–21, 323, 324; intramural
conciliarism, 319, 323, 327; finality of
standards, 321; Scripture, 326
Methodists, Oxford, 52
Meyer, Card. Albert G., 296–99
Ministry of Jesus, 84–86, 193–96; as sacri-
fice, 193; as servant, 194; as eschatologi-
cal, 205, 210; of the Synoptic Gospels,
206–12; to the Gentiles, 210; as mission,
210; as reconciler, 221–23
Miracle, xiii, 114, 115, 116, 120, 126, 136, 160;
relocation of, 105, 125, 128, 130, 132, 134,
144, 247, 251–52
Model Deed (Meth.), 320
Monism, metaphysical. *See* Ontology
Moral goodness, Christian, 85, 86, 89–90
Moralism, 92, 225
Mowinckel, Sigmund, 202, 208
Mystery, of holiness, 126, 181, 192, 195; revelation of, 198, 205, 212, 215–17

Natural conscience, 69
Natural man, 68–70, 72, 76, 81, 94, 98, 108,
182. *See also* Man
Natural theology, 8–9, 107, 109, 116. *See also*
Theology
Nature, xiii, 248
Nature and grace, 4, 69–70, 78, 84, 89, 93;
divorcement of, 88, 89, 167. *See also*
Grace
Nature and history, 35, 38, 124–25. *See also*
History

372

INDEX

Ruffini, Card. Ernesto, 223, 274, 285, 295, 297
Russell, Elbert, 331

Sacraments: Baptism, 193, 196, 211–12, 240; Eucharist, 196, 197, 235–42; *ex opere operato*, 235, 237; real presence, 237, 240; converting ordinance—Wesley, 238; participation, 241; sign and seal—Calvin, 337
Sacrifice of Christ, 193, 194–95
Sandmel, Samuel, 217, 219
Santayana, George, 86
Saybrook *Confession*, 237
Schleiermacher, Friedrich, 105, 116, 117, 156, 248; Cartesianism, 103, 105; immanent causality, 121; ontological monism, 245, 247. *See also* Monism
Schlink, Edmund, 261, 263
Schniewind, Julius, 137
Schweitzer, Albert, 92, 135, 141, 148
Skinner, John, 200
Smith, H. Shelton, 337
Socrates, ix, 38, 39; amendment of life, 12; practical and theoretical reason, 15; moral enlightenment, 42; humanism of, 43; moral consciousness, 87, 92–93
Soper, Edmund D., 331, 335
Spinoza, Benedict: ethics of, 81–84; of human bondage, 82; as beatitude, 82–84; acceptance of the divine determination, 83; of intellectual love of God, 83; resulting freedom for goodness, 83
Stoicism, 82, 205
Suenens, Card. Leo, 298
Syllabus of Errors (1864), 292, 295
Symonds, John A., 41–42, 49

Taylor, Jeremy, 56, 332
Temple, William, 102, 112, 134, 162, 168
Tertullian, 3, 249
Theologia crucis, 176
Theology, systematic: starting point of, 3–5, 18–19, 38, 42, 53–54, 98–99, 144, 247; method, 103–6, 243–47, 253–55
Theology, types of: Christo-centric, 19, 103, 119–20; confessional, 19–21, 181–83, 187–88, 190, 196, 253, et passim; biblical, 52–54; experiential, 103, 116, 121, 136–38, 142, 167; Cartesian, 104–6, 109, 112–16, 252; of the Word of God, 107–9, 117, 156, 158, 181, 250, 252, et passim; kerygmatic, 124–25, 146, 152, 154, 248; radical, 243, 245, 247, 251; liberation, 339–40. *See also* Natural Theology, Sacraments
Thomas à Kempis, 56

Tillich, Paul, 103–6, 247, 248, 334. *See also* Ontology
Time: Plato on, 22–26; Aristotle on, 26–30; Augustine on, 31–35; of theleological time, 35; of historical time, 36–39. *See also* History
Tindal, Matthew, 252
Tisserant, Card. Eugenio, 271, 298–99
Toland, John, 252
Tomkins, Oliver S., 261, 264, 265
Toplady, Augustus, 340
Tradition, 10–11, 51–52, 55, 87, 99, 250, 313
Transcendence of God, 42, 92, 108, 141, 185–88, 245, 247, 248, 249, 250, 251, et passim
Trinity, 6, 161–62
Triumphalism, 278, 311
Troeltsch, Ernst, 157

Unitarianism, 45
Universalism, 201, 204, 217
Utopia, 40, 45

Values, 80
Vatican Council I, *Dogmatic Decrees*, 292
Vatican Council II: Curia, 223, 274, 275, 277, 279, 292; objectives, 272, 273, 274, 275, 280; spirit of, 272, 273, 284–90; openness, 273, 308; inner dynamics, 274, 277, 279; collegiality, 279, 283, 312; non-Catholic observers, 280–82, 287–89, 306; Secretariat for Christian unity, 280, 283, 286, 292, 298, 299, 300, 306–7; papal absolutism, 283; ecumenical policy, 284, 285, 286, 289–90, 292, 301, 304; achievements of, 291, 308–9, 310–15
Vatican Council II, Constitutions and Decrees of: sacred liturgy, 271, 313; on the Church, 275, 278, 302, 312, 314–15; on Ecumenism, 275, 280, 282–83, 284, 285, 292, 293, 300; religious liberty, 275, 282, 294–99; non-Christian religions, 278, 282; on Church and modern world, 313, 315; of Divine Revelation, 313
Via moderna, 249
Voluntarism, 76, 110
Von Rad, Gerhard, 199

Weigel, Gustav, 285
Wesley, Charles, 62, 63
Wesley, John, Christian doctrine of: of the care of the doctrine, 51, 56; of Anglican tradition, 52; of Scripture, 52, 53; of Scriptural Christianity, 53, 54; of *sola gratia*, 53, 63; of justification by faith and forgiveness of sins, 54, 56, 57–59, 60, 64; of orthodoxy or right opinion, 54; of